Thomas Reid

Selected Philosophical Writings

Edited and Introduced
by Giovanni B. Grandi

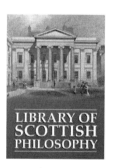

LIBRARY OF
SCOTTISH
PHILOSOPHY

IMPRINT ACADEMIC

Published in the UK by Imprint Academic
PO Box 200, Exeter EX5 5YX, UK

Published in the USA by Imprint Academic
Philosophy Documentation Center
PO Box 7147, Charlottesville, VA 22906-7147, USA

ISBN 9781845401603

A CIP catalogue record for this book is available from the
British Library and US Library of Congress

Full series details:

www.imprint-academic.com/losp

In memory of my father, Mario Grandi

Contents

Series Editor's Note

The principal purpose of volumes in this series is not to provide scholars with accurate editions, but to make the writings of Scottish philosophers accessible to a new generation of modern readers in an attractively produced and competitively priced format. In accordance with this purpose, certain changes have been made to the original texts:

- Spelling and punctuation have been modernized.
- In some cases the selections have been given new titles.
- Some original footnotes and references have not been included.
- Some extracts have been shortened from their original length.
- Quotations from Greek have been transliterated, and passages in languages other than English translated, or omitted altogether.

Care has been taken to ensure that in no instance do these amendments truncate the argument or alter the meaning intended by the original author. For readers who want to consult the original texts, full bibliographical details are provided for each extract.

The Library of Scottish Philosophy was originally an initiative of the Centre for the Study of Scottish Philosophy at the University of Aberdeen. The first six volumes, published in 2004, were commissioned with financial support from the Carnegie Trust for the Universities of Scotland. In 2006 the CSSP moved to Princeton where it became one of three research centers within the Special Collections of Princeton Theological Seminary, and with the Seminary's financial support more volumes have been published. *Selections from*

Thomas Reid is the fourteenth volume in the series and has been prepared for publication by Olivia Lane, to whom a special debt of gratitude is owed.

Acknowledgements

The CSSP gratefully acknowledges financial support from the Carnegie Trust and Princeton Theological Seminary, the enthusiasm and excellent service of the publisher Imprint Academic, and the permission of the University of Aberdeen Special Collections and Libraries to use the engraving of the Faculty of Advocates (1829) as the logo for the series.

Gordon Graham,
Princeton, January 2012

Giovanni B. Grandi

Introduction

Thomas Reid (1710–1796) is the main representative of the Scottish 'common sense' school of philosophy. His works were popular until the mid-nineteenth century, especially in Britain, France, and North America. Although Reid has been the object of recurring scholarly and philosophical interest, his reputation may have suffered from the quick and dismissive comments given by Kant in the introduction to the *Prolegomena to any Future Metaphysics* (1783). Kant criticized Reid, James Beattie (1735–1803), James Oswald (1703–1793), and Reid's opponent, Joseph Priestley (1703–1804), for having misconstrued Hume's question concerning causality, and also for their appeal to common sense — an appeal that Kant considers no different than having recourse to the judgment of the multitude.[1] Most likely, Kant never read Reid's works, nor had the opportunity to appreciate them in their real significance. Reid, on his part, thought that Hume's chief merit lay in having drawn out consistently the implications of a particular account our cognitive functions, the 'theory of ideas'.

I

In a letter to James Gregory (1753–1821), from 1790, Reid drew a summary balance of his contribution to philosophy:

> It would be want of candour not to own, that I think there is some merit in what you are pleased to call *my Philosophy*; but I think it lies chiefly in having called in question the common theory of *Ideas* or *Images of things in the mind* being the only object of thought; a theory founded on natural prejudices, and so universally received as to be interwoven with the structure of language. Yet were I to give you a detail of

what led me to call in question this theory, after I long held it
self-evident and unquestionable, you would think, as I do,
that there was much of chance in the matter. The discovery
was the birth of time, not of genius; and BERKELEY and
HUME did more to bring it to light than the man that hit
upon it. I think there is hardly any thing that can be called
mine in the philosophy of the mind, which does not follow
with ease from the detection of this prejudice.[2]

According to Reid, the theory of ideas was founded on 'natural prejudices', and 'interwoven with the structure of language'. Among the prejudices he alluded to was the analogy
drawn between the operations of the mind and the actions of
bodies. Some verbs expressing mental operations, such as 'to
apprehend', 'to conceive', 'to comprehend', and 'to grasp',
are indeed derived from descriptions of interactions between
bodies (or, more precisely, they are derived from the actions
of our own self-directed body on other physical objects).[3]
Reid thought that past philosophers had elevated to the
dignity of philosophical theory the analogy embedded in the
etymology of these expressions. They had taken for granted
that principles explaining the interaction of bodies — e.g. that
no body can act where it is not, and that no body can act on
another at a distance — could be equally applied to the cognitive relation between the mind and its objects.[4]

Philosophers also thought that consciousness clearly testifies the immediate presence to the mind itself of some of its
objects: 'Of those things that are observed with the mind, certain are present in the mind itself, such as thought, desire,
affection, and other operations of the mind; […] the mind by
its very nature is endowed with an awareness of its own
operations, so much so that it can perceive whatever is in
itself.'[5] After all, not even the worst sceptic of all, Hume,
doubted of the existence of impressions and ideas, conceived
as objects of consciousness.[6] The theory of ideas was thus
used primarily to explain other acts of the mind beside consciousness: the perception by our senses of objects that are
situated at a distance from (the seat of) the mind, the remembrance of past events to which we have been witnesses, and
the conception of objects that do not presently or ever exist.
Whenever an object cannot be immediately present to the
mind, a representative idea takes its place in the mind. But
what is present to the mind is an object of consciousness. In

this way — as Reid explained in the *Philosophical Orations* — all operations of the mind were resolved into the faculty of consciousness.[7] Nor was Reid unaware that philosophers might not necessarily conceive of this proxy object as an image of the original object. In the *Philosophical Orations*, he explicitly considered the possibility of ideas being symbols that do not resemble the original objects they stand for.[8]

Like many of his contemporaries — among them, his erstwhile teacher at Marischal College, George Turnbull (1698–1749), and his philosophical opponents, Hume and Joseph Priestley — Reid saw himself as trying to apply the new experimental method of reasoning to the philosophy of mind. He thought it was a great merit of Newton to have reduced to a system of rules the methodological principles already presented by Bacon.[9] He occasionally refers to the *regulæ philosophandi* (*rules for philosophizing*) that Newton listed at the beginning of Book III of the *Principia*. Newton's first rule states that the causes of natural phenomena must satisfy two conditions: causes must be real, and they must be sufficient to explain the phenomena in question.[10] According to Reid, the theory of ideas failed on both counts. There is no evidence for the existence of ideas, and even if, for the sake of argument, we assume that they do exist, they cannot explain the various operations of the mind, including consciousness, sensation, perception, memory, and conception.

Already Descartes and his followers had refuted the hypothesis of physical images sent forth from the external objects to the organs of sense.[11] But — Reid claimed — modern philosophers stopped short in their criticism: there is no evidence for the existence of images of external objects in the brain, nor is there any evidence that images can be transmitted from the organs of sense to the brain. Although no sensory perception occurs without some impression made by external objects, whether directly or indirectly, on sense organs, there is no evidence that sense organs are actually impressed with images of the external objects. The only sense organs where we find images of external objects are the eyes, but what we perceive in vision are not the images on the retinas: these are double and inverted in relation to the objects we actually see.[12]

If the existence of images in the brain is doubtful, the hypothesis of images in the mind is hardly intelligible, according to Reid. How indeed can we speak of images in the mind? If these images resemble external objects, they must have size, figure, and extension. Should we not then assume the mind, where these images are located, to have size, figure, and extension as well? This is a conclusion about the nature of the mind for which there is little or no evidence, according to Reid.[13] Moreover, how could we conceive of the sensations of smell, sound, and taste as images of something extended? They do not appear to us to have size, figure, and extension.[14]

What is most important, the theory of ideas does not make the cognitive operations of the mind any more intelligible. Ideas are supposed to play the role of immediate objects representing more remote objects that cannot be present by themselves to the mind. According to Reid, it is not clear how ideas can perform this function: how can we be certain that ideas represent other objects that are not present to the mind, and do so reliably, unless we are immediately aware of these objects and can compare them to the ideas themselves? How do we know that ideas 'speak' for something else, and that we are not, so to speak, trapped in a *camera obscura*? A dilemma then arises: either ideas are the *only* objects of the mind, and we cannot be certain that they represent anything else beside themselves, or we are immediately aware of the objects that ideas are supposed to represent. The first alternative leads us to scepticism about the external world perceived by the senses and about the past events we remember, while the second one makes the hypothesis of ideas utterly useless.[15] Moreover, the theory of ideas leaves unexplained our ability to be aware of ideas themselves.[16]

Nor would conceiving of ideas as symbols of a book rather than as images in a *camera obscura* be of any help. 'Who will interpret this book for us?' asks Reid.[17] Without a key to the interpretation of these symbols, that is, without already knowing what these symbols mean, they will remain forever 'dumb' to us: 'If you address someone in a foreign language, perhaps your words are symbols as far as you are concerned, but they mean nothing to him.'[18]

The outlines of this critique of the 'ideal system' can be found in Reid's second discourse to the Aberdeen Philosophical Society from 1759, and in his third and fourth graduation orations delivered at King's College, Aberdeen, in 1759 and 1762. Reid elaborated considerably on this criticism in his Glasgow lectures on the philosophy of mind (what was then called 'pneumatology'). These lectures would then be used for the compilation of the *Essays on the Intellectual Powers of Man* (1785).

In *An Inquiry into the Human Mind on the Principles of Common Sense* (1764) — a work largely based on seven discourses he delivered to the Aberdeen Philosophical Society between 1758 and 1763 — Reid presented his views on the workings of the senses, but he omitted some of the details of his critique of the theory of ideas.[19] He rather chose to highlight two theses about 'the hypothesis of ideas'. Firstly, he showed that sensations — or, in Hume's terms, impressions of sense — do not resemble the qualities of external objects we get to know by our senses. Thus, in Reid's view, sensations cannot play the role of ideas. Secondly, Reid demonstrated how the theory of ideas led by gradual steps to what he took to be the foremost expression of scepticism, the philosophy of Hume. Reid's account of the history of philosophy as the logical development of the theory of ideas will be further expanded in the later *Essays on the Intellectual Powers of Man*.

II

One of the first documents including Reid's objections to the hypothesis of ideas is a question he discussed for the Aberdeen Philosophical Society in July 1758. The question concerns Hume's division of the objects of the human mind into impressions and ideas: '[1] Are the objects of the human Mind properly divided into impressions and Ideas? [2] And must every Idea be a Copy of a preceding Impression?'[20] As we can see, Reid did not merely try to determine whether the objects of the human mind are exhaustively classified as either ideas or impressions. He also wanted to determine whether it is true, as Hume claimed, that all ideas are copies of preceding impressions. In this paper, along with other criticisms later reformulated in the second discourse and in the graduation orations, Reid explicitly addressed the second question, and claimed that '[t]here seems to be good ground to apprehend that we have many Ideas which are not copys [*sic*] of Impressions got either by Sensation or Reflexion'.[21]

In other unpublished papers from the same period, Reid methodically explores the nature of tactual sensations. According to Reid, these sensations do not resemble the notions of primary qualities we acquire by the sense of touch (the notions of extension, size, figure, motion, hardness or softness, roughness or smoothness, and solidity). He presents the first version of a thought experiment we find in the *Inquiry*: Reid asks us to imagine a blind man who has lost all the notions he got by touch of the size, figure, and extension of his own and other bodies, but who is left with the power of sensation and the ability to reason from his sensations. Reid argues that this blind man would not be able to reach any conclusion about the nature of the causes of his sensations. Indeed, none of his sensations, by itself or jointly with others, resembles the notions we normally acquire by touch of the primary qualities of external bodies.[22] As he would later say in the *Inquiry*, our reason cannot perceive the least tie or connection between our sensations and the notions we have by touch of these qualities.[23] In these manuscripts, Reid also tried to extend his analysis of the relation between tactual sensations and the ideas of primary qualities perceived by touch to the relation between the sensations of colour and visible figure. Reid, for example, speaks of our ability to conceive of a visible figure without having any sensation of colour.[24]

Some remarks in these early manuscripts may be read in a way that does not make them entirely compatible with Reid's mature views. As we have seen, the thought experiment of the blind man shows that we cannot acquire the notions of primary qualities from our own sensations of touch. Presumably, we cannot do so because these sensations do not resemble the ideas of those qualities. Perhaps, by the word 'idea', Reid could still have meant some proxy objects in the mind that resemble qualities in the external world. Reid would then only have objected to Hume's view that all our ideas are copies of some preceding sense impressions.

Reid, at times, seems to argue for a thesis concerning colour sensations and visible figure that appears to be weaker than his mature view. For example, he claims that we can perceive a 'dark' (and therefore colourless) triangle (or circle) against a coloured background, and from this fact he goes on to argue that we can have an idea of figure without sensation of colours. Although he does not explicitly say so, it appears we can have this idea of a colourless figure only because the colour sensations along the border of the dark spot are arranged in a certain figure. He also says that three distinct 'lucid' points against a dark background introduce into the mind 'a perception quite distinct from them all, and which remains after they are gone; and that is their place and distance'.[25] If these luminous points are colour sensations, as Reid seems to imply, then colour sensations are, after all, arranged in a spatial order—a view that appears to be at odds with the claim that not even the order of sensations is spatial.

Reid, as we have seen, argues that visible figure and extension are at first introduced into the mind by colour sensations but can abstracted from the sensations themselves. It seems that the target of this discussion is the thesis of Hume and Berkeley that we cannot abstract our ideas of primary qualities from our ideas of secondary qualities. This appears also from an early remark at the end of the first discourse to the Aberdeen Philosophical Society delivered on 14 June 1758:

> I think both Berkly [sic] & Hume affirm that there can be no idea of visible space without colour. I am of a contrary opinion & think I have a distinct conception of visible extension without colour. This idea seems indeed to be very refractory, & not easily made to ply with their systems. But as the same difficulties may occur with regard to tangible space, I shall refer them till that comes under consideration.[26]

Berkeley and Hume argued from the impossibility of separating ideas of primary qualities from our ideas of secondary qualities to the impossibility of proving the existence of an external world. Ideas of secondary qualities do not resemble the properties of matter, an inert and insensible substance, any more than pain resembles the point of a sword, as Locke had already shown. If ideas of primary qualities cannot be abstracted from ideas secondary qualities, then they cannot resemble properties of matter as well.

III

If we take the remarks we discussed in the early manuscripts uncharitably, Reid appears to reject the limited claim that all ideas are copies of impressions, but still appears to subscribe to the view that there are some ideas in our mind that resemble qualities of external bodies. But, in the same manuscripts, Reid's mature viewpoint unequivocally unfolds. Reid does not simply reject the claim that all ideas are copies of impressions, but rather the claim that all the objects of thought are properly divided in impressions and ideas. This will become evident by considering his answer to Hume's comments on a draft of the *Inquiry*.

Hume understood Reid's doctrine to be a return to the theory of innate ideas: 'If I comprehend the Author's Doctrine, which I own, I can hitherto do but imperfectly, it leads us back to innate Ideas.'[27] Hume saw Reid as simply denying that all our ideas are copies of preceding impressions, and so as simply objecting to the view that all our knowledge of the external world is derived from sense impressions. If that had been the point of the *Inquiry*, then Reid would not have rejected the theory of ideas as objects present in the mind. He simply would have distinguished two types of ideas: (1) sensations, which are ideas that do not resemble properties of external objects, and (2) notions, which are ideas that do not resemble sensations but that do resemble the properties of external objects.

Reid disposed of this possible misunderstanding in an abstract of the *Inquiry* he sent to Hume. Reid granted Hume's thesis that all ideas are faint copies of preceding impressions. Reid also implicitly assumed, perhaps wrongly, that Hume's impressions and ideas fit the description that Reid himself ascribes to the philosophical tradition: impressions and ideas are objects existing in the mind and of which we are directly aware. If we can find some conceptions or thoughts that do not resemble our impressions, then they cannot be ideas. According to Reid, we do find such thoughts and conceptions.[28] But what would be their nature, if they are not ideas in the philosophical sense, that is, objects existing in the mind of which we are directly aware? In the same writing, Reid at first speaks of dissimilarity between impressions and 'thoughts' or 'conceptions' of objects and their qualities. He then speaks of dissimilarity between impressions and 'sensible objects' and their qualities. This shift in language is compatible with his mature usage: to have a conception (a notion, a thought, or an idea) of an object and its qualities does not mean that in the mind there is some special entity of which we are aware and that allegedly resembles some other thing outside the mind. To say 'the mind has a conception (or a thought, or an idea) of an object (or a quality of an object)' is a mere pleonasm, a redundant expression ultimately equivalent to saying that 'the mind conceives of an object (or quality of an object)'.[29] We do directly conceive of the primary qualities in the external world without any need for ideas as intermediary objects. In perception, we not only have a conception but a belief in the present existence of a quality. Again, to have a belief in the existence of a quality simply means to believe in its present existence. According to Reid, both conception and belief are ingredients of the act of perception. As acts of the minds, conception and belief can be said to exist in the mind as a subject of inherence but not in a local sense. Moreover, the objects of these acts are distinct from the acts themselves: the objects of the acts of conception and belief, in our perception of primary qualities, are the qualities themselves of things existing in an external world. In Reid's view, sensations do regularly precede our conception and belief of the primary qualities we perceive, but they are not images of these qualities. By paying attention to the nature of sensations—what he also calls 'the way of reflection'—we can recognize that no sensations of ours resemble the properties of an extended, solid, and moveable substance such as matter is conceived to be. Reid appeals to an *experimentum crucis* to settle the point:

> This dissimilitude betwixt our Sensations and the sensible qualities known to us by their means, is the Foundation of my System, as their Similitude is the Foundation of all the Systems that went before. Aristotle makes all our Sensations to be Forms or Images of the sensible qualities that correspond to them. Locke makes the Sensations we have by primary Qualities to be resemblances, but not the sensations of the secondary. Berkley [sic] and Hume do not indeed admit the existence of sensible things, but they affirm that all the Notions we have of what we call sensible qualities are nothing else but copies & images of our Sensations. I have there-

fore proposed this as an *Experimentum Crucis* by which these Systems must stand or fall. If what we call Extension, Figure, Motion, Hardness or Softness, Roughness or Smoothness have any Resemblance to the Sensations that correspond to them, then I must Subscribe to Mr Humes [*sic*] Creed and cannot avoid it. But if there is no such resemblance then his System falls to pieces as well as all the other Systems I have named and we are to seek for a new one. The last Appeal in a Question of this kind must be to a mans [*sic*] own Perceptions. He that can attend to his {sensations} so far as to make them an object of thought, and can compare them with sensible qualities can be at no loss to judge in this question. And if he is at any loss this is an evident proof that he has no clear and distinct notions of the things he would compare. After taking much pains to attend to my Sensations and to form clear and distinct conceptions of them, it appears to me as clear and as certain that they are not like sensible qualities, as the pain of a toothach [*sic*] is not like a triangle.[30]

According to Reid, the theory of ideas was innocuous as long as philosophers working in the Aristotelian tradition thought that all our sensations are indeed resemblances of the qualities of objects in the external world. However, this confidence in the ability of our ideas to represent features of the external world was shaken by the modern revival of the Ancient atomists' distinction between ideas of primary qualities and secondary qualities. Descartes and Locke, among others, argued that some of our ideas do not resemble qualities in the external world that occasion them. Berkeley went on to argue that none of our ideas can resemble the qualities of an inanimate being such as matter is conceived to be. Reid then saw Berkeley's immaterialism as part of a 'brood of monsters' that resulted from the 'union' between the old hypothesis of ideas and the newly discovered dissimilarity between sensations and the qualities of external objects. The argument Reid sees at work would be the following one:

1. We can have no conception of anything but what resembles some sensation (or idea) in the mind [theory of ideas].
2. No sensation (or idea) can resemble the qualities of an inanimate substance such as matter is conceived to be [dissimilarity between sensations (or ideas) and the qualities of matter].
3. Therefore, we cannot have any conception of an inanimate

substance, such as matter is conceived to be, or of any of its
qualities.[31]

According to Reid, 'the progeny' that followed Berkeley's
system was an even more 'frightful' one, and Hume had the
courage 'to act the midwife, to rear it up, and usher it into
the world: no causes nor effects; no substances, material or
spiritual; no evidence even in mathematical demonstration;
no liberty nor active power; nothing existing in nature, but
impressions and ideas, following each other without time,
place, or subject'.[32] In particular, Reid saw Hume as applying
the sceptical argument to the idea of self and of active power:
we can only conceive of things by way of resembling ideas,
but do not have ideas of a self or of active power and therefore we cannot conceive of a self or active power.

IV

If we do not perceive things by means of ideas resembling
them, how can we explain our ability to perceive by our senses the qualities of external objects? Strictly speaking, no exp-
lanation is possible if we presume to discover necessary connections arising from the nature of things. Sensations can be
said to be caused by the action of the external qualities, and
by the ensuing physical impressions on the body, only in
what Reid calls the 'popular', 'vulgar', or 'physical' sense of
causation, but not in the sense of a real efficient causation.[33]
The constant conjunction between a particular sense impression and the ensuing sensation is a 'law of nature' regulating
our constitution. However, this regular succession does not
reveal any necessary connection between impression and
sensation: we could have had different sensations upon having the same impressions on the sense organs, had God established different laws of nature.[34]

Sensations, in their turn, regularly precede acts of perception whereby we conceive of an external quality and believe
in its present existence.[35] Again, the constant conjunction between a sensation and the ensuing conception and belief is a
'law of nature' regulating our own constitution.

Reid also speaks of sensations as 'natural signs' of the external objects, or as suggesting the conception and belief of
certain qualities of external objects by a natural principle of

the mind, but by these expressions he simply means that perceptions regularly follow sensations.[36]

This general scheme of 'the process of nature in perception' lends itself to specifications that account for the different ways of perceiving primary qualities and secondary qualities. In the perception of primary qualities, a sensation is immediately followed by an act of perception whereby we directly conceive of a quality residing in an object and believe in its existence. As Reid also says, we have 'direct and distinct notion' of primary qualities.[37]

The mechanism at work in the perception of secondary qualities is different. While primary qualities are 'manifest', that is, they are the express objects of acts of conception, secondary qualities are 'occult'.[38] Upon having a sensation, an innate principle of nature makes us think that it must be caused by something else. We look out for the cause of our sensation, and learn to distinguish objects in our surroundings that regularly accompany it: we end up locating some unknown and hidden power in the external object that occasions the sensation—a power that might eventually be explicated in terms of primary qualities only in the theories of natural science. Thus, we come to locate the hidden cause of the sensation we have upon smelling a rose in that familiar three-dimensional, shaped, solid, soft object perceived by the senses of sight and touch.[39] On the other hand, the sensation we have upon feeling a hard object is immediately followed by the clear conception of solid parts that resist relative motion.[40]

Sensations play an essential role in our cognition of secondary qualities, since we can start discriminating between different hidden qualities in the external objects only on the basis of the different sensations that they cause in the mind. But these qualities as they are in themselves are described by 'natural philosophy' in terms of primary qualities and therefore do not resemble the sensations we experience. Reid also says that we have a 'relative and obscure notion' of secondary qualities.[41] In our sensory perception, we conceive of them only as the unknown causes of known effects, our sensations.

Various innate principles of common sense, 'judgments of nature', are ultimately responsible for the acquisition of other relative notions. For example, we have direct notions of the operations of our minds while we are thinking, but we do only have a relative notion of our mind, and of its faculties and powers. We invariably and constantly ascribe all the operations of our mind to a power or faculty of thinking. In its turn, we consider this faculty or power to belong to a subject unknown in its intrinsic nature. Thus, all that we know of the mind is that it is a permanent subject of inherence for the various operations of which we are conscious.[42]

In a similar fashion, we do not have direct notions of matter and its powers. The only notion we have of matter or body is that of a substratum for the primary qualities we directly conceive (and the secondary qualities we indirectly conceive). What is matter in its intrinsic nature remains unknown.[43] Furthermore, other powers ascribed to matter are described as the unknown causes of manifest effects.[44] The only notion we have of an active power is a relative notion too. We are directly aware of some acts of the mind, what we normally call efforts and exertions of the will, and cannot help but conceive them as a manifestation of a power we do have.[45]

V

The longest part of the *Inquiry* is devoted to a discussion of sight. Reid tried to determine the relative role of innate mechanisms and learning at work in vision. He agreed with Berkeley and Robert Smith (1689–1768) that by sight we do not originally perceive the distance at which objects lie from the eyes. However, contrary to what Berkeley claimed, Reid thought there is at least one feature of the objects we touch that we do directly perceive by sight: we originally perceive their position with regard to the eyes — in other words, we directly perceive the degree of elevation and the compass direction that objects have with respect to the point in space where each eye is situated.[46] A law of vision regulates our perception of the position of objects with regard to each eye: we see a point on the surface of the object in the direction of a straight line originating from the point on the retina where its image falls and passing through the centre of the eye.[47] This law explains how we originally see objects erect even if their image on the retina is inverted. Reid also says that we directly perceive the 'visible figure' of an object, since this figure is constituted by the position that each point of the object that reflects light to the eye has with regard to the eye itself. Reid elsewhere says that visible figure is a partial notion of the very same object we touch: it is the very same object we touch in so far as it has position with regard to the eye.[48] A being endowed only with sight—an Idomenian, as Reid also called him—presented with a straight line in three dimensions would only have a partial view of this line. In perceiving a straight line, an Idomenian excludes curvature in the up and down direction and in the left and right direction, but cannot exclude curvature in the forward and backward dimension of which he is not aware. However, as Reid pointed out, the Idomenian's notion of the line is correct as far as it goes.[49] The geometry that an Idomenian would construct is the 'intrinsic' geometry of the surface of the sphere. In different terms, it is the geometry of the surface of the sphere described without reference to points and lines outside the surface itself. This geometry tracks the position of objects with regard to the eye without mentioning that these objects are at some distance from the eye. In this way, it goes beyond the geometry of the celestial sphere of observational astronomy, where objects are considered, so to speak, as all having the same undetermined distance from the eye. Since in the geometry of visibles great circles play the role of geodesics (the shortest lines between two points), this geometry is non-Euclidean: there are no parallel straight lines, and triangles have an angle sum of more than two right angles.[50]

Another innate law makes us see objects single, whenever rays of light fall on points of the retinas of the two eyes that are similarly situated. Reid here objects to both the various nativist solutions proposed by Newton, William Briggs (1650–1704), and William Porterfield (ca. 1696–1771), and to the empirist solution proposed by Robert Smith whereby we learn to perceive by sight objects as single by experience of the constant conjunction between two visual images and the single object as perceived by touch.[51] Reid finally explains the various means whereby we come to learn how to perceive the distance and real size of an object by sight.[52]

VI

In 1764, a few months after the publication of the *Inquiry*, Reid moved to Glasgow where he took up the chair of moral philosophy vacated by Adam Smith. Reid discussed at length both the intellectual and the active powers of the human mind in his lectures on pneumatology and in several discourses delivered to the Glasgow Literary Society. After his retirement from teaching duties in 1780, he finally had time to arrange these lectures and discourses in two volumes of essays. The first volume, the *Essays on the Intellectual Powers of Man*, was published in 1785. It not only included new lengthy discussions of the theory of ideas and of our external senses but also essays on memory, conception, abstraction, judgment and the principles of common sense, reasoning, and taste. We can only briefly hint at some of Reid's contributions.

Reid applies his critique of the theory of ideas to the other cognitive powers of the mind. There are no ideas that play the role of proxies between the mind's operations and objects that are not present to mind. Reid also maintains a strict distinction between act and object in the operations of our mind (a particular case is that of sensation, which is the only operation of the mind that has no object, or, at least, no object distinct from itself).[53]

At the beginning of the essay on conception, Reid claims that conception is an ingredient in all the operations of the mind. The object of the act of conception need not exist either inside or outside the mind. This allows Reid to avoid reintroducing ideas in the case of conception of non-existent objects.[54] Since he also accepts the principle that everything that exists is a particular, Reid makes clear in the essay on abstraction that we can conceive of universals attributes and kinds without thereby postulating their existence as special objects either within or without the mind.[55]

VII

Many themes in the *Essays on Active Powers of Man* (1788) had already been discussed by Reid in Aberdeen—for example, Reid's defence of the notion of justice as a natural virtue against Hume's view.[56] Reid's doctrine of active power and his defence of 'moral liberty' in the *Essays* are also the result of previous epistolary debates with his patron Henry Home, Lord Kames (1696–1782), and with James Gregory on the nature of power, and of his discussion of Priestley's determinism and materialism in the discourses delivered to the Glasgow Literary Society. According to Reid, various ingredients in our actions bear witness to the universal conviction we have of the existence of a power over the determinations of our will. The notion of moral responsibility, and our ability to decide and follow a plan of action are also arguments in favour of moral liberty.[57] Reid rejects the reduction made by Hume of the traditional 'combat of reason and passions' to a mere opposition between calm benevolent passions and violent malevolent passions. Reid also objects to Hume's view that 'reason is, and ought to be the servant of the passions' (in different terms, to the view that reason can only play a role in the choice of means to ends, but not in the determination of ends themselves).[58] According to Reid, there is an unbridgeable gap between animals and human beings: animals are only moved into action by whatever passion turns out to gain the upper hand at the moment, while humans have the power to resist passions and to act on the basis of rational judgments they can form about what is useful in the long-run and morally right. Animals may at best be subject to 'discipline', that is, to deliberate attempts to stir in them passions that restrain them. Humans, on the other hand, can also be subject of a 'moral government': they can freely submit to prescriptions that they understand to be just and opportune. Reid thought that this 'common sense' view was compatible with Christian doctrine: humans, being created in the image of God, hold a special place in the plan of creation. God's 'mechanical government' of nature is thus distinguished from his 'moral government', to which only intelligent and active beings are subject.[59] According to Reid, in moral evaluations there is not simply a feeling or sentiment at work arising from the observation of characters and actions, but a real judgment ascribing moral qualities to characters and actions.[60]

Among the various principles of actions common to humans and animals, the desire for esteem is naturally allied to virtue, and can thus be beneficial to a society. In a late discourse to the Glasgow Literary Society, Reid presented an ideal form of state that, among other things, required the abolition of private property.[61] In this system, the profit motive would be replaced by a system of state-conferred ranks and honours to which the best and brightest can aspire. Reid's political radicalism appears only obliquely in the *Essays*. He claims that '[t]he end of government is to make society happy, which can only be done by making it good and virtuous'.[62] He then extols the benefits of state-controlled education and discipline, thus foreshadowing what he had in mind for his utopia. He elsewhere argues that the right to property is an acquired right that follows naturally from the rights to life and liberty. However, he also makes clear that this right may be subject to 'limitations and restrictions' for the sake of the public good.[63]

VIII

This volume includes extracts from Reid's main philosophical works: *An Inquiry into the Human Mind on the Principles of Common Sense* (1764), *Essays on the Intellectual Powers of Man* (1785), and *Essays on the Active Powers of Man* (1785). The text is from the nineteenth-century edition by William Hamilton, with only minor amendments. I was guided in my choice of readings not only by my preferences, but also by the necessity of keeping this anthology within reasonable size and of diversifying it from the already excellent selection presented by Ronald E. Beanblossom and Keith Lehrer.[64]

I would like to thank Lorne Falkenstein for comments on the introduction, Ryan Nichols and Gideon Yaffe for allowing me to use the bibliography from their article on Reid in the *Stanford Encyclopedia of Philosophy* as the basis for the bibliography that is appended to this volume. I would also like to thank Olivia Lane for copyediting the text. In some selections from the *Essays on the Intellectual Powers of Man*, the abridgment made by A.D. Woozley has been of some help in guiding my choices. For the compilation of the chronology, I relied on the biographical studies by Paul Wood. Translations of Latin passages are based on the translations provided by the critical editions.[65]

---

[1] See Immanuel Kant, *Prolegomena to Any Future Metaphysics*, trans. Lewis White Beck (Indianapolis, IN: Bobbs-Merrill, 1950), pp. 6–7.

2   *The Correspondence of Thomas Reid*, ed. Paul Wood (Edinburgh: Edinburgh University Press, 2002), letter 114, pp. 210–211.

3   See *The Philosophical Orations of Thomas Reid Delivered at Graduation Ceremonies in King's College, Aberdeen, 1753, 1756, 1759, 1762*, ed. D.D. Todd, trans. Shirley Darcus Sullivan (Carbondale and Edwardsville, IL: Southern Illinois University Press, 1989), Oration IV (1762), p. 73. See also Thomas Reid, *Essays on the Intellectual Powers of Man* [1785], text edited by Derek R. Brookes, annotations by Derek R. Brookes and Knud Haakonssen, introduction by Knud Haakonssen (Edinburgh: Edinburgh University Press, 2002), I.4 [Essay I, Chapter 4], pp. 54–55.

4   See *Philosophical Orations*, Oration III (1759), pp. 64–65, and Oration IV (1762), p. 73. See also the question ('Are the Objects of the Human Mind properly divided into impressions and Ideas?') discussed by the Aberdeen Philosophical Society (July 1758) [APS Question 1758], in Thomas Reid, *Inquiry into the Human Mind on the Principles of Common Sense*, ed. Derek R. Brookes (Edinburgh: Edinburgh University Press, 1997), p. 290, and p. 292; *Essays on the Intellectual Powers of Man*, II.14, pp. 174–178.

5   *Philosophical Orations*, Oration III (1759), pp. 58–59.

6   See *Inquiry*, V.7, p. 79 [Chapter V, Section 7, page 79].

7   See *Philosophical Orations*, Oration III (1759), pp. 58–59. See also *ibid.*, p. 60: 'The doctrine of ideas maintains without any manifest proof that perception and memory are not primary faculties but have their origin from another faculty, namely, from the consciousness of the ideas that are present in the mind itself.' See also Reid's second discourse to the Aberdeen Philosophical Society (14 March 1759) [APS Discourse 2], in *Inquiry*, pp. 298–299, p. 303, and pp. 307–308. In other texts, Reid observes that philosophers rather speak of all the operations of the mind as involving 'the perception of ideas': see *Essays on the Intellectual Powers*, IV.2, p. 322. See also *Essays on the Intellectual Powers of Man*, II.14, pp. 184–185.

8   See *Philosophical Orations*, Oration III (1759), p. 62; APS Discourse 2, in *Inquiry*, pp. 297–298, and p. 311.

9   See Thomas Reid, 'A Brief Account of Aristotle's Logic, with Remarks' [1774], VI.2 [Chapter VI, Section 2] in *Thomas Reid on Logic, Rhetoric, and the Fine Arts: Papers on the Culture of Mind*, ed. Alexander Broadie (Edinburgh: Edinburgh University Press, 2004), pp. 145–147, and *Essays on the Intellectual Powers of Man*, VI.4, p. 457/27–36.

10 See Isaac Newton *The* Principia: *Mathematical Principles of Natural Philosophy*, trans. I. Bernard Cohen and Anne Whitman (Berkeley, CA: University of California Press, 1999), pp. 794–795. See *Essays on the Intellectual Powers of Man*, I.4, p. 51/11–18, and II.3, p. 80/13–18.

11 See *Philosophical Orations*, Oration III (1759), p. 59, and Oration IV (1762). p. 72; APS Discourse 2, in *Inquiry*, p. 312. Cf. *Essays on the Intellectual Powers of Man*, II.8, p. 125.

12 See *Philosophical Orations*, Oration IV (1762), pp. 70–71.

13 See *Philosophical Orations*, Oration III (1759), pp. 61–62.

14 See *Philosophical Orations,* Oration III (1759), pp. 62–63, on the impropriety of the expression 'image of sound'. See also APS Discourse 2, in *Inquiry*, pp. 310–311.

15 See *Philosophical Orations*, Oration III (1759), p. 62, and pp. 63–64.

16 See *Essays on the Intellectual Powers*, II.14, pp. 184–185.

17 *Philosophical Orations*, Oration III (1759), p. 62.

18 *Philosophical Orations*, Oration III (1759), p. 62; see also APS Discourse 2, in *Inquiry*, p. 311.

19 On the genesis of the *Inquiry*, see Derek R. Brookes, Introduction, in Reid, *Inquiry*, pp. xii–xxiii, and Paul B. Wood, Introduction, in Thomas Reid, *An Inquiry into the Human Mind on the Principles of Common Sense* (facsimile reprint of the 1785 edition, Bristol: Thoemmes Antiquarian Books, 1990), pp. v–xv.

20 Two versions of this question remain: see Reid APS Question 1758, in *Inquiry*, pp. 289–296.

21 APS Question 1758, in *Inquiry*, p. 294.

22 See Aberdeen University Library [hereafter referred to as AUL] MS 2131/8/II/21, fols. 1v–2r. On this manuscript see Ryan Nichols, *Thomas Reid's Theory of Perception* (Oxford: Oxford University Press, 2007), pp. 101–107, and Giovanni B. Grandi, 'Reid and Condillac on Sensation and Perception: A Thought Experiment on Sensory Deprivation', *Southwest Philosophy Review* 24 (2008), pp. 191–200. For the published version of the blind man thought experiment, see *Inquiry*, V.7, pp. 65–67.

23 See *Inquiry* V.5, p. 64.

24 See AUL MS 2131/8/II/21, fol. 2v, and MS 2131/6/III/8, in *Inquiry*, p. 324.

25 The example of the three luminous points appears in AUL MS 2131/8/II/21, fol. 2v. The dark triangle case appears both in AUL MS 2131/8/II/21, fol. 2v, and in MS 2131/6/III/8 (in *Inquiry*, p. 324).

26 APS Discourse 1, in *Inquiry*, p. 277.

27 The Hume-Reid Exchange, in *Inquiry*, p. 256.

28 See Hume-Reid Exchange, in *Inquiry*, pp. 257–258.

29 See APS Discourse 2, in *Inquiry*, p. 314.

30 The Hume-Reid Exchange, in *Inquiry*, pp. 259–260.

31 See *Inquiry*, V.8, p. 75.

32 *Inquiry*, VI.6, p. 94. In the *Essays on the Intellectual Powers*, Reid further explains the influence of Berkeley on his philosophical development: 'If I may presume to speak my own sentiments, I once believed this doctrine of ideas so firmly, as to embrace the whole of BERKELEY's system in consequence of it; till, finding other consequences to follow from it, which gave more uneasiness than the want of a material world, it came into my mind, more than forty years ago, to put this question, What evidence have I for this doctrine, that all the object of my knowledge are ideas in my own mind? From that time to the present, I have been candidly and impartially, as I think, seeking for the evidence of this principle, but can find none, excep-

ting the authority of Philosophers' (*Essays on the Intellectual Powers of Man*, II.10, p. 142).

33   See *Inquiry*, II.9, p. 40, V.3, p. 59, and VI.24, p. 198.

34   See *Inquiry*, VI.21, p. 176.

35   There is an exception to this general scheme of the process of perception: Reid claims that there is no sensation appropriated to visible figure. In different words, there is no sensation whose office is to introduce visible figure. Visible figure is suggested immediately by the impression on the retina. See *Inquiry*, VI.8, pp. 99–101, and VI.21, p. 176.

36   See Hume-Reid exchange, in *Inquiry*, p. 261.

37   See *Essays on the Intellectual Powers of Man*, II.17, pp. 201–202.

38   See *Inquiry*, V.5, p. 65, and *Essays on the Intellectual Powers of Man*, II.18, p. 217.

39   See *Inquiry*, II.8, pp. 39–40.

40   See *Inquiry*, V.2, pp. 55–58.

41   See *Essays on the Intellectual Powers of Man*, II.17, p. 202. See also *Inquiry*, V.5, p. 65.

42   See *Inquiry*, II.7, pp. 36–38.

43   See *Essays on the Intellectual Powers of Man*, II.19, pp. 217–219.

44   See *Inquiry*, VI.5, p. 88, and *Essays on the Intellectual Powers of Man*, II.18, pp. 211–217.

45   See *Essays on the Intellectual Powers of Man*, VI.5, pp. 478–480, and Thomas Reid, *Essays on the Active Powers of Man*, eds. Knud Haakonssen and James A. Harris (Edinburgh: Edinburgh University Press, 2010), I.1, pp. 7–13.

46   See *Inquiry*, VI.7, p. 96.

47   See *Inquiry*, VI.12, pp. 122–123.

48   See *Essays on the Intellectual Powers of Man*, II.19, pp. 222–223.

49   See *Inquiry*, VI.9, pp. 106–108.

50   See *Inquiry*, VI.9, pp. 103–106.

51   See *Inquiry*, VI.13–19, pp. 132–167. For the difference between 'empirism' and 'empiricism', see Gary Hatfield, *The Natural and the Normative: Theories of Spatial Perception from Kant to Helmholtz* (Cambridge, MA: MIT Press, 1990), pp. 281–284: empirism is opposed to nativism, while empiricism is opposed to naturalism.

52   See *Inquiry*, VI.22–23, pp. 178–190.

53   See *Essays on the Intellectual Powers of Man*, I.1, pp. 36–37, and *Inquiry*, VI.20, pp. 167–168.

54   See *Essays on the Intellectual Powers of Man*, IV.1, pp. 310–311.

55   See *Essays on the Intellectual Powers of Man*, V (especially V.6, pp. 388–405).

56   Reid discussed the question 'Whether justice be a natural or artificial virtue?' at a meeting of the Aberdeen Philosophical Society on 22 November 1758.

57   See *Essays on the Active Powers of Man*, III.6–8, pp. 228–243.

58   See *Essays on the Active Powers of Man*, III.ii.6, pp. 135–136, III.iii.1, p. 153, and III.iii.2, p. 157.

59 See *Essays on the Active Powers of Man*, IV.5, pp. 221–228.
60 See *Essays on the Intellectual Powers of Man*, V.6, pp. 494–495. See also *Essays on the Active Powers of Man*, III.iii.6, pp. 176–177, and III.iii.7, pp. 181–183.
61 See 'Some Thoughts on the Utopian System', in Thomas Reid, *Practical Ethics: Being Lectures and Papers on Natural Religion, Self-Government, Natural Jurisprudence, and the Law of Nations*, ed. Knud Haakonssen (Princeton, NJ: Princeton University Press, 1990), pp. 277–299; also reprinted in *Politics and Society in Scottish Thought*, ed. Shinichi Nagao, 'Library of Scottish Philosophy' (Exeter: Imprint Academic, 2007), pp. 179–200.
62 *Essays on the Active Powers of Man*, III.ii.8, p. 148.
63 See *Essays on the Active Powers of Man*, V.5, pp. 318–319.
64 See bibliography for references.
65 See bibliography for references.

Chronology

1710:   born on 26 April at Strachan, Kincardineshire, not far from Aberdeen, Scotland. His father, Lewes Reid, was minister of the local parish of the Church of Scotland. His mother, Margaret Gregory, belonged to a family renowned for scientific achievements: among her relatives, her uncle, James Gregory, invented the reflecting telescope; her brother, David Gregory, became Savilian Professor of astronomy at Oxford; two younger brothers, James and Charles, were professors of mathematics at Edinburgh and St. Andrews respectively.

1720–22:   attended the parish school of Kincardine O'Neil.

1722:   attended Aberdeen Grammar School; entered Marischal College at Aberdeen; taught by George Turnbull.

1726:   graduated MA from Marischal College; began his studies for ministry in the Church of Scotland. During these years at Marischal College, he also applied to a systematic study of Newton's *Principia* with his friend John Stewart.

1731:   licensed to preach by the presbytery of Kincardine O'Neil.

1732–33:   Clerk for the presbytery of Kincardine O'Neill.

1733:   appointed Librarian at Marischal College, a post he kept until 1736.

1736–37:   in 1736, legal action against Marischal College for mismanagement of the bequest from which his position as Librarian was paid (a bequest left by an ancestor). In the same year, with John Stewart, he visited London, Oxford, and Cambridge. Among the people he met was the Cambridge professor of mathematics, Nicholas Saunderson, (referred to in the *Inquiry* as example of a blind man who can understand the notion of visible figure). Between 1736 and 1737, he also attended the meetings of a philosophical club in Aberdeen.

1737: appointed to the parish of New Machar, a benefice of King's College, Aberdeen. Apparently, he was physically attacked when he first set foot in New Machar, and had to be protected by men with drawn swords while delivering his first sermon.

1740: travelled to London and married Elizabeth Reid (1724–1792), a cousin from the Gregory's side of the family.

1748: observed the eclipse of Venus with John Stewart and a group of Scottish observers. The results were sent to the *Philosophical Transactions* of the Royal Society. Later the same year, he published *An Essay on Quantity* in the *Philosophical Transactions*.

1751: appointed Regent at King's College, Aberdeen.

1758: founding member of the Aberdeen Philosophical Society (also known as the Wise Club); attended the inaugural meeting of the Gordon's Mill Farming Club.

1762: awarded Doctor of Divinity degree by Marischal College.

1764: publication of the *Inquiry into the Human Mind on the Principles of Common Sense*; appointed Professor of Moral Philosophy at the University of Glasgow; elected member of the Glasgow Literary Society, to which he delivered various discourses.

1774: publication of 'A Brief Account of Aristotle's Logic', as an appendix to the *Sketches of the History of Man* by Henry Home, Lord Kames.

1780: retired from teaching duties.

1783: elected Fellow of the Royal Society of Edinburgh.

1785: publication of the *Essays on the Intellectual Powers of Man*.

1788:   publication of the *Essays on the Active Powers of Man*. In February, he wrote to James Gregory: 'Our University has sent a petition to the House of Commons, in favour of the African slaves...'

1790:   founding member of the Glasgow Society of the Sons of Ministers of the Church of Scotland, a society designed to provide relief to the sons of the clergy in need. Later, he also became director of another charitable organization, the Humane Society.

1791:   convener at the dinner meeting of Society of the Friends of Liberty held on 14 July (Bastille Day) to celebrate the anniversary of the French Revolution.

1792:   contributed money to the French national assembly.

1794:   delivered the discourse 'Some thoughts on the Utopian System of Government', which was published, in an abridged form, with the title 'Observations on the Dangers of Political Innovation'.

1796:   portrait painted by Henry Raeburn in Edinburgh; died on 7 October, survived by only one of his children, Martha.

1799:   publication of 'University of Glasgow', in the *Statistical Account of Scotland*.

An Inquiry into the Human Mind on the Principles of Common Sense

Dedication

To the right honourable James, Earl of Findlater and Seafield, Chancellor of the University of Old Aberdeen.

[…] I acknowledge, my Lord, that I never thought of calling in question the principles commonly received with regard to the human understanding, until the *Treatise of Human Nature* was published in the year 1739. The ingenious author of that treatise upon the principles of Locke — who was no sceptic — hath built a system of scepticism, which leaves no ground to believe any one thing rather than its contrary. His reasoning appeared to me to be just; there was, therefore, a necessity to call in question the principles upon which it was founded, or to admit the conclusion.

But can any ingenuous mind admit this sceptical system without reluctance? I truly could not, my Lord; for I am persuaded, that absolute scepticism is not more destructive of the faith of a Christian than of the science of a philosopher, and of the prudence of a man of common understanding. I am persuaded, that the unjust *live by faith* as well as the *just*; that, if all belief could be laid aside, piety, patriotism, friendship, parental affection, and private virtue, would appear as ridiculous as knight-errantry; and that the pursuits of pleasure, of ambition, and of avarice, must be grounded upon belief, as well as those that are honourable or virtuous.

The day-labourer toils at his work, in the belief that he shall receive his wages at night; and, if he had not this belief, he would not toil. We may venture to say, that even the author of this sceptical system wrote it in the belief that it should be read and regarded. I hope he wrote it in the belief also that it would be useful to mankind; and, perhaps, it may prove so at last. For I conceive the sceptical writers to be a set of men whose business it is to pick holes in the fabric of knowledge wherever it is weak and faulty; and, when these places are properly repaired, the whole building becomes more firm and solid than it was formerly.

For my own satisfaction, I entered into a serious examination of the principles upon which this sceptical system is built; and was not a little surprised to find, that it leans with its whole weight upon a hypothesis, which is ancient indeed, and hath been very generally received by philosophers, but of which I could find no solid proof. The hypothesis I mean is, That nothing is perceived but what is in the mind which perceives it: That we do not really perceive things that are external, but only certain images and pictures of them imprinted upon the mind, which are called *impressions and ideas*.

If this be true, supposing certain impressions and ideas to exist in my mind, I cannot, from their existence, infer the existence of anything else: my impressions and ideas are the only existences of which I can have any knowledge or conception; and they are such fleeting and transitory beings, that they can have no existence at all, any longer than I am conscious of them. So that, upon this hypothesis, the whole universe about me, bodies and spirits, sun, moon, stars, and earth, friends and relations, all things without exception, which I imagined to have a permanent existence, whether I thought of them or not, vanish at once;

> And, like the baseless fabric of a vision,
> Leave not a track behind.[1]

I thought it unreasonable, my Lord, upon the authority of philosophers, to admit a hypothesis which, in my opinion, overturns all philosophy, all religion and virtue, and all common sense — and, finding that all the systems concerning the human understanding which I was acquainted with, were built upon this hypothesis, I resolved to inquire into this subject anew, without regard to any hypothesis.

What I now humbly present to your Lordship, is the fruit of this inquiry, so far only as it regards the five senses: in which I claim no other merit than that of having given great attention to the operations of my own mind, and of having expressed, with all the perspicuity I was able, what I conceive every man, who gives the same attention, will feel and perceive.[…]

Chapter I: Introduction

Section I

The importance of the subject, and the means of prosecuting it.

[…] Wise men now agree, or ought to agree, in this, that there is but one way to the knowledge of nature's works — the way of observation and experiment. By our constitution, we have a strong propensity to trace particular facts and observations to general rules, and to apply such general rules to account for other effects, or to direct us in the production of them. This procedure of the understanding is familiar to every human creature in the common affairs of life, and it is the only one by which any real discovery in philosophy can be made.

The man who first discovered that cold freezes water, and that heat turns it into vapour, proceeded on the same general principles, and in the same method by which Newton discovered the law of gravitation and the properties of light. His *regulæ philosophandi* are maxims of common sense, and are practised every day in common life; and he who philosophizes by other rules, either concerning the material system or concerning the mind, mistakes his aim.

Conjectures and theories are the creatures of men, and will always be found very unlike the creatures of God. If we would know the works of God, we must consult themselves with attention and humility, without daring to add anything of ours to what they declare. A just interpretation of nature is the only sound and orthodox philosophy: whatever we add of our own, is apocryphal, and of no authority.

All our curious theories of the formation of the earth, of the generation of animals, of the origin of natural and moral evil, so far as they go beyond a just induction from facts, are vanity and folly, no less than the Vortices of Des Cartes, or the Archeus of Paracelsus. Perhaps the philosophy of the mind hath been no less adulterated by theories, than that of the material system. The theory of Ideas is indeed very ancient, and hath been very universally received; but, as neither of these titles can give it authenticity, they ought not to screen it from a free and candid examination; especially in this age, when it hath produced a system of scepticism that seems to triumph over all science, and even over the dictates of common sense.

All that we know of the body, is owing to anatomical dissection and observation, and it must be by an anatomy of the mind that we can discover its powers and principles.

Section III

The present state of this part of philosophy – of Des Cartes, Malebranche, and Locke.

That our philosophy concerning the mind and its faculties is but in a very low state, may be reasonably conjectured even by those who never have narrowly examined it. Are there any principles, with regard to the mind, settled with that perspicuity and evidence which attends the principles of mechanics, astronomy and optics? These are really sciences built upon laws of nature which universally obtain. What is discovered in them is no longer matter of dispute: future ages may add to it; but, till the course of nature be changed, what is already established can never be overturned. But when we turn our attention inward, and consider the phænomena of human thoughts, opinions, and perceptions, and endeavour to trace them to the general laws and the first principles of our constitution, we are immediately involved in darkness and perplexity; and, if common sense, or the principles of education, happen not to be stubborn, it is odds but we end in absolute scepticism.

Des Cartes, finding nothing established in this part of philosophy, in order to lay the foundation of it deep, resolved not to believe his own existence till he should be able to give a good reason for it. He was, perhaps, the first that took up such a resolution; but, if he could indeed have effected his purpose, and really become diffident of his existence, his case would have been deplorable, and without any remedy from reason or philosophy. A man that disbelieves his own existence, is surely as unfit to be reasoned with as a man that believes he is made of glass. There may be disorders in the human frame that may produce such extravagancies, but they will never be cured by reasoning. Des Cartes, indeed, would make us believe that he got out of this delirium by this logical argument, *Cogito, ergo sum*; but it is evident he was in his senses all the time, and never seriously doubted of his existence; for he takes it for granted in this argument, and proves nothing at all. I am thinking, says he—therefore, I am. And is it not as good reasoning to say, I am sleeping—therefore, I am? or, I am doing nothing—therefore, I am? If a body moves, it must exist, no doubt; but, if it is at rest, it must exist likewise.

Perhaps Des Cartes meant not to assume his own existence in this enthymeme, but the existence of thought; and to infer from that the existence of a mind, or subject of thought. But why did he not prove the existence of his thought? Consciousness, it may be said, vouches that. But who is voucher for consciousness? Can any man prove that his consciousness may not deceive him? No man can; nor can we give a better reason for trusting to it, than that every man, while his mind is sound, is determined, by the constitution of his nature, to give implicit belief to it, and to laugh at or pity the man who doubts its testimony. And is not every man, in his wits, as much determined to take his existence upon trust as his consciousness?

The other proposition assumed in this argument, That thought cannot be without a mind or subject, is liable to the same objection: not that it wants evidence but that its evidence is no clearer, nor more immediate, than that of the proposition to be proved by it. And, taking all these propositions together—I think; I am conscious; Everything that thinks, exists; I exist—would not every sober man form the same opinion of the man who seriously doubted any one of them? And if he was his friend, would he not hope for his cure from physic and good regimen, rather than from metaphysic and logic?

But supposing it proved, that my thought and my consciousness must have a subject, and consequently that I exist, how do I know that all that train and succession of thoughts which I remember belong to one subject, and that the I of this moment is the very individual I of yesterday and of times past?

Des Cartes did not think proper to start this doubt; but Locke has done it; and, in order to resolve it, gravely determines that personal identity consists in consciousness — that is, if you are conscious that you did such a thing a twelvemonth ago, this consciousness makes you to be the very person that did it. Now, consciousness of what is past can signify nothing else but the remembrance that I did it; so that Locke's principle must be, That identity consists in remembrance; and, consequently, a man must lose his personal identity with regard to everything he forgets.

Nor are these the only instances whereby our philosophy concerning the mind appears to be very fruitful in creating doubts, but very unhappy in resolving them.

Des Cartes, Malebranche, and Locke, have all employed their genius and skill to prove the existence of a material world; and with very bad success. Poor untaught mortals believe undoubtedly that there is a sun, moon, and stars; an earth, which we inhabit; country, friends, and relations, which we enjoy; land, houses, and moveables, which we possess. But philosophers, pitying the credulity of the vulgar, resolve to have no faith but what is founded upon reason. They apply to philosophy to furnish them with reasons for the belief of those things which all mankind have believed, without being able to give any reason for it. And surely one would expect, that, in matters of such importance, the proof would not be difficult: but it is the most difficult thing in the world. For these three great men, with the best good will, have not been able, from all the treasures of philosophy, to draw one argument that is fit to convince a man that can reason, of the existence of any one thing without him. Admired Philosophy! daughter of light! parent of wisdom and knowledge! if thou art she, surely thou hast not yet arisen upon the human mind, nor blessed us with more of thy rays than are sufficient to shed a darkness visible upon the human faculties, and to disturb that repose and security which happier mortals enjoy, who never approached thine altar, nor felt thine influence! But if, indeed, thou hast not power to dispel those clouds and phantoms which thou hast discovered or created, withdraw this penurious and malignant ray; I despise Philosophy, and renounce its guidance — let my soul dwell with Common Sense.

Section IV

Apology for those philosophers.

But, instead of despising the dawn of light, we ought rather to hope for its increase: instead of blaming the philosophers I have mentioned for the defects and blemishes of their system we ought rather to honour their memories, as the first discoverers of a region in philosophy formerly unknown;[...]

It may be observed, that the defects and blemishes in the received philosophy concerning the mind, which have most exposed it to the contempt and ridicule of sensible men, have chiefly been owing to this — that the votaries of this Philosophy, from a natural prejudice in her favour, have endeavoured to extend her jurisdiction beyond its just limits, and to call to her bar the dictates of Common Sense. But these decline this jurisdiction; they disdain the trial of reasoning, and disown its authority; they neither claim its aid, nor dread its attacks.

In this unequal contest betwixt Common Sense and Philosophy, the latter will always come off both with dishonour and loss; nor can she ever thrive till this rivalship is dropt, these encroachments given up, and a cordial friendship restored: for, in reality, Common Sense holds nothing of Philosophy, nor needs her aid. But, on the other hand, Philosophy (if I may be permitted to change the metaphor) has no other root but the principles of Common Sense; it grows out of them, and draws its nourishment from them. Severed from this root, its honours wither, its sap is dried up, it dies and rots.

The philosophers of the last age, whom I have mentioned, did not attend to the preserving this union and subordination so carefully as the honour and interest of philosophy required: but those of the present have waged open war with

Common Sense, and hope to make a complete conquest of it by the subtilties of Philosophy — an attempt no less audacious and vain than that of the giants to dethrone almighty Jove.

Section V

Of Bishop Berkeley — the Treatise of Human Nature — and of scepticism.

The present age, I apprehend, has not produced two more acute or more practised in this part of philosophy, than the Bishop of Cloyne, and the author of the *Treatise of Human Nature*. The first was no friend to scepticism, but had that warm concern for religious and moral principles which became his order: yet the result of his inquiry was a serious conviction that there is no such thing as a material world — nothing in nature but spirits and ideas; and that the belief of material substances, and of abstract ideas, are the chief causes of all our errors in philosophy, and of all infidelity and heresy in religion. His arguments are founded upon the principles which were formerly laid down by Des Cartes, Malebranche, and Locke, and which have been very generally received.

And the opinion of the ablest judges seems to be, that they neither have been, nor can be confuted; and that he hath proved by unanswerable arguments what no man in his senses can believe.

The second proceeds upon the same principles, but carries them to their full length; and, as the Bishop undid the whole material world, this author, upon the same grounds, undoes the world of spirits, and leaves nothing in nature but ideas and impressions, without any subject on which they may be impressed.

It seems to be a peculiar strain of humour in this author, to set out in his introduction by promising, with a grave face, no less than a complete system of the sciences, upon a foundation entirely new — to wit, that of human nature — when the intention of the whole work is to show, that there is neither human nature nor science in the world. It may perhaps be unreasonable to complain of this conduct in an author who neither believes his own existence nor that of his reader; and therefore could not mean to disappoint him, or to laugh at his credulity. Yet I cannot imagine that the author of the *Treatise of Human Nature* is so sceptical as to plead this apology. He believed, against his principles, that he should be read, and that he should retain his personal identity, till he reaped the honour and reputation justly due to his metaphysical *acumen*. Indeed, he ingenuously acknowledges, that it was only in solitude and retirement that he could yield any assent to his own philosophy; society, like day-light, dispelled the darkness and fogs of scepticism, and made him yield to the dominion of common sense. Nor did I ever hear him charged with doing anything, even in solitude, that argued such a degree of scepticism as his principles maintain. Surely if his friends apprehended this, they would have the charity never to leave him alone.[…]

It is a bold philosophy that rejects, without ceremony, principles which irresistibly govern the belief and the conduct of all mankind in the common concerns of life; and to which the philosopher himself must yield, after he imagines he hath confuted them. Such principles are older, and of more authority, than Philosophy: she rests upon them as her basis, not they upon her. If she could overturn them, she must be buried in their ruins; but all the engines of philosophical subtilty are too weak for this purpose; and the attempt is no less ridiculous than if a mechanic should contrive an *axis in peritrochio* to remove the earth out of its place; or if a mathematician should pretend to demonstrate that things equal to the same thing are not equal to one another.[…]

Section VII

The system of all these authors is the same, and leads to scepticism.

But what if these profound disquisitions into the first principles of human nature, do naturally and necessarily plunge a man into this abyss of scepticism? May we not reasonably judge so from what hath happened? Des Cartes no sooner began to dig in this mine, than scepticism was ready to break in upon him. He did what he could to shut it out. Malebranche and Locke, who dug deeper, found the difficulty of keeping out this enemy still to increase; but they laboured honestly in the design. Then Berkeley, who carried on the work, despairing of securing all, bethought himself of an expedient: — By giving up the material world, which he thought might be spared without loss, and even with advantage, he hoped, by an impregnable partition, to secure the world of spirits. But, alas! the *Treatise of Human Nature* wantonly sapped the foundation of this partition, and drowned all in one universal deluge.

These facts, which are undeniable, do, indeed, give reason to apprehend that Des Cartes' system of the human understanding, which I shall beg leave to call *the ideal system*, and which, with some improvements made by later writers, is now generally received, hath some original defect; that this scepticism is inlaid in it, and reared along with it; and, therefore, that we must lay it open to the foundation, and examine the materials, before we can expect to raise any solid and useful fabric of knowledge on this subject.

Chapter II: Of Smelling

Section I

The order of proceeding – of the medium and organ of smell.

[…] [T]hat all bodies are smelled by means of effluvia which they emit, and which are drawn into the nostrils along with the air, there is no reason to doubt. So that there is manifest appearance of design in placing the organ of smell in the inside of that canal, through which the air is continually passing in inspiration and expiration.

Anatomy informs us, that the *membrana pituitaria*, and the olfactory nerves, which are distributed to the villous parts of this membrane, are the organs destined by the wisdom of nature to this sense; so that when a body emits no effluvia, or when they do not enter into the nose, or when the pituitary membrane or olfactory nerves are rendered unfit to perform their office, it cannot be smelled.

Yet, notwithstanding this, it is evident that neither the organ of smell, nor the medium, nor any motions we can conceive excited in the membrane above mentioned, or in the nerve or animal spirits, do in the least resemble the sensation of smelling; nor could that sensation of itself ever have led us to think of nerves, animal spirits, or effluvia.

Section II

The sensation considered abstractly.

Having premised these things, with regard to the medium and organ of this sense, let us now attend carefully to what the mind is conscious of when we smell a rose or a lily; and, since our language affords no other name for this sensation, we shall call it a *smell* or *odour*, carefully excluding from the meaning of those names everything but the sensation itself, at least till we have examined it.

Suppose a person who never had this sense before, to receive it all at once, and to smell a rose—can he perceive any similitude or agreement between the smell and the rose? or indeed between it and any other object whatsoever? Certainly he cannot. He finds himself affected in a new way, he knows not why or from what cause. Like a man that feels some pain or pleasure, formerly unknown to him, he is conscious that he is not the cause of it himself; but cannot, from the nature of the thing, determine whether it is caused by body or spirit, by something near, or by something at a distance. It has no similitude to anything else, so as to admit of a comparison; and, therefore, he can conclude nothing from it, unless, perhaps, that there must be some unknown cause of it.

It is evidently ridiculous to ascribe to it figure, colour, extension, or any other quality of bodies. He cannot give it a place, any more than he can give a place to melancholy or joy; nor can he conceive it to have any existence, but when it is smelled. So that it appears to be a simple and original affection or feeling of the mind, altogether inexplicable and unaccountable. It is, indeed, impossible that it can be in any body: it is a sensation, and a sensation can only be in a sentient thing.

The various odours have each their different degrees of strength or weakness. Most of them are agreeable or disagreeable; and frequently those that are agreeable when weak, are disagreeable when stronger. When we compare different smells together, we can perceive very few resemblances or contrarieties, or, indeed, relations of any kind between them. They are all so simple in themselves, and so different from each other, that it is hardly possible to divide

them into *genera* and *species*. Most of the names we give them
are particular; as the smell of a *rose*, of a *jessamine*, and the
like. Yet there are some general names — as *sweet, stinking,
musty, putrid, cadaverous, aromatic*. Some of them seem to ref-
resh and animate the mind, others to deaden and depress it.

Section III

Sensation and remembrance, natural principles of belief.

So far we have considered this sensation abstractly. Let us
next compare it with other things to which it bears some relation. And first I shall compare this sensation with the remembrance, and the imagination of it.

I can think of the smell of a rose when I do not smell it;
and it is possible that when I think of it, there is neither rose
nor smell anywhere existing. But when I smell it, I am necessarily determined to believe that the sensation really exists.
This is common to all sensations, that, as they cannot exist
but in being perceived, so they cannot be perceived but they
must exist. I could as easily doubt of my own existence, as of
the existence of my sensations. Even those profound philosophers who have endeavoured to disprove their own existence, have yet left their sensations to stand upon their own
bottom, stript of a subject, rather than call in question the
reality of their existence.

Here, then, a sensation, a smell, for instance, may be presented to the mind three different ways: it may be smelled, it
may be remembered, it may be imagined or thought of. In
the first case, it is necessarily accompanied with a belief of its
present existence; in the second, it is necessarily accompanied with a belief of its past existence; and in the last, it is not
accompanied with belief at all, but is what the logicians call *a
simple apprehension.*

Why sensation should compel our belief of the present
existence of the thing, memory a belief of its past existence,
and imagination no belief at all, I believe no philosopher can
give a shadow of reason, but that such is the nature of these
operations: they are all simple and original, and therefore
inexplicable acts of the mind.

Suppose that once, and only once, I smelled a tuberose in
a certain room, where it grew in a pot, and gave a very grate-
ful perfume. Next day I relate what I saw and smelled. When

I attend as carefully as I can to what passes in my mind in this case, it appears evident that the very thing I saw yesterday, and the fragrance I smelled, are now the immediate objects of my mind, when I remember it. Further, I can imagine this pot and flower transported to the room where I now sit, and yielding the same perfume. Here likewise it appears, that the individual thing which I saw and smelled, is the object of my imagination.

Philosophers indeed tell me, that the immediate object of my memory and imagination in this case, is not the past sensation, but an idea of it, an image, phantasm, or species, of the odour I smelled: that this idea now exists in my mind, or in my sensorium; and the mind, contemplating this present idea, finds it a representation of what is past, or of what may exist; and accordingly calls it memory, or imagination. This is the doctrine of the ideal philosophy; which we shall not now examine, that we may not interrupt the thread of the present investigation. Upon the strictest attention, memory appears to me to have things that are past, and not present ideas, for its object. We shall afterwards examine this system of ideas, and endeavour to make it appear, that no solid proof has ever been advanced of the existence of ideas; that they are a mere fiction and hypothesis, contrived to solve the phænomena of the human understanding; that they do not at all answer this end; and that this hypothesis of ideas or images of things in the mind, or in the sensorium, is the parent of those many paradoxes so shocking to common sense, and of that scepticism which disgrace our philosophy of the mind, and have brought upon it the ridicule and contempt of sensible men.

In the meantime, I beg leave to think, with the vulgar, that, when I remember the smell of the tuberose, that very sensation which I had yesterday, and which has now no more any existence, is the immediate object of my memory; and when I imagine it present, the sensation itself, and not any idea of it, is the object of my imagination. But, though the object of my sensation, memory, and imagination, be in this case the same, yet these acts or operations of the mind are as different, and as easily distinguishable, as smell, taste, and sound. I am conscious of a difference in kind between sensation and memory, and between both and imagination. I find this also, that the sensation compels my belief of the present existence of the smell, and memory my belief of its past existence. There is a smell, is the immediate testimony of sense; there was a smell, is the immediate testimony of memory. If you ask me, why I believe that the smell exists, I can give no other reason, nor shall ever be able to give any other, than that I smell it. If you ask, why I believe that it existed yesterday, I can give no other reason but that I remember it.

Sensation and memory, therefore, are simple, original, and perfectly distinct operations of the mind, and both of them are original principles of belief. Imagination is distinct from both, but is no principle of belief. Sensation implies the present existence of its object, memory its past existence, but imagination views its object naked, and without any belief of its existence or non-existence, and is therefore what the schools call *Simple Apprehension*.

Section IV

Judgment and belief in some cases precede simple apprehension.

But here, again, the ideal system comes in our way: it teaches us that the first operation of the mind about its ideas, is simple apprehension — that is, the bare conception of a thing without any belief about it; and that, after we have got simple apprehensions, by comparing them together, we perceive agreements or disagreements between them; and that this perception of the agreement or disagreement of ideas, is all that we call belief, judgment, or knowledge. Now, this appears to me to be all fiction, without any foundation in nature; for it is acknowledged by all, that sensation must go before memory and imagination; and hence it necessarily follows, that apprehension, accompanied with belief and knowledge, must go before simple apprehension, at least in the matters we are now speaking of. So that here, instead of saying that the belief or knowledge is got by putting together and comparing the simple apprehensions, we ought rather to say that the simple apprehension is performed by resolving and analysing a natural and original judgment. And it is with the operations of the mind, in this case, as with natural bodies, which are, indeed, compounded of simple principles or elements. Nature does not exhibit these elements separate, to be compounded by us; she exhibits them mixed and compounded in concrete bodies, and it is only by art and chemical analysis that they can be separated.

Section V

Two theories of the nature of belief refuted – conclusions from what hath been said.

But what is this belief or knowledge which accompanies sensation and memory? Every man knows what it is, but no man can define it. Does any man pretend to define sensation, or to define consciousness? It is happy, indeed, that no man does. And if no philosopher had endeavoured to define and explain belief, some paradoxes in philosophy, more incredible than ever were brought forth by the most abject superstition or the most frantic enthusiasm, had never seen the light. Of this kind surely is that modern discovery of the ideal philosophy, that sensation, memory, belief, and imagination, when they have the same object, are only different degrees of strength and vivacity in the idea. Suppose the idea to be that of a future state after death: one man believes it firmly – this means no more than that he hath a strong and lively idea of it; another neither believes nor disbelieves – that is, he has a weak and faint idea. Suppose, now, a third person believes firmly that there is no such thing, I am at a loss to know whether his idea be faint or lively: if it is faint, then there may be a firm belief where the idea is faint; if the idea is lively, then the belief of a future state and the belief of no future state must be one and the same. The same arguments that are used to prove that belief implies only a stronger idea of the object than simple apprehension, might as well be used to prove that love implies only a stronger idea of the object than indifference. And then what shall we say of hatred, which must upon this hypothesis be a degree of love, or a degree of indifference? If it should be said, that in love there is something more than an idea – to wit, an affection of the mind – may it not be said with equal reason, that in belief there is something more than an idea – to wit, an assent or persuasion of the mind?

But perhaps it may be thought as ridiculous to argue against this strange opinion, as to maintain it. Indeed, if a man should maintain that a circle, a square, and a triangle differ only in magnitude, and not in figure, I believe he would find nobody disposed either to believe him or to argue against him; and yet I do not think it less shocking to common sense, to maintain that sensation, memory, and imagination differ only in degree, and not in kind. I know it is said, that, in a delirium, or in dreaming, men are apt to mistake one for the other. But does it follow from this, that men who are neither dreaming nor in a delirium cannot distinguish them? But how does a man know that he is not in a delirium? I cannot tell: neither can I tell how a man knows that he exists. But, if any man seriously doubts whether he is in a delirium, I think it highly probable that he is, and that it is time to seek for a cure, which I am persuaded he will not find in the whole system of logic.

[…] I conclude, then, that the belief which accompanies sensation and memory, is a simple act of the mind, which cannot be defined. It is, in this respect, like seeing and hearing, which can never be so defined as to be understood by those who have not these faculties; and to such as have them, no definition can make these operations more clear than they are already. In like manner, every man that has any belief — and he must be a curiosity that has none — knows perfectly what belief is, but can never define or explain it. I conclude, also, that sensation, memory, and imagination, even where they have the same object, are operations of a quite different nature, and perfectly distinguishable by those who are sound and sober. A man that is in danger of confounding them, is indeed to be pitied; but whatever relief he may find from another art, he can find none from logic or metaphysic. I conclude further, that it is no less a part of the human constitution, to believe the present existence of our sensations, and to believe the past existence of what we remember, than it is to believe that twice two make four. The evidence of sense, the evidence of memory, and the evidence of the necessary relations of things, are all distinct and original kinds of evidence, equally grounded on our constitution: none of them depends upon, or can be resolved into another. To reason against any of these kinds of evidence, is absurd; nay, to reason for them is absurd. They are first principles; and such fall not within the province of reason, but of common sense.

Section VI

*Apology for metaphysical absurdities – sensation without a
sentient, a consequence of the theory of ideas – consequences
of this strange opinion.*

Having considered the relation which the sensation of smelling bears to the remembrance and imagination of it, I proceed to consider what relation it bears to a mind or sentient
principle. It is certain, no man can conceive or believe smelling to exist of itself, without a mind, or something that has
the power of smelling, of which it is called a sensation, an
operation, or feeling. Yet, if any man should demand a proof,
that sensation cannot be without a mind or sentient being, I
confess that I can give none; and that to pretend to prove it,
seems to me almost as absurd as to deny it.

This might have been said without any apology before
the *Treatise of Human Nature* appeared in the world. For till
that time, no man, as far as I know, ever thought either of
calling in question that principle, or of giving a reason for his
belief of it. Whether thinking beings were of an ethereal or
igneous nature, whether material or immaterial, was variously disputed; but that thinking is an operation of some
kind of being or other, was always taken for granted, as a
principle that could not possibly admit of doubt.

However, since the author above mentioned, who is
undoubtedly one of the most acute metaphysicians that this
or any age hath produced, hath treated it as a vulgar prejudice, and maintained that the mind is only a succession of
ideas and impressions without any subject; his opinion, however contrary to the common apprehensions of mankind,
deserves respect. I beg therefore, once for all, that no offence
may be taken at charging this or other metaphysical notions
with absurdity, or with being contrary to the common sense
of mankind. No disparagement is meant to the understandings of the authors or maintainers of such opinions. Indeed,
they commonly proceed, not from defect of understanding,
but from an excess of refinement; the reasoning that leads to
them often gives new light to the subject, and shows real
genius and deep penetration in the author; and the premises
do more than atone for the conclusion.

If there are certain principles, as I think there are, which the constitution of our nature leads us to believe, and which we are under a necessity to take for granted in the common concerns of life, without being able to give a reason for them these are what we call the principles of common sense; and what is manifestly contrary to them, is what we call absurd.

Indeed, if it is true, and to be received as a principle of philosophy, that sensation and thought may be without a thinking being, it must be acknowledged to be the most wonderful discovery that this or any other age hath produced. The received doctrine of ideas is the principle from which it is deduced, and of which indeed it seems to be a just and natural consequence. And it is probable, that it would not have been so late a discovery, but that it is so shocking and repugnant to the common apprehensions of mankind, that it required an uncommon degree of philosophical intrepidity to usher it into the world. It is a fundamental principle of the ideal system, that every object of thought must be an impression or an idea—that is, a faint copy of some preceding impression. This is a principle so commonly received, that the author above mentioned, although his whole system is built upon it, never offers the least proof of it. It is upon this principle, as a fixed point, that he erects his metaphysical engines, to overturn heaven and earth, body and spirit. And, indeed, in my apprehension, it is altogether sufficient for the purpose. For, if impressions and ideas are the only objects of thought, then heaven and earth, and body and spirit, and everything you please, must signify only impressions and ideas, or they must be words without any meaning. It seems, therefore, that this notion, however strange, is closely connected with the received doctrine of ideas, and we must either admit the conclusion, or call in question the premises.

Ideas seem to have something in their nature unfriendly to other existences. They were first introduced into philosophy, in the humble character of images or representatives of things: and in this character they seemed not only to be inoffensive, but to serve admirably well for explaining the operations of the human understanding. But, since men began to reason clearly and distinctly about them, they have by degrees supplanted their constituents, and undermined the existence of everything but themselves. First, they discarded all secondary qualities of bodies; and it was found out by their means, that fire is not hot, nor snow cold, nor honey sweet; and, in a word, that heat and cold, sound, colour, taste, and smell, are nothing but ideas or impressions. Bishop Berkeley advanced them a step higher, and found out, by just reasoning from the same principles, that extension, solidity, space, figure, and body, are ideas, and that there is nothing in nature but ideas and spirits. But the triumph of ideas was completed by the *Treatise of Human Nature*, which discards spirits also, and leaves ideas and impressions as the sole existences in the universe. What if, at last, having nothing else to contend with, they should fall foul of one another, and leave no existence in nature at all? This would surely bring philosophy into danger; for what should we have left to talk or to dispute about?

However, hitherto these philosophers acknowledge the existence of impressions and ideas; they acknowledge certain laws of attraction, or rules of precedence, according to which, ideas and impressions range themselves in various forms, and succeed one another: but that they should belong to a mind, as its proper goods and chattels, this they have found to be a vulgar error. These ideas are as free and independent as the birds of the air, or as Epicurus's atoms when they pursued their journey in the vast inane. Shall we conceive them like the films of things in the Epicurean system?[…]

Or do they rather resemble Aristotle's intelligible species, after they are shot forth from the object, and before they have yet struck upon the passive intellect? But why should we seek to compare them with anything, since there is nothing in nature but themselves? They make the whole furniture of the universe; starting into existence, or out of it, without any cause; combining into parcels, which the vulgar call *minds*; and succeeding one another by fixed laws, without time, place, or author of those laws.

Yet, after all, these self-existent and independent ideas look pitifully naked and destitute, when left thus alone in the universe, and seem, upon the whole, to be in a worse condition than they were before. Des Cartes, Malebranche, and Locke, as they made much use of ideas, treated them handsomely, and provided them in decent accommodation; lodging them either in the pineal gland, or in the pure intellect, or even in the divine mind. They moreover clothed them with a commission, and made them representatives of things, which gave them some dignity and character. But the *Treatise of Human Nature*, though no less indebted to them, seems to have made but a bad return, by bestowing upon them this independent existence: since thereby they are turned out of house and home, and set adrift in the world, without friend or connection, without a rag to cover their nakedness; and who knows but the whole system of ideas may perish by the indiscreet zeal of their friends to exalt them?

However this may be, it is certainly a most amazing discovery that thought and ideas may be without any thinking being – a discovery big with consequences which cannot easily be traced by those deluded mortals who think and reason in the common track. We were always apt to imagine, that thought supposed a thinker, and love a lover, and treason a traitor: but this, it seems, was all a mistake; and it is found out, that there may be treason without a traitor, and love without a lover, laws without a legislator, and punishment without a sufferer, succession without time, and motion without anything moved, or space in which it may move: or if, in these cases, ideas are the lover, the sufferer, the traitor, it were to be wished that the author of this discovery had farther condescended to acquaint us whether ideas can converse together, and be under obligations of duty or gratitude to each other; whether they can make promises and enter into leagues and covenants, and fulfil or break them, and be punished for the breach. If one set of ideas makes a covenant, another breaks it, and a third is punished for it, there is reason to think that justice is no natural virtue in this system.

It seemed very natural to think, that the *Treatise of Human Nature* required an author, and a very ingenious one too; but now we learn that it is only a set of ideas which came together and arranged themselves by certain associations and attractions.

After all, this curious system appears not to be fitted to the present state of human nature. How far it may suit some choice spirits, who are refined from the dregs of common sense, I cannot say. It is acknowledged, I think, that even these can enter into this system only in their most speculative hours, when they soar so high in pursuit of those self-existent ideas as to lose sight of all other things. But when they condescend to mingle again with the human race, and to converse with a friend, a companion, or a fellow-citizen, the ideal system vanishes; common sense, like an irresistible torrent, carries them along; and, in spite of all their reasoning and philosophy, they believe their own existence, and the existence of other things.

Indeed, it is happy they do so; for, if they should carry their closet belief into the world, the rest of mankind would consider them as diseased, and send them to an infirmary. Therefore, as Plato required certain previous qualifications of those who entered his school, I think it would be prudent for the doctors of this ideal philosophy to do the same, and to refuse admittance to every man who is so weak as to imagine that he ought to have the same belief in solitude and in company, or that his principles ought to have any influence upon his practice; for this philosophy is like a hobby-horse, which a man in bad health may ride in his closet, without hurting his reputation; but, if he should take him abroad with him to church, or to the exchange, or to the play-house, his heir would immediately call a jury, and seize his estate.

Section VII

The conception and belief of a sentient being or mind is suggested by our constitution — the notion of relations not always got by comparing the related ideas.

Leaving this philosophy, therefore, to those who have occasion for it, and can use it discreetly as a chamber exercise, we may still inquire how the rest of mankind, and even the adepts themselves, except in some solitary moments, have got so strong and irresistible a belief, that thought must have a subject, and be the act of some thinking being; how every man believes himself to be something distinct from his ideas and impressions — something which continues the same identical self when all his ideas and impressions are changed. It is impossible to trace the origin of this opinion in history; for all languages have it interwoven in their original construction. All nations have always believed it. The constitution of all laws and governments, as well as the common transactions of life, suppose it.

It is no less impossible for any man to recollect when he himself came by this notion; for, as far back as we can remember, we were already in possession of it, and as fully persuaded of our own existence, and the existence of other things, as that one and one make two. It seems, therefore, that this opinion preceded all reasoning, and experience, and instruction; and this is the more probable, because we could not get it by any of these means. It appears, then, to be an undeniable fact, that, from thought or sensation, all mankind, constantly and invariably, from the first dawning of reflection, do infer a power or faculty of thinking and a permanent being or mind to which that faculty belongs; and that we as invariably ascribe all the various kinds of sensation and thought we are conscious of, to one individual mind or self.

But by what rules of logic we make these inferences, it is impossible to show; nay, it is impossible to show how our sensations and thoughts can give us the very notion and conception either of a mind or of a faculty. The faculty of smelling is something very different from the actual sensation of smelling; for the faculty may remain when we have no sensation. And the mind is no less different from the faculty; for it continues the same individual being when that faculty is lost. Yet this sensation suggests to us both a faculty and a mind; and not only suggests the notion of them, but creates a belief of their existence; although it is impossible to discover, by reason, any tie or connection between one and the other.

What shall we say, then? Either those inferences which we draw from our sensations — namely, the existence of a mind, and of powers or faculties belonging to it — are prejudices of philosophy or education, mere fictions of the mind, which a wise man should throw off as he does the belief of fairies; or they are judgments of nature — judgments not got by comparing ideas, and perceiving agreements and disagreements, but immediately inspired by our constitution.

If this last is the case, as I apprehend it is, it will be impossible to shake off those opinions, and we must yield to them at last, though we struggle hard to get rid of them. And if we could, by a determined obstinacy, shake off the principles of our nature, this is not to act the philosopher, but the fool or the madman. It is incumbent upon those who think that these are not natural principles, to show, in the first place, how we can otherwise get the notion of a mind and its faculties; and then to show how we come to deceive ourselves into the opinion that sensation cannot be without a sentient being.

It is the received doctrine of philosophers, that our notions of relations can only be got by comparing the related ideas: but, in the present case, there seems to be an instance to the contrary. It is not by having first the notions of mind and sensation, and then comparing them together, that we perceive the one to have the relation of a subject or substratum, and the other that of an act or operation: on the contrary, one of the related things — to wit, sensation — suggests to us both the correlate and the relation.

I beg leave to make use of the word *suggestion*, because I know not one more proper, to express a power of the mind, which seems entirely to have escaped the notice of philosophers, and to which we owe many of our simple notions which are neither impressions nor ideas, as well as many original principles of belief. I shall endeavor to illustrate, by an example, what I understand by this word. We all know, that a certain kind of sound suggests immediately to the mind, a coach passing in the street; and not only produces the imagination, but the belief, that a coach is passing. Yet there is here no comparing of ideas, no perception of agreements or disagreements, to produce this belief: nor is there the least similitude between the sound we hear and the coach we imagine and believe to be passing.

It is true that this suggestion is not natural and original; it is the result of experience and habit. But I think it appears, from what hath been said, that there are natural suggestions: particularly, that sensation suggests the notion of present existence, and the belief that what we perceive or feel does now exist; that memory suggests the notion of past existence, and the belief that what we remember did exist in time past; and that our sensations and thoughts do also suggest the notion of a mind, and the belief of its existence, and of its relation to our thoughts. By a like natural principle it is, that a beginning of existence, or any change in nature, suggests to us the notion of a cause, and compels our belief of its existence. And, in like manner, as shall be shown when we come to the sense of touch, certain sensations of touch, by the constitution of our nature, suggest to us extension, solidity, and motion, which are nowise like to sensations, although they have been hitherto confounded with them.

Section VIII

There is a quality or virtue in bodies, which we call their smell — how this is connected in the imagination with the sensation.

We have considered smell as signifying a sensation, feeling, or impression upon the mind; and in this sense, it can only be in a mind, or sentient being: but it is evident that mankind gives the name of *smell* much more frequently to something which they conceive to be external, and to be a quality of body: they understand something by it which does not at all infer a mind; and have not the least difficulty in conceiving the air perfumed with aromatic odours in the deserts of Arabia, or in some uninhabited island, where the human foot never trod. Every sensible day-labourer hath as clear a notion of this, and as full a conviction of the possibility of it, as he hath of his own existence; and can no more doubt of the one than of the other.

Suppose that such a man meets with a modern philosopher, and wants to be informed what smell in plants is. The philosopher tells him, that there is no smell in plants, nor in anything but in the mind; that it is impossible there can be smell but in a mind; and that all this hath been demonstrated by modern philosophy. The plain man will, no doubt, be apt to think him merry: but, if he finds that he is serious, his next conclusion will be that he is mad; or that philosophy, like magic, puts men into a new world, and gives them different faculties from common men. And thus philosophy and common sense are set at variance. But who is to blame for it? In my opinion the philosopher is to blame. For if he means by smell, what the rest of mankind most commonly mean, he is certainly mad. But if he puts a different meaning upon the word, without observing it himself, or giving warning to others, he abuses language and disgraces philosophy, without doing any service to truth: as if a man should exchange the meaning of the words *daughter* and *cow*, and then endeavour to prove to his plain neighbour, that his cow is his daughter, and his daughter his cow.

I believe there is not much more wisdom in many of those paradoxes of the ideal philosophy, which to plain sensible men appear to be palpable absurdities, but with the adepts pass for profound discoveries. I resolve, for my own part, always to pay a great regard to the dictates of common sense, and not to depart from them without absolute necessity: and, therefore, I am apt to think that there is really something in the rose or lily, which is by the vulgar called *smell*, and which continues to exist when it is not smelled: and shall proceed to inquire what this is; how we come by the notion of it; and what relation this quality or virtue of smell hath to the sensation which we have been obliged to call by the same name, for want of another.

Let us therefore suppose, as before, a person beginning to exercise the sense of smelling; a little experience will discover to him that the nose is the organ of this sense, and that the air, or something in the air, is a medium of it. And finding, by farther experience, that, when a rose is near, he has a certain sensation, when it is removed, the sensation is gone, he finds a connection in nature betwixt the rose and this sensation. The rose is considered as a cause, occasion, or antecedent of the sensation; the sensation as an effect or consequence of the presence of the rose; they are associated in the mind, and constantly found conjoined in the imagination.

But here it deserves our notice, that, although the sensation may seem more closely related to the mind its subject, or to the nose its organ, yet neither of these connections operate so powerfully upon the imagination as its connection with the rose its concomitant. The reason of this seems to be, that its connection with the mind is more general, and noway distinguisheth it from other smells, or even from tastes, sounds, and other kinds of sensations. The relation it hath to the organ is likewise general, and doth not distinguish it from other smells; but the connection it hath with the rose is special and constant; by which means they become almost inseparable in the imagination, in like manner as thunder and lightning, freezing and cold.

Section IX

That there is a principle in human nature, from which the notion of this, as well as all other natural virtues or causes, is derived.

In order to illustrate further how we come to conceive a quality or virtue in the rose which we call *smell*, and what this smell is, it is proper to observe, that the mind begins very early to thirst after principles which may direct it in the exertion of its powers. The smell of a rose is a certain affection or feeling of the mind; and, as it is not constant, but comes and goes, we want to know when and where we may expect it; and are uneasy till we find something which, being present, brings this feeling along with it, and, being removed, removes it. This, when found, we call the cause of it; not in a strict and philosophical sense, as if the feeling were really effected or produced by that cause, but in a popular sense; for the mind is satisfied if there is a constant conjunction between them; and such causes are in reality nothing else but laws of nature. Having found the smell thus constantly conjoined with the rose, the mind is at rest, without inquiring whether this conjunction is owing to a real efficiency or not; that being a philosophical inquiry, which does not concern human life. But every discovery of such a constant conjunction is of real importance in life, and makes a strong impression upon the mind.

So ardently do we desire to find everything that happens within our observation thus connected with something else as its cause or occasion, that we are apt to fancy connections upon the slightest grounds; and this weakness is most remarkable in the ignorant, who know least of the real connections established in nature. A man meets with an unlucky accident on a certain day of the year, and, knowing no other cause of his misfortune, he is apt to conceive something unlucky in that day of the calendar; and, if he finds the same connection hold a second time, is strongly confirmed in his superstition. I remember, many years ago, a white ox was brought into this country, of so enormous a size that people came many miles to see him. There happened, some months after, an uncommon fatality among women in child-bearing. Two such uncommon events, following one another, gave a suspicion of their connection, and occasioned a common opinion among the country-people that the white ox was the cause of this fatality.

However silly and ridiculous this opinion was, it sprung from the same root in human nature on which all natural philosophy grows—namely, an eager desire to find out connections in things, and a natural, original, and unaccountable propensity to believe that the connections which we have observed in time past will continue in time to come. Omens, portents, good and bad luck, palmistry, astrology, all the numerous arts of divination and of interpreting dreams, false hypotheses and systems, and true principles in the philosophy of nature, are all built upon the same foundation in the human constitution, and are distinguished only according as we conclude rashly from too few instances, or cautiously from a sufficient induction.

As it is experience only that discovers these connections between natural causes and their effects; without inquiring further, we attribute to the cause some vague and indistinct notion of power or virtue to produce the effect. And, in many cases, the purposes of life do not make it necessary to give distinct names to the cause and the effect. Whence it happens, that, being closely connected in the imagination, although very unlike to each other, one name serves for both; and, in common discourse, is most frequently applied to that which, of the two, is most the object of our attention. This occasions an ambiguity in many words, which, having the same causes in all languages, is common to all, and is apt to be overlooked even by philosophers.[…]

Heat signifies a sensation, and cold a contrary one; but heat likewise signifies a quality or state of bodies, which hath no contrary, but different degrees. When a man feels the same water hot to one hand and cold to the other, this gives him occasion to distinguish between the feeling and the heat of the body; and, although he knows that the sensations are contrary, he does not imagine that the body can have contrary qualities at the same time. And when he finds a different taste in the same body in sickness and in health, he is easily convinced, that the quality in the body called *taste* is the same as before, although the sensations he has from it are perhaps opposite.

The vulgar are commonly charged by philosophers, with the absurdity of imagining the smell in the rose to be something like to the sensation of smelling; but I think unjustly; for they neither give the same epithets to both, nor do they reason in the same manner from them. What is smell in the rose? It is a quality or virtue of the rose, or of something proceeding from it, which we perceive by the sense of smelling; and this is all we know of the matter. But what is smelling? It is an act of the mind, but is never imagined to be a quality of the mind. Again, the sensation of smelling is conceived to infer necessarily a mind or sentient being; but smell in the rose infers no such thing. We say, this body smells sweet, that stinks; but we do not say, this mind smells sweet and that stinks. Therefore, smell in the rose, and the sensation which it causes, are not conceived, even by the vulgar, to be things of the same kind, although they have the same name.

From what hath been said, we may learn that the smell of a rose signifies two things: *First*, a sensation, which can have no existence but when it is perceived, and can only be in a sentient being or mind; *Secondly*, it signifies some power, quality, or virtue, in the rose, or in effluvia proceeding from it, which hath a permanent existence, independent of the mind, and which, by the constitution of nature, produces the sensation in us. By the original constitution of our nature, we are both led to believe that there is a permanent cause of the sensation, and prompted to seek after it; and experience determines us to place it in the rose. The names of all smells, tastes, sounds, as well as heat and cold, have a like ambiguity in all languages; but it deserves our attention, that these names are but rarely, in common language, used to signify the sensations; for the most part, they signify the external qualities which are indicated by the sensations — the cause of which phænomenon I take to be this. Our sensations have very different degrees of strength. Some of them are so quick and lively as to give us a great deal either of pleasure or of uneasiness. When this is the case, we are compelled to attend to the sensation itself, and to make it an object of thought and discourse; we give it a name, which signifies nothing but the sensation; and in this case we readily acknowledge, that the thing meant by that name is in the mind only, and not in anything external. Such are the various kinds of pain, sickness, and the sensations of hunger and other appetites. But, where the sensation is not so interesting as to require to be made an object of thought, our constitution leads us to consider it as a sign of something external, which hath a constant conjunction with it; and, having found what it indicates, we give a name to that: the sensation, having no proper name, falls in as an accessory to the thing signified by it, and is confounded under the same name. So that the name may, indeed, be applied to the sensation, but most properly and commonly is applied to the thing indicated by that sensation. The sensations of smell, taste, sound, and colour, are of infinitely more importance as signs or indications, than they are upon their own account; like the words of a language, wherein we do not attend to the sound but to the sense.

Section X

Whether in sensation the mind is active or passive?

There is one inquiry remains, Whether, in smelling, and in other sensations, the mind is active or passive? This possibly may seem to be a question about words, or, at least, of very small importance; however, if it leads us to attend more accurately to the operations of our minds than we are accustomed to do, it is, upon that very account, not altogether unprofitable. I think the opinion of modern philosophers is, that in sensation the mind is altogether passive. And this undoubtedly is so far true, that we cannot raise any sensation in our minds by willing it; and, on the other hand, it seems hardly possible to avoid having the sensation when the object is presented. Yet it seems likewise to be true, that, in proportion as the attention is more or less turned to a sensation or diverted from it, that sensation is more or less perceived and remembered. Every one knows that very intense pain may be diverted by a surprise, or by anything that entirely occupies the mind. When we are engaged in earnest conversation, the clock may strike by us without being heard; at least, we remember not, the next moment, that we did hear it. The noise and tumult of a great trading city is not heard by them who have lived in it all their days; but it stuns those strangers who have lived in the peaceful retirement of the country. Whether, therefore, there can be any sensation where the mind is purely passive, I will not say; but I think we are conscious of having given some attention to every sensation which we remember, though ever so recent.

No doubt, where the impulse is strong and uncommon, it is as difficult to withhold attention as it is to forbear crying out in racking pain, or starting in a sudden fright. But how far both might be attained by strong resolution and practice, is not easy to determine. So that, although the Peripatetics had no good reason to suppose an active and a passive intellect, since attention may be well enough accounted an act of the will, yet I think they came nearer to the truth, in holding the mind to be in sensation partly passive and partly active, than the moderns in affirming it to be purely passive. Sensation, imagination, memory and judgment, have, by the vulgar in all ages, been considered as acts of the mind. The manner in which they are expressed in all languages, shows this. When the mind is much employed in them, we say it is very active; whereas, if they were impressions only, as the ideal philosophy would lead us to conceive, we ought, in such a case, rather to say, that the mind is very passive; for, I suppose, no man would attribute great activity to the paper I write upon, because it receives variety of characters.

The relation which the sensation of smell bears to the memory and imagination of it, and to a mind or subject, is common to all our sensations, and, indeed, to all the operations of the mind: the relation it bears to the will is common to it with all the powers of understanding; and the relation it bears to that quality or virtue of bodies which it indicates, is common to it with the sensations of taste, hearing, colour, heat, and cold — so that what hath been said of this sense, may easily be applied to several of our senses, and to other operations of the mind; and this, I hope, will apologize for our insisting so long upon it.

Chapter IV: Of Hearing

Section I

Variety of sounds — their place and distance learned by custom, without reasoning.

Sounds have probably no less variety of modifications, than either tastes or odours.[…]

It seems to be by custom that we learn to distinguish both the place of things, and their nature, by means of their sound. That such a noise is in the street, such another in the room above me; that this is a knock at my door, that a person walking up stairs—is probably learnt by experience. I remember, that once lying a-bed, and having been put into a fright, I heard my own heart beat; but I took it to be one knocking at the door, and arose and opened the door oftener than once, before I discovered that the sound was in my own breast. It is probable, that, previous to all experience, we should as little know whether a sound came from the right or left, from above or below, from a great or a small distance, as we should know whether it was the sound of a drum, or a bell, or a cart. Nature is frugal in her operations, and will not be at the expense of a particular instinct, to give us that knowledge which experience will soon produce, by means of a general principle of human nature.

For a little experience, by the constitution of human nature, ties together, not only in our imagination, but in our belief, those things which were in their nature unconnected. When I hear a certain sound, I conclude immediately, without reasoning, that a coach passes by. There are no premises from which this conclusion is inferred by any rules of logic. It is the effect of a principle of our nature, common to us with the brutes.[…]

Section II

Of natural language.

One of the noblest purposes of sound undoubtedly is language, without which mankind would hardly be able to attain any degree of improvement above the brutes. Language is commonly considered as purely an invention of men, who by nature are no less mute than the brutes; but, having a superior degree of invention and reason, have been able to contrive artificial signs of their thoughts and purposes, and to establish them by common consent. But the origin of language deserves to be more carefully inquired into, not only as this inquiry may be of importance for the improvement of language, but as it is related to the present subject, and tends to lay open some of the first principles of human nature. I shall, therefore, offer some thoughts upon this subject.

By language I understand all those signs which mankind use in order to communicate to others their thoughts and intentions, their purposes and desires. And such signs may be conceived to be of two kinds: First, such as have no meaning but what is affixed to them by compact or agreement among those who use them — these are artificial signs; Secondly, such as, previous to all compact or agreement, have a meaning which every man understands by the principles of his nature. Language, so far as it consists of artificial signs, may be called *artificial*; so far as it consists of natural signs, I call it *natural*.

Having premised these definitions, I think it is demonstrable, that, if mankind had not a natural language, they could never have invented an artificial one by their reason and ingenuity. For all artificial language supposes some compact or agreement to affix a certain meaning to certain signs; therefore, there must be compacts or agreements before the use of artificial signs; but there can be no compact or agreement without signs, nor without language; and, therefore, there must be a natural language before any artificial language can be invented: which was to be demonstrated.

Had language in general been a human invention, as much as writing or printing, we should find whole nations as mute as the brutes. Indeed, even the brutes have some natural signs by which they express their own thoughts, affections, and desires, and understand those of others. A chick, as soon as hatched, understands the different sounds whereby its dam calls it to food, or gives the alarm of danger. A dog or a horse understands, by nature, when the human voice caresses, and when it threatens him. But brutes, as far as we know, have no notion of contracts or covenants, or of moral obligation to perform them. If nature had given them these notions, she would probably have given them natural signs to express them. And where nature has denied these notions, it is as impossible to acquire them by art, as it is for a blind man to acquire the notion of colours. Some brutes are sensible of honour or disgrace; they have resentment and gratitude; but none of them, as far as we know, can make a promise or plight their faith, having no such notions from their constitution. And if mankind had not these notions by nature, and natural signs to express them by, with all their wit and ingenuity they could never have invented language.

The elements of this natural language of mankind, or the signs that are naturally expressive of our thoughts, may, I think, be reduced to these three kinds: modulations of the voice, gestures, and features. By means of these, two savages who have no common artificial language, can converse together; can communicate their thoughts in some tolerable manner; can ask and refuse, affirm and deny, threaten and supplicate; can traffic, enter into covenants, and plight their faith. This might be confirmed by historical facts of undoubted credit, if it were necessary.

Mankind having thus a common language by nature, though a scanty one, adapted only to the necessities of nature, there is no great ingenuity required in improving it by the addition of artificial signs, to supply the deficiency of the natural. These artificial signs must multiply with the arts of life, and the improvements of knowledge. The articulations of the voice seem to be, of all signs, the most proper for artificial language; and as mankind have universally used them for that purpose, we may reasonably judge that nature intended them for it. But nature probably does not intend that we should lay aside the use of the natural signs; it is enough that we supply their defects by artificial ones. A man that rides always in a chariot, by degrees loses the use of his legs; and one who uses artificial signs only, loses both the knowledge and use of the natural. Dumb people retain much more of the natural language than others, because necessity obliges them to use it. And for the same reason, savages have much more of it than civilized nations. It is by natural signs chiefly that we give force and energy to language; and the less language has of them, it is the less expressive and persuasive. Thus, writing is less expressive than reading, and reading less expressive than speaking without book; speaking without the proper and natural modulations, force, and variations of the voice, is a frigid and dead language, compared with that which is attended with them; it is still more expressive when we add the language of the eyes and features; and is then only in its perfect and natural state, and attended with its proper energy, when to all these we superadd the force of action.

Where speech is natural, it will be an exercise, not of the voice and lungs only, but of all the muscles of the body; like that of dumb people and savages, whose language, as it has more of nature, is more expressive, and is more easily learned.

Is it not pity that the refinements of a civilized life, instead of supplying the defects of natural language, should root it out and plant in its stead dull and lifeless articulations of unmeaning sounds, or the scrawling of insignificant characters? The perfection of language is commonly thought to be, to express human thoughts and sentiments distinctly by these dull signs; but if this is the perfection of artificial language, it is surely the corruption of the natural.

Artificial signs signify, but they do not express; they speak to the understanding, as algebraical characters may do, but the passions, the affections, and the will, hear them not; these continue dormant and inactive, till we speak to them in the language of nature, to which they are all attention and obedience.

It were easy to show, that the fine arts of the musician, the painter, the actor, and the orator, so far as they are expressive—although the knowledge of them requires in us a delicate taste, a nice judgment, and much study and practice—yet they are nothing else but the language of nature, which we brought into the world with us, but have unlearned by disuse, and so find the greatest difficulty in recovering it.

Abolish the use of articulate sounds and writing among mankind for a century, and every man would be a painter, an actor, and an orator. We mean not to affirm that such an expedient is practicable; or, if it were, that the advantage would counterbalance the loss; but that, as men are led by nature and necessity to converse together, they will use every mean in their power to make themselves understood; and where they cannot do this by artificial signs, they will do it, as far as possible, by natural ones: and he that understands perfectly the use of natural signs, must be the best judge in all the expressive arts.

Chapter V: Of Touch

Section I

Of heat and cold.

[...] As to heat and cold, it will easily be allowed that they are secondary qualities, of the same order with smell, taste, and sound. And, therefore, what hath been already said of smell, is easily applicable to them; that is, that the words *heat* and *cold* have each of them two significations; they sometimes signify certain sensations of the mind, which can have no existence when they are not felt, nor can exist anywhere but in a mind or sentient being; but more frequently they signify a quality in bodies, which, by the laws of nature, occasions the sensations of heat and cold in us — a quality which, though connected by custom so closely with the sensation, that we cannot, without difficulty, separate them, yet hath not the least resemblance to it, and may continue to exist when there is no sensation at all.

The sensations of heat and cold are perfectly known; for they neither are, nor can be, anything else than what we feel them to be; but the qualities in bodies which we call *heat* and *cold* are unknown. They are only conceived by us, as unknown causes or occasions of the sensations to which we give the same names. But, though common sense says nothing of the nature of these qualities, it plainly dictates the existence of them; and to deny that there can be heat and cold when they are not felt, is an absurdity too gross to merit confutation. For what could be more absurd, than to say, that the thermometer cannot rise or fall, unless some person be present, or that the coast of Guinea would be as cold as Nova Zembla, if it had no inhabitants?[...]

[W]hatever be the nature of that quality in bodies which we call *heat*, we certainly know this, that it cannot in the least resemble the sensation of heat. It is no less absurd to suppose a likeness between the sensation and the quality, than it would be to suppose that the pain of the gout resembles a square or a triangle. The simplest man that hath common sense, does not imagine the sensation of heat, or anything that resembles that sensation, to be in the fire. He only imagines that there is something in the fire which makes him and other sentient beings feel heat. Yet, as the name of *heat*, in

common language, more frequently and more properly signifies this unknown something in the fire, than the sensation
occasioned by it, he justly laughs at the philosopher who
denies that there is any heat in the fire, and thinks that he
speaks contrary to common sense.

Section II

Of hardness and softness.

Let us next consider hardness and softness; by which words
we always understand real properties or qualities of bodies
of which we have a distinct conception.

When the parts of a body adhere so firmly that it cannot
easily be made to change its figure, we call it *hard*; when its
parts are easily displaced, we call it *soft*. This is the notion
which all mankind have of hardness and softness; they are
neither sensations, nor like any sensation; they were real
qualities before they were perceived by touch, and continue
to be so when they are not perceived; for if any man will
affirm that diamonds were not hard till they were handled,
who would reason with him?

There is, no doubt, a sensation by which we perceive a
body to be hard or soft. This sensation of hardness may easily be had, by pressing one's hand against the table, and attending to the feeling that ensues, setting aside, as much as
possible, all thought of the table and its qualities, or of any
external thing. But it is one thing to have the sensation, and
another to attend to it, and make it a distinct object of reflection. The first is very easy; the last, in most cases, extremely
difficult.

We are so accustomed to use the sensation as a sign, and
to pass immediately to the hardness signified, that, as far as
appears, it was never made an object of thought, either by
the vulgar or by philosophers; nor has it a name in any language. There is no sensation more distinct, or more frequent;
yet it is never attended to, but passes through the mind
instantaneously, and serves only to introduce that quality in
bodies, which, by a law of our constitution, it suggests.[...]

[H]owever difficult it may be to attend to this fugitive
sensation, to stop its rapid progress, and to disjoin it from the
external quality of hardness, in whose shadow it is apt immediately to hide itself; this is what a philosopher by pains and

practice must attain, otherwise it will be impossible for him to reason justly upon this subject, or even to understand what is here advanced. For the last appeal, in subjects of this nature, must be to what a man feels and perceives in his own mind.[…]

The firm cohesion of the parts of a body, is no more like that sensation by which I perceive it to be hard, than the vibration of a sonorous body is like the sound I hear: nor can I possibly perceive, by my reason, any connection between the one and the other. No man can give a reason, why the vibration of a body might not have given the sensation of smelling, and the effluvia of bodies affected our hearing, if it had so pleased our Maker. In like manner, no man can give a reason why the sensations of smell, or taste, or sound, might not have indicated hardness, as well as that sensation which, by our constitution, does indicate it. Indeed, no man can conceive any sensation to resemble any known quality of bodies. Nor can any man show, by any good argument, that all our sensations might not have been as they are, though no body, nor quality of body, had ever existed.

Here, then, is a phænomenon of human nature, which comes to be resolved. Hardness of bodies is a thing that we conceive as distinctly, and believe as firmly, as anything in nature. We have no way of coming at this conception and belief, but by means of a certain sensation of touch, to which hardness hath not the least similitude; nor can we, by any rules of reasoning, infer the one from the other. The question is, How we come by this conception and belief?

First, as to the conception: Shall we call it an idea of sensation, or of reflection? The last will not be affirmed; and as little can the first, unless we will call that an idea of sensation which hath no resemblance to any sensation. So that the origin of this idea of hardness, one of the most common and most distinct we have, is not to be found in all our systems of the mind: not even in those which have so copiously endeavoured to deduce all our notions from sensation and reflection.

But, secondly, supposing we have got the conception of hardness, how come we by the belief of it? Is it self-evident, from comparing the ideas, that such a sensation could not be felt, unless such a quality of bodies existed? No. Can it be proved by probable or certain arguments? No; it cannot. Have we got this belief, then, by tradition, by education, or by experience? No; it is not got in any of these ways. Shall we then throw off this belief as having no foundation in reason? Alas! it is not in our power; it triumphs over reason, and laughs at all the arguments of a philosopher. Even the author of the *Treatise of Human Nature*, though he saw no reason for this belief, but many against it, could hardly conquer it in his speculative and solitary moments; at other times, he fairly yielded to it, and confesses that he found himself under a necessity to do so.

What shall we say, then, of this conception, and this belief, which are so unaccountable and untractable? I see nothing left, but to conclude, that, by an original principle of our constitution, a certain sensation of touch both suggests to the mind the conception of hardness, and creates the belief of it: or, in other words, that this sensation is a natural sign of hardness. And this I shall endeavour more fully to explain.

Section III

Of natural signs.

As in artificial signs there is often neither similitude between the sign and thing signified, nor any connection that arises necessarily from the nature of the things, so it is also in natural signs. The word *gold* has no similitude to the substance signified by it; nor is it in its own nature more fit to signify this than any other substance; yet, by habit and custom, it suggests this and no other. In like manner, a sensation of touch suggests hardness, although it hath neither similitude to hardness, nor, as far as we can perceive, any necessary connection with it. The difference betwixt these two signs lies only in this — that, in the first, the suggestion is the effect of habit and custom; in the second, it is not the effect of habit, but of the original constitution of our minds.

It appears evident from what hath been said on the subject of language, that there are natural signs as well as artificial; and particularly, that the thoughts, purposes, and dispositions of the mind, have their natural signs in the features of the face, the modulation of the voice, and the motion and attitude of the body: that, without a natural knowledge of the connection between these signs and the things signified by them, language could never have been invented and established among men: and, that the fine arts are all founded upon this connection, which we may call *the natural language of mankind*. It is now proper to observe, that there are different orders of natural signs, and to point out the different classes into which they may be distinguished, that we may more distinctly conceive the relation between our sensations and the things they suggest, and what we mean by calling sensations signs of external things.

The first class of natural signs comprehends those whose connection with the thing signified is established by nature, but discovered only by experience. The whole of genuine philosophy consists in discovering such connections, and reducing them to general rules. The great Lord Verulam had a perfect comprehension of this, when he called it *an interpretation of nature*. No man ever more distinctly understood or happily expressed the nature and foundation of the philosophic art. What is all we know of mechanics, astronomy, and optics, but connections established by nature, and discovered by experience or observation, and consequences deduced from them? All the knowledge we have in agriculture, gardening, chemistry, and medicine, is built upon the same foundation. And if ever our philosophy concerning the human mind is carried so far as to deserve the name of science, which ought never to be despaired of, it must be by observing facts, reducing them to general rules, and drawing just conclusions from them. What we commonly call natural *causes* might, with more propriety, be called natural *signs*, and what we call *effects*, the things signified. The causes have no proper efficiency or causality, as far as we know; and all we can certainly affirm is, that nature hath established a constant conjunction between them and the things called their effects; and hath given to mankind a disposition to observe those connections, to confide in their continuance, and to make use of them for the improvement of our knowledge, and increase of our power.

A second class is that wherein the connection between the sign and thing signified, is not only established by nature, but discovered to us by a natural principle, without reasoning or experience. Of this kind are the natural signs of human thoughts, purposes, and desires, which have been already mentioned as the natural language of mankind. An infant may be put into a fright by an angry countenance, and soothed again by smiles and blandishments. A child that has a good musical ear, may be put to sleep or to dance, may be made merry or sorrowful, by the modulation of musical sounds. The principles of all the fine arts, and of what we call *a fine taste*, may be resolved into connections of this kind. A fine taste may be improved by reasoning and experience; but if the first principles of it were not planted in our minds by nature, it could never be acquired. Nay, we have already made it appear, that a great part of this knowledge which we have by nature, is lost by the disuse of natural signs, and the substitution of artificial in their place.

A third class of natural signs comprehends those which, though we never before had any notion or conception of the thing signified, do suggest it, or conjure it up, as it were, by a natural kind of magic, and at once give us a conception and create a belief of it. I showed formerly, that our sensations suggest to us a sentient being or mind to which they belong — a being which hath a permanent existence, although the sensations are transient and of short duration — a being which is still the same, while its sensations and other operations are varied ten thousand ways — a being which hath the same relation to all that infinite variety of thoughts, purposes, actions, affections, enjoyments, and sufferings, which we are conscious of, or can remember. The conception of a mind is neither an idea of sensation nor of reflection; for it is neither like any of our sensations, nor like anything we are conscious of. The first conception of it, as well as the belief of it, and of the common relation it bears to all that we are conscious of, or remember, is suggested to every thinking being, we do not know how.

The notion of hardness in bodies, as well as the belief of it, are got in a similar manner; being, by an original principle of our nature, annexed to that sensation which we have when we feel a hard body. And so naturally and necessarily does the sensation convey the notion and belief of hardness, that hitherto they have been confounded by the most acute inquirers into the principles of human nature, although they appear, upon accurate reflection, not only to be different things, but as unlike as pain is to the point of a sword.

It may be observed, that, as the first class of natural signs I have mentioned is the foundation of true philosophy, and the second the foundation of the fine arts, or of taste — so the last is the foundation of common sense — a part of human nature which hath never been explained.

I take it for granted, that the notion of hardness, and the belief of it, is first got by means of that particular sensation which, as far back as we can remember, does invariably suggest it; and that, if we had never had such a feeling, we should never have had any notion of hardness. I think it is evident, that we cannot, by reasoning from our sensations, collect the existence of bodies at all, far less any of their qualities. This hath been proved by unanswerable arguments by the Bishop of Cloyne, and by the author of the *Treatise of Human Nature*. It appears as evident that this connection between our sensations and the conception and belief of external existences cannot be produced by habit, experience, education, or any principle of human nature that hath been admitted by philosophers. At the same time, it is a fact that such sensations are invariably connected with the conception and belief of external existences. Hence, by all rules of just reasoning, we must conclude that this connection is the effect of our constitution, and ought to be considered as an original principle of human nature, till we find some more general principle into which it may be resolved.

Section IV

Of hardness, and other primary qualities.

Further, I observe that hardness is a quality, of which we have as clear and distinct a conception as of anything whatsoever. The cohesion of the parts of a body with more or less force, is perfectly understood, though its cause is not; we know what it is, as well as how it affects the touch. It is, therefore, a quality of a quite different order from those secondary qualities we have already taken notice of, whereof we know no more naturally than that they are adapted to raise certain sensations in us. If hardness were a quality of the same kind, it would be a proper inquiry for philosophers, what hardness in bodies is? and we should have had various hypotheses about it, as well as about colour and heat. But it is evident that any such hypothesis would be ridiculous.[…]

The distinction betwixt primary and secondary qualities hath had several revolutions. Democritus and Epicurus, and their followers, maintained it. Aristotle and the Peripatetics abolished it. Des Cartes, Malebranche, and Locke, revived it, and were thought to have put it in a very clear light. But Bishop Berkeley again discarded this distinction, by such proofs as must be convincing to those that hold the received doctrine of ideas. Yet, after all, there appears to be a real foundation for it in the principles of our nature.

What hath been said of hardness, is so easily applicable not only to its opposite, softness, but likewise to roughness and smoothness, to figure and motion, that we may be excused from making the application, which would only be a repetition of what hath been said. All these, by means of certain corresponding sensations of touch, are presented to the mind as real external qualities; the conception and the belief of them are invariably connected with the corresponding sensations, by an original principle of human nature. Their sensations have no name in any language; they have not only been overlooked by the vulgar, but by philosophers; or, if they have been at all taken notice of, they have been confounded with the external qualities which they suggest.

Section V

Of extension.

It is further to be observed, that hardness and softness, roughness and smoothness, figure and motion, do all suppose extension, and cannot be conceived without it; yet, I think it must, on the other hand, be allowed that, if we had never felt any thing hard or soft, rough or smooth, figured or moved, we should never have had a conception of extension; so that, as there is good ground to believe that the notion of extension could not be prior to that of other primary qualities, so it is certain that it could not be posterior to the notion of any of them, being necessarily implied in them all.

Extension, therefore, seems to be a quality *suggested* to us, by the very same sensations which suggest the other qualities above mentioned. When I grasp a ball in my hand, I perceive it at once hard, figured, and extended. The feeling is very simple, and hath not the least resemblance to any quality of body. Yet it suggests to us three primary qualities perfectly distinct from one another, as well as from the sensation which indicates them. When I move my hand along the table, the feeling is so simple that I find it difficult to distinguish it into things of different natures; yet, it immediately suggests hardness, smoothness, extension, and motion—things of very different natures, and all of them as distinctly under-stood as the feeling which suggests them.

We are commonly told by philosophers, that we get the idea of extension by feeling along the extremities of a body, as if there was no manner of difficulty in the matter. I have sought, with great pains, I confess, to find out how this idea can be got by feeling; but I have sought in vain. Yet it is one of the clearest and most distinct notions we have; nor is there anything whatsoever about which the human understanding can carry on so many long and demonstrative trains of reasoning.

The notion of extension is so familiar to us from infancy, and so constantly obtruded by everything we see and feel, that we are apt to think it obvious how it comes into the mind; but upon a narrower examination we shall find it utt-erly inexplicable. It is true we have feelings of touch, which every moment present extension to the mind; but how they come to do so, is the question; for those feelings do no more resemble extension, than they resemble justice or courage—nor can the existence of extended things be inferred from those feelings by any rules of reasoning; so that the feelings we have by touch, can neither explain how we get the notion, nor how we come by the belief of extended things.

What hath imposed upon philosophers in this matter is, that the feelings of touch, which suggest primary qualities, have no names, nor are they ever reflected upon. They pass through the mind instantaneously, and serve only to intro-duce the notion and belief of external things, which, by our constitution, are connected with them. They are natural signs, and the mind immediately passes to the thing sig-nified, without making the least reflection upon the sign, or observing that there was any such thing. Hence it hath always been taken for granted, that the ideas of extension, figure, and motion, are ideas of sensation, which enter into the mind by the sense of touch, in the same manner as the sensations of sound and smell do by the ear and nose. The sensations of touch are so connected, by our constitution, with the notions of extension, figure, and motion, that philosophers have mistaken the one for the other, and never have been able to discern that they were not only distinct things, but altogether unlike. However, if we will reason distinctly upon this subject, we ought to give names to those feelings of touch; we must accustom ourselves to attend to them, and to reflect upon them, that we may be able to disjoin them from, and to compare them with, the qualities signified or suggested by them.

The habit of doing this is not to be attained without pains and practice; and till a man hath acquired this habit, it will be impossible for him to think distinctly, or to judge right, upon this subject.

Let a man press his hand against the table—*he feels it hard.* But what is the meaning of this?—The meaning undoubtedly is, that he hath a certain feeling of touch, from which he concludes, without any reasoning, or comparing ideas, that there is something external really existing, whose parts stick so firmly together, that they cannot be displaced without considerable force.

There is here a feeling, and a conclusion drawn from it, or some way suggested by it. In order to compare these, we must view them separately, and then consider by what tie they are connected, and wherein they resemble one another. The hardness of the table is the conclusion, the feeling is the medium by which we are led to that conclusion. Let a man attend distinctly to this medium, and to the conclusion, and he will perceive them to be as unlike as any two things in nature. The one is a sensation of the mind, which can have no existence but in a sentient being; nor can it exist one moment longer than it is felt; the other is in the table, and we conclude, without any difficulty, that it was in the table before it was felt, and continues after the feeling is over. The one implies no kind of extension, nor parts, nor cohesion; the other implies all these. Both, indeed, admit of degrees, and the feeling, beyond a certain degree, is a species of pain; but adamantine hardness does not imply the least pain.

And as the feeling hath no similitude to hardness, so neither can our reason perceive the least tie or connection between them; nor will the logician ever be able to show a reason why we should conclude hardness from this feeling, rather than softness, or any other quality whatsoever. But, in reality, all mankind are led by their constitution to conclude hardness from this feeling.

The sensation of heat, and the sensation we have by pressing a hard body, are equally feelings; nor can we, by reasoning, draw any conclusion from the one but what may be drawn from the other: but, by our constitution, we conclude from the first an obscure or occult quality, of which we have only this relative conception, that it is something adapted to raise in us the sensation of heat; from the second, we conclude a quality of which we have a clear and distinct conception — to wit, the hardness of the body.

Section VI

Of extension.

To put this matter in another light, it may be proper to try, whether from sensation alone we can collect any notion of extension, figure, motion, and space. I take it for granted, that a blind man hath the same notions of extension, figure, and motion, as a man that sees; that Dr Saunderson[2] had the same notion of a cone, a cylinder, and a sphere, and of the motions and distances of the heavenly bodies, as Sir Isaac Newton.

As sight, therefore, is not necessary for our acquiring those notions, we shall leave it out altogether in our inquiry into the first origin of them; and shall suppose a blind man, by some strange distemper, to have lost all the experience, and habits, and notions he had got by touch; not to have the least conception of the existence, figure, dimensions, or extension, either of his own body, or of any other; but to have all his knowledge of external things to acquire anew, by means of sensation, and the power of reason, which we suppose to remain entire.

We shall, first, suppose his body fixed immovably in one place, and that he can only have the feelings of touch, by the application of other bodies to it. Suppose him first to be pricked with a pin — this will, no doubt, give a smart sensation: he feels pain; but what can he infer from it? Nothing, surely, with regard to the existence or figure of a pin. He can infer nothing from this species of pain, which he may not as well infer from the gout or sciatica. Common sense may lead him to think that this pain has a cause; but whether this cause is body or spirit, extended or unextended, figured or not figured, he cannot possibly, from any principles he is supposed to have, form the least conjecture. Having had formerly no notion of body or of extension, the prick of a pin can give him none.

Suppose, next, a body not pointed, but blunt, is applied to his body with a force gradually increased until it bruises him. What has he got by this, but another sensation or train of sensations, from which he is able to conclude as little as from the former? A scirrhous tumour in any inward part of the body, by pressing upon the adjacent parts, may give the same kind of sensation as the pressure of an external body, without conveying any notion but that of pain, which, surely, hath no resemblance to extension.

Suppose, thirdly, that the body applied to him touches a larger or a lesser part of his body. Can this give him any notion of its extension or dimensions? To me it seems impossible that it should, unless he had some previous notion of the dimensions and figure of his own body, to serve him as a measure. When my two hands touch the extremities of a body, if I know them to be a foot asunder, I easily collect that the body is a foot long; and, if I know them to be five feet asunder, that it is five feet long; but, if I know not what the distance of my hands is, I cannot know the length of the object they grasp; and, if I have no previous notion of hands at all, or of distance between them, I can never get that notion by their being touched.

Suppose, again, that a body is drawn along his hands or face, while they are at rest. Can this give him any notion of space or motion? It no doubt gives a new feeling; but how it should convey a notion of space or motion to one who had none before, I cannot conceive. The blood moves along the arteries and veins, and this motion, when violent, is felt: but I imagine no man, by this feeling, could get the conception of space or motion, if he had it not before. Such a motion may give a certain succession of feelings, as the colic may do; but no feelings, nor any combination of feelings, can ever resemble space or motion.

Let us next suppose, that he makes some instinctive effort to move his head or his hand; but that no motion follows, either on account of external resistance, or of palsy. Can this effort convey the notion of space and motion to one who never had it before? Surely it cannot.

Last of all, let us suppose that he moves a limb by instinct, without having had any previous notion of space or motion. He has here a new sensation, which accompanies the flexure of joints, and the swelling of muscles. But how this sensation can convey into his mind the idea of space and motion, is still altogether mysterious and unintelligible. The motions of the heart and lungs are all performed by the contraction of muscles, yet give no conception of space or motion. An embryo in the womb has many such motions, and probably the feelings that accompany them, without any idea of space or motion.

Upon the whole, it appears that our philosophers have imposed upon themselves and upon us, in pretending to deduce from sensation the first origin of our notions of external existences, of space, motion, and extension, and all the primary qualities of body — that is, the qualities whereof we have the most clear and distinct conception. These qualities do not at all tally with any system of the human faculties that hath been advanced. They have no resemblance to any sensation, or to any operation of our minds; and, therefore, they cannot be ideas either of sensation or of reflection. The very conception of them is irreconcilable to the principles of all our philosophic systems of the understanding. The belief of them is no less so.

Section VII

Of the existence of a material world.

It is beyond our power to say when, or in what order, we came by our notions of these qualities. When we trace the operations of our minds as far back as memory and reflection can carry us, we find them already in possession of our imagination and belief, and quite familiar to the mind: but how they came first into its acquaintance, or what has given them so strong a hold of our belief, and what regard they deserve, are, no doubt, very important questions in the philosophy of human nature.

Shall we, with the Bishop of Cloyne, serve them with a *quo warranto*, and have them tried at the bar of philosophy, upon the statute of the ideal system? Indeed, in this trial they seem to have come off very pitifully; for, although they had very able counsel, learned in the law—viz., Des Cartes, Malebranche, and Locke, who said everything they could for their clients—the Bishop of Cloyne, believing them to be aiders and abetters of heresy and schism, prosecuted them with great vigour, fully answered all that had been pleaded in their defence, and silenced their ablest advocates, who seem, for half a century past, to decline the argument, and to trust to the favour of the jury rather than to the strength of their pleadings.

Thus, the wisdom of *philosophy* is set in opposition to the *common sense* of mankind. The first pretends to demonstrate, *a priori*, that there can be no such thing as a material world; that sun, moon, stars, and earth, vegetable and animal bodies, are, and can be nothing else, but sensations in the mind, or images of those sensations in the memory and imagination; that, like pain and joy, they can have no existence when they are not thought of. The last can conceive no otherwise of this opinion, than as a kind of metaphysical lunacy, and concludes that too much learning is apt to make men mad; and that the man who seriously entertains this belief, though in other respects he may be a very good man, as a man may be who believes that he is made of glass; yet, surely he hath a soft place in his understanding, and hath been hurt by much thinking.

This opposition betwixt philosophy and common sense, is apt to have a very unhappy influence upon the philosopher himself. He sees human nature in an odd, unamiable, and mortifying light. He considers himself, and the rest of his species, as born under a necessity of believing ten thousand absurdities and contradictions, and endowed with such a pittance of reason as is just sufficient to make this unhappy discovery: and this is all the fruit of his profound speculations. Such notions of human nature tend to slacken every nerve of the soul, to put every noble purpose and sentiment out of countenance, and spread a melancholy gloom over the whole face of things.

If this is wisdom, let me be deluded with the vulgar. I find something within me that recoils against it, and inspires more reverent sentiments of the human kind, and of the universal administration. Common Sense and Reason have both one author; that Almighty Author in all whose other works we observe a consistency, uniformity, and beauty which charm and delight the understanding: there must, therefore, be some order and consistency in the human faculties, as well as in other parts of his workmanship. A man that thinks reverently of his own kind, and esteems true wisdom and philosophy, will not be fond, nay, will be very suspicious, of such strange and paradoxical opinions. If they are false, they disgrace philosophy; and, if they are true, they degrade the human species, and make us justly ashamed of our frame.

To what purpose is it for philosophy to decide against common sense in this or any other matter? The belief of a material world is older, and of more authority, than any principles of philosophy. It declines the tribunal of reason, and laughs at all the artillery of the logician. It retains its sovereign authority in spite of all the edicts of philosophy, and reason itself must stoop to its orders. Even those philosophers who have disowned the authority of our notions of an external material world, confess that they find themselves under a necessity of submitting to their power.

Methinks, therefore, it were better to make a virtue of necessity; and, since we cannot get rid of the vulgar notion and belief of an external world, to reconcile our reason to it as well as we can; for, if Reason should stomach and fret ever so much at this yoke, she cannot throw it off; if she will not be the servant of Common Sense, she must be her slave.

In order, therefore, to reconcile Reason to Common Sense in this matter, I beg leave to offer to the consideration of philosophers these two observations. First, That, in all this debate about the existence of a material world, it hath been taken for granted on both sides, that this same material world, if any such there be, must be the express image of our sensations; that we can have no conception of any material thing which is not like some sensation in our minds; and particularly that the sensations of touch are images of extension, hardness, figure, and motion. Every argument brought against the existence of a material world, either by the Bishop of Cloyne, or by the author of the *Treatise of Human Nature*, supposeth this. If this is true, their arguments are conclusive and unanswerable; but, on the other hand, if it is not true, there is no shadow of argument left. Have those philosophers, then, given any solid proof of this hypothesis, upon which the whole weight of so strange a system rests? No. They have not so much as attempted to do it. But, because ancient and modern philosophers have agreed in this opinion, they have taken it for granted. But let us, as becomes philosophers, lay aside authority; we need not, surely, consult Aristotle or Locke, to know whether pain be like the point of a sword. I have as clear a conception of extension, hardness, and motion, as I have of the point of a sword; and, with some pains and practice, I can form as clear a notion of the other sensations of touch as I have of pain. When I do so, and compare them together, it appears to me clear as daylight, that the former are not of kin to the latter, nor resemble them in any one feature. They are as unlike, yea as certainly and manifestly unlike, as pain is to the point of a sword. It may be true, that those sensations first introduced the material world to our acquaintance; it may be true, that it seldom or never appears without their company; but, for all that, they are as unlike as the passion of anger is to those features of the countenance which attend it.

So that, in the sentence those philosophers have passed against the material world, there is an *error personæ*. Their proof touches not matter, or any of its qualities; but strikes directly against an idol of their own imagination, a material world made of ideas and sensations, which never had nor can have an existence.

Secondly, The very existence of our conceptions of extension, figure, and motion, since they are neither ideas of sensation nor reflection, overturns the whole ideal system, by which the material world hath been tried and condemned; so that there hath been likewise in this sentence an *error juris*.

It is a very fine and a just observation of Locke, that, as no human art can create a single particle of matter, and the whole extent of our power over the material world consists in compounding, combining, and disjoining the matter made to our hands; so, in the world of thought, the materials are all made by nature, and can only be variously combined and disjoined by us. So that it is impossible for reason or prejudice, true or false philosophy, to produce one simple notion or conception, which is not the work of nature, and the result of our constitution. The conception of extension, motion, and the other attributes of matter, cannot be the effect of error or prejudice; it must be the work of nature. And the power or faculty by which we acquire those conceptions, must be something different from any power of the human mind that hath been explained, since it is neither sensation nor reflection.

This I would, therefore, humbly propose, as an *experimentum crucis*, by which the ideal system must stand or fall; and it brings the matter to a short issue: Extension, figure, motion, may, any one or all of them, be taken for the subject of this experiment. Either they are ideas of sensation, or they are not. If any one of them can be shown to be an idea of sensation, or to have the least resemblance to any sensation, I lay my hand upon my mouth, and give up all pretense to reconcile reason to common sense in this matter, and must suffer the ideal scepticism to triumph. But if, on the other hand, they are not ideas of sensation, nor like to any sensation, then the ideal system is a rope of sand, and all the laboured arguments of the sceptical philosophy against a material world, and against the existence of everything but impressions and ideas, proceed upon a false hypothesis.

If our philosophy concerning the mind be so lame with regard to the origin of our notions of the clearest, most simple, and most familiar objects of thought, and the powers from which they are derived, can we expect that it should be more perfect in the account it gives of the origin of our opinions and belief? We have seen already some instances of its imperfection in this respect: and, perhaps, that same nature which hath given us the power to conceive things altogether unlike to any of our sensations, or to any operation of our minds, hath likewise provided for our belief of them, by some part of our constitution hitherto not explained.

Bishop Berkeley hath proved, beyond the possibility of reply, that we cannot by reasoning infer the existence of matter from our sensations; and the author of the *Treatise of Human Nature* hath proved no less clearly, that we cannot by reasoning infer the existence of our own or other minds from our sensations. But are we to admit nothing but what can be proved by reasoning? Then we must be sceptics indeed, and believe nothing at all. The author of the *Treatise of Human Nature* appears to me to be but a half-sceptic. He hath not followed his principles so far as they lead him; but, after having, with unparalleled intrepidity and success, combated vulgar prejudices, when he had but one blow to strike, his courage fails him, he fairly lays down his arms, and yields himself a captive to the most common of all vulgar prejudices — I mean the belief of the existence of his own impressions and ideas.

I beg, therefore, to have the honour of making an addition to the sceptical system, without which I conceive it cannot hang together. I affirm, that the belief of the existence of impressions and ideas, is as little supported by reason, as that of the existence of minds and bodies. No man ever did or could offer any reason for this belief. Des Cartes took it for granted, that he thought, and had sensations and ideas; so have all his followers done. Even the hero of scepticism hath yielded this point, I crave leave to say, weakly and imprudently. I say so, because I am persuaded that there is no principle of his philosophy that obliged him to make this concession. And what is there in impressions and ideas so formidable, that this all-conquering philosophy, after triumphing over every other existence, should pay homage to them? Besides, the concession is dangerous: for belief is of such a nature, that, if you leave any root, it will spread; and you may more easily pull it up altogether, than say, Hitherto shalt thou go and no further: the existence of impressions and ideas I give up to thee; but see thou pretend to nothing more. A thorough and consistent sceptic will never, therefore, yield this point; and while he holds it, you can never oblige him to yield anything else.

To such a sceptic I have nothing to say; but of the semi-sceptics, I should beg to know, why they believe the existence of their impressions and ideas. The true reason I take to be, because they cannot help it; and the same reason will lead them to believe many other things.

All reasoning must be from first principles; and for first principles no other reason can be given but this, that, by the constitution of our nature, we are under a necessity of assenting to them. Such principles are parts of our constitution, no less than the power of thinking: reason can neither make nor destroy them; nor can it do anything without them: it is like a telescope, which may help a man to see farther, who hath eyes; but, without eyes, a telescope shows nothing at all. A mathematician cannot prove the truth of his axioms, nor can he prove anything, unless he takes them for granted. We cannot prove the existence of our minds, nor even of our thoughts and sensations. A historian, or a witness, can prove nothing, unless it is taken for granted that the memory and senses may be trusted. A natural philosopher can prove nothing, unless it is taken for granted that the course of nature is steady and uniform.

How or when I got such first principles, upon which I build all my reasoning, I know not; for I had them before I can remember: but I am sure they are parts of my constitution, and that I cannot throw them off. That our thoughts and sensations must have a subject, which we call *ourself*, is not therefore an opinion got by reasoning, but a natural principle. That our sensations of touch indicate something external, extended, figured, hard or soft, is not a deduction of reason, but a natural principle. The belief of it, and the very conception of it, are equally parts of our constitution. If we are deceived in it, we are deceived by Him that made us, and there is no remedy.

I do not mean to affirm, that the sensations of touch do, from the very first, suggest the same notions of body and its qualities which they do when we are grown up. Perhaps Nature is frugal in this, as in her other operations. The passion of love, with all its concomitant sentiments and desires, is naturally suggested by the perception of beauty in the other sex; yet the same perception does not suggest the tender passion till a certain period of life. A blow given to an infant, raises grief and lamentation; but when he grows up, it as naturally stirs resentment, and prompts him to resistance. Perhaps a child in the womb, or for some short period of its existence, is merely a sentient being; the faculties by which it perceives an external world, by which it reflects on its own thoughts, and existence, and relation to other things, as well as its reasoning and moral faculties, unfold themselves by degrees; so that it is inspired with the various principles of common sense, as with the passions of love and resentment, when it has occasion for them.

Section VIII

Of the systems of philosophers concerning the senses.

All the systems of philosophers about our senses and their objects have split upon this rock, of not distinguishing properly sensations which can have no existence but when they are felt, from the things suggested by them. Aristotle—with as distinguishing a head as ever applied to philosophical disquisitions—confounds these two; and makes every sensation to be the form, without the matter, of the thing perceived by it. As the impression of a seal upon wax has the form of the seal but nothing of the matter of it, so he conceived our sensations to be impressions upon the mind, which bear the image, likeness, or form of the external thing perceived, without the matter of it. Colour, sound, and smell, as well as extension, figure, and hardness, are, according to him, various forms of matter: our sensations are the same forms imprinted on the mind, and perceived in its own intellect. It is evident from this, that Aristotle made no distinction between primary and secondary qualities of bodies, although that distinction was made by Democritus, Epicurus, and others of the ancients.

Des Cartes, Malebranche, and Locke, revived the distinction between primary and secondary qualities; but they made the secondary qualities mere sensations, and the primary ones resemblances of our sensations. They maintained that colour, sound, and heat, are not anything in bodies, but sensations of the mind; at the same time, they acknowledged some particular texture or modification of the body to be the cause or occasion of those sensations; but to this modification they gave no name. Whereas, by the vulgar, the names of colour, heat, and sound, are but rarely applied to the sensations, and most commonly to those unknown causes of them, as hath been already explained. The constitution of our nature leads us rather to attend to the things signified by the sensation than to the sensation itself, and to give a name to the former rather than to the latter. Thus we see, that, with regard to secondary qualities, these philosophers thought with the vulgar, and with common sense. Their paradoxes were only an abuse of words; for when they maintain, as an important modern discovery, that there is no heat in the fire, they mean no more, than that the fire does not feel heat, which every one knew before.

With regard to primary qualities, these philosophers erred more grossly. They indeed believed the existence of those qualities; but they did not at all attend to the sensations that suggest them, which, having no names, have been as little considered as if they had no existence. They were aware that figure, extension, and hardness, are perceived by means of sensations of touch; whence they rashly concluded, that these sensations must be images and resemblances of figure, extension, and hardness.

The received hypothesis of ideas naturally led them to this conclusion: and indeed cannot consist with any other; for, according to that hypothesis, external things must be perceived by means of images of them in the mind; and what can those images of external things in the mind be, but the sensations by which we perceive them?

This, however, was to draw a conclusion from a hypothesis against fact. We need not have recourse to any hypothesis to know what our sensations are, or what they are like. By a proper degree of reflection and attention we may understand them perfectly, and be as certain that they are not like any quality of body, as we can be, that the toothache is not like a triangle. How a sensation should instantly make us conceive and believe the existence of an external thing altogether unlike to it, I do not pretend to know; and when I say that the one suggests the other, I mean not to explain the manner of their connection, but to express a fact, which every one may be conscious of—namely, that, by a law of our nature, such a conception and belief constantly and immediately follow the sensation.

Bishop Berkeley gave new light to this subject, by showing, that the qualities of an inanimate thing, such as matter is conceived to be, cannot resemble any sensation; that it is impossible to conceive anything like the sensations of our minds, but the sensations of other minds. Every one that attends properly to his sensations must assent to this; yet it had escaped all the philosophers that came before Berkeley; it had escaped even the ingenious Locke, who had so much practised reflection on the operations of his own mind. So difficult it is to attend properly even to our own feelings. They are so accustomed to pass through the mind unobserved and instantly to make way for that which nature intended them to signify, that it is extremely difficult to stop, and survey them; and when we think we have acquired this power, perhaps the mind still fluctuates between the sensation and its associated quality, so that they mix together, and present something to the imagination that is compounded of both. Thus, in a globe or cylinder, whose opposite sides are quite unlike in colour, if you turn it slowly, the colours are perfectly distinguishable and their dissimilitude is manifest; but if it is turned fast, they lose their distinction, and seem to be of one and the same colour.

No succession can be more quick than that of tangible qualities to the sensations with which nature has associated them; but when one has once acquired the art of making them separate and distinct objects of thought, he will then clearly perceive that the maxim of Bishop Berkeley, abovementioned, is self-evident; and that the features of the face are not more unlike to a passion of the mind which they indicate, than the sensations of touch are to the primary qualities of body.

But let us observe what use the Bishop makes of this important discovery. Why, he concludes, that we can have no conception of an inanimate substance, such as matter is conceived to be, or of any of its qualities; and that there is the strongest ground to believe that there is no existence in nature but minds, sensations, and ideas: if there is any other kind of existence, it must be what we neither have nor can have any conception of. But how does this follow? Why, thus: We can have no conception of anything but what resembles some sensation or idea in our minds; but the sensations and ideas in our minds can resemble nothing but the sensations and ideas in other minds; therefore, the conclusion is evident. This argument, we see, leans upon two propositions. The last of them the ingenious author hath, indeed, made evident to all that understand his reasoning, and can attend to their own sensations: but the first proposition he never attempts to prove; it is taken from the doctrine of ideas, which hath been so universally received by philosophers, that it was thought to need no proof.

We may here again observe, that this acute writer argues from a hypothesis against fact, and against the common sense of mankind. That we can have no conception of anything, unless there is some impression, sensation, or idea, in our minds which resembles it, is indeed an opinion which hath been very generally received among philosophers; but it is neither self-evident, nor hath it been clearly proved; and therefore it had[3] been more reasonable to call in question this doctrine of philosophers, than to discard the material world, and by that means expose philosophy to the ridicule of all men who will not offer up common sense as a sacrifice to metaphysics.

We ought, however, to do this justice both to the Bishop of Cloyne and to the author of the *Treatise of Human Nature*, to acknowledge, that their conclusions are justly drawn from the doctrine of ideas, which has been so universally received. On the other hand, from the character of Bishop Berkeley, and of his predecessors, Des Cartes, Locke, and Malebranche, we may venture to say, that, if they had seen all the consequences of this doctrine, as clearly as the author before mentioned did, they would have suspected it vehemently, and examined it more carefully than they appear to have done.

The theory of ideas, like the Trojan horse, had a specious appearance both of innocence and beauty; but if those philosophers had known that it carried in its belly death and destruction to all science and common sense, they would not have broken down their walls to give it admittance.

That we have clear and distinct conceptions of extension, figure, motion, and other attributes of body, which are neither sensations, nor like any sensation, is a fact of which we may be as certain as that we have sensations. And that all mankind have a fixed belief of an external material world — a belief which is neither got by reasoning nor education, and a belief which we cannot shake off, even when we seem to have strong arguments against it and no shadow of argument for it — is likewise a fact, for which we have all the evidence that the nature of the thing admits. These facts are phænomena of human nature, from which we may justly argue against any hypothesis, however generally received.

But to argue from a hypothesis against facts, is contrary to the rules of true philosophy.

Chapter VI: Of Seeing

Section II

Sight discovers almost nothing which the blind may not comprehend – the reason of this.

[…] [I]t is worthy of our observation, that there is very little of the knowledge acquired by sight, that may not be communicated to a man born blind. One who never saw the light, may be learned and knowing in every science, even in optics; and may make discoveries in every branch of philosophy. He may understand as much as another man, not only of the order, distances, and motions of the heavenly bodies; but of the nature of light, and of the laws of the reflection and refraction of its rays. He may understand distinctly how those laws produce the phænomena of the rainbow, the prism, the camera obscura, and the magic lanthorn, and all the powers of the microscope and telescope. This is a fact sufficiently attested by experience.

In order to perceive the reason of it, we must distinguish the appearance that objects make to the eye, from the things suggested by that appearance: and again, in the visible appearance of objects, we must distinguish the appearance of colour from the appearance of extension, figure, and motion. First, then, as to the visible appearance of the figure, and motion, and extension of bodies, I conceive that a man born blind may have a distinct notion, if not of the very things, at least of something extremely like to them. May not a blind man be made to conceive that a body moving directly from the eye, or directly towards it, may appear to be at rest? and that the same motion may appear quicker or slower, according as it is nearer to the eye or farther off, more direct or more oblique? May he not be made to conceive, that a plain surface, in a certain position, may appear as a straight line, and vary its visible figure, as its position, or the position of the eye, is varied? – that a circle seen obliquely will appear an ellipse; and a square, a rhombus, or an oblong rectangle? Dr Saunderson understood the projection of the sphere, and the common rules of perspective; and if he did, he must have understood all that I have mentioned.[…]

As to the appearance of colour, a blind man must be more at a loss; because he hath no perception that resembles it. Yet he may, by a kind of analogy, in part supply this defect. To those who see, a scarlet colour signifies an unknown quality in bodies, that makes to the eye an appearance which they are well acquainted with and have often observed — to a blind man, it signifies an unknown quality, that makes to the eye an appearance which he is unacquainted with. But he can conceive the eye to be variously affected by different colours, as the nose is by different smells, or the ear by different sounds. Thus he can conceive scarlet to differ from blue, as the sound of a trumpet does from that of a drum; or as the smell of an orange differs from that of an apple. It is impossible to know whether a scarlet colour has the same appearance to me which it hath to another man; and, if the appearances of it to different persons differed as much as colour does from sound, they might never be able to discover this difference. Hence it appears obvious, that a blind man might talk long about colours distinctly and pertinently; and, if you were to examine him in the dark about the nature, composition, and beauty of them, he might be able to answer, so as not to betray his defect.

We have seen how far a blind man may go in the knowledge of the appearances which things make to the eye. As to the things which are suggested by them or inferred from them, although he could never discover them of himself, yet he may understand them perfectly by the information of others. And everything of this kind that enters into our minds by the eye, may enter into his by the ear. Thus, for instance, he could never, if left to the direction of his own faculties, have dreamed of any such thing as light; but he can be informed of everything we know about it. He can conceive, as distinctly as we, the minuteness and velocity of its rays, their various degrees of refrangibility and reflexibility, and all the magical powers and virtues of that wonderful element. He could never of himself have found out, that there are such bodies as the sun, moon, and stars; but he may be informed of all the noble discoveries of astronomers, about their motions, and the laws of nature by which they are

regulated. Thus, it appears, that there is very little knowledge got by the eye, which may not be communicated by
language to those who have no eyes.[…]

The distinction we have made between the visible
appearances of the objects of sight, and things suggested by
them, is necessary to give us a just notion of the intention of
nature in giving us eyes. If we attend duly to the operation of
our mind in the use of this faculty, we shall perceive that the
visible appearance of objects is hardly ever regarded by us. It
is not at all made an object of thought or reflection, but
serves only as a sign to introduce to the mind something else,
which may be distinctly conceived by those who never saw.

Thus, the visible appearance of things in my room varies
almost every hour, according as the day is clear or cloudy, as
the sun is in the east, or south, or west, and as my eye is in
one part of the room or in another; but I never think of these
variations, otherwise than as signs of morning, noon, or
night, of a clear or cloudy sky. A book or a chair has a different appearance to the eye, in every different distance and
position; yet we conceive it to be still the same; and, over-
looking the appearance, we immediately conceive the real
figure, distance, and position of the body, of which its visible
or perspective appearance is a sign and indication.

When I see a man at the distance of ten yards, and afterwards see him at the distance of a hundred yards, his visible
appearance, in its length, breadth, and all its linear proportions, is ten times less in the last case than it is in the first; yet
I do not conceive him one inch diminished by this diminution of his visible figure. Nay, I do not in the least attend to
this diminution, even when I draw from it the conclusion of
his being at a greater distance. For such is the subtilty of the
mind's operation in this case, that we draw the conclusion,
without perceiving that ever the premises entered into the
mind. A thousand such instances might be produced, in
order to show that the visible appearances of objects are intended by nature only as signs or indications; and that the
mind passes instantly to the things signified, without making
the least reflection upon the sign, or even perceiving that
there is any such thing. It is in a way somewhat similar, that
the sounds of a language, after it is become familiar, are

overlooked, and we attend only to the things signified by them.

It is therefore a just and important observation of the Bishop of Cloyne, That the visible appearance of objects is a kind of language used by nature, to inform us of their distance, magnitude, and figure.[…]

[W]e shall avail ourselves of the distinction between the signs that nature useth in this visual language, and the things signified by them; and in what remains to be said of sight, shall first make some observations upon the signs.

Section III

Of the visible appearances of objects.

In this section we must speak of things which are never made the object of reflection, though almost every moment presented to the mind. Nature intended them only for signs; and in the whole course of life they are put to no other use. The mind has acquired a confirmed and inveterate habit of inattention to them; for they no sooner appear, than quick as lightning the thing signified succeeds, and engrosses all our regard. They have no name in language; and, although we are conscious of them when they pass through the mind, yet their passage is so quick and so familiar, that it is absolutely unheeded; nor do they leave any footsteps of themselves, either in the memory or imagination. That this is the case with regard to the sensations of touch, hath been shown in the last chapter; and it holds no less with regard to the visible appearances of objects.

I cannot therefore entertain the hope of being intelligible to those readers who have not, by pains and practice, acquired the habit of distinguishing the appearance of objects to the eye, from the judgment which we form by sight of their colour, distance, magnitude, and figure. The only profession in life wherein it is necessary to make this distinction, is that of painting. The painter hath occasion for an abstraction, with regard to visible objects, somewhat similar to that which we here require: and this indeed is the most difficult part of his art. For it is evident, that, if he could fix in his imagination the visible appearance of objects, without confounding it with the things signified by that appearance, it would be as easy for him to paint from the life, and to give every figure its proper shading and relief, and its perspective proportions, as it is to paint from a copy. Perspective, shading, giving relief, and colouring, are nothing else but copying the appearance which things make to the eye. We may therefore borrow some light on the subject of visible appearance from this art.

Let one look upon any familiar object, such as a book, at different distances and in different positions: is he not able to affirm, upon the testimony of his sight, that it is the same book, the same object, whether seen at the distance of one foot or of ten, whether in one position or another; that the colour is the same, the dimensions the same, and the figure the same, as far as the eye can judge? This surely must be acknowledged. The same individual object is presented to the mind, only placed at different distances and in different positions. Let me ask, in the next place, Whether this object has the same appearance to the eye in these different distances? Infallibly it hath not. For,

First, However certain our judgment may be that the colour is the same, it is as certain that it hath not the same appearance at different distances. There is a certain degradation of the colour, and a certain confusion and indistinctness of the minute parts, which is the natural consequence of the removal of the object to a greater distance. Those that are not painters, or critics in painting, overlook this; and cannot easily be persuaded, that the colour of the same object hath a different appearance at the distance of one foot and of ten, in the shade and in the light But the masters in painting know how, by the degradation of the colour and the confusion of the minute parts, figures which are upon the same canvas, and at the same distance from the eye, may be made to represent objects which are at the most unequal distances. They know how to make the objects appear to be of the same colour, by making their pictures really of different colours, according to their distances or shades.

Secondly, Every one who is acquainted with the rules of perspective, knows that the appearance of the figure of the book must vary in every different position: yet if you ask a man that has no notion of perspective, whether the figure of it does not appear to his eye to be the same in all its different positions? he can with a good conscience affirm that it does.

He hath learned to make allowance for the variety of visible figure arising from the difference of position, and to draw the proper conclusions from it. But he draws these conclusions so readily and habitually, as to lose sight of the premises: and therefore where he hath made the same conclusion, he conceives the visible appearance must have been the same.

Thirdly, Let us consider the apparent magnitude or dimensions of the book. Whether I view it at the distance of one foot or of ten feet, it seems to be about seven inches long, five broad, and one thick. I can judge of these dimensions very nearly by the eye, and I judge them to be the same at both distances. But yet it is certain, that, at the distance of one foot, its visible length and breadth is about ten times as great as at the distance of ten feet; and consequently its surface is about a hundred times as great. This great change of apparent magnitude is altogether overlooked, and every man is apt to imagine, that it appears to the eye of the same size at both distances. Further, when I look at the book, it seems plainly to have three dimensions, of length, breadth, and thickness: but it is certain that the visible appearance hath no more than two, and can be exactly represented upon a canvas which hath only length and breadth.

In the last place, does not every man, by sight, perceive the distance of the book from his eye? Can he not affirm with certainty, that in one case it is not above one foot distant, that in another it is ten? Nevertheless, it appears certain, that distance from the eye is no immediate object of sight. There are certain things in the visible appearance, which are signs of distance from the eye, and from which, as we shall afterwards show, we learn by experience to judge of that distance within certain limits; but it seems beyond doubt, that a man born blind, and suddenly made to see, could form no judgment at first of the distance of the objects which he saw. The young man couched by Cheselden thought, at first, that everything he saw touched his eye, and learned only by experience to judge of the distance of visible objects.[4]

I have entered into this long detail, in order to show that the visible appearance of an object is extremely different from the notion of it which experience teaches us to form by sight; and to enable the reader to attend to the visible appearance of colour, figure, and extension, in visible things, which is no common object of thought, but must be carefully attended to by those who would enter into the philosophy of this sense, or would comprehend what shall be said upon it. To a man newly made to see, the visible appearance of objects would be the same as to us; but he would see nothing at all of their real dimensions, as we do. He could form no conjecture, by means of his sight only, how many inches or feet they were in length, breadth, or thickness. He could perceive little or nothing of their real figure; nor could he discern that this was a cube, that a sphere; that this was a cone, and that a cylinder. His eye could not inform him that this object was near, and that more remote. The habit of a man or of a woman, which appeared to us of one uniform colour, variously folded and shaded, would present to his eye neither fold nor shade, but variety of colour. In a word, his eyes, though ever so perfect, would at first give him almost no information of things without him. They would indeed present the same appearances to him as they do to us, and speak the same language; but to him it is an unknown language; and, therefore, he would attend only to the signs, without knowing the signification of them, whereas to us it is a language perfectly familiar; and, therefore, we take no notice of the signs, but attend only to the thing signified by them.

Section IV

That colour is a quality of bodies, not a sensation of the mind.

By colour, all men, who have not been tutored by modern philosophy, understand, not a sensation of the mind, which can have no existence when it is not perceived, but a quality or modification of bodies, which continues to be the same whether it is seen or not. The scarlet-rose which is before me, is still a scarlet-rose when I shut my eyes, and was so at midnight when no eye saw it. The colour remains when the appearance ceases; it remains the same when the appearance changes. For when I view this scarlet-rose through a pair of green spectacles, the appearance is changed; but I do not conceive the colour of the rose changed. To a person in the jaundice, it has still another appearance; but he is easily convinced that the change is in his eye, and not in the colour of the object. Every different degree of light makes it have a different appearance, and total darkness takes away all appearance, but makes not the least change in the colour of the body. We may, by a variety of optical experiments, change the appearance of figure and magnitude in a body, as well as that of colour; we may make one body appear to be ten. But all men believe, that, as a multiplying glass does not really produce ten guineas out of one, nor a microscope turn a guinea into a ten-pound piece, so neither does a coloured glass change the real colour of the object seen through it, when it changes the appearance of that colour.

The common language of mankind shows evidently, that we ought to distinguish between the colour of a body, which is conceived to be a fixed and permanent quality in the body, and the appearance of that colour to the eye, which may be varied a thousand ways, by a variation of the light, of the medium, or of the eye itself. The permanent colour of the body is the cause which, by the mediation of various kinds or degrees of light, and of various transparent bodies interposed, produces all this variety of appearances. When a coloured body is presented, there is a certain apparition to the eye, or to the mind, which we have called *the appearance of colour*. Mr Locke calls it *an idea*; and, indeed, it may be called so with the greatest propriety. This idea can have no existence but when it is perceived. It is a kind of thought, and can only be the act of a percipient or thinking being. By the constitution of our nature, we are led to conceive this idea as a sign of something external, and are impatient till we learn its meaning. A thousand experiments for this purpose are made every day by children, even before they come to the use of reason. They look at things, they handle them, they put them in various positions, at different distances, and in different lights. The ideas of sight, by these means, come to be associated with, and readily to suggest, things external, and altogether unlike them. In particular, that idea which we have called *the appearance of colour*, suggests the conception and belief of some unknown quality in the body which occasions the idea; and it is to this quality, and not to the idea, that we give the name of *colour*. The various colours, although in their nature equally unknown, are easily distinguished when we think or speak of them, by being associated with the ideas which they excite. In like manner, gravity, magnetism, and electricity, although all unknown qualities, are distinguished by their different effects. As we grow up, the mind acquires a habit of passing so rapidly from the ideas of sight to the external things suggested by them, that the ideas are not in the least attended to, nor have they names given them in common language.

When we think or speak of any particular colour, however simple the notion may seem to be which is presented to the imagination, it is really in some sort compounded. It involves an unknown cause and a known effect. The name of *colour* belongs indeed to the cause only, and not to the effect. But as the cause is unknown, we can form no distinct conception of it but by its relation to the known effect; and, therefore, both go together in the imagination, and are so closely united, that they are mistaken for one simple object of thought. When I would conceive those colours of bodies which we call *scarlet* and *blue* — if I conceived them only as unknown qualities, I could perceive no distinction between the one and the other. I must, therefore, for the sake of distinction, join to each of them, in my imagination, some effect or some relation that is peculiar; and the most obvious distinction is, the appearance which one and the other makes to the eye. Hence the appearance is, in the imagination, so closely united with the quality called *a scarlet-colour*, that they are apt to be mistaken for one and the same thing, although they are in reality so different and so unlike, that one is an idea in the mind, and the other is a quality of body.

I conclude, then, that colour is not a sensation, but a secondary quality of bodies, in the sense we have already explained; that it is a certain power or virtue in bodies, that in fair daylight exhibits to the eye an appearance which is very familiar to us, although it hath no name. Colour differs from other secondary qualities in this, that, whereas the name of the quality is sometimes given to the sensation which indicates it, and is occasioned by it, we never, as far as I can judge, give the name of *colour* to the sensation, but to the quality only. Perhaps the reason of this may be, that the appearances of the same colour are so various and changeable, according to the different modifications of the light, of the medium, and of the eye, that language could not afford names for them. And, indeed, they are so little interesting that they are never attended to, but serve only as signs to introduce the things signified by them. Nor ought it to appear incredible, that appearances so frequent and so familiar should have no names, nor be made objects of thought; since we have before shown that this is true of many sensations of touch, which are no less frequent nor less familiar.

Section V

An inference from the preceding.

From what hath been said about colour, we may infer two things. The first is, that one of the most remarkable paradoxes of modern philosophy, which hath been universally esteemed as a great discovery, is, in reality, when examined to the bottom, nothing else but an abuse of words. The paradox I mean is, That colour is not a quality of bodies, but only an idea in the mind. We have shown, that the word *colour*, as used by the vulgar, cannot signify an idea in the mind, but a permanent quality of body. We have shown that there is really a permanent quality of body, to which the common use of this word exactly agrees. Can any stronger proof be desired, that this quality is that to which the vulgar give the name of *colour*? If it should be said, that this quality, to which we give the name of *colour*, is unknown to the vulgar, and, therefore, can have no name among them, I answer, it is, indeed, known only by its effects — that is, by its exciting a certain idea in us; but are there not numberless qualities of bodies which are known only by their effects, to which, notwithstanding, we find it necessary to give names? Medicine alone might furnish us with a hundred instances of this kind. Do not the words *astringent, narcotic, epispastic, caustic,* and innumerable others, signify qualities of bodies, which are known only by their effects upon animal bodies? Why, then, should not the vulgar give a name to a quality, whose effects are every moment perceived by their eyes? We have all the reason, therefore, that the nature of the thing admits, to think that the vulgar apply the name of *colour* to that quality of bodies which excites in us what the philosophers call the *idea of colour*. And that there is such a quality in bodies, all philosophers allow, who allow that there is any such thing as body. Philosophers have thought fit to leave that quality of bodies which the vulgar call *colour*, without a name, and to give the name of *colour* to the idea or appearance, to which, as we have shown, the vulgar give no name, because they never make it an object of thought or reflection. Hence it appears, that, when philosophers affirm that colour is not in bodies, but in the mind, and the vulgar affirm that colour is not in the mind, but is a quality of bodies, there is no difference between them about things, but only about the meaning of a word.

The vulgar have undoubted right to give names to things which they are daily conversant about; and philosophers seem justly chargeable with an abuse of language, when they change the meaning of a common word, without giving warning.

If it is a good rule, to think with philosophers and speak with the vulgar, it must be right to speak with the vulgar when we think with them, and not to shock them by philosophical paradoxes, which, when put into common language, express only the common sense of mankind.

If you ask a man that is no philosopher, what colour is, or what makes one body appear white, another scarlet, he cannot tell. He leaves that inquiry to philosophers, and can embrace any hypothesis about it, except that of our modern philosophers, who affirm that colour is not in body, but only in the mind.

Nothing appears more shocking to his apprehension, than that visible objects should have no colour, and that colour should be in that which he conceives to be invisible. Yet this strange paradox is not only universally received, but considered as one of the noblest discoveries of modern philosophy.[…]

[I]t is just to acknowledge that Locke, and other modern philosophers, on the subject of secondary qualities, have the merit of distinguishing more accurately than those that went before them, between the sensation in the mind, and that constitution or quality of bodies which gives occasion to the sensation. They have shown clearly that these two things are not only distinct, but altogether unlike: that there is no similitude between the effluvia of an odorous body and the sensation of smell, or between the vibrations of a sounding body and the sensation of sound: that there can be no resemblance between the feeling of heat, and the constitution of the heated body which occasions it; or between the appearance which a coloured body makes to the eye, and the texture of the body which causes that appearance.

Nor was the merit small of distinguishing these things accurately; because, however different and unlike in their nature, they have been always so associated in the imagination, as to coalesce, as it were, into one two-faced form, which, from its amphibious nature, could not justly be appropriated either to body or mind; and, until it was properly distinguished into its different constituent parts, it was impossible to assign to either their just shares in it. None of the ancient philosophers had made this distinction. The followers of Democritus and Epicurus conceived the forms of heat, and sound, and colour, to be in the mind only; but that our senses fallaciously represented them as being in bodies. The Peripatetics imagined that those forms are really in bodies; and that the images of them are conveyed to the mind by our senses.

The one system made the senses naturally fallacious and deceitful; the other made the qualities of body to resemble the sensations of the mind. Nor was it possible to find a third, without making the distinction we have mentioned; by which, indeed, the errors of both these ancient systems are avoided, and we are not left under the hard necessity of believing, either, on the one hand, that our sensations are like to the qualities of body, or, on the other, that God hath given us one faculty to deceive us, and another to detect the cheat.

We desire, therefore, with pleasure, to do justice to the doctrine of Locke, and other modern philosophers, with regard to colour and other secondary qualities, and to ascribe to it its due merit, while we beg leave to censure the language in which they have expressed their doctrine. When they had explained and established the distinction between the appearance which colour makes to the eye, and the modification of the coloured body which, by the laws of nature, causes that appearance, the question was, whether to give the name of *colour* to the cause or to the effect? By giving it, as they have done, to the effect, they set philosophy apparently in opposition to common sense, and expose it to the ridicule of the vulgar. But had they given the name of *colour* to the cause, as they ought to have done, they must then have affirmed, with the vulgar, that colour is a quality of bodies; and that there is neither colour nor anything like it in the mind. Their language, as well as their sentiments, would have been perfectly agreeable to the common apprehensions of mankind, and true Philosophy would have joined hands with Common Sense. As Locke was no enemy to common sense, it may be presumed, that, in this instance, as in some others, he was seduced by some received hypothesis; and that this was actually the case, will appear in the following section.

Section VI

That none of our sensations are resemblances of any of the qualities of bodies.

A second inference is, that, although colour is really a quality of body, yet it is not represented to the mind by an idea or sensation that resembles it; on the contrary, it is suggested by an idea which does not in the least resemble it. And this inference is applicable, not to colour only, but to all the qualities of body which we have examined.

It deserves to be remarked, that, in the analysis we have hitherto given of the operations of the five senses, and of the qualities of bodies discovered by them, no instance hath occurred, either of any sensation which resembles any quality of body, or of any quality of body whose image or resemblance is conveyed to the mind by means of the senses.

There is no phænomenon in nature more unaccountable than the intercourse that is carried on between the mind and the external world — there is no phænomenon which philosophical spirits have shown greater avidity to pry into, and to resolve. It is agreed by all, that this intercourse is carried on by means of the senses; and this satisfies the vulgar curiosity, but not the philosophic. Philosophers must have some system, some hypothesis, that shows the manner in which our senses make us acquainted with external things. All the fertility of human invention seems to have produced only one hypothesis for this purpose, which, therefore, hath been universally received; and that is, that the mind, like a mirror, receives the images of things from without, by means of the senses; so that their use must be to convey these images into the mind.

Whether to these images of external things in the mind, we give the name of *sensible forms*, or *sensible species*, with the Peripatetics, or the name of *ideas of sensation*, with Locke; or whether, with later philosophers, we distinguish *sensations*, which are immediately conveyed by the senses, from *ideas of sensation*, which are faint copies of our sensations retained in the memory and imagination; these are only differences about words. The hypothesis I have mentioned is common to all these different systems.

The necessary and allowed consequence of this hypothesis is, *that no material thing, nor any quality of material things, can be conceived by us, or made an object of thought, until its image is conveyed to the mind by means of the senses*. We shall examine this hypothesis particularly afterwards, and at this time only observe, that, in consequence of it, one would naturally expect, that to every quality and attribute of body we know or can conceive, there should be a sensation corresponding, which is the image and resemblance of that quality; and that the sensations which have no similitude or resemblance to body, or to any of its qualities, should give us no conception of a material world, or of anything belonging to it. These things might be expected as the natural consequences of the hypothesis we have mentioned.

Now, we have considered, in this and the preceding chapters, Extension, Figure, Solidity, Motion, Hardness, Roughness, as well as Colour, Heat, and Cold, Sound, Taste, and Smell. We have endeavoured to show that our nature and constitution lead us to conceive these as qualities of body, as all mankind have always conceived them to be. We have likewise examined with great attention the various sensations we have by means of the five senses, and are not able to find among them all one single image of body, or of any of its qualities. From whence, then, come those images of body and of its qualities into the mind? Let philosophers resolve this question. All I can say is, that they come not by the senses. I am sure that, by proper attention and care, I may know my sensations, and be able to affirm with certainty what they resemble, and what they do not resemble. I have examined them one by one, and compared them with matter and its qualities; and I cannot find one of them that confesses a resembling feature.

A truth so evident as this — that our sensations are not images of matter, or of any of its qualities — ought not to yield to a hypothesis such as that above-mentioned, however ancient, or however universally received by philosophers; nor can there be any amicable union between the two. This will appear by some reflections upon the spirit of the ancient and modern philosophy concerning sensation.

During the reign of the Peripatetic philosophy, our sensations were not minutely or accurately examined. The attention of philosophers, as well as of the vulgar, was turned to the things signified by them: therefore, in consequence of the common hypothesis, it was taken for granted, that all the sensations we have from external things, are the forms or images of these external things. And thus the truth we have mentioned yielded entirely to the hypothesis, and was altogether suppressed by it.

Des Cartes gave a noble example of turning our attention inward, and scrutinizing our sensations; and this example hath been very worthily followed by modern philosophers, particularly by Malebranche, Locke, Berkeley, and Hume. The effect of this scrutiny hath been, a gradual discovery of the truth above-mentioned — to wit, the dissimilitude between the sensations of our minds, and the qualities or attributes of an insentient inert substance, such as we conceive matter to be. But this valuable and useful discovery, in its different stages, hath still been unhappily united to the ancient hypothesis — and from this inauspicious match of opinions, so unfriendly and discordant in their natures, have arisen those monsters of paradox and scepticism with which the modern philosophy is too justly chargeable.

Locke saw clearly, and proved incontestably, that the sensations we have by taste, smell, and hearing, as well as the sensations of colour, heat, and cold, are not resemblances of anything in bodies; and in this he agrees with Des Cartes and Malebranche. Joining this opinion with the hypothesis, it follows necessarily, that three senses of the five are cut off from giving us any intelligence of the material world, as being altogether inept for that office. Smell, and taste, and sound, as well as colour and heat, can have no more relation to body, than anger or gratitude; nor ought the former to be called qualities of body, whether primary or secondary, any more than the latter. For it was natural and obvious to argue thus from that hypothesis: If heat, and colour, and sound are real qualities of body, the sensations by which we perceive them must be resemblances of those qualities; but these sensations are not resemblances; therefore, those are not real qualities of body.

We see, then, that Locke, having found that the ideas of secondary qualities are no resemblances, was compelled, by a hypothesis common to all philosophers, to deny that they are real qualities of body. It is more difficult to assign a reason why, after this, he should call them *secondary qualities*; for this name, if I mistake not, was of his invention. Surely he did not mean that they were secondary qualities of the mind; and I do not see with what propriety, or even by what tolerable license, he could call them secondary qualities of body, after finding that they were no qualities of body at all. In this, he seems to have sacrificed to Common Sense, and to have been led by her authority even in opposition to his hypothesis. The same sovereign mistress of our opinions that led this philosopher to call those things secondary qualities of body, which, according to his principles and reasonings, were no qualities of body at all, hath led, not the vulgar of all ages only, but philosophers also, and even the disciples of Locke, to believe them to be real qualities of body — she hath led them to investigate, by experiments, the nature of colour, and sound, and heat, in bodies. Nor hath this investigation been fruitless, as it must have been if there had been no such thing in bodies; on the contrary, it hath produced very noble and useful discoveries, which make a very considerable part of natural philosophy. If, then, natural philosophy be not a dream, there is something in bodies which we call *colour*, and *heat*, and *sound*. And if this be so, the hypothesis from which the contrary is concluded, must be false: for the argument, leading to a false conclusion, recoils against the hypothesis from which it was drawn, and thus directs its force backward. If the qualities of body were known to us only by sensations that resemble them, then colour, and sound, and heat could be no qualities of body; but these are real qualities of body; and, therefore, the qualities of body are not known only by means of sensations that resemble them.

But to proceed. What Locke had proved with regard to the sensations we have by smell, taste, and hearing, Bishop Berkeley proved no less unanswerably with regard to all our other sensations; to wit, that none of them can in the least resemble the qualities of a lifeless and insentient being, such as matter is conceived to be. Mr Hume hath confirmed this by his authority and reasoning. This opinion surely looks with a very malign aspect upon the old hypothesis; yet that hypothesis hath still been retained, and conjoined with it. And what a brood of monsters hath this produced!

The first-born of this union, and, perhaps, the most harmless, was, that the secondary qualities of body were mere sensations of the mind. To pass by Malebranche's notion of seeing all things in the ideas of the divine mind, as a foreigner, never naturalized in this island; the next was Berkeley's system, That extension, and figure, and hardness, and motion—that land, and sea, and houses, and our own bodies, as well as those of our wives, and children, and friends—are nothing but ideas of the mind: and that there is nothing existing in nature, but minds and ideas.

The progeny that followed, is still more frightful; so that it is surprising, that one could be found who had the courage to act the midwife, to rear it up, and to usher it into the world. No causes nor effects; no substances, material or spiritual; no evidence, even in mathematical demonstration; no liberty nor active power; nothing existing in nature, but impressions and ideas following each other, without time, place, or subject. Surely no age ever produced such a system of opinions, justly deduced with great acuteness, perspicuity, and elegance, from a principle universally received. The hypothesis we have mentioned is the father of them all. The dissimilitude of our sensations and feelings to external things, is the innocent mother of most of them.

As it happens sometimes, in an arithmetical operation, that two errors balance one another, so that the conclusion is little or nothing affected by them; but when one of them is corrected, and the other left, we are led farther from the truth than by both together: so it seems to have happened in the Peripatetic philosophy of sensation, compared with the modern. The Peripatetics adopted two errors; but the last served as a corrective to the first, and rendered it mild and gentle; so that their system had no tendency to scepticism. The moderns have retained the first of those errors, but have gradually detected and corrected the last. The consequence hath been, that the light we have struck out hath created darkness, and scepticism hath advanced hand in hand with knowledge, spreading its melancholy gloom, first over the material world, and at last over the whole face of nature. Such a phænomenon as this, is apt to stagger even the lovers of light and knowledge, while its cause is latent; but, when that is detected, it may give hopes that this darkness shall not be everlasting, but that it shall be succeeded by a more permanent light.

Section VII

Of visible figure and extension.

Although there is no resemblance, nor, as far as we know, any necessary connection, between that quality in a body which we call its *colour*, and the appearance which that colour makes to the eye, it is quite otherwise with regard to its *figure* and *magnitude*. There is certainly a resemblance, and a necessary connection, between the visible figure and magnitude of a body, and its real figure and magnitude; no man can give a reason why a scarlet colour affects the eye in the manner it does; no man can be sure that it affects his eye in the same manner as it affects the eye of another, and that it has the same appearance to him as it has to another man; — but we can assign a reason why a circle placed obliquely to the eye, should appear in the form of an ellipse. The visible figure, magnitude, and position may, by mathematical reasoning, be deduced from the real; and it may be demonstrated, that every eye that sees distinctly and perfectly, must, in the same situation, see it under this form, and no other. Nay, we may venture to affirm, that a man born blind, if he were instructed in mathematics, would be able to determine the visible figure of a body when its real figure, distance, and position, are given. Dr Saunderson understood the projection of the sphere, and perspective. Now, I require no more knowledge in a blind man, in order to his being able to determine the visible figure of bodies, than that he can project the outline of a given body, upon the surface of a hollow sphere, whose centre is in the eye. This projection is the visible figure he wants: for it is the same figure with that which is projected upon the *tunica retina* in vision.

A blind man can conceive lines drawn from every point of the object to the centre of the eye, making angles. He can conceive that the length of the object will appear greater or less, in proportion to the angle which it subtends at the eye; and that, in like manner, the breadth, and in general the distance, of any one point of the object from any other point, will appear greater or less, in proportion to the angles which those distances subtend. He can easily be made to conceive, that the visible appearance has no thickness, any more than a projection of the sphere, or a perspective draught. He may be informed, that the eye, until it is aided by experience, does not represent one object as nearer or more remote than another. Indeed, he would probably conjecture this of himself, and be apt to think that the rays of light must make the same impression upon the eye, whether they come from a greater or a less distance.

These are all the principles which we suppose our blind mathematician to have; and these he may certainly acquire by information and reflection. It is no less certain, that, from these principles, having given the real figure and magnitude of a body, and its position and distance with regard to the eye, he can find out its visible figure and magnitude. He can demonstrate in general, from these principles, that the visible figure of all bodies will be the same with that of their projection upon the surface of a hollow sphere, when the eye is placed in the centre. And he can demonstrate that their visible magnitude will be greater or less, according as their projection occupies a greater or less part of the surface of this sphere.

To set this matter in another light, let us distinguish betwixt the *position* of objects with regard to the eye, and their *distance* from it. Objects that lie in the same right line drawn from the centre of the eye, have the same position, however different their distances from the eye may be: but objects which lie in different right lines drawn from the eye's centre, have a different position; and this difference of position is greater or less in proportion to the angle made at the eye by the right lines mentioned. Having thus defined what we mean by the position of objects with regard to the eye, it is evident that, as the real figure of a body consists in the situation of its several parts with regard to one another, so its visible figure consists in the position of its several parts with regard to the eye; and, as he that hath a distinct conception of the situation of the parts of the body with regard to one another, must have a distinct conception of its real figure; so he that conceives distinctly the position of its several parts with regard to the eye, must have a distinct conception of its visible figure. Now, there is nothing, surely, to hinder a blind man from conceiving the position of the several parts of a body with regard to the eye, any more than from conceiving their situation with regard to one another; and, therefore, I conclude, that a blind man may attain a distinct conception of the visible figure of bodies.[...]

Section VIII

Some queries concerning visible figure answered.

It may be asked, What kind of thing is this visible figure? Is it a Sensation, or an Idea? If it is an idea, from what sensation is it copied? These questions may seem trivial or impertinent to one who does not know that there is a tribunal of inquisition erected by certain modern philosophers, before which everything in nature must answer. The articles of inquisition are few indeed, but very dreadful in their consequences. They are only these: Is the prisoner an Impression or an Idea? If an idea, from what impression copied? Now, if it appears that the prisoner is neither an impression, nor an idea copied from some impression, immediately, without being allowed to offer anything in arrest of judgment, he is sentenced to pass out of existence, and to be, in all time to come, an empty unmeaning sound, or the ghost of a departed entity.

Before this dreadful tribunal, cause and effect, time and place, matter and spirit, have been tried and cast: how then shall such a poor flimsy form as visible figure stand before it? It must even plead guilty, and confess that it is neither an impression nor an idea. For, alas! it is notorious, that it is extended in length and breadth; it may be long or short, broad or narrow, triangular, quadrangular, or circular; and, therefore, unless ideas and impressions are extended and figured, it cannot belong to that category.

If it should still be asked, To what category of beings does visible figure then belong? I can only, in answer, give some tokens, by which those who are better acquainted with the categories, may chance to find its place. It is, as we have said, the position of the several parts of a figured body with regard to the eye. The different positions of the several parts of the body with regard to the eye, when put together, make a real figure, which is truly extended in length and breadth, and which represents a figure that is extended in length, breadth, and thickness. In like manner, a projection of the sphere is a real figure, and hath length and breadth, but represents the sphere, which hath three dimensions. A projection of the sphere, or a perspective view of a palace, is a representative in the very same sense as visible figure is; and wherever they have their lodgings in the categories, this will be found to dwell next door to them.

It may farther be asked, Whether there be any sensation proper to visible figure, by which it is suggested in vision? — or by what means it is presented to the mind? This is a question of some importance, in order to our having a distinct notion of the faculty of seeing: and to give all the light to it we can, it is necessary to compare this sense with other senses, and to make some suppositions, by which we may be enabled to distinguish things that are apt to be confounded, although they are totally different.

There are three of our senses which give us intelligence of things at a distance: smell, hearing, and sight. In smelling and in hearing, we have a sensation or impression upon the mind, which, by our constitution, we conceive to be a sign of something external: but the position of this external thing, with regard to the organ of sense, is not presented to the mind along with the sensation. When I hear the sound of a coach, I could not, previous to experience, determine whether the sounding body was above or below, to the right hand or to the left. So that the sensation suggests to me some external object as the cause or occasion of it; but it suggests not the position of that object, whether it lies in this direction or in that. The same thing may be said with regard to smelling. But the case is quite different with regard to seeing.

When I see an object, the appearance which the colour of it makes, may be called *the sensation*, which suggests to me some external thing as its cause; but it suggests likewise the individual direction and position of this cause with regard to the eye. I know it is precisely in such a direction, and in no other. At the same time, I am not conscious of anything that can be called *sensation*, but the sensation of colour. The position of the coloured thing is no sensation; but it is by the laws of my constitution presented to the mind along with the colour, without any additional sensation.

Let us suppose that the eye were so constituted that the rays coming from any one point of the object were not, as they are in our eyes, collected in one point of the *retina*, but diffused over the whole: it is evident to those who understand the structure of the eye, that such an eye as we have supposed, would show the colour of a body as our eyes do, but that it would neither show figure nor position. The operation of such an eye would be precisely similar to that of hearing and smell; it would give no perception of figure or extension, but merely of colour. Nor is the supposition we have made altogether imaginary: for it is nearly the case of most people who have cataracts, whose crystalline, as Mr Cheselden observes, does not altogether exclude the rays of light, but diffuses them over the *retina*, so that such persons see things as one does through a glass of broken gelly: they perceive the colour, but nothing of the figure or magnitude of objects.

Again, if we should suppose that smell and sound were conveyed in right lines from the objects, and that every sensation of hearing and smell suggested the precise direction or position of its object; in this case, the operations of hearing and smelling would be similar to that of seeing: we should smell and hear the figure of objects, in the same sense as now we see it; and every smell and sound would be associated with some figure in the imagination, as colour is in our present state.

We have reason to believe, that the rays of light make some impression upon the *retina*; but we are not conscious of this impression; nor have anatomists or philosophers been able to discover the nature and effects of it; whether it produces a vibration in the nerve, or the motion of some subtile fluid contained in the nerve, or something different from either, to which we cannot give a name. Whatever it is, we shall call it the *material impression*; remembering carefully, that it is not an impression upon the mind, but upon the body; and that it is no sensation, nor can resemble sensation, any more than figure or motion can resemble thought. Now, this material impression, made upon a particular point of the retina, by the laws of our constitution, suggests two things to the mind — namely, the colour and the position of some external object. No man can give a reason why the same material impression might not have suggested sound, or smell, or either of these, along with the position of the object. That it should suggest colour and position, and nothing else, we can resolve only into our constitution, or the will of our Maker. And since there is no necessary connection between these two things suggested by this material impression, it might, if it had so pleased our Creator, have suggested one of them without the other. Let us suppose, therefore, since it plainly appears to be possible, that our eyes had been so framed as to suggest to us the position of the object, without suggesting colour, or any other quality: What is the consequence of this supposition? It is evidently this, that the person endued with such an eye, would perceive the visible figure of bodies, without having any sensation or impression made upon his mind. The figure he perceives is altogether external; and therefore cannot be called an impression upon the mind, without the grossest abuse of language. If it should be said, that it is impossible to perceive a figure, unless there be some impression of it upon the mind, I beg leave not to admit the impossibility of this without some proof: and I can find none. Neither can I conceive what is meant by an impression of figure upon the mind. I can conceive an impression of figure upon wax, or upon any body that is fit to receive it; but an impression of it upon the mind, is to me quite unintelligible; and, although I form the most distinct conception of the figure, I cannot, upon the strictest examination, find any impression of it upon my mind.

If we suppose, last of all, that the eye hath the power restored of perceiving colour, I apprehend that it will be allowed, that now it perceives figure in the very same manner as before, with this difference only, that colour is always joined with it.

In answer, therefore, to the question proposed, there seems to be no sensation that is appropriated to visible figure, or whose office it is to suggest it. It seems to be suggested immediately by the material impression upon the organ, of which we are not conscious: and why may not a material impression upon the *retina* suggest visible figure, as well as the material impression made upon the hand, when we grasp a ball, suggests real figure? In the one case, one and the same material impression, suggests both colour and visible figure; and in the other case, one and the same material impression suggests hardness, heat, or cold, and real figure, all at the same time.

We shall conclude this section with another question upon this subject. Since the visible figure of bodies is a real and external object to the eye, as their tangible figure is to the touch, it may be asked, Whence arises the difficulty of attending to the first, and the facility of attending to the last? It is certain that the first is more frequently presented to the eye, than the last is to the touch; the first is as distinct and determinate an object as the last, and seems in its own nature as proper for speculation. Yet so little hath it been attended to, that it never had a name in any language, until Bishop Berkeley gave it that which we have used after his example, to distinguish it from the figure which is the object of touch.

The difficulty of attending to the visible figure of bodies, and making it an object of thought, appears so similar to that which we find in attending to our sensations, that both have probably like causes. Nature intended the visible figure as a sign of the tangible figure and situation of bodies, and hath taught us, by a kind of instinct, to put it always to this use. Hence it happens, that the mind passes over it with a rapid motion, to attend to the things signified by it. It is as unnatural to the mind to stop at the visible figure, and attend to it, as it is to a spherical body to stop upon an inclined plane. There is an inward principle, which constantly carries it forward, and which cannot be overcome but by a contrary force.

There are other external things which nature intended for signs; and we find this common to them all, that the mind is disposed to overlook them, and to attend only to the things signified by them. Thus there are certain modifications of the human face, which are natural signs of the present disposition of the mind. Every man understands the meaning of these signs, but not one of a hundred ever attended to the signs themselves, or knows anything about them. Hence you may find many an excellent practical physiognomist who knows nothing of the proportions of a face nor can delineate or describe the expression of any one passion.

An excellent painter or statuary can tell, not only what are the proportions of a good face, but what changes every passion makes in it. This, however, is one of the chief mysteries of his art, to the acquisition of which infinite labour and attention, as well as a happy genius, are required; but when he puts his art in practice, and happily expresses a passion by its proper signs, every one understands the meaning of these signs, without art, and without reflection.

What has been said of painting, might easily be applied to all the fine arts. The difficulty in them all consists in knowing and attending to those natural signs whereof every man understands the meaning.

We pass from the sign to the thing signified, with ease, and by natural impulse; but to go backward from the thing signified to the sign, is a work of labour and difficulty. Visible figure, therefore, being intended by nature to be a sign, we pass on immediately to the thing signified, and cannot easily return to give any attention to the sign.

Nothing shows more clearly our indisposition to attend to visible figure and visible extension than this — that, although mathematical reasoning is no less applicable to them, than to tangible figure and extension, yet they have entirely escaped the notice of mathematicians. While that figure and that extension which are objects of touch, have been tortured ten thousand ways for twenty centuries, and a very noble system of science has been drawn out of them, not a single proposition do we find with regard to the figure and extension which are the immediate objects of sight!

When the geometrician draws a diagram with the most perfect accuracy — when he keeps his eye fixed upon it, while he goes through a long process of reasoning, and demonstrates the relations of the several parts of his figure — he does not consider that the visible figure presented to his eye, is only the representative of a tangible figure, upon which all his attention is fixed; he does not consider that these two figures have really different properties; and that, what he demonstrates to be true of the one, is not true of the other.

This, perhaps, will seem so great a paradox, even to mathematicians, as to require demonstration before it can be believed. Nor is the demonstration at all difficult, if the reader will have patience to enter but a little into the mathematical consideration of visible figure, which we shall call *the geometry of visibles*.

Of the geometry of visibles.

In this geometry, the definitions of a point; of a line, whether straight or curve; of an angle, whether acute, or right, or obtuse; and of a circle—are the same as in common geometry. The mathematical reader will easily enter into the whole mystery of this geometry, if he attends duly to these few evident principles.

1. Supposing the eye placed in the centre of a sphere, every great circle of the sphere will have the same appearance to the eye as if it was a straight line; for the curvature of the circle being turned directly toward the eye, is not perceived by it. And, for the same reason, any line which is drawn in the plane of a great circle of the sphere, whether it be in reality straight or curve, will appear straight to the eye.

2. Every visible right line will appear to coincide with some great circle of the sphere; and the circumference of that great circle, even when it is produced until it returns into itself, will appear to be a continuation of the same visible right line, all the parts of it being visibly *in directum*. For the eye, perceiving only the position of objects with regard to itself, and not their distance, will see those points in the same visible place which have the same position with regard to the eye, how different soever their distances from it may be. Now, since a plane passing through the eye and a given visible right line, will be the plane of some great circle of the sphere, every point of the visible right line will have the same position as some point of the great circle; therefore, they will both have the same visible place, and coincide to the eye; and the whole circumference of the great circle,

continued even until it returns into itself, will appear to be a continuation of the same visible right line.

Hence it follows—

3. That every visible right line, when it is continued *in directum*, as far as it may be continued, will be represented by a great circle of a sphere, in whose centre the eye is placed. It follows—

4. That the visible angle comprehended under two visible right lines, is equal to the spherical angle comprehended under the two great circles, which are the representatives of these visible lines. For, since the visible lines appear to coincide with the great circles, the visible angle comprehended under the former must be equal to the visible angle comprehended under the latter. But the visible angle comprehended under the two great circles, when seen from the centre, is of the same magnitude with the spherical angle which they really comprehend, as mathematicians know; therefore, the visible angle made by any two visible lines is equal to the spherical angle made by the two great circles of the sphere which are their representatives.

5. Hence it is evident, that every visible right-lined triangle will coincide in all its parts with some spherical triangle. The sides of the one will appear equal to the sides of the other, and the angles of the one to the angles of the other, each to each; and, therefore, the whole of the one triangle will appear equal to the whole of the other. In a word, to the eye they will be one and the same, and have the same mathematical properties. The properties, therefore, of visible right-lined triangles are not the same with the properties of plain triangles, but are the same with those of spherical triangles.

6. Every lesser circle of the sphere will appear a circle to the eye, placed, as we have supposed all along, in the centre of the sphere; and, on the other hand, every visible circle will appear to coincide with some lesser circle of the sphere.

7. Moreover, the whole surface of the sphere will represent the whole of visible space; for, since every visible point coincides with some point of the surface of the sphere, and has the same visible place, it follows, that all the parts of the spherical surface taken together, will represent all poss-

ible visible places—that is, the whole of visible space. And from this it follows, in the last place—

8. That every visible figure will be represented by that part of the surface of the sphere on which it might be projected, the eye being in the centre. And every such visible figure will bear the same *ratio* to the whole of visible space, as the part of the spherical surface which represents it, bears to the whole spherical surface.

The mathematical reader, I hope, will enter into these principles with perfect facility, and will as easily perceive that the following propositions with regard to visible figure and space, which we offer only as a specimen, may be mathematically demonstrated from them, and are not less true nor less evident than the propositions of Euclid, with regard to tangible figures.

Prop. 1. Every right line being produced, will at last return into itself.

2. A right line returning into itself, is the longest possible right line; and all other right lines bear a finite *ratio* to it.

3. A right line returning into itself, divides the whole of visible space into two equal parts, which will both be comprehended under this right line.

4. The whole of visible space bears a finite *ratio* to any part of it.

5. Any two right lines being produced, will meet in two points, and mutually bisect each other.

6. If two lines be parallel—that is, everywhere equally distant from each other—they cannot both be straight.

7. Any right line being given, a point may be found, which is at the same distance from all the points of the given right line.

8. A circle may be parallel to a right line—that is, may be equally distant from it in all its parts.

9. Right-lined triangles that are similar, are also equal.

10. Of every right-lined triangle, the three angles taken together, are greater than two right angles.

11. The angles of a right-lined triangle, may all be right angles, or all obtuse angles.

12. Unequal circles are not as the squares of their diameters, nor are their circumferences in the *ratio* of their diameters.

This small specimen of the geometry of visibles, is intended to lead the reader to a clear and distinct conception of the figure and extension which is presented to the mind by vision; and to demonstrate the truth of what we have affirmed above—namely, that those figures and that extension which are the immediate objects of sight, are not the figures and the extension about which common geometry is employed; that the geometrician, while he looks at his diagram, and demonstrates a proposition, hath a figure presented to his eye, which is only a sign and representative of a tangible figure; that he gives not the least attention to the first, but attends only to the last; and that these two figures have different properties, so that what he demonstrates of the one, is not true of the other.

It deserves, however, to be remarked, that, as a small part of a spherical surface differs not sensibly from a plain surface, so a small part of visible extension differs very little from that extension in length and breadth, which is the object of touch. And it is likewise to be observed, that the human eye is so formed, that an object which is seen distinctly and at one view, can occupy but a small part of visible space; for we never see distinctly what is at a considerable distance from the axis of the eye; and, therefore, when we would see a large object at one view, the eye must be at so great a distance, that the object occupies but a small part of visible space. From these two observations, it follows, that plain figures which are seen at one view, when their planes are not oblique, but direct to the eye, differ little from the visible figures which they present to the eye. The several lines in the tangible figure, have very nearly the same proportion to each other as in the visible; and the angles of the one are very nearly, although not strictly and mathematically, equal to those of the other. Although, therefore, we have found many instances of natural signs which have no similitude to the things signified, this is not the case with regard to visible figure. It hath, in all cases, such a similitude to the thing signified by it, as a plan or profile hath to that which it represents; and, in some cases, the sign and thing signified have to all sense the same figure and the same proportions. If we could find a being endued with sight only, without any other external sense, and capable of reflecting and reasoning upon what he sees, the notions and philosophical speculations of such a being, might assist us in the difficult task of distinguishing the perceptions which we have purely by sight, from those which derive their origin from other senses. Let us suppose such a being, and conceive, as well as we can, what notion he would have of visible objects, and what conclusions he would deduce from them. We must not conceive him disposed by his constitution, as we are, to consider the visible appearance as a sign of something else: it is no sign to him, because there is nothing signified by it; and, therefore, we must suppose him as much disposed to attend to the visible figure and extension of bodies, as we are disposed to attend to their tangible figure and extension.

If various figures were presented to his sense, he might, without doubt, as they grow familiar, compare them together, and perceive wherein they agree, and wherein they differ. He might perceive visible objects to have length and breadth, but could have no notion of a third dimension, any more than we can have of a fourth. All visible objects would appear to be terminated by lines, straight or curve; and objects terminated by the same visible lines, would occupy the same place, and fill the same part of visible space. It would not be possible for him to conceive one object to be behind another, or one to be nearer, another more distant.

To us, who conceive three dimensions, a line may be conceived straight; or it may be conceived incurvated in one dimension, and straight in another; or, lastly, it may be incurvated in two dimensions. Suppose a line to be drawn upwards and downwards, its length makes one dimension, which we shall call *upwards and downwards*; and there are two dimensions remaining, according to which it may be straight or curve. It may be bent to the right or to the left, and, if it has no bending either to right or left, it is straight in this dimension. But supposing it straight in this dimension of right and left, there is still another dimension remaining, in which it may be curve; for it may be bent backwards or forwards. When we conceive a tangible straight line, we exclude curvature in either of these two dimensions: and as what is conceived to be excluded, must be conceived, as well as what is conceived to be included, it follows that all the three dimensions enter into our conception of a straight line. Its length is one dimension, its straightness in two other dimensions is included, or curvature in these two dimensions excluded, in the conception of it.

The being we have supposed, having no conception of more than two dimensions, of which the length of a line is one, cannot possibly conceive it either straight or curve in more than one dimension; so that, in his conception of a right line, curvature to the right hand or left is excluded; but curvature backwards or forwards cannot be excluded, because he neither hath, nor can have any conception of such curvature. Hence we see the reason that a line which is straight to the eye, may return into itself; for its being straight to the eye, implies only straightness in one dimension; and a line which is straight in one dimension may, notwithstanding, be curve in another dimension, and so may return into itself.

To us, who conceive three dimensions, a surface is that which hath length and breadth, excluding thickness; and a surface may be either plain in this third dimension, or it maybe incurvated: so that the notion of a third dimension enters into our conception of a surface; for it is only by means of this third dimension that we can distinguish surfaces into plain and curve surfaces; and neither one nor the other can be conceived without conceiving a third dimension.

The being we have supposed, having no conception of a third dimension, his visible figures have length and breadth indeed; but thickness is neither included nor excluded, being a thing of which he has no conception. And, therefore, visible figures, although they have length and breadth, as surfaces have, yet they are neither plain surfaces nor curve surfaces. For a curve surface implies curvature in a third dimension, and a plain surface implies the want of curvature in a third dimension; and such a being can conceive neither of these, because he has no conception of a third dimension. Moreover, although he hath a distinct conception of the inclination of two lines which make an angle, yet he can neither conceive a plain angle nor a spherical angle. Even his notion of a point is somewhat less determined than ours. In the notion of a point, we exclude length, breadth, and thickness; he excludes length and breadth, but cannot either exclude, or include thickness, because he hath no conception of it.

Having thus settled the notions which such a being as we have supposed might form of mathematical points, lines, angles, and figures, it is easy to see, that, by comparing these together, and reasoning about them, he might discover their relations, and form geometrical conclusions built upon self-evident principles. He might likewise, without doubt, have the same notions of numbers as we have, and form a system of arithmetic. It is not material to say in what order he might proceed in such discoveries, or how much time and pains he might employ about them, but what such a being, by reason and ingenuity, without any materials of sensation but those of sight only, might discover.

As it is more difficult to attend to a detail of possibilities than of facts, even of slender authority, I shall beg leave to give an extract from the travels of Johannes Rudolphus Anepigraphus, a Rosicrucian philosopher, who having, by deep study of the occult sciences, acquired the art of transporting himself to various sublunary regions, and of conversing with various orders of intelligences, in the course of his adventures became acquainted with an order of beings exactly such as I have supposed.

How they communicate their sentiments to one another, and by what means he became acquainted with their language, and was initiated into their philosophy, as well as of many other particulars, which might have gratified the curiosity of his readers, and, perhaps, added credibility to his relation, he hath not thought fit to inform us; these being matters proper for adepts only to know. His account of their philosophy is as follows: —

'The Idomenians,' saith he, 'are many of them very ingenious, and much given to contemplation. In arithmetic, geometry, metaphysics, and physics, they have most elaborate systems. In the two latter, indeed, they have had many disputes carried on with great subtilty, and are divided into various sects; yet in the two former there hath been no less unanimity than among the human species. Their principles relating to numbers and arithmetic, making allowance for their notation, differ in nothing from ours — but their geometry differs very considerably.'

As our author's account of the geometry of the Idomenians agrees in everything with the geometry of visibles, of which we have already given a specimen, we shall pass over it. He goes on thus: — 'Colour, extension, and figure, are conceived to be the essential properties of body. A very considerable sect maintains, that colour is the essence of body. If there had been no colour, say they, there had been no perception or sensation. Colour is all that we perceive, or can conceive, that is peculiar to body; extension and figure being modes common to body and to empty space. And if we should suppose a body to be annihilated, colour is the only thing in it that can be annihilated; for its place, and consequently the figure and extension of that place, must remain, and cannot be imagined not to exist. These philosophers hold space to be the place of all bodies, immoveable and indestructible, without figure and similar in all its parts, incapable of increase or diminution, yet not unmeasurable; for every the least part of space bears a finite *ratio* to the whole. So that with them the whole extent of space is the common and natural measure of everything that hath length and breadth; and the magnitude of every body and of every figure is expressed by its being such a part of the universe. In like manner, the common and natural measure of length is an infinite right line, which, as hath been before observed, returns into itself, and hath no limits, but bears a finite *ratio* to every other line.

'As to their natural philosophy, it is now acknowledged by the wisest of them to have been for many ages in a very low state. The philosophers observing, that body can differ from another only in colour, figure, or magnitude, it was taken for granted, that all their particular qualities must arise from the various combinations of these their essential attributes; and, therefore, it was looked upon as the end of natural philosophy, to show how the various combinations of these three qualities in different bodies produced all the phænomena of nature. It were endless to enumerate the various systems that were invented with this view, and the disputes that were carried on for ages; the followers of every system exposing the weak sides of other systems, and palliating those of their own, with great art.

'At last, some free and facetious spirits, wearied with eternal disputation, and the labour of patching and propping weak systems, began to complain of the subtilty of nature; of the infinite changes that bodies undergo in figure, colour, and magnitude; and of the difficulty of accounting for these appearances—making this a pretence for giving up all inquiries into the causes of things, as vain and fruitless.

'These wits had ample matter of mirth and ridicule in the systems of philosophers; and, finding it an easier task to pull down than to build or support, and that every sect furnished them with arms and auxiliaries to destroy another, they began to spread mightily, and went on with great success. Thus philosophy gave way to scepticism and irony, and those systems which had been the work of ages, and the admiration of the learned, became the jest of the vulgar: for even the vulgar readily took part in the triumph over a kind of learning which they had long suspected, because it produced nothing but wrangling and altercation. The wits, having now acquired great reputation, and being flushed with success, began to think their triumph incomplete, until every pretence to knowledge was overturned; and accordingly began their attacks upon arithmetic, geometry, and even upon the common notions of untaught Idomenians. So difficult it hath always been,' says our author, 'for great conquerors to know where to stop.

'In the meantime, natural philosophy began to rise from its ashes, under the direction of a person of great genius, who is looked upon as having had something in him above Idomenian nature.' He observed, that the Idomenian faculties were certainly intended for contemplation, and that the works of nature were a nobler subject to exercise them upon, than the follies of systems, or the errors of the learned; and being sensible of the difficulty of finding out the causes of natural things, he proposed, by accurate observation of the phænomena of nature, to find out the rules according to which they happen, without inquiring into the causes of those rules. In this he made considerable progress himself, and planned out much work for his followers, who call themselves *inductive philosophers*. The sceptics look with envy upon this rising sect, as eclipsing their reputation, and threatening to limit their empire; but they are at a loss on what hand to attack it. The vulgar begin to reverence it as producing useful discoveries.

'It is to be observed, that every Idomenian firmly believes, that two or more bodies may exist in the same place.
For this they have the testimony of sense, and they can no
more doubt of it, than they can doubt whether they have any
perception at all. They often see two bodies meet and coincide in the same place, and separate again, without having
undergone any change in their sensible qualities by this
penetration. When two bodies meet, and occupy the same
place, commonly one only appears in that place, and the
other disappears. That which continues to appear is said to
overcome, the other to be overcome.'

To this quality of bodies they gave a name, which our
author tells us hath no word answering to it in any human
language. And, therefore, after making a long apology,
which I omit, he begs leave to call it *the overcoming quality of
bodies*. He assures us, that 'the speculations which had been
raised about this single quality of bodies, and the hypotheses
contrived to account for it, were sufficient to fill many volumes. Nor have there been fewer hypotheses invented by
their philosophers, to account for the changes of magnitude
and figure; which, in most bodies that move, they perceive to
be in a continual fluctuation. The founder of the inductive
sect, believing it to be above the reach of Idomenian faculties,
to discover the real causes of these phænomena, applied
himself to find from observation, by what laws they are connected together; and discovered many mathematical ratios
and relations concerning the motions, magnitudes, figures,
and overcoming quality of bodies, which constant experience
confirms. But the opposers of this sect choose rather to content themselves with feigned causes of these phænomena,
than to acknowledge the real laws whereby they are governed, which humble their pride, by being confessedly
unaccountable.'

Thus far Johannes Rudolphus Anepigraphus. Whether
this Anepigraphus be the same who is recorded among the
Greek alchemistical writers not yet published, by Borrichius,
Fabricius, and others, I do not pretend to determine. The
identity of their name, and the similitude of their studies,
although no slight arguments, yet are not absolutely conclusive. Nor will I take upon me to judge of the narrative of
this learned traveller, by the *external* marks of his credibility;

I shall confine myself to those which the critics call *internal*. It would even be of small importance to inquire, whether the Idomenians have a real, or only an ideal existence; since this is disputed among the learned with regard to things with which we are more nearly connected. The important question is, whether the account above given, is a just account of their geometry and philosophy? We have all the faculties which they have, with the addition of others which they have not; we may, therefore, form some judgment of their philosophy and geometry, by separating from all others, the perceptions we have by sight and reasoning upon them. As far as I am able to judge in this way, after a careful examination, their geometry must be such as Anepigraphus hath described. Nor does his account of their philosophy appear to contain any evident marks of imposture; although here, no doubt, proper allowance is to be made for liberties which travellers take, as well as for involuntary mistakes which they are apt to fall into.

Section XIX

Of Dr Briggs's theory and Sir Isaac Newton's conjecture on this subject.

[...] [I]t was observed, in the beginning of this chapter, that the visible appearances of objects serve only as signs of their distance, magnitude, figure, and other tangible qualities. The visible appearance is that which is presented to the mind by nature, according to those laws of our constitution which have been explained. But the thing signified by that appearance, is that which is presented to the mind by custom.

When one speaks to us in a language that is familiar, we hear certain sounds, and this is all the effect that his discourse has upon us by nature; but by custom we understand the meaning of these sounds; and, therefore, we fix our attention, not upon the sounds, but upon the things signified by them. In like manner, we see only the visible appearance of objects by nature; but we learn by custom to interpret these appearances, and to understand their meaning. And when this visual language is learned, and becomes familiar, we attend only to the things signified; and cannot, without great difficulty, attend to the signs by which they are presented. The mind passes from one to the other so rapidly and so familiarly, that no trace of the sign is left in the memory, and we seem immediately, and without the intervention of any sign, to perceive the thing signified.

When I look at the apple-tree which stands before my window, I perceive, at the first glance, its distance and magnitude, the roughness of its trunk, the disposition of its branches, the figure of its leaves and fruit. I seem to perceive all these things immediately. The visible appearance which presented them all to the mind, has entirely escaped me; I cannot, without great difficulty, and painful abstraction, attend to it, even when it stands before me. Yet it is certain that this visible appearance only is presented to my eye by nature, and that I learned by custom to collect all the rest from it. If I had never seen before now, I should not perceive either the distance or tangible figure of the tree; and it would have required the practice of seeing for many months, to change that original perception which nature gave me by my eyes, into that which I now have by custom.

The objects which we see naturally and originally, as hath been before observed, have length and breadth, but no thickness nor distance from the eye. Custom, by a kind of legerdemain, withdraws gradually these original and proper objects of sight, and substitutes in their place objects of touch, which have length, breadth, and thickness, and a determinate distance from the eye. By what means this change is brought about, and what principles of the human mind concur in it, we are next to inquire.

Section XX

Of perception in general.

Sensation, and the perception of external objects by the senses, though very different in their nature, have commonly been considered as one and the same thing. The purposes of common life do not make it necessary to distinguish them, and the received opinions of philosophers tend rather to confound them; but, without attending carefully to this distinction, it is impossible to have any just conception of the operations of our senses. The most simple operations of the mind, admit not of a logical definition: all we can do is to describe them, so as to lead those who are conscious of them in themselves, to attend to them, and reflect upon them; and it is often very difficult to describe them so as to answer this intention.

The same mode of expression is used to denote sensation and perception; and, therefore, we are apt to look upon them as things of the same nature. Thus, *I feel a pain; I see a tree*: the first denoteth a sensation, the last a perception. The grammatical analysis of both expressions is the same: for both consist of an active verb and an object. But if we attend to the things signified by these expressions, we shall find that, in the first, the distinction between the act and the object is not real but grammatical; in the second, the distinction is not only grammatical but real.

The form of the expression, *I feel pain*, might seem to imply that the feeling is something distinct from the pain felt; yet, in reality, there is no distinction. As *thinking a thought* is an expression which could signify no more than *thinking*, so *feeling a pain* signifies no more than *being pained*. What we have said of pain is applicable to every other mere sensation. It is difficult to give instances, very few of our sensations having names; and, where they have, the name being common to the sensation, and to something else which is associated with it. But, when we attend to the sensation by itself, and separate it from other things which are conjoined with it in the imagination, it appears to be something which can have no existence but in a sentient mind, no distinction from the act of the mind by which it is felt.

Perception, as we here understand it, hath always an object distinct from the act by which it is perceived; an object which may exist whether it be perceived or not. I perceive a tree that grows before my window; there is here an object which is perceived, and an act of the mind by which it is perceived; and these two are not only distinguishable, but they are extremely unlike in their natures. The object is made up of a trunk, branches, and leaves; but the act of the mind by which it is perceived hath neither trunk, branches, nor leaves. I am conscious of this act of my mind, and I can reflect upon it; but it is too simple to admit of an analysis, and I cannot find proper words to describe it. I find nothing that resembles it so much as the remembrance of the tree, or the imagination of it. Yet both these differ essentially from perception; they differ likewise one from another. It is in vain that a philosopher assures me, that the imagination of the tree, the remembrance of it, and the perception of it, are all one, and differ only in degree of vivacity. I know the contrary; for I am as well acquainted with all the three as I am with the apartments of my own house. I know this also, that the perception of an object implies both a conception of its form, and a belief of its present existence. I know, moreover, that this belief is not the effect of argumentation and reasoning; it is the immediate effect of my constitution.

I am aware that this belief which I have in perception stands exposed to the strongest batteries of scepticism. But they make no great impression upon it. The sceptic asks me, Why do you believe the existence of the external object which you perceive? This belief, sir, is none of my manufacture; it came from the mint of Nature; it bears her image and superscription; and, if it is not right, the fault is not mine: I even took it upon trust, and without suspicion. Reason, says the sceptic, is the only judge of truth, and you ought to throw off every opinion and every belief that is not grounded on reason. Why, sir, should I believe the faculty of reason more than that of perception? — they came both out of the same shop, and were made by the same artist; and if he puts one piece of false ware into my hands, what should hinder him from putting another?

Perhaps the sceptic will agree to distrust reason, rather than give any credit to perception. For, says he, since, by your own concession, the object which you perceive, and that act of your mind by which you perceive it, are quite different things, the one may exist without the other; and, as the object may exist without being perceived, so the perception may exist without an object. There is nothing so shameful in a philosopher as to be deceived and deluded; and, therefore, you ought to resolve firmly to withhold assent, and to throw off this belief of external objects, which may be all delusion. For my part, I will never attempt to throw it off; and, although the sober part of mankind will not be very anxious to know my reasons, yet, if they can be of use to any sceptic, they are these: —

First, because it is not in my power: why, then, should I make a vain attempt? It would be agreeable to fly to the moon, and to make a visit to Jupiter and Saturn; but, when I know that Nature has bound me down by the law of gravitation to this planet which I inhabit, I rest contented, and quietly suffer myself to be carried along in its orbit. My belief is carried along by perception, as irresistibly as my body by the earth. And the greatest sceptic will find himself to be in the same condition. He may struggle hard to disbelieve the informations of his senses, as a man does to swim against a torrent; but, ah! it is in vain. It is in vain that he strains every nerve, and wrestles with nature, and with every object that strikes upon his senses. For, after all, when his strength is spent in the fruitless attempt, he will be carried down the torrent with the common herd of believers.

Secondly, I think it would not be prudent to throw off this belief, if it were in my power. If Nature intended to deceive me, and impose upon me by false appearances, and I, by my great cunning and profound logic, have discovered the imposture, prudence would dictate to me, in this case, even to put up [with] this indignity done me, as quietly as I could, and not to call her an impostor to her face, lest she should be even with me in another way. For what do I gain by resenting this injury? You ought at least not to believe what she says. This indeed seems reasonable, if she intends to impose upon me. But what is the consequence? I resolve not to believe my senses. I break my nose against a post that comes in my way; I step into a dirty kennel; and, after twenty such wise and rational actions, I am taken up and clapped into a mad-house. Now, I confess I would rather make one of the credulous fools whom Nature imposes upon, than of those wise and rational philosophers who resolve to withhold assent at all this expense. If a man pretends to be a sceptic with regard to the informations of sense, and yet prudently keeps out of harm's way as other men do, he must excuse my suspicion, that he either acts the hypocrite, or imposes upon himself. For, if the scale of his belief were so evenly poised as to lean no more to one side than to the contrary, it is impossible that his actions could be directed by any rules of common prudence.

Thirdly, Although the two reasons already mentioned are perhaps two more than enough, I shall offer a third. I gave implicit belief to the informations of Nature by my senses, for a considerable part of my life, before I had learned so much logic as to be able to start a doubt concerning them. And now, when I reflect upon what is past, I do not find that I have been imposed upon by this belief. I find that without it I must have perished by a thousand accidents. I find that without it I should have been no wiser now than when I was born. I should not even have been able to acquire that logic which suggests these sceptical doubts with regard to my senses. Therefore, I consider this instinctive belief as one of the best gifts of Nature. I thank the Author of my being, who bestowed it upon me before the eyes of my reason were opened, and still bestows it upon me, to be my guide where reason leaves me in the dark. And now I yield to the direction of my senses, not from instinct only, but from confidence and trust in a faithful and beneficent Monitor, grounded upon the experience of his paternal care and goodness.

In all this, I deal with the Author of my being, no otherwise than I thought it reasonable to deal with my parents and tutors. I believed by instinct whatever they told me, long before I had the idea of a lie, or thought of the possibility of their deceiving me. Afterwards, upon reflection, I found they had acted like fair and honest people, who wished me well. I found that, if I had not believed what they told me, before I could give a reason of my belief, I had to this day been little better than a changeling. And although this natural credulity hath sometimes occasioned my being imposed upon by deceivers, yet it hath been of infinite advantage to me upon the whole; therefore, I consider it as another good gift of Nature. And I continue to give that credit, from reflection, to those of whose integrity and veracity I have had experience, which before I gave from instinct.

There is a much greater similitude than is commonly imagined, between the testimony of nature given by our senses, and the testimony of men given by language. The credit we give to both is at first the effect of instinct only. When we grow up, and begin to reason about them, the credit given to human testimony is restrained and weakened, by the experience we have of deceit. But the credit given to the testimony of our senses, is established and confirmed by the uniformity and constancy of the laws of nature.

Our perceptions are of two kinds: some are natural and original; others acquired, and the fruit of experience. When I perceive that this is the taste of cyder, that of brandy; that this is the smell of an apple, that of an orange; that this is the noise of thunder, that the ringing of bells; this the sound of a coach passing, that the voice of such a friend: these perceptions, and others of the same kind, are not original—they are acquired. But the perception which I have, by touch, of the hardness and softness of bodies, of their extension, figure, and motion, is not acquired—it is original.

In all our senses, the acquired perceptions are many more than the original, especially in sight. By this sense we perceive originally the visible figure and colour of bodies only, and their visible place: but we learn to perceive by the eye, almost everything which we can perceive by touch. The original perceptions of this sense serve only as signs to introduce the acquired.

The signs by which objects are presented to us in perception, are the language of Nature to man; and as, in many respects, it hath great affinity with the language of man to man, so particularly in this, that both are partly natural and original, partly acquired by custom. Our original or natural perceptions are analogous to the natural language of man to man, of which we took notice in the fourth chapter; and our acquired perceptions are analogous to artificial language, which, in our mother-tongue, is got very much in the same manner with our acquired perceptions—as we shall afterwards more fully explain.

Not only men, buf children, idiots, and brutes, acquire by habit many perceptions which they had not originally. Almost every employment in life hath perceptions of this kind that are peculiar to it. The shepherd knows every sheep of his flock, as we do our acquaintance, and can pick them out of another flock one by one. The butcher knows by sight the weight and quality of his beeves and sheep before they are killed. The farmer perceives by his eye, very nearly, the quantity of hay in a rick, or of corn in a heap. The sailor sees the burthen, the built, and the distance of a ship at sea, while she is a great way off. Every man accustomed to writing, distinguishes his acquaintance by their handwriting, as he does by their faces. And the painter distinguishes, in the works of his art, the style of all the great masters. In a word, acquired perception is very different in different persons, according to the diversity of objects about which they are employed, and the application they bestow in observing them.

Perception ought not only to be distinguished from sensation, but likewise from that knowledge of the objects of sense which is got by reasoning. There is no reasoning in perception, as hath been observed. The belief which is implied in it, is the effect of instinct. But there are many things, with regard to sensible objects, which we can infer from what we perceive; and such conclusions of reason ought to be distinguished from what is merely perceived. When I look at the moon, I perceive her to be sometimes circular, sometimes horned, and sometimes gibbous. This is simple perception, and is the same in the philosopher and in the clown: but from these various appearances of her enlightened part, I infer that she is really of a spherical figure. This conclusion is not obtained by simple perception, but by reasoning. Simple perception has the same relation to the conclusions of reason drawn from our perceptions, as the axioms in mathematics have to the propositions. I cannot demonstrate that two quantities which are equal to the same quantity, are equal to each other; neither can I demonstrate that the tree which I perceive, exists. But, by the constitution of my nature, my belief is irresistibly carried along by my apprehension of the axiom; and, by the constitution of my nature, my belief is no less irresistibly carried along by my perception of the tree. All reasoning is from principles. The first principles of mathematical reasoning are mathematical axioms and definitions; and the first principles of all our reasoning about existences, are our perceptions. The first principles of every kind of reasoning are given us by Nature, and are of equal authority with the faculty of reason itself, which is also the gift of Nature. The conclusions of reason are all built upon first principles, and can have no other foundation. Most justly, therefore, do such principles disdain to be tried by reason, and laugh at all the artillery of the logician, when it is directed against them.

When a long train of reasoning is necessary in demonstrating a mathematical proposition, it is easily distinguished from an axiom; and they seem to be things of a very different nature. But there are some propositions which lie so near to axioms, that it is difficult to say whether they ought to be held as axioms, or demonstrated as propositions. The same thing holds with regard to perception, and the conclusions drawn from it. Some of these conclusions follow our perceptions so easily, and are so immediately connected with them, that it is difficult to fix the limit which divides the one from the other.

Perception, whether original or acquired, implies no exercise of reason; and is common to men, children, idiots, and brutes. The more obvious conclusions drawn from our perceptions, by reason, make what we call *common understanding*; by which men conduct themselves in the common affairs of life, and by which they are distinguished from idiots. The more remote conclusions which are drawn from our perceptions, by reason, make what we commonly call *science* in the various parts of nature, whether in agriculture, medicine, mechanics, or in any part of natural philosophy. When I see a garden in good order, containing a great variety of things of the best kinds, and in the most flourishing condition, I immediately conclude from these signs the skill and industry of the gardener. A farmer, when he rises in the morning, and perceives that the neighbouring brook overflows his field, concludes that a great deal of rain hath fallen in the night. Perceiving his fence broken, and his corn trodden down, he concludes that some of his own or his neighbours' cattle have broke loose. Perceiving that his stable-door is broke open, and some of his horses gone, he concludes that a thief has carried them off. He traces the prints of his horses' feet in the soft ground, and by them discovers which road the thief hath taken. These are instances of common understanding, which dwells so near to perception that it is difficult to trace the line which divides the one from the other. In like manner, the science of nature dwells so near to common understanding that we cannot discern where the latter ends and the former begins. I perceive that bodies lighter than water swim in water, and that those which are heavier sink. Hence I conclude, that, if a body remains wherever it is put under water, whether at the top or bottom, it is precisely of the same weight with water. If it will rest only when part of it is above water, it is lighter than water. And the greater the part above water is, compared with the whole, the lighter is the body. If it had no gravity at all, it would make no impression upon the water, but stand wholly above it. Thus, every man, by common understanding, has a rule by which he judges of the specific gravity of bodies which swim in water; and a step or two more leads him into the science of hydrostatics.

All that we know of nature, or of existences, may be compared to a tree, which hath its root, trunk, and branches. In this tree of knowledge, perception is the root, common understanding is the trunk, and the sciences are the branches.

Section XXI

Of the process of nature in perception.

Although there is no reasoning in perception, yet there are certain means and instruments, which, by the appointment of nature, must intervene between the object and our perception of it; and, by these, our perceptions are limited and regulated. First, if the object is not in contact with the organ of sense, there must be some medium which passes between them. Thus, in vision, the rays of light; in hearing, the vibrations of elastic air; in smelling, the effluvia of the body smelled—must pass from the object to the organ; otherwise we have no perception. Secondly, There must be some action or impression upon the organ of sense, either by the immediate application of the object, or by the medium that goes between them. Thirdly, The nerves which go from the brain to the organ must receive some impression by means of that which was made upon the organ; and, probably, by means of the nerves, some impression must be made upon the brain. Fourthly, The impression made upon the organ, nerves, and brain, is followed by a sensation. And, last of all, This sensation is followed by the perception of the object.

Thus, our perception of objects is the result of a train of operations; some of which affect the body only, others affect the mind. We know very little of the nature of some of these operations; we know not at all how they are connected together, or in what way they contribute to that perception which is the result of the whole; but, by the laws of our constitution, we perceive objects in this, and in no other way.

There may be other beings who can perceive external objects without rays of light, or vibrations of air, or effluvia of bodies—without impressions on bodily organs, or even without sensations; but we are so framed by the Author of Nature, that even when we are surrounded by external objects, we may perceive none of them. Our faculty of perceiving an object lies dormant, until it is roused and stimulated by a certain corresponding sensation. Nor is this sensation always at hand to perform its office; for it enters into the mind only in consequence of a certain corresponding impression made on the organ of sense by the object.

Let us trace this correspondence of impressions, sensations, and perceptions, as far as we can — beginning with that which is first in order, the impression made upon the bodily organ. But, alas! we know not of what nature these impressions are, far less how they excite sensations in the mind.

We know that one body may act upon another by pressure, by percussion, by attraction, by repulsion, and, probably, in many other ways which we neither know nor have names to express. But in which of these ways objects, when perceived by us, act upon the organs of sense, these organs upon the nerves, and the nerves upon the brain, we know not. Can any man tell me how in vision, the rays of light act upon the *retina*, how the *retina* acts upon the optic nerve, and how the optic nerve acts upon the brain? No man can. When I feel the pain of the gout in my toe, I know that there is some unusual impression made upon that part of my body. But of what kind is it? Are the small vessels distended with some redundant elastic, or unelastic fluid? Are the fibres unusually stretched? Are they torn asunder by force, or gnawed and corroded by some acrid humour? I can answer none of these questions. All that I feel is pain, which is not an impression upon the body, but upon the mind; and all that I perceive by this sensation is, that some distemper in my toe occasions this pain. But as I know not the natural temper and texture of my toe when it is at ease, I know as little what change or disorder of its parts occasions this uneasy sensation. In like manner, in every other sensation, there is, without doubt, some impression made upon the organ of sense; but an impression of which we know not the nature. It is too subtile to be discovered by our senses, and we may make a thousand conjectures without coming near the truth. If we understood the structure of our organs of sense so minutely as to dis-

cover what effects are produced upon them by external objects, this knowledge would contribute nothing to our perception of the object; for they perceive as distinctly who
know least about the manner of perception, as the greatest
adepts. It is necessary that the impression be made upon our
organs, but not that it be known. Nature carries on this part
of the process of perception, without our consciousness or
concurrence.

But we cannot be unconscious of the next step in this process — the sensation of the mind, which always immediately
follows the impression made upon the body. It is essential to
a sensation to be felt, and it can be nothing more than we feel
it to be. If we can only acquire the habit of attending to our
sensations, we may know them perfectly. But how are the
sensations of the mind produced by impressions upon the
body? Of this we are absolutely ignorant, having no means
of knowing how the body acts upon the mind, or the mind
upon the body. When we consider the nature and attributes
of both, they seem to be so different, and so unlike, that we
can find no handle by which the one may lay hold of the
other. There is a deep and a dark gulf between them, which
our understanding cannot pass; and the manner of their
correspondence and intercourse is absolutely unknown.

Experience teaches us, that certain impressions upon the
body are constantly followed by certain sensations of the
mind; and that, on the other hand, certain determinations of
the mind are constantly followed by certain motions in the
body; but we see not the chain that ties these things together.
Who knows but their connection may be arbitrary, and
owing to the will of our Maker? Perhaps the same sensations
might have been connected with other impressions, or other
bodily organs. Perhaps we might have been so made as to
taste with our fingers, to smell with our ears, and to hear by
the nose. Perhaps we might have been so made as to have all
the sensations and perceptions which we have, without any
impression made upon our bodily organs at all.

However these things may be, if Nature had given us
nothing more than impressions made upon the body, and
sensations in our minds corresponding to them, we should,
in that case, have been merely sentient, but not percipient
beings. We should never have been able to form a conception

of any external object, far less a belief of its existence. Our sensations have no resemblance to external objects; nor can we discover, by our reason, any necessary connection between the existence of the former, and that of the latter.

We might, perhaps, have been made of such a constitution as to have our present perceptions connected with other sensations. We might, perhaps, have had the perception of external objects, without either impressions upon the organs of sense, or sensations. Or, lastly, The perceptions we have, might have been immediately connected with the impressions upon our organs, without any intervention of sensations. This last seems really to be the case in one instance — to wit, in our perception of the visible figure of bodies, as was observed in the eighth section of this chapter.

The process of Nature, in perception by the senses, may, therefore, be conceived as a kind of drama, wherein some things are performed behind the scenes, others are represented to the mind in different scenes, one succeeding another. The impression made by the object upon the organ, either by immediate contact or by some intervening medium, as well as the impression made upon the nerves and brain, is performed behind the scenes, and the mind sees nothing of it. But every such impression, by the laws of the drama, is followed by a sensation, which is the first scene exhibited to the mind; and this scene is quickly succeeded by another, which is the perception of the object.

In this drama, Nature is the actor, we are the spectators. We know nothing of the machinery by means of which every different impression upon the organ, nerves, and brain, exhibits its corresponding sensation; or of the machinery by means of which each sensation exhibits its corresponding perception. We are inspired with the sensation, and we are inspired with the corresponding perception, by means unknown. And, because the mind passes immediately from the sensation to that conception and belief of the object which we have in perception, in the same manner as it passes from signs to the things signified by them, we have, therefore, called our sensations *signs of external objects*; finding no word more proper to express the function which Nature hath assigned them in perception, and the relation which they bear to their corresponding objects.

There is no necessity of a resemblance between the sign and the thing signified; and indeed no sensation can resemble any external object. But there are two things necessary to our knowing things by means of signs. First, That a real connection between the sign and thing signified be established, either by the course of nature, or by the will and appointment of men. When they are connected by the course of nature, it is a natural sign; when by human appointment, it is an artificial sign. Thus, smoke is a natural sign of fire; certain features are natural signs of anger: but our words, whether expressed by articulate sounds or by writing, are artificial signs of our thoughts and purposes.

Another requisite to our knowing things by signs is, that the appearance of the sign to the mind, be followed by the conception and belief of the thing signified. Without this, the sign is not understood or interpreted; and, therefore, is no sign to us, however fit in its own nature for that purpose.

Now, there are three ways in which the mind passes from the appearance of a natural sign to the conception and belief of the thing signified — by *original principles of our constitution*, by *custom,* and by *reasoning*.

Our original perceptions are got in the first of these ways, our acquired perceptions in the second, and all that reason discovers of the course of nature, in the third. In the first of these ways, Nature, by means of the sensations of touch, informs us of the hardness and softness of bodies; of their extension, figure, and motion; and of that space in which they move and are placed — as hath been already explained in the fifth chapter of this inquiry. And, in the second of these ways, she informs us, by means of our eyes, of almost all the same things which originally we could perceive only by touch.

In order, therefore, to understand more particularly how we learn to perceive so many things by the eye, which originally could be perceived only by touch, it will be proper, First, To point out the signs by which those things are exhibited to the eye, and their connection with the things signified by them; and, Secondly, To consider how the experience of this connection produces that habit by which the mind, without any reasoning or reflection, passes from the sign to the conception and belief of the thing signified.

Of all the acquired perceptions which we have by sight, the most remarkable is the perception of the distance of objects from the eye; we shall, therefore, particularly consider the signs by which this perception is exhibited, and only make some general remarks with regard to the signs which are used in other acquired perceptions.

Section XXIV

Of the analogy between perception and the credit we give to human testimony.

The objects of human knowledge are innumerable; but the channels by which it is conveyed to the mind are few. Among these, the perception of external things by our senses, and the informations which we receive upon human testimony, are not the least considerable; and so remarkable is the analogy between these two, and the analogy between the principles of the mind which are subservient to the one and those which are subservient to the other, that, without further apology, we shall consider them together.

In the testimony of Nature given by the senses, as well as in human testimony given by language, things are signified to us by signs: and in one as well as the other, the mind, either by original principles or by custom, passes from the sign to the conception and belief of the things signified.

We have distinguished our perceptions into original and acquired; and language, into natural and artificial. Between acquired perception and artificial language, there is a great analogy; but still a greater between original perception and natural language.

The signs in original perception are sensations, of which Nature hath given us a great variety, suited to the variety of the things signified by them. Nature hath established a real connection between the signs and the things signified; and Nature hath also taught us the interpretation of the signs — so that, previous to experience, the sign suggests the thing signified, and creates the belief of it.

The signs in natural language are features of the face, gestures of the body, and modulations of the voice; the variety of which is suited to the variety of the things signified by them. Nature hath established a real connection between these signs, and the thoughts and dispositions of the mind which are signified by them; and Nature hath taught us the interpretation of these signs; so that, previous to experience, the signs suggest the thing signified, and create the belief of it.

A man in company, without doing good or evil, without uttering an articulate sound, may behave himself gracefully, civilly, politely; or, on the contrary, meanly, rudely, and impertinently. We see the dispositions of his mind by their natural signs in his countenance and behavior, in the same manner as we perceive the figure and other qualities of bodies by the sensations which nature hath connected with them.

The signs in the natural language of the human countenance and behaviour, as well as the signs in our original perceptions, have the same signification in all climates and in all nations; and the skill of interpreting them is not acquired, but innate.

In acquired perception, the signs are either sensations, or things which we perceive by means of sensations. The connection between the sign and the thing signified, is established by nature; and we discover this connection by experience; but not without the aid of our original perceptions, or of those which we have already acquired. After this connection is discovered, the sign, in like manner as in original perception, always suggests the thing signified, and creates the belief of it.

In artificial language, the signs are articulate sounds, whose connection with the things signified by them, is established by the will of men; and, in learning our mother tongue, we discover this connection by experience; but not without the aid of natural language, or of what we had before attained of artificial language. And after this connection is discovered, the sign, as in natural language, always suggests the thing signified, and creates the belief of it.

Our original perceptions are few, compared with the acquired; but, without the former, we could not possibly attain the latter. In like manner, natural language is scanty, compared with artificial; but, without the former we could not possibly attain the latter.

Our original perceptions, as well as the natural language of human features and gestures, must be resolved into particular principles of the human constitution. Thus, it is by one particular principle of our constitution that certain features express anger; and, by another particular principle, that certain features express benevolence. It is, in like manner, by one particular principle of our constitution that a certain sensation signifies hardness in the body which I handle; and it is by another particular principle that a certain sensation signifies motion in that body.

But our acquired perceptions, and the information we receive by means of artificial language, must be resolved into general principles of the human constitution. When a painter perceives that this picture is the work of Raphael, that the work of Titian; a jeweller, that this is a true diamond, that a counterfeit; a sailor, that this is a ship of five hundred ton, that of four hundred; these different acquired perceptions are produced by the same general principles of the human mind, which have a different operation in the same person, according as they are variously applied, and in different persons according to the diversity of their education and manner of life. In like manner, when certain articulate sounds convey to my mind the knowledge of the battle of Pharsalia, and others, the knowledge of the battle of Poltowa — when a Frenchman and an Englishman receive the same information by different articulate sounds — the signs used in these different cases, produce the knowledge and belief of the things signified, by means of the same general principles of the human constitution.

Now, if we compare the general principles of our constitution, which fit us for receiving information from our fellow-creatures by language, with the general principles which fit us for acquiring the perception of things by our senses, we shall find them to be very similar in their nature and manner of operation.

When we begin to learn our mother tongue, we perceive, by the help of natural language, that they who speak to us use certain sounds to express certain things, we imitate the same sounds when we would express the same things; and find that we are understood.

But here a difficulty occurs which merits our attention, because the solution of it leads to some original principles of the human mind, which are of great importance, and of very extensive influence. We know by experience that men *have*

used such words to express such things; but all experience is
of the *past*, and can, of itself, give no notion or belief of what
is *future*. How come we, then, to believe, and to rely upon it
with assurance, that men, who have it in their power to do
otherwise, will continue to use the same words when they
think the same things? Whence comes this knowledge and
belief — this foresight, we ought rather to call it — of the future
and voluntary actions of our fellow-creatures? Have they
promised that they will never impose upon us by equivocation or falsehood? No, they have not. And, if they had, this
would not solve the difficulty; for such promise must be
expressed by words or by other signs; and, before we can
rely upon it, we must be assured that they put the usual
meaning upon the signs which express that promise. No man
of common sense ever thought of taking a man's own word
for his honesty; and it is evident that we take his veracity for
granted when we lay any stress upon his word or promise. I
might add, that this reliance upon the declarations and
testimony of men is found in children long before they know
what a promise is.

There is, therefore, in the human mind an early anticipation, neither derived from experience, nor from reason, nor
from any compact or promise, that our fellow-creatures will
use the same signs in language, when they have the same
sentiments.

This is, in reality, a kind of prescience of human actions;
and it seems to me to be an original principle of the human
constitution, without which we should be incapable of language, and consequently incapable of instruction.

The wise and beneficent Author of Nature, who intended
that we should be social creatures, and that we should
receive the greatest and most important part of our knowledge by the information of others, hath, for these purposes,
implanted in our natures two principles that tally with each
other.

The first of these principles is, a propensity to speak
truth, and to use the signs of language so as to convey our
real sentiments. This principle has a powerful operation,
even in the greatest liars; for, where they lie once, they speak
truth a hundred times. Truth is always uppermost, and is the
natural issue of the mind. It requires no art or training, no

inducement or temptation, but only that we yield to a natural impulse. Lying, on the contrary, is doing violence to our nature; and is never practised, even by the worst men, without some temptation. Speaking truth is like using our natural food, which we would do from appetite, although it answered no end; but lying is like taking physic, which is nauseous to the taste, and which no man takes but for some end which he cannot otherwise attain.

If it should be objected, That men may be influenced by moral or political considerations to speak truth, and, therefore, that their doing so is no proof of such an original principle as we have mentiond—I answer, First, That moral or political considerations can have no influence until we arrive at years of understanding and reflection; and it is certain, from experience, that children keep to truth invariably, before they are capable of being influenced by such considerations. Secondly, When we are influenced by moral or political considerations, we must be conscious of that influence, and capable of perceiving it upon reflection. Now, when I reflect upon my actions most attentively, I am not conscious that, in speaking truth, I am influenced on ordinary occasions by any motive, moral or political. I find that truth is always at the door of my lips, and goes forth spontaneously, if not held back. It requires neither good nor bad intention to bring it forth, but only that I be artless and undesigning. There may indeed be temptations to falsehood, which would be too strong for the natural principle of veracity, unaided by principles of honor or virtue; but where there is no such temptation, we speak truth by instinct—and this instinct is the principle I have been explaining.

By this instinct, a real connection is formed between our words and our thoughts, and thereby the former became fit to be signs of the latter, which they could not otherwise be. And although this connection is broken in every instance of lying and equivocation, yet these instances being comparatively few, the authority of human testimony is only weakened by them, but not destroyed.

Another original principle implanted in us by the Supreme Being, is a disposition to confide in the veracity of others, and to believe what they tell us. This is the counterpart to the former; and, as that may be called *the principle of veracity*, we shall, for want of a more proper name, call this *the principle of credulity*. It is unlimited in children, until they meet with instances of deceit and falsehood; and it retains a very considerable degree of strength through life.

If Nature had left the mind of the speaker in *æquilibrio*, without any inclination to the side of truth more than to that of falsehood, children would lie as often as they speak truth, until reason was so far ripened as to suggest the imprudence of lying, or conscience, as to suggest its immorality. And if Nature had left the mind of the hearer in *aequilibrio*, without any inclination to the side of belief more than to that of disbelief, we should take no man's word until we had positive evidence that he spoke truth. His testimony would, in this case, have no more authority than his dreams; which may be true or false, but no man is disposed to believe them, on this account, that they were dreamed. It is evident that, in the matter of testimony, the balance of human judgment is by nature inclined to the side of belief; and turns to that side of itself, when there is nothing put into the opposite scale. If it was not so, no proposition that is uttered in discourse would be believed, until it was examined and tried by reason; and most men would be unable to find reasons for believing the thousandth part of what is told them. Such distrust and incredulity would deprive us of the greatest benefits of society, and place us in a worse condition than that of savages.

Children, on this supposition, would be absolutely incredulous, and, therefore, absolutely incapable of instruction: those who had little knowledge of human life, and of the manners and characters of men, would be in the next degree incredulous: and the most credulous men would be those of greatest experience, and of the deepest penetration; because, in many cases, they would be able to find good reasons for believing testimony, which the weak and the ignorant could not discover.

In a word, if credulity were the effect of reasoning and experience, it must grow up and gather strength, in the same proportion as reason and experience do. But, if it is the gift of Nature, it will be strongest in childhood, and limited and restrained by experience; and the most superficial view of human life shows, that the last is really the case, and not the first.

It is the intention of Nature, that we should be carried in arms before we are able to walk upon our legs; and it is likewise the intention of Nature, that our belief should be guided by the authority and reason of others, before it can be guided by our own reason. The weakness of the infant, and the natural affection of the mother, plainly indicate the former; and the natural credulity of youth, and authority of age, as plainly indicate the latter. The infant, by proper nursing and care, acquires strength to walk without support. Reason hath likewise her infancy, when she must be carried in arms: then she leans entirely upon authority, by natural instinct, as if she was conscious of her own weakness; and, without this support, she becomes vertiginous. When brought to maturity by proper culture, she begins to feel her own strength, and leans less upon the reason of others; she learns to suspect testimony in some cases, and to disbelieve it in others; and sets bounds to that authority to which she was at first entirely subject. But still, to the end of life, she finds a necessity of borrowing light from testimony, where she has none within herself, and of leaning, in some degree, upon the reason of others, where she is conscious of her own imbecility.

And as, in many instances, Reason, even in her maturity, borrows aid from testimony, so in others she mutually gives aid to it, and strengthens its authority. For, as we find good reason to reject testimony in some cases, so in others we find good reason to rely upon it with perfect security, in our most important concerns. The character, the number, and the disinterestedness of witnesses, the impossibility of collusion, and the incredibility of their concurring in their testimony without collusion, may give an irresistible strength to testimony, compared to which its native and intrinsic authority is very inconsiderable.

Having now considered the general principles of the human mind which fit us for receiving information from our fellow-creatures, by the means of language, let us next consider the general principles which fit us for receiving the information of Nature by our acquired perceptions.

It is undeniable, and indeed is acknowledged by all, that when we have found two things to have been constantly conjoined in the course of nature, the appearance of one of them is immediately followed by the conception and belief of the other. The former becomes a natural sign of the latter; and the knowledge of their constant conjunction in time past, whether got by experience or otherwise, is sufficient to make us rely with assurance upon the continuance of that conjunction.

This process of the human mind is so familiar that we never think of inquiring into the principles upon which it is founded. We are apt to conceive it as a self-evident truth, that what is to come must be similar to what is past. Thus, if a certain degree of cold freezes water today, and has been known to do so in all time past, we have no doubt but the same degree of cold will freeze water tomorrow, or a year hence. That this is a truth which all men believe as soon as they understand it, I readily admit; but the question is, Whence does its evidence arise? Not from comparing the ideas, surely. For, when I compare the idea of cold with that of water hardened into a transparent solid body, I can perceive no connection between them: no man can show the one to be the necessary effect of the other; no man can give a shadow of reason why Nature hath conjoined them. But do we not learn their conjunction from experience? True; experience informs us that they have been conjoined in time *past* but no man ever had any experience of what is *future*: and this is the very question to be resolved, How we come to believe that the *future* will be like the *past*? Hath the Author of nature promised this? Or were we admitted to his council, when he established the present laws of nature, and determined the time of their continuance? No, surely. Indeed, if we believe that there is a wise and good Author of nature, we may see a good reason why he should continue the same laws of nature, and the same connections of things, for a long time: because, if he did otherwise, we could learn nothing from what is past, and all our experience would be of no use to us. But, though this consideration, when we come to the use of reason, may confirm our belief of the continuance of the present course of nature, it is certain that it did not give rise to this belief; for children and idiots have this belief as

soon as they know that fire will burn them. It must, therefore, be the effect of instinct, not of reason.

The wise Author of our nature intended, that a great and
necessary part of our knowledge should be derived from
experience, before we are capable of reasoning, and he hath
provided means perfectly adequate to this intention. For,
First, He governs nature by fixed laws, so that we find
innumerable connections of things which continue from age
to age. Without this stability of the course of nature, there
could be no experience; or, it would be a false guide, and
lead us into error and mischief. If there were not a principle
of veracity in the human mind, men's words would not be
signs of their thoughts: and if there were no regularity in the
course of nature, no one thing could be a natural sign of
another. Secondly, He hath implanted in human minds an
original principle by which we believe and expect the continuance of the course of nature, and the continuance of those
connections which we have observed in time past. It is by
this general principle of our nature, that, when two things
have been found connected in time past, the appearance of
the one produces the belief of the other.[…]

[W]e agree with the author of the *Treatise of Human
Nature*, in this, That our belief of the continuance of nature's
laws is not derived from reason. It is an instinctive prescience
of the operations of nature very like to that prescience of
human actions which makes us rely upon the testimony of
our fellow-creatures; and as, without the latter, we should be
incapable of receiving information from men by language,
so, without the former, we should be incapable of receiving
the information of nature by means of experience.

All our knowledge of nature beyond our original perceptions, is got by experience, and consists in the interpretation
of natural signs. The constancy of nature's laws connects the
sign with the thing signified; and, by the natural principle
just now explained, we rely upon the continuance of the
connections which experience hath discovered; and thus the
appearance of the sign is followed by the belief of the thing
signified.

Upon this principle of our constitution, not only acquired
perception, but all inductive reasoning, and all our reasoning
from analogy, is grounded; and, therefore, for want of

another name, we shall beg leave to call it *the inductive principle*. It is from the force of this principle that we immediately assent to that axiom upon which all our knowledge of nature is built, That effects of the same kind must have the same cause; for *effects* and *causes*, in the operations of nature, mean nothing but signs and the things signified by them. We perceive no proper causality or efficiency in any natural cause; but only a connection established by the course of nature between it and what is called its effect. Antecedently to all reasoning, we have, by our constitution, an anticipation that there is a fixed and steady course of nature: and we have an eager desire to discover this course of nature. We attend to every conjunction of things which presents itself, and expect the continuance of that conjunction. And, when such a conjunction has been often observed, we conceive the things to be naturally connected, and the appearance of one, without any reasoning or reflection, carries along with it the belief of the other.

If any reader should imagine that the inductive principle may be resolved into what philosophers usually call the *association of ideas*, let him observe, that, by this principle, natural signs are not associated with the idea only, but with the belief of the things signified. Now, this can with no propriety be called an association of ideas, unless ideas and belief be one and the same thing. A child has found the prick of a pin conjoined with pain; hence he believes, and knows, that these things are naturally connected; he knows that the one will always follow the other. If any man will call this only an association of ideas, I dispute not about words, but I think he speaks very improperly. For, if we express it in plain English, it is a prescience that things which he hath found conjoined in time past, will be conjoined in time to come. And this prescience is not the effect of reasoning, but of an original principle of human nature, which I have called *the inductive principle*.

This principle, like that of credulity, is unlimited in infancy, and gradually restrained and regulated as we grow up. It leads us often into mistakes; but is of infinite advantage upon the whole. By it, the child once burnt shuns the fire; by it, he likewise runs away from the surgeon by whom he was inoculated. It is better that he should do the last, than that he should not do the first.

But the mistakes we are led into by these two natural principles, are of a different kind. Men sometimes lead us into mistakes, when we perfectly understand their language, by speaking lies. But Nature never misleads us in this way: her language is always true; and it is only by misinterpreting it that we fall into error. There must be many accidental conjunctions of things, as well as natural connections; and the former are apt to be mistaken for the latter. Thus, in the instance above mentioned, the child connected the pain of inoculation with the surgeon; whereas it was really connected with the incision only. Philosophers, and men of science are not exempted from such mistakes; indeed, all false reasoning in philosophy is owing to them; it is drawn from experience and analogy, as well as just reasoning, otherwise it could have no verisimilitude; but the one is an unskilful and rash, the other a just and legitimate interpretation of natural signs. If a child, or a man of common understanding, were put to interpret a book of science, written in his mother tongue, how many blunders and mistakes would he be apt to fall into? Yet he knows as much of this language as is necessary for his manner of life.

The language of Nature is the universal study; and the students are of different classes. Brutes, idiots, and children employ themselves in this study, and owe to it all their acquired perceptions. Men of common understanding make a greater progress, and learn, by a small degree of reflection, many things of which children are ignorant.

Philosophers fill up the highest form in this school, and are critics in the language of nature. All these different classes have one teacher — Experience, enlightened by the inductive principle. Take away the light of this inductive principle, and Experience is as blind as a mole: she may, indeed, feel what is present, and what immediately touches her; but she sees nothing that is either before or behind, upon the right hand or upon the left, future or past.[…]

They that are unskilful in inductive reasoning, are more apt to fall into error in their *reasonings* from the phænomena of nature than in their *acquired perceptions*; because we often reason from a few instances, and thereby are apt to mistake accidental conjunctions of things for natural connections: but that habit of passing, without reasoning, from the sign to the thing signified, which constitutes acquired perception, must be learned by many instances or experiments; and the number of experiments serves to disjoin those things which have been accidentally conjoined, as well as to confirm our belief of natural connections.

From the time that children begin to use their hands, Nature directs them to handle everything over and over, to look at it while they handle it, and to put it in various positions, and at various distances from the eye. We are apt to excuse this as a childish diversion, because they must be doing something, and have not reason to entertain themselves in a more manly way. But, if we think more justly, we shall find, that they are engaged in the most serious and important study; and, if they had all the reason of a philosopher, they could not be more properly employed. For it is this childish employment that enables them to make the proper use of their eyes. They are thereby every day acquiring habits of perception, which are of greater importance than anything we can teach them. The original perceptions which Nature gave them are few, and insufficient for the purposes of life; and, therefore, she made them capable of acquiring many more perceptions by habit. And, to complete her work, she hath given them an unwearied assiduity in applying to the exercises by which those perceptions are acquired.[...]

Chapter VII: Conclusion

Containing reflections upon the opinions of philosophers on this subject.

There are two ways in which men may form their notions and opinions concerning the mind, and concerning its powers and operations. The first is the only way that leads to truth; but it is narrow and rugged, and few have entered upon it. The second is broad and smooth, and hath been much beaten, not only by the vulgar, but even by philosophers; it is sufficient for common life, and is well adapted to the purposes of the poet and orator: but, in philosophical disquisitions concerning the mind, it leads to error and delusion.

We may call the first of these ways, *the way of reflection*. When the operations of the mind are exerted, we are conscious of them; and it is in our power to attend to them; and to reflect upon them, until they become familiar objects of thought. This is the only way in which we can form just and accurate notions of those operations. But this attention and reflection is so difficult to man, surrounded on all hands by external objects which constantly solicit his attention, that it has been very little practised, even by philosophers. In the course of this inquiry, we have had many occasions to show how little attention hath been given to the most familiar operations of the senses.

The second, and the most common way, in which men form their opinions concerning the mind and its operations, we may call *the way of analogy*. There is nothing in the course of nature so singular, but we can find some resemblance, or at least some analogy, between it and other things with which we are acquainted. The mind naturally delights in hunting after such analogies, and attends to them with pleasure. From them, poetry and wit derive a great part of their charms; and eloquence, not a little of its persuasive force.

Besides the pleasure we receive from analogies, they are of very considerable use, both to facilitate the conception of things, when they are not easily apprehended without such a handle, and to lead us to probable conjectures about their nature and qualities, when we want the means of more direct and immediate knowledge. When I consider that the planet Jupiter, in like manner as the earth, rolls round his own axis, and revolves round the sun, and that he is enlightened by several secondary planets, as the earth is enlightened by the moon, I am apt to conjecture, from analogy, that, as the earth by these means is fitted to be the habitation of various orders of animals, so the planet Jupiter is, by the like means, fitted for the same purpose; and, having no argument more direct and conclusive to determine me in this point, I yield, to this analogical reasoning, a degree of assent proportioned to its strength. When I observe that the potato plant very much resembles the *solanum* in its flower and fructification, and am informed that the last is poisonous, I am apt from analogy to have some suspicion of the former: but, in this case, I have access to more direct and certain evidence; and, therefore, ought not to trust to analogy, which would lead me into an error.

Arguments from analogy are always at hand, and grow up spontaneously in a fruitful imagination; while arguments that are more direct and more conclusive often require painful attention and application; and therefore mankind in general have been very much disposed to trust to the former. If one attentively examines the systems of the ancient philosophers, either concerning the material world, or concerning the mind, he will find them to be built solely upon the foundation of analogy. Lord Bacon first delineated the strict and severe method of induction; since his time, it has been applied with very happy success in some parts of natural philosophy — and hardly in anything else. But there is no subject in which mankind are so much disposed to trust to the analogical way of thinking and reasoning, as in what concerns the mind and its operations; because, to form clear and distinct notions of those operations in the direct and proper way, and to reason about them, requires a habit of attentive reflection, of which few are capable, and which, even by those few, cannot be attained without much pains and labour.

Every man is apt to form his notions of things difficult to be apprehended, or less familiar, from their analogy to things which are more familiar. Thus, if a man bred to the seafaring life, and accustomed to think and talk only of matters relating to navigation, enters into discourse upon any other subject, it is well known that the language and the notions proper to his own profession are infused into every subject, and all things are measured by the rules of navigation; and, if he should take it into his head to philosophize concerning the faculties of the mind, it cannot be doubted but he would draw his notions from the fabric of his ship, and would find in the mind, sails, masts, rudder, and compass.

Sensible objects, of one kind or other; do no less occupy and engross the rest of mankind, than things relating to navigation the seafaring man. For a considerable part of life, we can think of nothing but the objects of sense; and, to attend to objects of another nature, so as to form clear and distinct notions of them, is no easy matter, even after we come to years of reflection. The condition of mankind, therefore, affords good reason to apprehend that their language, and their common notions concerning the mind and its operations, will be analogical, and derived from the objects of sense; and that these analogies will be apt to impose upon philosophers, as well as upon the vulgar, and to lead them to materialize the mind and its faculties: and experience abundantly confirms the truth of this.

How generally men of all nations, and in all ages of the world, have conceived the soul, or thinking principle in man, to be some subtile matter, like breath or wind, the names given to it almost in all languages sufficiently testify. We have words which are proper, and not analogical, to express the various ways in which we perceive external objects by the senses—such as *feeling, sight, taste;* but we are often obliged to use these words analogically, to express other powers of the mind which are of a very different nature. And the powers which imply some degree of reflection, have generally no names but such as are analogical. The objects of thought are said to be *in the mind*—to be *apprehended, comprehended, conceived, imagined, retained, weighed, ruminated.*

It does not appear that the notions of the ancient philosophers, with regard to the nature of the soul, were much more refined than those of the vulgar, or that they were formed in any other way. We shall distinguish the philosophy that regards our subject into the *old* and the *new*. The old reached down to Des Cartes, who gave it a fatal blow, of which it has been gradually expiring ever since, and is now almost extinct. Des Cartes is the father of the new philosophy that relates to this subject; but it hath been gradually improving since his time, upon the principles laid down by him. The old philosophy seems to have been purely analogical; the new is more derived from reflection, but still with a very considerable mixture of the old analogical notions.

[…] The system which is now generally received, with regard to the mind and its operations, derives not only its spirit from Des Cartes, but its fundamental principles; and, after all the improvements made by Malebranche, Locke, Berkeley, and Hume, may still be called *the Cartesian system*: we shall, therefore, make some remarks upon its spirit and tendency in general, and upon its doctrine concerning ideas in particular.

1. It may be observed, That the method which Des Cartes pursued, naturally led him to attend more to the operations of the mind by accurate reflection, and to trust less to analogical reasoning upon this subject, than any philosopher had done before him. Intending to build a system upon a new foundation, he began with a resolution to admit nothing but what was absolutely certain and evident. He supposed that his senses, his memory, his reason, and every other faculty to which we trust in common life, might be fallacious; and resolved to disbelieve everything, until he was compelled by irresistible evidence to yield assent.

In this method of proceeding, what appeared to him, first of all, certain and evident, was, That he thought—that he doubted—that he deliberated. In a word, the operations of his own mind, of which he was conscious, must be real, and no delusion; and, though all his other faculties should deceive him, his consciousness could not. This, therefore, he looked upon as the first of all truths. This was the first firm ground upon which he set his foot, after being tossed in the ocean of scepticism; and he resolved to build all knowledge upon it, without seeking after any more first principles.

As every other truth, therefore, and particularly the existence of the objects of sense, was to be deduced by a train of strict argumentation from what he knew by consciousness, he was naturally led to give attention to the operations of which he was conscious, without borrowing his notions of them from external things.

It was not in the way of analogy, but of attentive reflection, that he was led to observe, That thought, volition, remembrance, and the other attributes of the mind, are altogether unlike to extension, to figure, and to all the attributes of body; that we have no reason, therefore, to conceive thinking substances to have any resemblance to extended substances; and that, as the attributes of the thinking substance are things of which we are conscious, we may have a more certain and immediate knowledge of them by reflection, than we can have of external objects by our senses.

These observations, as far as I know, were first made by Des Cartes; and they are of more importance, and throw more light upon the subject, than all that had been said upon it before. They ought to make us diffident and jealous of every notion concerning the mind and its operations, which is drawn from sensible objects in the way of analogy, and to make us rely only upon accurate reflection, as the source of all real knowledge upon this subject.

2. I observe that, as the Peripatetic system has a tendency to materialize the mind and its operations, so the Cartesian has a tendency to spiritualize body and its qualities. One error, common to both systems, leads to the first of these extremes in the way of analogy, and to the last in the way of reflection. The error I mean is, That we can know nothing about body, or its qualities, but as far as we have sensations which resemble those qualities. Both systems agreed in this: but, according to their differing methods of reasoning, they drew very different conclusions from it; the Peripatetic drawing his notions of sensation from the qualities of body; the Cartesian, on the contrary, drawing his notions of the qualities of body from his sensations.

The Peripatetic, taking it for granted that bodies and their qualities do really exist, and are such as we commonly take them to be, inferred from them the nature of his sensations, and reasoned in this manner: — Our sensations are the impressions which sensible objects make upon the mind, and may be compared to the impression of a seal upon wax: the impression is the image or form of the seal, without the matter of it; in like manner, every sensation is the image or form of some sensible quality of the object. This is the reasoning of Aristotle: and it has an evident tendency to materialize the mind and its sensations.

The Cartesian, on the contrary, thinks that the existence of body, or of any of its qualities, is not to be taken as a first principle; and that we ought to admit nothing concerning it, but what, by just reasoning, can be deduced from our sensations; and he knows that, by reflection, we can form clear and distinct notions of our sensations, without borrowing our notions of them by analogy from the objects of sense. The Cartesians, therefore, beginning to give attention to their sensations, first discovered that the sensations corresponding to secondary qualities, cannot resemble any quality of body. Hence, Des Cartes and Locke inferred, that sound, taste, smell, colour, heat, and cold, which the vulgar took to be qualities of body, were not qualities of body, but mere sensations of the mind. Afterwards, the ingenious Berkeley, considering more attentively the nature of sensation in general, discovered and demonstrated, that no sensation whatever could possibly resemble any quality of an insentient being, such as body is supposed to be; and hence he inferred, very justly, that there is the same reason to hold extension, figure, and all the primary qualities, to be mere sensations, as there is to hold the secondary qualities to be mere sensations. Thus, by just reasoning upon the Cartesian principles, matter was stripped of all its qualities; the new system, by a kind of metaphysical sublimation, converted all the qualities of matter into sensations, and spiritualized body, as the old had materialized spirit.

The way to avoid both these extremes, is to admit the existence of what we see and feel as a first principle, as well as the existence of things whereof we are conscious; and to take our notions of the qualities of body, from the testimony of our senses, with the Peripatetics; and our notions of our sensations from the testimony of consciousness, with the Cartesians.

3. I observe, That the modern scepticism is the natural issue of the new system; and that, although it did not bring forth this monster until the year 1739, it may be said to have carried it in its womb from the beginning.

The old system admitted all the principles of common sense as first principles, without requiring any proof of them; and, therefore, though its reasoning was commonly vague, analogical, and dark, yet it was built upon a broad foundation, and had no tendency to scepticism. We do not find that any Peripatetic thought it incumbent upon him to prove the existence of a material world; but every writer upon the Cartesian system attempted this, until Berkeley clearly demonstrated the futility of their arguments; and thence concluded that there was no such thing as a material world; and that the belief of it ought to be rejected as a vulgar error.

The new system admits only one of the principles of common sense as a first principle; and pretends, by strict argumentation, to deduce all the rest from it. That our thoughts, our sensations, and every thing of which we are conscious, hath a real existence, is admitted in this system as a first principle; but everything else must be made evident by the light of reason. Reason must rear the whole fabric of knowledge upon this single principle of consciousness.

There is a disposition in human nature to reduce things to as few principles as possible; and this, without doubt, adds to the beauty of a system, if the principles are able to support what rests upon them. The mathematicians glory, very justly, in having raised so noble and magnificent a system of science, upon the foundation of a few axioms and definitions. This love of simplicity, and of reducing things to few principles, hath produced many a false system; but there never was any system in which it appears so remarkably as that of Des Cartes. His whole system concerning matter and spirit is built upon one axiom, expressed in one word, *cogito*. Upon the foundation of conscious thought, with ideas for his materials, he builds his system of the human understanding, and attempts to account for all its phænomena; and having, as he imagined, from his consciousness, proved the existence of matter; upon the existence of matter, and of a certain quantity of motion originally impressed upon it, he builds his system of the material world, and attempts to account for all its phænomena.

These principles, with regard to the material system, have been found insufficient; and it has been made evident that, besides matter and motion, we must admit gravitation, cohesion, corpuscular attraction, magnetism, and other centripetal and centrifugal forces, by which the particles of matter attract and repel each other. Newton, having discovered this, and demonstrated that these principles cannot be resolved into matter and motion, was led, by analogy and the love of simplicity, to conjecture, but with a modesty and caution peculiar to him, that all the phænomena of the material world depended upon attracting and repelling forces in the particles of matter. But we may now venture to say, that this conjecture fell short of the mark. For, even in the unorganized kingdom, the powers by which salts, crystals, spars, and many other bodies, concrete into regular forms, can never be accounted for by attracting and repelling forces in the particles of matter. And in the vegetable and animal kingdoms, there are strong indications of powers of a different nature from all the powers of unorganized bodies. We see, then, that, although, in the structure of the material world, there is, without doubt, all the beautiful simplicity consistent with the purposes for which it was made, it is not so simple as the great Des Cartes determined it to be; nay, it is not so simple as the greater Newton modestly conjectured it to be. Both were misled by analogy, and the love of simplicity. One had been much conversant about extension, figure, and motion; the other had enlarged his views to attracting and repelling forces; and both formed their notions of the unknown parts of nature, from those with which they were acquainted.[…]

But to come to the system of Des Cartes, concerning the human understanding. It was built, as we have observed, upon consciousness as its sole foundation, and with ideas as its materials; and all his followers have built upon the same foundation and with the same materials. They acknowledge that Nature hath given us various simple ideas. These are analogous to the matter, of Des Cartes's physical system. They acknowledge, likewise, a natural power, by which ideas are compounded, disjoined, associated, compared. This is analogous to the original quantity of motion in Des Cartes's physical system. From these principles, they attempt to explain the phænomena of the human understanding, just as in the physical system the phænomena of nature were to be explained by matter and motion. It must, indeed, be acknowledged, that there is great simplicity in this system, as well as in the other. There is such a similitude between the two, as may be expected between children of the same father; but, as the one has been found to be the child of Des Cartes, and not of Nature, there is ground to think that the other is so likewise.

That the natural issue of this system is scepticism with regard to everything except the existence of our ideas, and of their necessary relations, which appear upon comparing them, is evident; for ideas, being the only objects of thought, and having no existence but when we are conscious of them, it necessarily follows that there is no object of our thought which can have a continued and permanent existence. Body and spirit, cause and effect, time and space, to which we were wont to ascribe an existence independent of our thought, are all turned out of existence by this short dilemma. Either these things are ideas of sensation or reflection, or they are not; if they are ideas of sensation or reflection, they can have no existence but when we are conscious of them; if they are not ideas of sensation or reflection, they are words without any meaning.

Neither Des Cartes nor Locke perceived this consequence of their system concerning ideas. Bishop Berkeley was the first who discovered it. And what followed upon this discovery? Why, with regard to the material world, and with regard to space and time, he admits the consequence, That these things are mere ideas, and have no existence but in our minds; but with regard to the existence of spirits or minds, he does not admit the consequence; and, if he had admitted it, he must have been an absolute sceptic. But how does he evade this consequence with regard to the existence of spirits? The expedient which the good Bishop uses on this occasion is very remarkable, and shows his great aversion to scepticism. He maintains that we have no ideas of spirits; and that we can think, and speak, and reason about them, and about their attributes, without having any ideas of them. If this is so, my Lord, what should hinder us from thinking and reasoning about bodies, and their qualities, without having ideas of them? The Bishop either did not think of this question, or did not think fit to give any answer to it. However, we may observe, that, in order to avoid scepticism, he fairly starts out of the Cartesian system, without giving any reason why he did so in this instance, and in no other. This, indeed, is the only instance of a deviation from Cartesian principles which I have met with in the successors of Des Cartes; and it seems to have been only a sudden start, occasioned by the terror of scepticism; for, in all other things, Berkeley's system is founded upon Cartesian principles.

Thus we see that Des Cartes and Locke take the road that leads to scepticism, without knowing the end of it; but they stop short for want of light to carry them farther. Berkeley, frighted at the appearance of the dreadful abyss, starts aside, and avoids it. But the author of the *Treatise of Human Nature*, more daring and intrepid, without turning aside to the right hand or to the left, shoots directly into the gulf.[...]

4. We may observe, That the account given by the new system, of that furniture of the human understanding which is the gift of Nature, and not the acquisition of our own reasoning faculty, is extremely lame and imperfect.

The natural furniture of the human understanding is of two kinds: First, The *notions* or simple apprehensions which we have of things; and, secondly, The *judgments* or the belief which we have concerning them. As to our notions, the new system reduces them to two classes — *ideas of sensation*, and *ideas of reflection*: the first are conceived to be copies of our sensations, retained in the memory or imagination; the second, to be copies of the operations of our minds whereof we are conscious, in like manner retained in the memory or imagination: and we are taught that these two comprehend all the materials about which the human understanding is, or can be employed. As to our judgment of things, or the belief which we have concerning them, the new system allows no part of it to be the gift of nature, but holds it to be the acquisition of reason, and to be got by comparing our ideas, and perceiving their agreements or disagreements. Now I take this account, both of our notions, and of our judgments or belief, to be extremely imperfect; and I shall briefly point out some of its capital defects.

The division of our notions into ideas of sensation, and ideas of reflection, is contrary to all rules of logic; because the second member of the division includes the first. For, can we form clear and just notions of our sensations any other way than by reflection? Surely we cannot. Sensation is an operation of the mind of which we are conscious; and we get the notion of sensation by reflecting upon that which we are conscious of. In like manner, doubting and believing are operations of the mind whereof we are conscious; and we get the notion of them by reflecting upon what we are conscious of. The ideas of sensation, therefore, are ideas of reflection, as much as the ideas of doubting, or believing, or any other ideas whatsoever.

But, to pass over the inaccuracy of this division, it is extremely incomplete. For, since sensation is an operation of the mind, as well as all the other things of which we form our notions by reflection, when it is asserted that all our notions are either ideas of sensation or ideas of reflection, the plain English of this is, That mankind neither do nor can think of anything but of the operations of their own minds. Nothing can be more contrary to truth, or more contrary to the experience of mankind. I know that Locke, while he maintained this doctrine, believed the notions which we have of body and of its qualities, and the notions which we have of motion and of space, to be ideas of sensation. But why did he believe this? Because he believed those notions to be nothing else but images of our sensations. If, therefore, the notions of body and its qualities, of motion and space, be not images of our sensations, will it not follow that those notions are not ideas of sensation? Most certainly.

There is no doctrine in the new system which more directly leads to scepticism than this. And the author of the *Treatise of Human Nature* knew very well how to use it for that purpose; for, if you maintain that there is any such existence as body or spirit, time or place, cause or effect, he immediately catches you between the horns of this dilemma; your notions of these existences are either ideas of sensation, or ideas of reflection: if of sensation, from what sensation are they copied? if of reflection, from what operation of the mind are they copied?

It is indeed to be wished that those who have written much about sensation, and about the other operations of the mind, had likewise thought and reflected much, and with great care, upon those operations; but is it not very strange that they will not allow it to be possible for mankind to think of anything else?

The account which this system gives of our judgment and belief concerning things, is as far from the truth as the account it gives of our notions or simple apprehensions. It represents our senses as having no other office but that of furnishing the mind with notions or simple apprehensions of things; and makes our judgment and belief concerning those things to be acquired by comparing our notions together, and perceiving their agreements or disagreements.

We have shown, on the contrary, that every operation of the senses, in its very nature, implies judgment or belief, as well as simple apprehension. Thus, when I feel the pain of the gout in my toe, I have not only a notion of pain, but a belief of its existence, and a belief of some disorder in my toe which occasions it; and this belief is not produced by comparing ideas, and perceiving their agreements and disagreements; it is included in the very nature of the sensation. When I perceive a tree before me, my faculty of seeing gives me not only a notion or simple apprehension of the tree, but a belief of its existence, and of its figure, distance, and magnitude; and this judgment or belief is not got by comparing ideas, it is included in the very nature of the perception. We have taken notice of several original principles of belief in the course of this inquiry; and when other faculties of the mind are examined, we shall find more, which have not occurred in the examination of the five senses.

Such original and natural judgments are, therefore, a part of that furniture which Nature hath given to the human understanding. They are the inspiration of the Almighty no less than our notions or simple apprehensions. They serve to direct us in the common affairs of life, where our reasoning faculty would leave us in the dark. They are a part of our constitution; and all the discoveries of our reason are grounded upon them. They make up what is called *the common sense of mankind*; and, what is manifestly contrary to any of those first principles, is what we call *absurd*. The strength of them is *good sense*, which is often found in those who are not acute in reasoning. A remarkable deviation from them, arising from a disorder in the constitution, is what we call *lunacy*; as when a man believes that he is made of glass. When a man suffers himself to be reasoned out of the principles of common sense, by metaphysical arguments, we may call this *metaphysical lunacy*; which differs from the other species of the distemper in this, that it is not continued, but intermittent: it is apt to seize the patient in solitary and speculative moments: but, when he enters into society, Common Sense recovers her authority. A clear explication and enumeration of the principles of common sense, is one of the chief *desiderata* in logic. We have only considered such of them as occurred in the examination of the five senses.

5. The last observation that I shall make upon the new system, is, that, although it professes to set out in the way of reflection, and not of analogy, it hath retained some of the old analogical notions concerning the operations of the mind; particularly, that things which do not now exist in the mind itself, can only be perceived, remembered, or imagined, by means of ideas or images of them in the mind, which are the immediate objects of perception, remembrance, and imagination. This doctrine appears evidently to be borrowed from

the old system; which taught that external things make impressions upon the mind, like the impressions of a seal upon wax; that it is by means of those impressions that we perceive, remember, or imagine them; and that those impressions must resemble the things from which they are taken. When we form our notions of the operations of the mind by analogy, this way of conceiving them seems to be very natural, and offers itself to our thoughts; for, as everything which is felt must make some impression upon the body, we are apt to think that everything which is understood must make some impression upon the mind.

From such analogical reasoning, this opinion of the existence of ideas or images of things in the mind, seems to have taken its rise, and to have been so universally received among philosophers. It was observed already, that Berkeley, in one instance, apostatizes from this principle of the new system, by affirming that we have no ideas of spirits, and that we can think of them immediately, without ideas. But I know not whether in this he has had any followers. There is some difference, likewise, among modern philosophers with regard to the ideas or images by which we perceive, remember, or imagine sensible things. For, though all agree in the existence of such images, they differ about their place; some placing them in a particular part of the brain, where the soul is thought to have her residence, and others placing them in the mind itself. Des Cartes held the first of these opinions; to which Newton seems likewise to have inclined; for he proposes this query in his *Optics*: — 'Annon sensorium animalium est locus cui substantia sentiens adest, et in quem sensibiles rerum species per nervos et cerebrum deferuntur, ut ibi præsentes a præsente sentiri possint?'[5] But Locke seems to place the ideas of sensible things in the mind; and that Berkeley, and the author of the *Treatise of Human Nature*, were of the same opinion, is evident. The last makes a very curious application of this doctrine, by endeavouring to prove from it, That the mind either is no substance, or that it is an extended and divisible substance; because the ideas of extension cannot be in a subject which is indivisible and unextended.

I confess I think his reasoning in this, as in most cases, is clear and strong. For whether the idea of extension be only another name for extension itself, as Berkeley and this author assert; or whether the idea of extension be an image and resemblance of extension, as Locke conceived; I appeal to any man of common sense, whether extension, or any image of extension, can be in an unextended and indivisible subject. But while I agree with him in his reasoning, I would make a different application of it. He takes it for granted, that there are ideas of extension in the mind; and thence infers, that, if it is at all a substance, it must be an extended and divisible substance. On the contrary, I take it for granted, upon the testimony of common sense, that my mind is a substance—that is, a permanent subject of thought; and my reason convinces me that it is an unextended and indivisible substance; and hence I infer that there cannot be in it anything that resembles extension. If this reasoning had occurred to Berkeley, it would probably have led him to acknowledge that we may think and reason concerning bodies, without having ideas of them in the mind, as well as concerning spirits.

I intended to have examined more particularly and fully this doctrine of the existence of ideas or images of things in the mind; and likewise another doctrine, which is founded upon it—to wit, That judgment or belief is nothing but a perception of the agreement or disagreement of our ideas; but, having already shown, through the course of this inquiry, that the operations of the mind which we have examined, give no countenance to either of these doctrines, and in many things contradict them, I have thought it proper to drop this part of my design. It may be executed with more advantage, if it is at all necessary, after inquiring into some other powers of the human understanding.

Although we have examined only the five senses, and the principles of the human mind which are employed about them, or such as have fallen in our way in the course of this examination, we shall leave the further prosecution of this inquiry to future deliberation. The powers of memory, of imagination, of taste, of reasoning, of moral perception, the will, the passions, the affections, and all the active powers of the soul, present a vast and boundless field of philosophical disquisition, which the author of this inquiry is far from thinking himself able to survey with accuracy. Many authors of ingenuity, ancient and modern, have made excursions into this vast territory, and have communicated useful observations: but there is reason to believe that those who have pretended to give us a map of the whole, have satisfied themselves with a very inaccurate and incomplete survey. If Galileo had attempted a complete system of natural philosophy, he had, probably, done little service to mankind: but by confining himself to what was within his comprehension, he laid the foundation of a system of knowledge, which rises by degrees, and does honour to the human understanding. Newton, building upon this foundation, and, in like manner, confining his inquiries to the law of gravitation and the properties of light, performed wonders. If he had attempted a great deal more, he had done a great deal less, and perhaps nothing at all. Ambitious of following such great examples, with unequal steps, alas! and unequal force, we have attempted an inquiry only into one little corner of the human mind — that corner which seems to be most exposed to vulgar observation, and to be most easily comprehended; and yet, if we have delineated it justly, it must be acknowledged that the accounts heretofore given of it were very lame, and wide of the truth.

---

[1]   William Shakespeare, *The Tempest*, IV, i, 151–156: 'And, like the baseless fabric of this vision,… Leave not a track behind.'

[2]   Dr Nicholas Saunderson was the blind Lucasian Professor of Mathematics at Cambridge.

[3]   Hamilton and the 4th edition, 1785 (the last one published in Reid's lifetime), have 'it hath been' instead of 'it had been'. In the critical edition, Brookes reintroduces the reading of the first three editions: 'it had been'.

[4]   William Cheselden (1688–1752), surgeon, author of 'An account of some obervations made by a young gentleman, who was born blind, or lost his sight so early, that he had no remembrance of ever having seen, and was couch'd between 13 and 14 year of age', published in the *Philosophical Transactions*, in 1728.

[5]   Isaac Newton, *Optice: sive de Reflexionibus, Refractionibus, Inflexionibus & Coloribus Lucis* (London, 1791), p. 373, trans. in *Opticks: Or, A Treatise of the Reflections, Refractions, Inflections and Colours of Light*, 4th ed. (London, Printed for William Innys at the West-End of St. Paul, 1730), pp. 344–345: 'Is not the Sensory of Animals that place to which the sensitive substance is present, and into which the sensible Species of Things are carried through the Nerves and Brain, that there they may be perceived by their immediate presence to that Substance?'

II

Essays on the Intellectual Powers of Man

Essay II: Of the Powers We Have by Means of Our External Senses

Chapter XIV

Reflections on the common theory of ideas.

After so long a detail of the sentiments of philosophers, ancient and modern, concerning ideas, it may seem presumptuous to call in question their existence. But no philosophical opinion, however ancient, however generally received, ought to rest upon authority. There is no presumption in requiring evidence for it, or in regulating our belief by the evidence we can find.

To prevent mistakes, the reader must again be reminded that if by ideas are meant only the acts or operations of our minds in perceiving, remembering, or imagining objects, I am far from calling in question the existence of those acts; we are conscious of them every day and every hour of life; and I believe no man of a sound mind ever doubted of the real existence of the operations of mind, of which he is conscious. Nor is it to be doubted that, by the faculties which God has given us, we can conceive things that are absent as well as perceive those that are within the reach of our senses; and that such conceptions may be more or less distinct, and more or less lively and strong. We have reason to ascribe to the all-knowing and all-perfect Being distinct conceptions of all things existent and possible, and of all their relations; and if these conceptions are called his eternal ideas, there ought to be no dispute among philosophers about a word. The ideas, of whose existence I require the proof, are not the operations of any mind, but supposed objects of those operations. They are not perception, remembrance, or conception, but things that are said to be perceived, or remembered, or imagined.

Nor do I dispute the existence of what the vulgar call the objects of perception. These, by all who acknowledge their existence, are called real things, not ideas. But philosophers maintain that, besides these, there are immediate objects of perception in the mind itself: that, for instance, we do not see the sun immediately, but an idea; or, as Mr Hume calls it, an impression in our own minds. This idea is said to be the image, the resemblance, the representative of the sun, if there be a sun. It is from the existence of the idea that we must infer the existence of the sun. But the idea, being immediately perceived, there can be no doubt, as philosophers think, of its existence.

In like manner, when I remember, or when I imagine anything, all men acknowledge that there must be something that is remembered or that is imagined; that is, some object of those operations. The object remembered must be something that did exist in time past: the object imagined may be something that never existed. But, say the philosophers, besides these objects which all men acknowledge, there is a more immediate object which really exists in the mind at the same time we remember or imagine. This object is an idea or image of the thing remembered or imagined.

The *first* reflection I would make on this philosophical opinion is, that it is directly contrary to the universal sense of men who have not been instructed in philosophy. When we see the sun or moon, we have no doubt that the very objects which we immediately see are very far distant from us, and from one another. We have not the least doubt that this is the sun and moon which God created some thousands of years ago, and which have continued to perform their revolutions in the heavens ever since. But how are we astonished when the philosopher informs us that we are mistaken in all this; that the sun and moon which we see are not, as we imagine, many miles distant from us, and from each other, but that they are in our own mind; that they had no existence before we saw them, and will have none when we cease to perceive and to think of them; because the objects we perceive are only ideas in our own mind, which can have no existence a moment longer than we think of them!

If a plain man, uninstructed in philosophy, has faith to receive these mysteries, how great must be his astonishment! He is brought into a new world where everything he sees, tastes, or touches, is an idea—a fleeting kind of being which he can conjure into existence, or can annihilate in the twinkling of an eye.

After his mind is somewhat composed, it will be natural for him to ask his philosophical instructor, Pray, sir, are there then no substantial and permanent beings called the sun and moon, which continue to exist whether we think of them or not?

Here the philosophers differ. Mr Locke, and those that were before him, will answer to this question that it is very true there are substantial and permanent beings called the sun and moon; but they never appear to us in their own person, but by their representatives, the ideas in our own minds, and we know nothing of them but what we can gather from those ideas.

Bishop Berkeley and Mr Hume would give a different answer to the question proposed. They would assure the querist that it is a vulgar error, a mere prejudice of the ignorant and unlearned, to think that there are any permanent and substantial beings called the sun and moon; that the heavenly bodies, our own bodies, and all bodies whatsoever, are nothing but ideas in our minds; and that there can be nothing like the ideas of one mind, but the ideas of another mind. There is nothing in nature but minds and ideas, says the Bishop;—nay, says Mr Hume, there is nothing in nature but ideas only; for what we call a mind is nothing but a train of ideas connected by certain relations between themselves.

In this representation of the theory of ideas there is nothing exaggerated or misrepresented, as far as I am able to judge; and surely nothing further is necessary to show that, to the uninstructed in philosophy, it must appear extravagant and visionary, and most contrary to the dictates of common understanding.

222222222222

There is the less need of any further proof of this, that it is very amply acknowledged by Mr Hume in his Essay on the Academical or Sceptical Philosophy.[1] 'It seems evident,' says he, 'that men are carried, by a natural instinct or prepossession, to repose faith in their senses; and that, without any reasoning, or even almost before the use of reason, we always suppose an external universe, which depends not on our perception, but would exist though we and every sensible creature were absent or annihilated. Even the animal creation are governed by a like opinion, and preserve this belief of external objects in all their thoughts, designs, and actions.'

'It seems also evident that, when men follow this blind and powerful instinct of nature, they always suppose the very images presented by the senses to be the external objects, and never entertain any suspicion that the one are nothing but representations of the other. This very table which we see white, and feel hard, is believed to exist independent of our perception, and to be something external to the mind which perceives it; our presence bestows not being upon it; our absence annihilates it not: it preserves its existence uniform and entire, independent of the situation of intelligent beings who perceive or contemplate it.'

'But this universal and primary notion of all men is soon destroyed by the slightest philosophy, which teaches us that nothing can ever be present to the mind, but an image or perception; and that the senses are only the inlets through which these images are received, without being ever able to produce any immediate intercourse between the mind and the object.'

It is therefore acknowledged by this philosopher to be a natural instinct or prepossession, a universal and primary opinion of all men, a primary instinct of nature, that the objects which we immediately perceive by our senses are not images in our minds, but external objects, and that their existence is independent of us and our perception.

In this acknowledgment, Mr Hume indeed seems to me more generous, and even more ingenuous, than Bishop Berkeley, who would persuade us that his opinion does not oppose the vulgar opinion, but only that of the philosophers; and that the external existence of a material world is a philosophical hypothesis, and not the natural dictate of our perceptive powers. The Bishop shows a timidity of engaging such an adversary, as a primary and universal opinion of all men. He is rather fond to court its patronage. But the philosopher intrepidly gives a defiance to this antagonist, and seems to glory in a conflict that was worthy of his arm. *Optat aprum aut fulvum descendere monte leonem.*[2] After all, I suspect that a philosopher who wages war with this adversary, will find himself in the same condition as a mathematician who should undertake to demonstrate that there is no truth in the axioms of mathematics.

A *second* reflection upon this subject is — that the authors who have treated of ideas have generally taken their existence for granted, as a thing that could not be called in question; and such arguments as they have mentioned incidentally, in order to prove it, seem too weak to support the conclusion.

Mr Locke, in the Introduction to his *Essay*, tells us that he uses the word idea to signify whatever is the immediate object of thought; and then adds, 'I presume it will be easily granted me that there are such ideas in men's minds; everyone is conscious of them in himself; and men's words and actions will satisfy him that they are in others.' I am indeed conscious of perceiving, remembering, imagining; but that the objects of these operations are images in my mind, I am not conscious. I am satisfied, by men's words and actions, that they often perceive the same objects which I perceive, which could not be if those objects were ideas in their own minds.

Mr Norris is the only author I have met with who professedly puts the question whether material things can be perceived by us immediately. He has offered four arguments to show that they cannot. *First*, 'Material objects are without the mind, and therefore there can be no union between the object and the percipient.' *Answer*, This argument is lame, until it is shown to be necessary that in perception there should be a union between the object and the percipient. *Second*, 'Material objects are disproportioned to the mind, and removed from it by the whole diameter of Being.' This argument I cannot answer, because I do not understand it. *Third*, 'Because, if material objects were immediate objects of perception, there could be no physical science – things necessary and immutable being the only object of science.' *Answer*, Although things necessary and immutable be not the immediate objects of perception, they may be immediate objects of other powers of the mind. *Fourth*, 'If material things were perceived by themselves, they would be a true light to our minds, as being the intelligible form of our understandings, and consequently perfective of them, and indeed superior to them.' If I comprehend anything of this mysterious argument, it follows from it that the Deity perceives nothing at all, because nothing can be superior to his understanding or perfective of it.

There is an argument which is hinted at by Malebranche, and by several other authors, which deserves to be more seriously considered. As I find it most clearly expressed and most fully urged by Dr Samuel Clarke, I shall give it in his words, in his second reply to Leibniz, sect. 4: 'The soul, without being present to the images of the things perceived, could not possibly perceive them. A living substance can only there perceive, where it is present, either to the things themselves (as the omnipresent God is to the whole universe) or to the images of things, as the soul is in its proper *sensorium*.'

Sir Isaac Newton expresses the same sentiment, but with his usual reserve, in a query only.

The ingenious Dr Porterfield, in his 'Essay concerning the Motions of our Eyes', adopts this opinion with more confidence. His words are: 'How body acts upon mind, or mind upon body, I know not; but this I am very certain of, that nothing can act, or be acted upon, where it is not; and therefore our mind can never perceive anything but its own proper modifications, and the various states of the sensorium, to which it is present: so that it is not the external sun and moon which are in the heavens, which our mind perceives, but only their image or representation impressed upon the sensorium. How the soul of a seeing man sees these images, or how it receives those ideas, from such agitations in the sensorium, I know not; but I am sure it can never perceive the external bodies themselves, to which it is not present.'

These, indeed, are great authorities: but in matters of philosophy we must not be guided by authority, but by reason. Dr Clarke, in the place cited, mentions slightly, as the reason of his opinion, that 'nothing can any more act, or be acted upon when it is not present, that it can be where it is not.' And again, in his third reply to Leibniz, sect. 11: 'We are sure the soul cannot perceive what it is not present to, because nothing can act, or be acted upon, where it is not.' The same reason we see is urged by Dr Porterfield.

That nothing can act immediately where it is not, I think must be admitted: for I agree with Sir Isaac Newton, that power without substance is inconceivable. It is a consequence of this, that nothing can be acted upon immediately where the agent is not present: let this, therefore, be granted. To make the reasoning conclusive, it is further necessary that, when we perceive objects, either they act upon us or we act upon them. This does not appear self-evident, nor have I ever met with any proof of it. I shall briefly offer the reasons why I think it ought not to be admitted.

When we say that one being acts upon another, we mean that some power or force is exerted by the agent which produces, or has a tendency to produce, a change in the thing acted upon. If this be the meaning of the phrase, as I conceive it is, there appears no reason for asserting that, in perception, either the object acts upon the mind or the mind upon the object.

An object, in being perceived, does not act at all. I perceive the walls of the room where I sit; but they are perfectly inactive, and therefore act not upon the mind. To be perceived, is what logicians call an external denomination, which implies neither action nor quality in the object perceived. Nor could men ever have gone into this notion, that perception is owing to some action of the object upon the mind, were it not that we are so prone to form our notions of the mind from some similitude we conceive between it and body. Thought in the mind is conceived to have some analogy to motion in a body: and, as a body is put in motion, by being acted upon by some other body; so we are apt to think the mind is made to perceive, by some impulse it receives from the object. But reasonings, drawn from such analogies, ought never to be trusted. They are, indeed, the cause of most of our errors with regard to the mind. And we might as well conclude, that minds may be measured by feet and inches, or weighed by ounces and drachms, because bodies have those properties.

I see as little reason, in the second place, to believe that in perception the mind acts upon the object. To perceive an object is one thing, to act upon it is another; nor is the last at all included in the first. To say that I act upon the wall by looking at it, is an abuse of language, and has no meaning. Logicians distinguish two kinds of operations of mind: the first kind produces no effect without the mind; the last does. The first they call *immanent* acts, the second *transitive*. All intellectual operations belong to the first class; they produce no effect upon any external object. But, without having recourse to logical distinctions, every man of common sense knows, that to think of an object, and to act upon it, are very different things.

As we have, therefore, no evidence that, in perception, the mind acts upon the object, or the object upon the mind, but strong reasons to the contrary, Dr Clarke's argument against our perceiving external objects immediately falls to the ground.

This notion, that, in perception, the object must be contiguous to the percipient, seems, with many other prejudices, to be borrowed from analogy. In all the external senses, there must, as has been before observed, be some impression made upon the organ of sense by the object, or by something coming from the object. An impression supposes contiguity. Hence we are led by analogy to conceive something similar in the operations of the mind. Many philosophers resolve almost every operation of mind into impressions and feelings, words manifestly borrowed from the sense of touch. And it is very natural to conceive contiguity necessary between that which makes the impression, and that which receives it; between that which feels, and that which is felt. And though no philosopher will now pretend to justify such analogical reasoning as this, yet it has a powerful influence upon the judgment, while we contemplate the operations of our minds, only as they appear through the deceitful medium of such analogical notions and expressions.

When we lay aside those analogies, and reflect attentively upon our perception of the object of sense, we must acknowledge that, though we are conscious of perceiving objects, we are altogether ignorant how it is brought about; and know as little how we perceive objects as how we were made. And, if we should admit an image in the mind, or contiguous to it, we know as little how perception may be produced by this image as by the most distant object. Why, therefore, should we be led, by a theory which is neither grounded on evidence, nor, if admitted, can explain any one phænomenon of perception, to reject the natural and immediate dictates of those perceptive powers, to which, in the conduct of life, we find a necessity of yielding implicit submission?

There remains only one other argument that I have been able to find urged against our perceiving external objects immediately. It is proposed by Mr Hume, who, in the essay already quoted, after acknowledging that it is an universal and primary opinion of all men, that we perceive external objects immediately, subjoins what follows:—

'But this universal and primary opinion of all men is soon destroyed by the slightest philosophy, which teaches us that nothing can ever be present to the mind but an image or perception; and that the senses are only the inlets through which these images are received, without being ever able to produce any immediate intercourse between the mind and the object. The table, which we see, seems to diminish as we remove farther from it: but the real table, which exists independent of us, suffers no alteration. It was, therefore, nothing but its image which was present to the mind. These are the obvious dictates of reason; and no man who reflects ever doubted that the existences which we consider, when we say *this house,* and *that tree*, are nothing but perceptions in the mind, and fleeting copies and representations of other existences, which remain uniform and independent. So far, then, we are necessitated, by reasoning, to depart from the primary instincts of nature, and to embrace a new system with regard to the evidence of our senses.'

We have here a remarkable conflict between two contradictory opinions, wherein all mankind are engaged. On the one side stand all the vulgar, who are unpractised in philosophical researches, and guided by the uncorrupted primary

instincts of nature. On the other side stand all the philosophers, ancient and modern; every man, without exception,
who reflects. In this division, to my great humiliation, I find
myself classed with the vulgar.

The passage now quoted is all I have found in Mr Hume's
writings upon this point: and, indeed, there is more reasoning in it than I have found in any other author. I shall, therefore, examine it minutely.

First, He tells us that 'this universal and primary opinion
of all men is soon destroyed by the slightest philosophy,
which teaches us that nothing can ever be present to the
mind but an image or perception.'

The phrase of being present to the mind has some obscur-
ity; but I conceive he means being an immediate object of
thought; an immediate object, for instance, of perception, of
memory, or of imagination. If this be the meaning, (and it is
the only pertinent one I can think of,) there is no more in this
passage but an assertion of the proposition to be proved, and
an assertion that philosophy teaches it. If this be so, I beg
leave to dissent from philosophy till she gives me reason for
what she teaches. For, though common sense and my external senses demand my assent to their dictates upon their
own authority, yet philosophy is not entitled to this privilege. But, that I may not dissent from so grave a personage
without giving a reason, I give this as the reason of my dissent: — I see the sun when he shines; I remember the battle of
Culloden; and neither of these objects is an image or perception.

He tells us, in the next place, 'That the senses are only the
inlets, through which these images are received.'

I know that Aristotle and the schoolmen taught that
images or species flow from objects, and are let in by the senses, and strike upon the mind; but this has been so effectually
refuted by Descartes, by Malebranche, and many others, that
nobody now pretends to defend it. Reasonable men consider
it as one of the most unintelligible and unmeaning parts of
the ancient system. To what cause is it owing that modern
philosophers are so prone to fall back into this hypothesis, as
if they really believed it? For, of this proneness I could give
many instances besides this of Mr Hume; and I take the
cause to be, that images in the mind, and images let in by the

senses, are so nearly allied, and so strictly connected, that they must stand or fall together. The old system consistently maintained both: but the new system has rejected the doctrine of images let in by the senses, holding, nevertheless, that there are images in the mind; and, having made this unnatural divorce of two doctrines which ought not to be put asunder, that which they have retained often leads them back involuntarily to that which they have rejected.

Mr Hume surely did not seriously believe that an image of sound is let in by the ear, an image of smell by the nose, an image of hardness and softness, of solidity and resistance, by the touch. For, besides the absurdity of the thing, which has often been shown, Mr Hume and all modern philosophers maintain that the images which are the immediate objects of perception have no existence when they are not perceived; whereas if they were let in by the senses, they must be, before they are perceived, and have a separate existence.

He tells us, further, that philosophy teaches that the senses are unable to produce any immediate intercourse between the mind and the object. Here I still require the reasons that philosophy gives for this; for, to my apprehension, I immediately perceive external objects, and this I conceive is the immediate intercourse here meant.

Hitherto I see nothing that can be called an argument. Perhaps it was intended only for illustration. The argument, the only argument, follows: —

The table which we see, seems to diminish as we remove farther from it; but the real table, which exists independent of us, suffers no alteration. It was, therefore, nothing but its image which was presented to the mind. These are the obvious dictates of reason.

To judge of the strength of this argument, it is necessary to attend to a distinction which is familiar to those who are conversant in the mathematical sciences — I mean the distinction between real and apparent magnitude. The real magnitude of a line is measured by some known measure of length — as inches, feet, or miles: the real magnitude of a surface or solid, by known measures of surface or of capacity. This magnitude is an object of touch only, and not of sight; nor could we even have had any conception of it, without the sense of touch; and Bishop Berkeley, on that account, calls it *tangible magnitude*.

Apparent magnitude is measured by the angle which an object subtends at the eye. Supposing two right lines drawn from the eye to the extremities of the object making an angle, of which the object is the subtense, the apparent magnitude is measured by this angle. This apparent magnitude is an object of sight, and not of touch. Bishop Berkeley calls it *visible magnitude*.

If it is asked what is the apparent magnitude of the sun's diameter, the answer is, that it is about thirty-one minutes of a degree. But, if it is asked what is the real magnitude of the sun's diameter, the answer must be, so many thousand miles, or so many diameters of the earth. From which it is evident that real magnitude, and apparent magnitude, are things of a different nature, though the name of magnitude is given to both. The first has three dimensions, the last only two; the first is measured by a line, the last by an angle.

From what has been said, it is evident that the real magnitude of a body must continue unchanged, while the body is unchanged. This we grant. But is it likewise evident, that the apparent magnitude must continue the same while the body is unchanged? So far otherwise, that every man who knows anything of mathematics can easily demonstrate, that the same individual object, remaining in the same place, and unchanged, must necessarily vary in its apparent magnitude, according as the point from which it is seen is more or less distant; and that its apparent length or breadth will be nearly in a reciprocal proportion to the distance of the spectator. This is as certain as the principles of geometry.

We must likewise attend to this—that, though the real magnitude of a body is not originally an object of sight, but of touch, yet we learn by experience to judge of the real magnitude in many cases by sight. We learn by experience to judge of the distance of a body from the eye within certain limits; and, from its distance and apparent magnitude taken together, we learn to judge of its real magnitude.

And this kind of judgment, by being repeated every hour and almost every minute of our lives, becomes, when we are grown up, so ready and so habitual, that it very much resembles the original perceptions of our senses, and may not improperly be called *acquired perception.*

Whether we call it judgment or acquired perception is a verbal difference. But it is evident that, by means of it, we often discover by one sense things which are properly and naturally the objects of another. Thus I can say, without impropriety, I hear a drum, I hear a great bell, or I hear a small bell; though it is certain that the figure or size of the sounding body is not originally an object of hearing. In like manner, we learn by experience how a body of such a real magnitude and at such a distance appears to the eye. But neither its real magnitude, nor its distance from the eye, are properly objects of sight, any more than the form of a drum or the size of a bell, are properly objects of hearing.

If these things be considered, it will appear that Mr Hume's argument hath no force to support his conclusion — nay, that it leads to a contrary conclusion. The argument is this: the table we see seems to diminish as we remove farther from it; that is, its apparent magnitude is diminished; but the real table suffers no alteration — to wit, in its real magnitude; therefore, it is not the real table we see. I admit both the premises in this syllogism, but I deny the conclusion. The syllogism has what the logicians call two middle terms: apparent magnitude is the middle term in the first premise; real magnitude in the second. Therefore, according to the rules of logic, the conclusion is not justly drawn from the premises; but, laying aside the rules of logic, let us examine it by the light of common sense.

Let us suppose, for a moment, that it is the real table we see: Must not this real table seem to diminish as we remove farther from it? It is demonstrable that it must. How then can this apparent diminution be an argument that it is not the real table? When that which must happen to the real table, as we remove farther from it, does actually happen to the table we see, it is absurd to conclude from this, that it is not the real table we see. It is evident, therefore, that this ingenious author has imposed upon himself by confounding real magnitude with apparent magnitude, and that his argument is a mere sophism.

I observed that Mr Hume's argument not only has no strength to support his conclusion, but that it leads to the contrary conclusion—to wit, that it is the real table we see; for this plain reason, that the table we see has precisely that apparent magnitude which it is demonstrable the real table must have when placed at that distance.

This argument is made much stronger by considering that the real table may be placed successively at a thousand different distances, and, in every distance, in a thousand different positions; and it can be determined demonstratively, by the rules of geometry and perspective, what must be its apparent magnitude and apparent figure in each of those distances and positions. Let the table be placed successively in as many of those different distances and different positions as you will, or in them all; open your eyes and you shall see a table precisely of that apparent magnitude, and that apparent figure, which the real table must have in that distance and in that position. Is not this a strong argument that it is the real table you see?

In a word, the appearance of a visible object is infinitely diversified, according to its distance and position. The visible appearances are innumerable, when we confine ourselves to one object, and they are multiplied according to the variety of objects. Those appearances have been matter of speculation to ingenious men, at least since the time of Euclid. They have accounted for all this variety, on the supposition that the objects we see are external and not in the mind itself. The rules they have demonstrated about the various projections of the sphere, about the appearances of the planets in their progressions, stations, and retrogradations, and all the rules of perspective, are built on the supposition that the objects of sight are external. They can each of them be tried in thousands of instances. In many arts and professions innumerable trials are daily made; nor were they ever found to fail in a single instance. Shall we say that a false supposition, invented by the rude vulgar, has been so lucky in solving an infinite number of phænomena of nature? This, surely, would be a greater prodigy than philosophy ever exhibited: add to this, that, upon the contrary hypothesis—to wit, that the objects of sight are internal—no account can be given of any one of those appearances, nor any physical cause assigned why a visible object should, in any one case, have one apparent figure and magnitude rather than another.

Thus, I have considered every argument I have found advanced to prove the existence of ideas, or images of external things, in the mind; and, if no better arguments can be found, I cannot help thinking that the whole history of philosophy has never furnished an instance of an opinion so unanimously entertained by philosophers upon so slight grounds.

A *third* reflection I would make upon this subject is, that philosophers, notwithstanding their unanimity as to the existence of ideas, hardly agree in any one thing else concerning them. If ideas be not a mere fiction, they must be, of all objects of human knowledge, the things we have best access to know, and to be acquainted with; yet there is nothing about which men differ so much.

Some have held them to be self-existent, others to be in the Divine mind, others in our own minds, and others in the brain or *sensorium*. I considered the hypothesis of images in the brain, in the fourth chapter of this essay. As to images in the mind, if anything more is meant by the image of an object in the mind than the thought of that object, I know not what it means. The distinct conception of an object may, in a metaphorical or analogical sense, be called an *image* of it in the mind. But this image is only the conception of the object, and not the object conceived. It is an act of the mind, and not the object of that act.

Some philosophers will have our ideas, or a part of them, to be innate; others will have them all to be adventitious: some derive them from the senses alone; others from sensation and reflection: some think they are fabricated by the mind itself; others that they are produced by external objects; others that they are the immediate operation of the Deity; others say that impressions are the causes of ideas, and that the causes of impressions are unknown: some think that we have ideas only of material objects, but none of minds, of their operations, or of the relations of things; others will have the immediate object of every thought to be an idea: some think we have abstract ideas, and that by this chiefly we are distinguished from the brutes; others maintain an abstract idea to be an absurdity, and that there can be no such thing: with some they are the immediate objects of thought, with others the only objects.

A *fourth* reflection is, that ideas do not make any of the operations of the mind to be better understood, although it was probably with that view that they have been first invented, and afterwards so generally received.

We are at a loss to know how we perceive distant objects; how we remember things past; how we imagine things that have no existence. Ideas in the mind seem to account for all these operations: they are all by the means of ideas reduced to one operation—to a kind of feeling, or immediate perception of things present and in contact with the percipient; and feeling is an operation so familiar that we think it needs no explication, but may serve to explain other operations.

But this feeling, or immediate perception, is as difficult to be comprehended as the things which we pretend to explain by it. Two things may be in contact without any feeling or perception; there must therefore be in the percipient a power to feel or to perceive. How this power is produced, and how it operates, is quite beyond the reach of our knowledge. As little can we know whether this power must be limited to things present, and in contact with us. Nor can any man pretend to prove that the Being who gave us the power to perceive things present may not give us the power to perceive things that are distant, to remember things past, and to conceive things that never existed.

Some philosophers have endeavoured to make all our senses to be only different modifications of touch; a theory which serves only to confound things that are different, and to perplex and darken things that are clear. The theory of ideas resembles this, by reducing all the operations of the human understanding to the perception of ideas in our own minds. This power of perceiving ideas is as inexplicable as any of the powers explained by it; and the contiguity of the object contributes nothing at all to make it better understood; because there appears no connection between contiguity and perception, but what is grounded on prejudices drawn from some imagined similitude between mind and body, and from the supposition that, in perception, the object acts upon the mind, or the mind upon the object. We have seen how this theory has led philosophers to confound those operations of mind which experience teaches all men to be different, and teaches them to distinguish in common language;

and that it has led them to invent a language inconsistent with the principles upon which all language is grounded.[...]

Essay III: Of Memory

Chapter I

Things obvious and certain with regard to memory.

[...] It is by memory that we have an immediate knowledge of things past. The senses give us information of things only as they exist in the present moment; and this information, if it were not preserved by memory, would vanish instantly and leave us as ignorant as if it had never been.

Memory must have an object. Every man who remembers must remember something, and that which he remembers is called the object of his remembrance. In this, memory agrees with perception but differs from sensation, which has no object but the feeling itself.

Every man can distinguish the thing remembered from the remembrance of it. We may remember anything which we have seen, or heard, or known, or done, or suffered; but the remembrance of it is a particular act of the mind which now exists, and of which we are conscious. To confound these two is an absurdity, which a thinking man could not be led into, but by some false hypothesis which hinders him from reflecting upon the thing which he would explain by it.

In memory we do not find such a train of operations connected by our constitution as in perception. When we perceive an object by our senses, there is, first, some impression made by the object upon the organ of sense, either immediately or by means of some medium. By this, an impression is made upon the nerves and brain, in consequence of which we feel some sensation; and that sensation is attended by that conception and belief of the external object which we call perception. These operations are so connected in our constitution, that it is difficult to disjoin them in our conceptions, and to attend to each without confounding it with the others. But, in the operations of memory, we are free from this embarrassment; they are easily distinguished from all other acts of the mind, and the names which denote them are free from all ambiguity.

The object of memory, or thing remembered, must be something that is past; as the object of perception and of consciousness must be something which is present. What now is, cannot be an object of memory; neither can that which is past and gone be an object of perception or of consciousness.

Memory is always accompanied with the belief of that which we remember, as perception is accompanied with the belief of that which we perceive, and consciousness with the belief of that whereof we are conscious. Perhaps in infancy, or in a disorder of mind, things remembered may be confounded with those which are merely imagined; but in mature years, and in a sound state of mind, every man feels that he must believe what he distinctly remembers, though he can give no other reason of his belief, but that he remembers the thing distinctly; whereas, when he merely imagines a thing ever so distinctly, he has no belief of it upon that account.

This belief, which we have from distinct memory, we account real knowledge, no less certain than if it was grounded on demonstration; no man in his wits calls it in question, or will hear any argument against it. The testimony of witnesses in causes of life and death depends upon it, and all the knowledge of mankind of past events is built on this foundation.

There are cases in which a man's memory is less distinct and determinate, and where he is ready to allow that it may have failed him; but this does not in the least weaken its credit, when it is perfectly distinct.

Memory implies a conception and belief of past duration; for it is impossible that a man should remember a thing distinctly, without believing some interval of duration, more or less, to have passed between the time it happened, and the present moment; and I think it is impossible to show how we could acquire a notion of duration if we had no memory. Things remembered must be things formerly perceived or known. I remember the transit of Venus over the sun in the year 1769. I must therefore have perceived it at the time it happened, otherwise I could not now remember it. Our first acquaintance with any object of thought cannot be by remembrance. Memory can only produce a continuance or renewal of a former acquaintance with the thing remembered.

The remembrance of a past event is necessarily accompanied with the conviction of our own existence at the time the event happened. I cannot remember a thing that happened a year ago, without a conviction as strong as memory can give, that I, the same identical person who now remember that event, did then exist.

What I have hitherto said concerning memory, I consider as principles which appear obvious and certain to every man who will take the pains to reflect upon the operations of his own mind. They are facts of which every man must judge by what he feels; and they admit of no other proof but an appeal to every man's own reflection.[…]

Chapter IV

Of identity.

The conviction which every man has of his Identity, as far back as his memory reaches, needs no aid of philosophy to strengthen it; and no philosophy can weaken it, without first producing some degree of insanity.

The philosopher, however, may very properly consider this conviction as a phænomenon of human nature worthy of his attention. If he can discover its cause, an addition is made to his stock of knowledge. If not, it must be held as a part of our original constitution, or an effect of that constitution produced in a manner unknown to us.

We may observe, first of all, that this conviction is indispensably necessary to all exercise of reason. The operations of reason, whether in action or in speculation, are made up of successive parts. The antecedent are the foundation of the consequent, and, without the conviction that the antecedent have been seen or don by me, I could have no reason to proceed to the consequent, in any speculation, or in any active project whatever.

There can be no memory of what is past without the conviction that we existed at the time remembered. There may be good arguments to convince me that I existed before the earliest thing I can remember; but to suppose that my memory reaches a moment farther back than my belief and conviction of my existence, is a contradiction.

The moment a man loses this conviction, as if he had drunk the water of Lethe, past things are done away; and, in his own belief, he then begins to exist. Whatever was thought, or said, or done, or suffered before that period, may belong to some other person; but he can never impute it to himself, or take any subsequent step that supposes it to be his doing.

From this it is evident that we must have the conviction of our own continued existence and identity, as soon as we are capable of thinking or doing anything, on account of what we have thought, or done, or suffered before; that is, as soon as we are reasonable creatures.

That we may form as distinct a notion as we are able of this phænomenon of the human mind, it is proper to consider what is meant by identity in general, what by our own personal identity, and how we are led into that invincible belief and conviction which every man has of his own personal identity, as far as his memory reaches.

Identity in general, I take to be a relation between a thing which is known to exist at one time, and a thing which is known to have existed at another time. If you ask whether they are one and the same, or two different things, every man of common sense understands the meaning of your question perfectly. Whence we may infer with certainty, that every man of common sense has a clear and distinct notion of identity.

If you ask a definition of identity, I confess I can give none; it is too simple a notion to admit of logical definition. I can say it is a relation; but I cannot find words to express the specific difference between this and other relations, though I am in no danger of confounding it with any other. I can say that diversity is a contrary relation, and that similitude and dissimilitude are another couple of contrary relations, which every man easily distinguishes in his conception from identity and diversity.

I see evidently that identity supposes an uninterrupted continuance of existence. That which hath ceased to exist, cannot be the same with that which afterwards begins to exist; for this would be to suppose a being to exist after it ceased to exist, and to have had existence before it was produced, which are manifest contradictions. Continued uninterrupted existence is therefore necessarily implied in identity.

Hence we may infer that identity cannot, in its proper sense, be applied to our pains, our pleasures, our thoughts, or any operation of our minds. The pain felt this day is not the same individual pain which I felt yesterday, though they may be similar in kind and degree, and have the same cause. The same may be said of every feeling and of every operation of mind: they are all successive in their nature, like time itself, no two moments of which can be the same moment.

It is otherwise with the parts of absolute space. They always are, and were, and will be the same. So far, I think, we proceed upon clear ground in fixing the notion of identity in general.

It is, perhaps, more difficult to ascertain with precision the meaning of Personality; but it is not necessary in the present subject: it is sufficient for our purpose to observe, that all mankind place their personality in something that cannot be divided, or consist of parts. A part of a person is a manifest absurdity.

When a man loses his estate, his health, his strength, he is still the same person and has lost nothing of his personality. If he has a leg or an arm cut off, he is the same person he was before. The amputated member is no part of his person, otherwise it would have a right to a part of his estate and be liable for a part of his engagements; it would be entitled to a share of his merit and demerit — which is manifestly absurd. A person is something indivisible, and is what Leibniz calls a *monad*.

My personal identity, therefore, implies the continued existence of that indivisible thing which I call myself. Whatever this self may be, it is something which thinks, and deliberates, and resolves, and acts, and suffers. I am not thought, I am not action, I am not feeling; I am something that thinks, and acts, and suffers. My thoughts, and actions, and feelings, change every moment — they have no continued, but a successive existence; but that *self* or *I* to which they belong, is permanent, and has the same relation to all the succeeding thoughts, actions, and feelings, which I call mine.

Such are the notions that I have of my personal identity. But perhaps it may be said, this may all be fancy without reality. How do you know? — what evidence have you that there is such a permanent self which has a claim to all the thoughts, actions, and feelings, which you call yours?

To this I answer, that the proper evidence I have of all this is remembrance. I remember that, twenty years ago, I conversed with such a person; I remember several things that passed in that conversation; my memory testifies not only that this was done, but that it was done by me who now remember it. If it was done by me, I must have existed at that time, and continued to exist from that time to the present: if the identical person whom I call myself had not a part in that conversation, my memory is fallacious—it gives a distinct and positive testimony of what is not true. Every man in his senses believes what he distinctly remembers, and everything he remembers convinces him that he existed at the time remembered.

Although memory gives the most irresistible evidence of my being the identical person that did such a thing, at such a time, I may have other good evidence of things which befell me, and which I do not remember: I know who bare me and suckled me, but I do not remember these events.

It may here be observed, (though the observation would have been unnecessary if some great philosophers had not contradicted it,) that it is not my remembering any action of mine that makes me to be the person who did it. This remembrance makes me to know assuredly that I did it; but I might have done it though I did not remember it. That relation to me, which is expressed by saying that I did it, would be the same though I had not the least remembrance of it. To say that my remembering that I did such a thing, or, as some choose to express it, my being conscious that I did it, makes me to have done it, appears to me as great an absurdity as it would be to say that my belief that the world was created made it to be created.

When we pass judgment on the identity of other persons besides ourselves, we proceed upon other grounds, and determine from a variety of circumstances, which sometimes produce the firmest assurance and sometimes leave room for doubt. The identity of persons has often furnished matter of serious litigation before tribunals of justice. But no man of a sound mind ever doubted of his own identity, as far as he distinctly remembered.

The identity of a person is a perfect identity; wherever it is real, it admits of no degrees; and it is impossible that a person should be in part the same, and in part different; because a person is a *monad,* and is not divisible into parts. The evidence of identity in other persons besides ourselves does indeed admit of all degrees, from what we account certainty to the least degree of probability. But still it is true that the same person is perfectly the same, and cannot be so in part, or in some degree only.

For this cause, I have first considered personal identity, as that which is perfect in its kind, and the natural measure of that which is imperfect.

We probably at first derive our notion of identity from that natural conviction which every man has from the dawn of reason of his own identity and continued existence. The operations of our minds are all successive, and have no continued existence. But the thinking being has a continued existence; and we have an invincible belief that it remains the same when all its thoughts and operations change.

Our judgments of the identity of objects of sense seem to be formed much upon the same grounds as our judgments of the identity of other persons besides ourselves.

Wherever we observe great similarity, we are apt to presume identity, if no reason appears to the contrary. Two objects ever so like, when they are perceived at the same time, cannot be the same; but, if they are presented to our senses at different times, we are apt to think them the same, merely from their similarity.

Whether this be a natural prejudice, or from whatever cause it proceeds, it certainly appears in children from infancy; and, when we grow up, it is confirmed in most instances by experience; for we rarely find two individuals of the same species that are not distinguishable by obvious differences.

A man challenges a thief whom he finds in possession of his horse or his watch, only on similarity. When the watchmaker swears that he sold this watch to such a person, his testimony is grounded on similarity. The testimony of witnesses to the identity of a person is commonly grounded on no other evidence.

Thus it appears that the evidence we have of our own identity, as far back as we remember, is totally of a different kind from the evidence we have of the identity of other persons, or of objects of sense. The first is grounded on memory, and gives undoubted certainty. The last is grounded on similarity, and on other circumstances, which in many cases are not so decisive as to leave no room for doubt.

It may likewise be observed, that the identity of objects of sense is never perfect. All bodies, as they consist of innumerable parts that may be disjoined from them by a great variety of causes, are subject to continual changes of their substance, increasing, diminishing, changing insensibly. When such alterations are gradual, because language could not afford a different name for every different state of such a changeable being, it retains the same name and is considered as the same thing. Thus we say of an old regiment that it did such a thing a century ago, though there now is not a man alive who then belonged to it. We say a tree is the same in the seed-bed and in the forest. A ship of war, which has successively changed her anchors, her tackle, her sails, her masts, her planks, and her timbers, while she keeps the same name, is the same.

The identity, therefore, which we ascribe to bodies, whether natural or artificial, is not perfect identity; it is rather something which, for the conveniency of speech, we call identity. It admits of a great change of the subject, providing the change be gradual, sometimes even of a total change. And the changes which in common language are made consistent with identity, differ from those that are thought to destroy it, not in kind, but in number and degree. It has no fixed nature when applied to bodies; and questions about the identity of a body are very often questions about words. But identity, when applied to persons, has no ambiguity, and admits not of degrees, or of more and less. It is the foundation of all rights and obligations, and of all accountableness; and the notion of it is fixed and precise.

Chapter VI

Of Mr Locke's account of our personal identity.

In a long chapter upon Identity and Diversity, Mr Locke has made many ingenious and just observations, and some which I think cannot be defended. I shall only take notice of

the account he gives of our own *Personal Identity*. His doctrine upon this subject has been censured by Bishop Butler, in
a short essay subjoined to his *Analogy*, with whose sentiments I perfectly agree.

Identity, as was observed, Chap. 4 of this Essay, supposes
the continued existence of the being of which it is affirmed,
and therefore can be applied only to things which have a
continued existence. While any being continues to exist, it is
the same being: but two beings which have a different beginning or a different ending of their existence, cannot possibly
be the same. To this I think Mr Locke agrees.

He observes, very justly, that to know what is meant by
the same person we must consider what the word *person*
stands for; and he defines a person to be an intelligent being
endowed with reason and with consciousness, which last he
thinks inseparable from thought.

From this definition of a person, it must necessarily follow, that, while the intelligent being continues to exist and to
be intelligent, it must be the same person. To say that the intelligent being is the person, and yet that the person ceases to
exist, while the intelligent being continues, or that the person
continues while the intelligent being ceases to exist, is to my
apprehension a manifest contradiction.

One would think that the definition of a person should
perfectly ascertain the nature of personal identity, or wherein
it consists, though it might still be a question how we come
to know and be assured of our personal identity.

Mr Locke tells us, however, 'that personal identity—that
is, the sameness of a rational being—consists in consciousness alone, and, as far as this consciousness can be extended
backwards to any past action or thought, so far reaches the
identity of that person. So that, whatever hath the consciousness of present and past actions, is the same person to whom
they belong.'

This doctrine hath some strange consequences, which the
author was aware of, Such as, that, if the same consciousness
can be transferred from one intelligent being to another,
which he thinks we cannot show to be impossible, then two
or twenty intelligent beings may be the same person. And if
the intelligent being may lose the consciousness of the
actions done by him, which surely is possible, then he is not

the person that did those actions; so that one intelligent being may be two or twenty different persons, if he shall so often lose the consciousness of his former actions.

There is another consequence of this doctrine, which follows no less necessarily, though Mr Locke probably did not see it. It is, that a man may be, and at the same time not be, the person that did a particular action.

Suppose a brave officer to have been flogged when a boy at school, for robbing an orchard, to have taken a standard from the enemy in his first campaign, and to have been made a general in advanced life: Suppose also, which must be admitted to be possible, that, when he took the standard, he was conscious of his having been flogged at school, and that when made a general he was conscious of his taking the standard, but had absolutely lost the consciousness of his flogging.

These things being supposed, it follows, from Mr Locke's doctrine, that he who was flogged at school is the same person who took the standard, and that he who took the standard is the same person who was made a general. Whence it follows, if there be any truth in logic, that the general is the same person with him who was flogged at school. But the general's consciousness does not reach so far back as his flogging—therefore, according to Mr Locke's doctrine, he is not the person who was flogged. Therefore the general is, and at the same time is not the same person with him who was flogged at school.[…]

Secondly, It may be observed, that, in this doctrine, not only is consciousness confounded with memory, but, which is still more strange, personal identity is confounded with the evidence which we have of our personal identity.

It is very true that my remembrance that I did such a thing is the evidence I have that I am the identical person who did it. And this, I am apt to think, Mr Locke meant. But, to say that my remembrance that I did such a thing, or my consciousness, makes me the person who did it, is, in my apprehension, an absurdity too gross to be entertained by any man who attends to the meaning of it; for it is to attribute to memory or consciousness a strange magical power of producing its object, though that object must have existed before the memory or consciousness which produced it.[…]

Thirdly, Is it not strange that the sameness or identity of a person should consist in a thing which is continually changing, and is not any two minutes the same?

Our consciousness, our memory, and every operation of the mind, are still flowing like the water of a river, or like time itself. The consciousness I have this moment can no more be the same consciousness I had last moment, than this moment can be the last moment. Identity can only be affirmed of things which have a continued existence. Consciousness, and every kind of thought, is transient and momentary, and has no continued existence; and, therefore, if personal identity consisted in consciousness, it would certainly follow that no man is the same person any two moments of his life; and, as the right and justice of reward and punishment is founded on personal identity, no man could be responsible for his actions.

But, though I take this to be the unavoidable consequence of Mr Locke's doctrine concerning personal identity, and though some persons may have liked the doctrine the better on this account, I am far from imputing anything of this kind to Mr Locke. He was too good a man not to have rejected with abhorrence a doctrine which he believed to draw this consequence after it.

Fourthly, There are many expressions used by Mr Locke, in speaking of personal identity, which, to me, are altogether unintelligible, unless we suppose that he confounded that sameness or identity which we ascribe to an individual, with the identity which, in common discourse, is often ascribed to many individuals of the same species.

When we say that pain and pleasure, consciousness and memory, are the same in all men, this sameness can only mean similarity, or sameness of kind; but that the pain of one man can be the same individual pain with that of another man, is no less impossible than that one man should be another man; the pain felt by me yesterday can no more be the pain I feel today, than yesterday can be this day; and the same thing may be said of every passion and of every operation of the mind. The same kind or species of operation may be in different men, or in the same man at different times; but it is impossible that the same individual operation should be in different men, or in the same man at different times.

When Mr Locke, therefore, speaks of 'the same consciousness being continued through a succession of different substances;' when he speaks of 'repeating the idea of a past action, with the same consciousness we had of it at the first,' and of 'the same consciousness extending to actions past and to come' — these expressions are to me unintelligible, unless he means not the same individual consciousness, but a consciousness that is similar, or of the same kind.

If our personal identity consists in consciousness, as this consciousness cannot be the same individually any two moments, but only of the same kind, it would follow that we are not for any two moments the same individual persons, but the same kind of persons.

As our consciousness sometimes ceases to exist, as in sound sleep, our personal identity must cease with it. Mr Locke allows, that the same thing cannot have two beginnings of existence; so that our identity would be irrecoverably gone every time we cease to think, if it was but for a moment.

Essay IV: Of Conception

Chapter I

Of conception, or simple apprehension in general.

Conceiving, imagining, apprehending, understanding, having a notion of a thing, are common words used, to express that operation of the understanding which the logicians call *simple apprehension*. The *having an idea of a thing*, is, in common language, used in the same sense, chiefly, I think, since Mr Locke's time.

Logicians define Simple Apprehension to be the bare conception of a thing without any judgment or belief about it. If this were intended for a strictly logical definition, it might be a just objection to it, that conception and apprehension are only synonymous words; and that we may as well define conception by apprehension, as apprehension by conception; but it ought to be remembered that the most simple operations of the mind cannot be logically defined. To have a distinct notion of them, we must attend to them as we feel them in our own minds. He that would have a distinct notion of a scarlet colour, will never attain it by a definition; he must set it before his eye, attend to it, compare it with the colours that come nearest to it, and observe the specific difference, which he will in vain attempt to define.

Every man is conscious that he can conceive a thousand things, of which he believes nothing at all—as a horse with wings, a mountain of gold; but, although conception may be without any degree of belief, even the smallest belief cannot be without conception. He that believes must have some conception of what he believes.

Without attempting a definition of this operation of the mind, I shall endeavour to explain some of its properties; consider the theories about it; and take notice of some mistakes of philosophers concerning it.

1. It may be observed that conception enters as an ingredient in every operation of the mind. Our senses cannot give us the belief of any object, without giving some conception of it at the same time. No man can either remember or reason about things of which he hath no conception. When we will to exert any of our active powers, there must be some conception of what we will to do. There can be no desire nor aversion, love nor hatred, without some conception of the object. We cannot feel pain without conceiving it, though we can conceive it without feeling it. These things are self-evident.[…]

As all the operations of our mind are expressed by language, everyone knows that it is one thing to understand what is said, to conceive or apprehend its meaning, whether it be a word, a sentence, or a discourse; it is another thing to judge of it, to assent or dissent, to be persuaded or moved. The first is simple apprehension, and may be without the last; but the last cannot be without the first.

2. In bare conception there can neither be truth nor falsehood, because it neither affirms nor denies. Every judgment, and every proposition by which judgment is expressed, must be true or false; and the qualities of true and false, in their proper sense, can belong to nothing but to judgments, or to propositions which express judgment. In the bare conception of a thing there is no judgment, opinion, or belief included, and therefore it cannot be either true or false.[…]

I grant that there are some states of the mind, wherein a man may confound his conceptions with what he perceives or remembers, and mistake the one for the other; as in the delirium of a fever, in some cases of lunacy and of madness, in dreaming, and perhaps in some momentary transports of devotion, or of other strong emotions, which cloud his intellectual faculties, and, for a time, carry a man out of himself, as we usually express it.

Even in a sober and sound state of mind, the memory of a thing may be so very weak that we may be in doubt whether we only dreamed or imagined it.

It may be doubted whether children, when their imagination first begins to work, can distinguish what they barely conceive from what they remember. I have been told, by a man of knowledge and observation, that one of his sons, when he began to speak, very often told lies with great assurance, without any intention, as far as appeared, or any consciousness of guilt. From which the father concluded, that it is natural to some children to lie. I am rather inclined to think that the child had no intention to deceive, but mistook the rovings of his own fancy for things which he remembered. This, however, I take to be very uncommon, after children can communicate their sentiments by language, though perhaps not so in a more early period.

Granting all this, if any man will affirm that they whose intellectual faculties are sound, and sober, and ripe, cannot with certainty distinguish what they perceive or remember, from what they barely conceive, when those operations have any degree of strength and distinctness, he may enjoy his opinion; I know not how to reason with him. Why should philosophers confound those operations in treating of ideas, when they would be ashamed to do it on other occasions? To distinguish the various powers of our minds, a certain degree of understanding is necessary. And if some, through a defect of understanding, natural or accidental, or from unripeness of understanding, may be apt to confound different powers, will it follow that others cannot clearly distinguish them?

To return from this digression—into which the abuse of the word perception, by philosophers, has led me—it appears evident that the bare conception of an object, which includes no opinion or judgment, can neither be true nor false. Those qualities, in their proper sense, are altogether inapplicable to this operation of the mind.

3. Of all the analogies between the operations of body and those of the mind, there is none so strong and so obvious to all mankind as that which there is between painting, or other plastic arts, and the power of conceiving objects in the mind. Hence, in all languages, the words by which this power of the mind and its various modifications are expressed, are analogical, and borrowed from those arts. We consider this power of the mind as a plastic power, by which we form to ourselves images of the objects of thought.

In vain should we attempt to avoid this analogical language, for we have no other language upon the subject; yet it is dangerous, and apt to mislead. All analogical and figurative words have a double meaning; and, if we are not very much upon our guard, we slide insensibly from the borrowed and figurative meaning into the primitive. We are prone to carry the parallel between the things compared further than it will hold, and thus very naturally to fall into error.

To avoid this as far as possible in the present subject, it is proper to attend to the dissimilitude between conceiving a thing in the mind, and painting it to the eye, as well as to their similitude. The similitude strikes and gives pleasure. The dissimilitude we are less disposed to observe; but the philosopher ought to attend to it, and to carry it always in mind, in his reasonings on this subject, as a monitor, to warn him against the errors into which the analogical language is apt to draw him.

When a man paints, there is some work done, which remains when his hand is taken off, and continues to exist though he should think no more of it. Every stroke of his pencil produces an effect, and this effect is different from his action in making it; for it remains and continues to exist when the action ceases. The action of painting is one thing; the picture produced is another thing. The first is the cause, the second is the effect.

Let us next consider what is done when he only conceives this picture. He must have conceived it before he painted it; for this is a maxim universally admitted, that every work of art must first be conceived in the mind of the operator. What is this conception? It is an act of the mind, a kind of thought. This cannot be denied. But does it produce any effect besides the act itself? Surely common sense answers this question in the negative; for every one knows that it is one thing to conceive, another thing to bring forth into effect. It is one thing to project, another to execute. A man may think for a long time what he is to do, and after all do nothing. Conceiving, as well as projecting or resolving, are what the schoolmen called *immanent* acts of the mind, which produce nothing beyond themselves. But painting is a transitive act, which produces an effect distinct from the operation, and this effect is the picture. Let this, therefore, be always remembered, that what is commonly called the image of a thing in the mind, is no more than the act or operation of the mind in conceiving it.[…]

4. Taking along with us what is said in the last article, to guard us against the seduction of the analogical language used on this subject, we may observe a very strong analogy, not only between conceiving and painting in general, but between the different kinds of our conceptions and the different works of the painter. He either makes fancy pictures, or he copies from the painting of others, or he paints from the life; that is, from real objects of art or nature which he has seen. I think our conceptions admit of a division very similar.

First, There are conceptions which may be called fancy pictures. They are commonly called creatures of fancy or of imagination. They are not the copies of any original that exists, but are originals themselves. Such was the conception which Swift formed of the island of Laputa and of the country of the Lilliputians; Cervantes of Don Quixote and his Squire; Harrington of the Government of Oceana; and Sir Thomas More of that of Utopia. We can give names to such creatures of imagination, conceive them distinctly, and reason consequentially concerning them, though they never had an existence. They were conceived by their creators, and may be conceived by others, but they never existed. We do not ascribe the qualities of true or false to them, because they are not accompanied with any belief, nor do they imply any affirmation or negation.

Setting aside those creatures of imagination, there are other conceptions, which may be called copies, because they have an original or archetype to which they refer, and with which they are believed to agree; and we call them true or false conceptions, according as they agree or disagree with the standard to which they are referred. These are of two kinds, which have different standards or originals.

The *first* kind is analogous to pictures taken from the life. We have conceptions of individual things that really exist such as the city of London, or the government of Venice. Here the things conceived are the originals; and our conceptions are called true when they agree with the thing conceived. Thus, my conception of the city of London is true when I conceive it to be what it really is.

Individual things which really exist, being the creatures of God, (though some of them may receive their outward form from man,) he only who made them knows their whole nature; we know them but in part, and therefore our conceptions of them must in all cases be imperfect and inadequate; yet they may be true and just, as far as they reach.

The *second* kind is analogous to the copies which the painter makes from pictures done before. Such I think are the conceptions we have of what the ancients called universals; that is, of things which belong or may belong to many individuals. These are kinds and species of things; such as man or elephant, which are species of substances; wisdom or courage, which are species of qualities; equality or similitude, which are species of relations. It may be asked — From what original are these conceptions formed? And when are they said to be true or false?

It appears to me that the original from which they are copied — that is, the thing conceived — is the conception or meaning which other men, who understand the language, affix to the same words.

Things are parcelled into kinds and sorts, not by nature, but by men. The individual things we are connected with, are so many, that to give a proper name to every individual would be impossible. We could never attain the knowledge of them that is necessary, nor converse and reason about them, without sorting them according to their different attributes. Those that agree in certain attributes are thrown into one parcel, and have a general name given them, which belongs equally to every individual in that parcel. This common name must therefore signify those attributes which have been observed to be common to every individual in that parcel, and nothing else.

That such general words may answer their intention, all that is necessary is that those who use them should affix the same meaning or notion—that is, the same conception to them. The common meaning is the standard by which such conceptions are formed, and they are said to be true or false according as they agree or disagree with it. Thus, my conception of felony is true and just when it agrees with the meaning of that word in the laws relating to it, and in authors who understand the law.[…]

Our conceptions, therefore, appear to be of *three* kinds. They are either the conceptions of individual things, the creatures of God; or they are conceptions of the meaning of general words; or they are the creatures of our own imagination: and these different kinds have different properties, which we have endeavoured to describe.

5. Our conception of things may be strong and lively, or it may be faint and languid in all degrees. These are qualities which properly belong to our conceptions, though we have no names for them but such as are analogical. Every man is conscious of such a difference in his conceptions, and finds his lively conceptions most agreeable when the object is not of such a nature as to give pain.[…]

6. Our conceptions of things may be clear, distinct, and steady; or they may be obscure, indistinct, and wavering. The liveliness of our conceptions gives pleasure, but it is their distinctness and steadiness that enables us to judge right, and to express our sentiments with perspicuity.[…]

7. It has been observed by many authors, that, when we barely conceive any object, the ingredients of that conception must either be things with which we were before acquainted by some other original power of the mind, or they must be parts or attributes of such things. Thus, a man cannot conceive colours if he never saw, nor sounds if he never heard. If a man had not a conscience, he could not conceive what is meant by moral obligation, or by right and wrong in conduct.

Fancy may combine things that never were combined in reality. It may enlarge or diminish, multiply or divide, compound and fashion the objects which nature presents; but it cannot, by the utmost effort of that creative power which we ascribe to it, bring any one simple ingredient into its productions which Nature has not framed and brought to our knowledge by some faculty.[…]

It is proper to observe, that our most simple conceptions are not those which nature immediately presents to us. When we come to years of understanding, we have the power of analysing the objects of nature, of distinguishing their several attributes and relations, of conceiving them one by one, and of giving a name to each, whose meaning extends only to that single attribute or relation: and thus our most simple conceptions are not those of any object in nature, but of some single attribute or relation of such objects.

Thus, nature presents to our senses bodies that are extended in three dimensions, and solid. By analysing the notion we have of body from our senses, we form to ourselves the conceptions of extension, solidity, space, a point, a line, a surface—all which are more simple conceptions than that of a body. But they are the elements, as it were, of which our conception of a body is made up and into which it may be analysed. This power of analysing objects we propose to consider particularly in another place. It is only mentioned here, that what is said in this article may not be understood so as to be inconsistent with it.

8. Though our conceptions must be confined to the ingredients mentioned in the last article, we are unconfined with regard to the arrangement of those ingredients. Here we may pick and choose, and form an endless variety of combinations and compositions, which we call creatures of the imagination. These may be clearly conceived, though they never existed: and, indeed, everything that is made, must have been conceived before it was made. Every work of human art, and every plan of conduct, whether in public or in private life, must have been conceived before it was brought to execution. And we cannot avoid thinking, that the Almighty, before he created the universe by his power, had a distinct conception of the whole and of every part, and saw it to be good, and agreeable to his intention.[…]

9. The last property I shall mention of this faculty, is that which essentially distinguishes it from every other power of the mind; and it is, that it is not employed solely about things which have existence. I can conceive a winged horse or a centaur as easily and as distinctly as I can conceive a man whom I have seen. Nor does this distinct conception incline my judgment in the least to the belief that a winged horse or a centaur ever existed.

It is not so with the other operations of our minds. They are employed about real existences and carry with them the belief of their objects. When I feel pain, I am compelled to believe that the pain that I feel has a real existence. When I perceive any external object, my belief of the real existence of the object is irresistible. When I distinctly remember any event, though that event may not now exist, I can have no doubt but it did exist. That consciousness which we have of the operations of our own minds, implies a belief of the real existence of those operations.

Thus we see, that the powers of sensation, of perception, of memory, and of consciousness, are all employed solely about objects that do exist, or have existed. But conception is often employed about objects that neither do, nor did, nor will exist. This is the very nature of this faculty, that its object, though distinctly conceived, may have no existence. Such an object we call a creature of imagination; but this creature never was created.

That we may not impose upon ourselves in this matter, we must distinguish between that act or operation of the mind which we call conceiving an object, and the object which we conceive. When we conceive anything, there is a real act or operation of the mind. Of this we are conscious, and can have no doubt of its existence. But every such act must have an object; for he that conceives must conceive something. Suppose he conceives a centaur, he may have a distinct conception of this object, though no centaur ever existed.

I am afraid that, to those who are unacquainted with the doctrine of philosophers upon this subject, I shall appear in a very ridiculous light for insisting upon a point so very evident as that men may barely conceive things that never existed. They will hardly believe that any man in his wits ever doubted of it. Indeed, I know no truth more evident to the common sense and to the experience of mankind. But, if the authority of philosophy, ancient and modern, opposes it, as I think it does, I wish not to treat that authority so fastidiously as not to attend patiently to what may be said in support of it.

Chapter II

Theories concerning conception.

[...] There are two prejudices which seem to me to have given rise to the theory of ideas in all the various forms in which it has appeared in the course of above two thousand years; and, though they have no support from the natural dictates of our faculties, or from attentive reflection upon their operations, they are prejudices which those who speculate upon this subject are very apt to be led into by analogy.

The *first* is—That, in all the operations of the understanding, there must be some immediate intercourse between the mind and its object, so that the one may act upon the other. The *second*, That, in all the operations of understanding, there must be an object of thought, which really exists while we think of it; or, as some philosophers have expressed it, that which is not cannot be intelligible.

Had philosophers perceived that these are prejudices grounded only upon analogical reasoning, we had never heard of ideas in the philosophical sense of that word.

The *first* of these principles has led philosophers to think that, as the external objects of sense are too remote to act upon the mind immediately, there must be some image or shadow of them that is present to the mind, and is the immediate object of perception. That there is such an immediate object of perception, distinct from the external object, has been very unanimously held by philosophers, though they have differed much about the name, the nature, and the origin of those immediate objects.

We have considered what has been said in the support of this principle, Essay II. chap. 14, to which the reader is referred, to prevent repetition.

I shall only add to what is there said, That there appears no shadow of reason why the mind must have an object immediately present to it in its intellectual operations, any more than in its affections and passions. Philosophers have not said that ideas are the immediate objects of love or resentment, of esteem or disapprobation. It is, I think, acknowledged, that persons and not ideas are the immediate objects of those affections; persons who are as far from being immediately present to the mind as other external objects, and, sometimes, persons who have now no existence, in this world at least, and who can neither act upon the mind, nor be acted upon by it.

The *second* principle, which I conceive to be likewise a prejudice of philosophers grounded upon analogy, is now to be considered.

It contradicts directly what was laid down in the last article of the preceding chapter — to wit, that we may have a distinct conception of things which never existed. This is undoubtedly the common belief of those who have not been instructed in philosophy; and they will think it as ridiculous to defend it by reasoning, as to oppose it.

The philosopher says, Though there may be a remote object which does not exist, there must be an immediate object which really exists; for that which is not, cannot be an object of thought. The idea must be perceived by the mind, and, if it does not exist there, there can be no perception of it, no operation of the mind about it.

This principle deserves the more to be examined, because the other before mentioned depends upon it; for, although the last may be true, even if the first was false, yet, if the last be not true, neither can the first. If we can conceive objects which have no existence, it follows that there may be objects of thought which neither act upon the mind, nor are acted upon by it; because that which has no existence can neither act nor be acted upon.

It is by these principles that philosophers have been led to think that, in every act of memory and of conception, as well as of perception, there are two objects — the one, the immediate object, the idea, the species, the form; the other, the mediate or external object. The vulgar know only of one object, which, in perception, is something external that exists; in memory, something that did exist; and, in conception, may be something that never existed. But the immediate object of the philosophers, the idea, is said to exist and to be perceived in all these operations.

These principles have not only led philosophers to split objects into two, where others can find but one, but likewise have led them to reduce the three operations now mentioned to one, making memory and conception, as well as perception, to be the perception of ideas. But nothing appears more evident to the vulgar, than that what is only remembered, or only conceived, is not perceived; and, to speak of the perceptions of memory, appears to them as absurd as to speak of the hearing of sight.

In a word, these two principles carry us into the whole philosophical theory of ideas, and furnish every argument that ever was used for their existence. If they are true, that system must be admitted with all its consequences. If they are only prejudices grounded upon analogical reasoning, the whole system must fall to the ground with them.

It is, therefore, of importance to trace those principles, as far as we are able, to their origin, and to see, if possible, whether they have any just foundation in reason, or whether they are rash conclusions drawn from a supposed analogy between matter and mind.

The unlearned, who are guided by the dictates of nature, and express what they are conscious of concerning the operations of their own mind, believe that the object which they distinctly perceive certainly exists; that the object which they distinctly remember certainly did exist, but now may not; but as to things that are barely conceived, they know that they can conceive a thousand things that never existed, and that the bare conception of a thing does not so much as afford a presumption of its existence. They give themselves no trouble to know how these operations are performed, or to account for them from general principles.

But philosophers, who wish to discover the causes of things, and to account for these operations of mind, observing that in other operations there must be not only an agent, but something to act upon, have been led by analogy to conclude that it must be so in the operations of the mind.

The relation between the mind and its conceptions bears a very strong and obvious analogy to the relation between a man and his work. Every scheme he forms, every discovery he makes by his reasoning powers, is very properly called the work of his mind. These works of the mind are sometimes great and important works, and draw the attention and admiration of men.

It is the province of the philosopher to consider how such works of the mind are produced, and of what materials they are composed. He calls the materials ideas. There must therefore be ideas, which the mind can arrange and form into a regular structure. Everything that is produced, must be produced of something; and from nothing, nothing can be produced.

Some such reasoning as this seems to me to have given the first rise to the philosophical notions of ideas. Those notions were formed into a system by the Pythagoreans, two thousand years ago; and this system was adopted by Plato, and embellished with all the powers of a fine and lofty imagination. I shall, in compliance with custom, call it the Platonic system of ideas, though in reality it was the invention of the Pythagorean school.

The most arduous question which employed the wits of men in the infancy of the Grecian philosophy was — What was the origin of the world? — from what principles and causes did it proceed? To this question very different answers were given in the different schools. Most of them appear to us very ridiculous. The Pythagoreans, however, judged, very rationally, from the order and beauty of the universe, that it must be the workmanship of an eternal, intelligent, and good being: and therefore they concluded the Deity to be one first principle or cause of the universe.

But they conceived there must be more. The universe must be made of something. Every workman must have materials to work upon. That the world should be made out of nothing seemed to them absurd, be cause everything that is made must be made of something.[…]

From this it followed, that an eternal uncreated matter was another first principle of the universe. But this matter they believed had no form nor quality. It was the same with the *materia prima* or first matter of Aristotle, who borrowed this part of his philosophy from his predecessors.

To us it seems more rational to think that the Deity created matter with its qualities, than that the matter of the universe should be eternal and self-existent. But so strong was the prejudice of the ancient philosophers against what we call creation, that they rather chose to have recourse to this eternal and unintelligible matter, that the Deity might have materials to work upon.

The same analogy which led them to think that there must be an eternal matter of which the world was made, led them also to conclude that there must be an eternal pattern or model according to which it was made. Works of design and art must be distinctly conceived before they are made. The Deity, as an intelligent Being, about to execute a work of perfect beauty and regularity, must have had a distinct conception of his work before it was made. This appears very rational.

But this conception, being the work of the Divine intellect, something must have existed as its object. This could only be ideas, which are the proper and immediate object of intellect.

From this investigation of the principles or causes of the universe, those philosophers concluded them to be three in number—to wit, an eternal matter as the material cause, eternal ideas as the model or exemplary cause, and an eternal intelligent mind as the efficient cause.[...]

Such was the most ancient system concerning ideas, of which we have any account. And, however different from the modern, it appears to be built upon the prejudices we have mentioned—to wit, that in every operation there must be something to work upon; and that even in conception there must be an object which really exists.

For, if those ancient philosophers had thought it possible that the Deity could operate without materials in the formation of the world, and that he could conceive the plan of it without a model, they could have seen no reason to make matter and ideas eternal and necessarily existent principles, as well as the Deity himself.

Whether they believed that the ideas were not only eternal, but eternally, and without a cause, arranged in that beautiful and perfect order which they ascribe to this intelligible world of ideas, I cannot say; but this seems to be a necessary consequence of the system: for, if the Deity could not conceive the plan of the world which he made, without a model which really existed, that model could not be his work, nor contrived by his wisdom; for, if he made it, he must have conceived it before it was made; it must therefore have existed in all its beauty and order independent of the Deity; and this I think they acknowledged, by making the model and the matter of this world, first principles, no less than the Deity.[…]

Aristotle rejected the ideas of his master Plato as visionary, but he retained the prejudices that gave rise to them, and therefore substituted something in their place, but under a different name and of a different origin.[…]

Modern philosophers, still persuaded that of every thought there must be an immediate object that really exists, have not deemed it necessary to distinguish by different names the immediate objects of intellect, of imagination, and of the senses, but have given the common name of *idea* to them all.[…]

So much is this opinion fixed in the minds of philosophers that I doubt not but it will appear to most a very strange paradox, or rather a contradiction, that men should think without ideas.

That it has the appearance of a contradiction, I confess. But this appearance arises from the ambiguity of the word idea. If the idea of a thing means only the thought of it, or the operation of the mind in thinking about it, which is the most common meaning of the word, to think without ideas is to think without thought, which is undoubtedly a contradiction.

But an idea, according to the definition given of it by philosophers, is not thought, but an object of thought, which really exists and is perceived. Now, whether is it a contradiction to say, that a man may think of an object that does not exist?

I acknowledge that a man cannot perceive an object that does not exist; nor can he remember an object that did not exist, but there appears to me no contradiction in his conceiving an object that neither does nor ever did exist.

Let us take an example. I conceive a centaur. This conception is an operation of the mind, of which I am conscious, and to which I can attend. The sole object of it is a centaur, an

animal which, I believe, never existed. I can see no contradiction in this.

The philosopher says, I cannot conceive a centaur without
having an idea of it in my mind. I am at a loss to understand
what he means. He surely does not mean that I cannot conceive it without conceiving it. This would make me no wiser.
What then is this idea? Is it an animal, half horse and half
man? No. Then I am certain it is not the thing I conceive. Perhaps he will say, that the idea is an image of the animal, and
is the immediate object of my conception, and that the
animal is the mediate or remote object.

To this I answer — *First*, I am certain there are not two objects of this conception, but one only, and that one is as immediate an object of my conception as any can be.

Secondly, This one object which I conceive is not the image
of an animal — it is an animal. I know what it is to conceive
an image of an animal, and what it is to conceive an animal;
and I can distinguish the one of these from the other without
any danger of mistake. The thing I conceive is a body of a
certain figure and colour, having life and spontaneous
motion. The philosopher says, that the idea is an image of the
animal; but that it has neither body, nor colour, nor life, nor
spontaneous motion. This I am not able to comprehend.

Thirdly, I wish to know how this idea comes to be an object of my thought, when I cannot even conceive what it
means; and, if I did conceive it, this would be no evidence of
its existence, any more than my conception of a centaur is of
its existence. Philosophers sometimes say that we perceive
ideas, sometimes that we are conscious of them. I can have
no doubt of the existence of anything which I either perceive
or of which I am conscious; but I cannot find that I either
perceive ideas or am conscious of them.

Perception and consciousness are very different operations, and it is strange that philosophers have never determined by which of them ideas are discerned. This is as if a
man should positively affirm that he perceived an object; but
whether by his eyes, or his ears, or his touch, he could not
say.

But may not a man who conceives a centaur say, that he
has a distinct image of it in his mind? I think he may. And if
he means by this way of speaking what the vulgar mean,

who never heard of the philosophical theory of ideas, I find no fault with it. By a distinct image in the mind, the vulgar mean a distinct conception; and it is natural to call it so, on account of the analogy between an image of a thing and the conception of it. On account of this analogy, obvious to all mankind, this operation is called imagination, and an image in the mind is only a periphrasis for imagination. But to infer from this that there is really an image in the mind, distinct from the operation of conceiving the object, is to be misled by an analogical expression; as if, from the phrases of deliberating and balancing things in the mind, we should infer that there is really a balance existing in the mind for weighing motives and arguments.

The analogical words and phrases used in all languages to express conception do, no doubt, facilitate their being taken in a literal sense. But, if we only attend carefully to what we are conscious of in this operation, we shall find no more reason to think that images do really exist in our minds, than that balances and other mechanical engines do.

We know of nothing that is in the mind but by consciousness, and we are conscious of nothing but various modes of thinking; such as understanding, willing, affection, passion, doing, suffering. If philosophers choose to give the name of an idea to any mode of thinking of which we are conscious, I have no objection to the name but that it introduces a foreign word into our language without necessity, and a word that is very ambiguous, and apt to mislead. But, if they give that name to images in the mind, which are not thought, but only objects of thought, I can see no reason to think that there are such things in nature. If they be, their existence and their nature must be more evident than anything else, because we know nothing but by their means. I may add that, if they be, we can know nothing besides them. For, from the existence of images, we can never, by any just reasoning, infer the existence of anything else, unless perhaps the existence of an intelligent Author of them. In this, Bishop Berkeley reasoned right.[…]

If now it should be asked, What is the idea of a circle? I answer, It is the conception of a circle. What is the immediate object of this conception? The immediate and the only object of it is a circle. But where is this circle? It is nowhere. If it was an individual and had a real existence, it must have a place; but, being a universal, it has no existence and therefore no place. Is it not in the mind of him that conceives it? The conception of it is in the mind, being an act of the mind; and in common language, a thing being in the mind is a figurative expression signifying that the thing is conceived or remembered.

It may be asked, Whether this conception is an image or resemblance of a circle? I answer, I have already accounted for its being, in a figurative sense, called the image of a circle in the mind. If the question is meant in the literal sense, we must observe that the word *conception* has two meanings. Properly it signifies that operation of the mind which we have been endeavouring to explain; but sometimes it is put for the object of conception, or thing conceived.

Now, if the question be understood in the last of these senses, the object of this conception is not an image or resemblance of a circle; for it is a circle, and nothing can be an image of itself.

If the question be — Whether the operation of mind in conceiving a circle be an image or resemblance of a circle, I think it is not; and that no two things can be more perfectly unlike than a species of thought and a species of figure. Nor is it more strange that conception should have no resemblance to the object conceived, than that desire should have no resemblance to the object desired, or resentment to the object of resentment.

I can likewise conceive an individual object that really exists, such as St. Paul's Church in London. I have an idea of it; that is, I conceive it. The immediate object of this conception is four hundred miles distant; and I have no reason to think that it acts upon me or that I act upon it; but I can think of it notwithstanding. I can think of the first year or the last year of the Julian period.[…]

This account of the faculty of conception, by images in the mind or in the brain, will deserve the regard of those who have a true taste in philosophy, when it is proved by solid arguments — *First*, That there are images in the mind, or in the brain, of the things we conceive. *Secondly*, That there is a faculty in the mind of perceiving such images. *Thirdly*, That the perception of such images produces the conception of

things most distant, and even of things that have no existence. And, *fourthly*, That the perception of individual images
in the mind or in the brain gives us the conception of universals, which are the attributes of many individuals. Until
this is done, the theory of images existing in the mind or in
the brain ought to be placed in the same category with the
sensible species, *materia prima* of Aristotle, and the *vortices* of
Des Cartes.

Chapter III

Mistakes concerning conception.

[...] 3. Simple apprehension is commonly represented as the
first operation of the understanding; and judgment, as being
a composition or combination of simple apprehensions.

This mistake has probably arisen from the taking sensation, and the perception of objects by the senses, to be nothing but simple apprehension. They are, very probably, the
first operations of the mind; but they are not simple apprehensions.

It is generally allowed, that we cannot conceive sounds if
we have never heard, nor colours if we have never seen; and
the same thing may be said of the objects of the other senses.
In like manner, we must have judged or reasoned before we
have the conception or simple apprehension of judgment
and of reasoning.

Simple apprehension, therefore, though it be the simplest,
is not the first operation of the understanding; and, instead
of saying that the more complex operations of the mind are
formed by compounding simple apprehensions, we ought
rather to say, that simple apprehensions are got by analysing
more complex operations.[...]

4. There remains another mistake concerning conception
which deserves to be noticed. It is—That our conception of
things is a test of their possibility, so that, what we can distinctly conceive, we may conclude to be possible; and of what
is impossible, we can have no conception.

This opinion has been held by philosophers for more than
a hundred years without contradiction or dissent, as far as I
know; and, if it be an error, it may be of some use to inquire
into its origin, and the causes that it has been so generally

received as a maxim whose truth could not be brought into doubt.[…]

'Impossibile est cujus nullam notionem formare possumus; possibile e contra, cui aliqua respondet notio.' — WOLFII ONTOLOGIA[…][3]

If the maxim be true in the extent which the famous Wolfius has given it, in the passage quoted above, we shall have a short road to the determination of every question about the possibility or impossibility of things. We need only look into our breast, and that […] will give an infallible answer. If we can conceive the thing, it is possible; if not, it is impossible. And surely every man may know whether he can conceive what is affirmed or not.

Other philosophers have been satisfied with one half of the maxim of Wolfius. They say, that whatever we can conceive is possible, but they do not say that whatever we cannot conceive is impossible.

I cannot help thinking even this to be a mistake, which philosophers have been unwarily led into, from the causes before mentioned. My reasons are these: —

1. Whatever is said to be possible or impossible is expressed by a proposition. Now, what is it to conceive a proposition? I think it is no more than to understand distinctly its meaning. I know no more that can be meant by simple apprehension or conception when applied to a proposition. The axiom, therefore, amounts to this: — Every proposition, of which you understand the meaning distinctly, is possible. I am persuaded that I understand as distinctly the meaning of this proposition, *Any two sides of a triangle are together equal to the third*, as of this — *Any two sides of a triangle are together greater than the third*; yet the first of these is impossible.

Perhaps it will be said, that, though you understand the meaning of the impossible proposition, you cannot suppose or conceive it to be true.

Here we are to examine the meaning of the phrases of *supposing* and *conceiving* a proposition to be true. I can certainly suppose it to be true, because I can draw consequences from it which I find to be impossible, as well as the proposition itself.

If, by conceiving it to be true, be meant giving some degree of assent to it, however small, this, I confess, I cannot do.

But will it be said that every proposition to which I can give any degree of assent, is possible? This contradicts experience, and, therefore, the maxim cannot be true in this sense.

Sometimes, when we say that *we cannot conceive a thing to be true*, we mean by that expression, that *we judge it to be impossible*. In this sense I cannot, indeed, conceive it to be true, that two sides of a triangle are equal to the third. I judge it to be impossible. If, then, we understand, in this sense, that maxim, that nothing we can conceive is impossible, the meaning will be, that nothing is impossible which we judge to be possible. But does it not often happen, that what one man judges to be possible, another man judges to be impossible? The maxim, therefore, is not true in this sense.

I am not able to find any other meaning of *conceiving a proposition*, or of *conceiving it to be true*, besides these I have mentioned. I know nothing that can be meant by having the idea of a proposition, but either the understanding its meaning or the judging of its truth. I can understand a proposition that is false or impossible, as well as one that is true or possible; and I find that men have contradictory judgments about what is possible or impossible, as well as about other things. In what sense then can it be said, that the having an idea of a proposition gives certain evidence that it is possible?

If it be said, that the idea of a proposition is an image of it in the mind, I think indeed there cannot be a distinct image, either in the mind or elsewhere, of that which is impossible; but what is meant by the image of a proposition I am not able to comprehend, and I shall be glad to be informed.

2. Every proposition that is necessarily true stands opposed to a contradictory proposition that is impossible; and he that conceives one conceives both. Thus, a man who believes that two and three necessarily make five, must believe it to be impossible that two and three should not make five. He conceives both propositions when he believes one. Every proposition carries its contradictory in its bosom, and both are conceived at the same time. 'It is confessed,' says Mr Hume, 'that, in all cases where we dissent from any person, we conceive both sides of the question; but we can believe only one.' From this, it certainly follows that, when we dissent from any person about a necessary proposition, we conceive one that is impossible; yet I know no philosopher who

has made so much use of the maxim, that whatever we conceive is possible, as Mr Hume. A great part of his peculiar tenets is built upon it; and, if it is true, they must be true. But he did not perceive that, in the passage now quoted, the truth of which is evident, he contradicts it himself.

3. Mathematicians have, in many cases, proved some things to be possible, and others to be impossible, which, without demonstration, would not have been believed. Yet I have never found that any mathematician has attempted to prove a thing to be possible, because it can be conceived; or impossible, because it cannot be conceived. Why is not this maxim applied to determine whether it is possible to square the circle? a point about which very eminent mathematicians have differed. It is easy to conceive that, in the infinite series of numbers, and intermediate fractions, some one number, integral or fractional, may bear the same ratio to another, as the side of a square bears to its diagonal; yet, however conceivable this may be, it may be demonstrated to be impossible.

4. Mathematicians often require us to conceive things that are impossible, in order to prove them to be so. This is the case in all their demonstrations *ad absurdum*. Conceive, says Euclid, a right line drawn from one point of the circumference of a circle to another, to fall without the circle: I conceive this—I reason from it until I come to a consequence that is manifestly absurd; and from thence conclude that the thing which I conceived is impossible.

Having said so much to show that our power of conceiving a proposition is no criterion of its possibility or impossibility, I shall add a few observations on the extent of our knowledge of this kind.

1. There are many propositions which, by the faculties God has given us, we judge to be necessary, as well as true. All mathematical propositions are of this kind, and many others. The contradictories of such propositions must be impossible. Our knowledge, therefore, of what is impossible, must, at least, be as extensive as our knowledge of necessary truth.

2. By our senses, by memory, by testimony, and by other means, we know many things to be true which do not appear to be necessary. But whatever is true is possible. Our know-

ledge, therefore, of what is possible must, at least, extend as far as our knowledge of truth.

3. If a man pretends to determine the possibility or impossibility of things beyond these limits, let him bring proof. I do not say that no such proof can be brought. It has been brought in many cases, particularly in mathematics. But I say that his being able to conceive a thing, is no proof that it is possible. Mathematics afford many instances of impossibilities in the nature of things, which no man would have believed if they had not been strictly demonstrated. Perhaps, if we were able to reason demonstratively in other subjects, to as great extent as in mathematics, we might find many things to be impossible, which we conclude without hesitation, to be possible.

It is possible, you say, that God might have made an universe of sensible and rational creatures, into which neither natural nor moral evil should ever enter. It may be so, for what I know. But how do you know that it is possible? That you can conceive it, I grant; but this is no proof. I cannot admit, as an argument, or even as a pressing difficulty, what is grounded on the supposition that such a thing is possible, when there is no good evidence that it is possible, and, for anything we know, it may, in the nature of things, be impossible.

Essay VI: Of Judgment

Chapter I

Of judgment in general.

Judging is an operation of the mind so familiar to every man who hath understanding, and its name is so common and so well understood, that it needs no definition.

As it is impossible by a definition to give a notion of colour to a man who never saw colours; so it is impossible by any definition to give a distinct notion of judgment to a man who has not often judged, and who is not capable of reflecting attentively upon this act of his mind. The best use of a definition is to prompt him to that reflection; and without it the best definition will be apt to mislead him.

The definition commonly given of judgment by the more ancient writers in logic, was, that it is *an act of the mind, whereby one thing is affirmed or denied of another*. I believe this is as good a definition of it as can be given. Why I prefer it to some later definitions, will afterwards appear. Without pretending to give any other, I shall make two remarks upon it, and then offer some general observations on this subject.

1. It is true that it is by affirmation or denial that we express our judgments; but there may be judgment which is not expressed. It is a solitary act of the mind, and the expression of it by affirmation or denial is not at all essential to it. It may be tacit, and not expressed. Nay, it is well known that men may judge contrary to what they affirm or deny; the definition therefore must be understood of mental affirmation or denial, which indeed is only another name for judgment.

2. Affirmation and denial is very often the expression of testimony, which is a different act of the mind, and ought to be distinguished from judgment.

A judge asks of a witness what he knows of such a matter to which he was an eye or ear-witness. He answers, by affirming or denying something. But his answer does not express his judgment; it is his testimony. Again, I ask a man his opinion in a matter of science or of criticism. His answer is not testimony; it is the expression of his judgment.

Testimony is a social act, and it is essential to it to be expressed by words or signs. A tacit testimony is a contradiction: but there is no contradiction in a tacit judgment; it is complete without being expressed.

In testimony a man pledges his veracity for what he affirms; so that a false testimony is a lie: but a wrong judgment is not a lie; it is only an error.

I believe, in all languages, testimony and judgment are expressed by the same form of speech. A proposition affirmative or negative, with a verb in what is called the indicative mood, expresses both. To distinguish them by the form of speech, it would be necessary that verbs should have two indicative moods, one for testimony, and another to express judgment. I know not that this is found in any language. And the reason is—not surely that the vulgar cannot distinguish the two, for every man knows the difference between a lie and an error of judgment—but that, from the matter and circumstances, we can easily see whether a man intends to give his testimony, or barely to express his judgment.

Although men must have judged in many cases before tribunals of justice were erected, yet it is very probable that there were tribunals before men began to speculate about judgment, and that the word may be borrowed from the practice of tribunals. As a judge, after taking the proper evidence, passes sentence in a cause, and that sentence is called his judgment, so the mind, with regard to whatever is true or false, passes sentence, or determines according to the evidence that appears. Some kinds of evidence leave no room for doubt. Sentence is passed immediately, without seeking or hearing any contrary evidence, because the thing is certain and notorious. In other cases, there is room for weighing evidence on both sides before sentence is passed. The analogy between a tribunal of justice, and this inward tribunal of the mind, is too obvious to escape the notice of any man who ever appeared before a judge. And it is probable that the word *judgment*, as well as many other words we use in speaking of this operation of mind, is grounded on this analogy.

Having premised these things, that it may be clearly understood what I mean by judgment, I proceed to make some general observations concerning it.

First, Judgment is an act of the mind, specifically different from simple apprehension, or the bare conception of a thing. It would be unnecessary to observe this, if some philosophers had not been led by their theories to a contrary opinion.

Although there can be no judgment without a conception of the things about which we judge, yet conception may be without any judgment. Judgment can be expressed by a proposition only, and a proposition is a complete sentence; but simple apprehension may be expressed by a word or words, which make no complete sentence. When simple apprehension is employed about a proposition, every man knows that it is one thing to apprehend a proposition — that is, to conceive what it means — but it is quite another thing to judge it to be true or false.

It is self-evident that every judgment must be either true or false; but simple apprehension, or conception, can neither be true nor false, as was shown before.

One judgment may be contradictory to another; and it is impossible for a man to have two judgments at the same time, which he perceives to be contradictory. But contradictory propositions may be conceived at the same time without any difficulty. That the sun is greater than the earth, and that the sun is not greater than the earth, are contradictory propositions. He that apprehends the meaning of one, apprehends the meaning of both. But it is impossible for him to judge both to be true at the same time. He knows that, if the one is true, the other must be false. For these reasons, I hold it to be certain that judgment and simple apprehension are acts of the mind specifically different.

Secondly, There are notions or ideas that ought to be referred to the faculty of judgment as their source; because, if we had not that faculty, they could not enter into our minds; and to those that have that faculty, and are capable of reflecting upon its operations, they are obvious and familiar.

Among these we may reckon the notion of judgment itself; the notions of a proposition — of its subject, predicate, and copula; of affirmation and negation, of true and false; of knowledge, belief, disbelief, opinion, assent, evidence. From no source could we acquire these notions, but from reflecting upon our judgments. Relations of things make one great class of our notions or ideas; and we cannot have the idea of any relation without some exercise of judgment, as will appear afterwards.

Thirdly, In persons come to years of understanding, judgment necessarily accompanies all sensation, perception by the senses, consciousness, and memory, but not conception.

I restrict this to persons come to the years of understanding, because it may be a question, whether infants, in the first period of life, have any judgment or belief at all. The same question may be put with regard to brutes and some idiots. This question is foreign to the present subject; and I say nothing here about it, but speak only of persons who have the exercise of judgment.[…]

A fourth observation is, that some exercise of judgment is necessary in the formation of all abstract and general conceptions, whether more simple or more complex; in dividing, in defining, and, in general, in forming all clear and distinct conceptions of things, which are the only fit materials of reasoning.

These operations are allied to each other, and therefore I bring them under one observation. They are more allied to our rational nature than those mentioned in the last observation, and therefore are considered by themselves.

That I may not be mistaken, it may be observed that I do not say that abstract notions, or other accurate notions of things, after they have been formed, cannot be barely conceived without any exercise of judgment about them. I doubt not that they may: but what I say is, that, in their formation in the mind at first, there must be some exercise of judgment.

It is impossible to distinguish the different attributes belonging to the same subject, without judging that they are really different and distinguishable, and that they have that relation to the subject which logicians express, by saying that they may be predicated of it. We cannot generalise, without judging that the same attribute does or may belong to many individuals. It has been shown that our simplest general notions are formed by these two operations of distinguishing and generalising; judgment therefore is exercised in forming the simplest general notions.

In those that are more complex, and which have been shown to be formed by combining the more simple, there is another act of the judgment required; for such combinations are not made at random, but for an end; and judgment is employed in fitting them to that end. We form complex general notions for conveniency of arranging our thoughts in discourse and reasoning; and, therefore, of an infinite number of combinations that might be formed, we choose only those that are useful and necessary.[…]

I add in general, that, without some degree of judgment we can form no accurate and distinct notions of things; so that one province of judgment is, to aid us in forming clear and distinct conceptions of things, which are the only fit materials for reasoning.

This will probably appear to be a paradox to philosophers, who have always considered the formation of ideas of every kind as belonging to simple apprehension; and that the sole province of judgment is to put them together in affirmative or negative propositions; and therefore it requires some confirmation.

First, I think it necessarily follows, from what has been already said in this observation. For if, without some degree of judgment, a man can neither distinguish, nor divide, nor define, nor form any general notion, simple or complex, he surely, without some degree of judgment, cannot have in his mind the materials necessary to reasoning.

There cannot be any proposition in language which does not involve some general conception. The proposition, *that I exist*, which Des Cartes thought the first of all truths, and the foundation of all knowledge, cannot be conceived without the conception of existence, one of the most abstract general conceptions. A man cannot believe his own existence, or the existence of anything he sees or remembers, until he has so much judgment as to distinguish things that really exist from things which are only conceived. He sees a man six feet high; he conceives a man sixty feet high: he judges the first object to exist, because he sees it; the second he does not judge to exist, because he only conceives it. Now, I would ask, whether he can attribute existence to the first object, and not to the second, without knowing what existence means. It is impossible.

How early the notion of existence enters into the mind, I cannot determine; but it must certainly be in the mind as soon as we can affirm of anything, with understanding, that it exists.

In every other proposition, the predicate, at least, must be a general notion—a predicable and a universal being one and the same. Besides this, every proposition either affirms or denies. And no man can have a distinct conception of a proposition, who does not understand distinctly the meaning of affirming or denying. But these are very general conceptions, and, as was before observed, are derived from judgment, as their source and origin.

I am sensible that a strong objection may be made to this reasoning, and that it may seem to lead to an absurdity or a contradiction. It may be said, that every judgment is a mental affirmation or negation. If, therefore, some previous exercise of judgment be necessary to understand what is meant by affirmation or negation, the exercise of judgment must go before any judgment which is absurd.

In like manner, every judgment may be expressed by a proposition, and a proposition must be conceived before we can judge of it. If, therefore, we cannot conceive the meaning of a proposition without a previous exercise of judgment, it follows that judgment must be previous to the conception of any proposition, and at the same time that the conception of a proposition must be previous to all judgment, which is a contradiction.

The reader may please to observe, that I have limited what I have said to distinct conception, and some degree of judgment; and it is by this means I hope to avoid this labyrinth of absurdity and contradiction. The faculties of conception and judgment have an infancy and a maturity as man has. What I have said is limited to their mature state. I believe in their infant state they are very weak and indistinct; and that, by imperceptible degrees, they grow to maturity, each giving aid to the other and, receiving aid from it. But which of them first began this friendly intercourse, is beyond my ability to determine. It is like the question concerning the bird and the egg.

In the present state of things, it is true that every bird comes from an egg, and every egg from a bird; and each may be said to be previous to the other. But, if we go back to the origin of things, there must have been some bird that did not come from any egg, or some egg that did not come from any bird.

In like manner, in the mature state of man, distinct conception of a proposition supposes some previous exercise of judgment, and distinct judgment supposes distinct conception. Each may truly be said to come from the other, as the bird from the egg, and the egg from the bird. But, if we trace back this succession to its origin—that is, to the first proposition that was ever conceived by the man, and the first judgment he ever formed—I determine nothing about them, nor do I know in what order, or how, they were produced, any more than how the bones grow in the womb of her that is with child.

The first exercise of these faculties of conception and judgment is hid, like the sources of the Nile, in an unknown region.

The necessity of some degree of judgment to clear and distinct conceptions of things, may, I think, be illustrated by this similitude.

An artist, suppose a carpenter, cannot work in his art without tools, and these tools must be made by art. The exercise of the art, therefore, is necessary to make the tools, and the tools are necessary to the exercise of the art. There is the same appearance of contradiction, as in what I have advanced concerning the necessity of some degree of judgment, in order to form clear and distinct conceptions of things. These are the tools we must use in judging and in reasoning, and without them must make very bungling work; yet these tools cannot be made without some exercise of judgment.

The necessity of some degree of judgment in forming accurate and distinct notions of things will further appear, if we consider attentively what notions we can form, without any aid of judgment, of the objects of sense, of the operations of our own minds, or of the relations of things.

To begin with the objects of sense. It is acknowledged, on all hands, that the first notions we have of sensible objects are got by the external senses only, and probably before judgment is brought forth; but these first notions are neither simple, nor are they accurate and distinct: they are gross and indistinct and, like the *chaos*, a *rudis indigestaque moles*.[4] Before we can have any distinct notion of this mass, it must be analysed; the heterogeneous parts must be separated in our conception, and the simple elements, which before lay hid in the common mass, must first be distinguished, and then put together into one whole.

In this way it is that we form distinct notions even of the objects of sense; but this process of analysis and composition by habit becomes so easy, and is performed so readily, that we are apt to overlook it, and to impute the distinct notion we have formed of the object to the senses alone; and this we are the more prone to do because, when once we have distinguished the sensible qualities of the object from one another, the sense gives testimony to each of them.

You perceive, for instance, an object white, round, and a foot in diameter. I grant that you perceive all these attributes of the object by sense; but, if you had not been able to distinguish the colour from the figure, and both from the magnitude, your senses would only have given you one complex and confused notion of all these mingled together.

A man who is able to say with understanding, or to determine in his own mind, that this object is white, must have distinguished whiteness from other attributes. If he has not made this distinction, he does not understand what he says.

Suppose a cube of brass to be presented at the same time to a child of a year old and to a man. The regularity of the figure will attract the attention of both. Both have the senses of sight and of touch in equal perfection; and, therefore, if anything be discovered in this object by the man, which cannot be discovered by the child, it must be owing, not to the senses, but to some other faculty which the child has not yet attained.

First, then, the man can easily distinguish the body from the surface which terminates it; this the child cannot do. *Secondly*, The man can perceive that this surface is made up of six planes of the same figure and magnitude; the child cannot discover this. *Thirdly*, The man perceives that each of these planes has four equal sides and four equal angles; and that the opposite sides of each plane and the opposite planes are parallel.

It will surely be allowed, that a man of ordinary judgment may observe all this in a cube which he makes an object of contemplation, and takes time to consider; that he may give the name of a square to a plane terminated by four equal sides and four equal angles; and the name of a cube to a solid terminated by six equal squares: all this is nothing else but analysing the figure of the object presented to his senses into its simplest elements, and again compounding it of those elements.

By this analysis and composition two effects are produced. *First*, From the one complex object which his senses presented, though one of the most simple the senses can present, he educes many simple and distinct notions of right lines, angles, plain surface, solid, equality, parallelism — notions which the child has not yet faculties to attain. *Sec-*

ondly, When he considers the cube as compounded of these elements put together in a certain order, he has then, and not before, a distinct and scientific notion of a cube. The child neither conceives those elements, nor in what order they must be put together in order to make a cube; and therefore has no accurate notion of a cube which can make it a subject of reasoning.

Whence I think we may conclude, that the notion which we have from the senses alone, even of the simplest objects of sense, is indistinct and incapable of being either described or reasoned upon, until it is analysed into its simple elements, and considered as compounded of those elements.

If we should apply this reasoning to more complex objects of sense, the conclusion would be still more evident. A dog may be taught to turn a jack, but he can never be taught to have a distinct notion of a jack. He sees every part as well as a man; but the relation of the parts to one another and to the whole, he has not judgment to comprehend.

A distinct notion of an object, even of sense, is never got in an instant; but the sense performs its office in an instant. Time is not required to see it better, but to analyse it, to distinguish the different parts, and their relation to one another and to the whole.

Hence it is that, when any vehement passion or emotion hinders the cool application of judgment, we get no distinct notion of an object, even though the sense be long directed to it. A man who is put into a panic, by thinking he sees a ghost, may stare at it long without having any distinct notion of it; it is his understanding, and not his sense, that is disturbed by his horror. If he can lay that aside, judgment immediately enters upon its office, and examines the length and breadth, the colour, and figure, and distance of the object. Of these, while his panic lasted, he had no distinct notion, though his eyes were open all the time.

When the eye of sense is open, but that of judgment shut by a panic, or any violent emotion that engrosses the mind, we see things confusedly, and probably much in the same manner that brutes and perfect idiots do, and infants before the use of judgment.

There are, therefore, notions of the objects of sense which are gross and indistinct, and there are others that are distinct and scientific. The former may be got from the senses alone, but the latter cannot be obtained without some degree of judgment.

The clear and accurate notions which geometry presents to us of a point, a right line, an angle, a square, a circle, of ratios direct and inverse, and others of that kind, can find no admittance into a mind that has not some degree of judgment. They are not properly ideas of the senses, nor are they got by compounding ideas of the senses, but by analysing the ideas or notions we get by the senses into their simplest elements, and again combining these elements into various accurate and elegant forms, which the senses never did nor can exhibit.

Had Mr Hume attended duly to this, it ought to have prevented a very bold attempt, which he has prosecuted through fourteen pages of his *Treatise of Human Nature* to prove that geometry is founded upon ideas that are not exact, and axioms that are not precisely true.

A mathematician might be tempted to think that the man who seriously undertakes this has no great acquaintance with geometry; but I apprehend it is to be imputed to another cause, to a zeal for his own system. We see that even men of genius may be drawn into strange paradoxes, by an attachment to a favourite idol of the understanding, when it demands so costly a sacrifice.

We Protestants think that the devotees of the Roman Church pay no small tribute to her authority when they renounce their five senses in obedience to her decrees. Mr Hume's devotion to his system carries him even to trample upon mathematical demonstration.

The fundamental articles of his system are, that all the perceptions of the human mind are either impressions or ideas, and that ideas are only faint copies of impressions. The idea of a right line, therefore, is only a faint copy of some line that has been seen, or felt by touch; and the faint copy cannot be more perfect than the original. Now of such right lines, it is evident that the axioms of geometry are not precisely true; for two lines that are straight to our sight or touch may include a space, or they may meet in more points than one. If, therefore, we cannot form any notion of a straight line more accurate than that which we have from the senses of sight and touch, geometry has no solid foundation. If, on the other hand, the geometrical axioms are precisely true, the idea of a right line is not copied from any impression of sight or touch, but must have a different origin and a more perfect standard.

As the geometrician, by reflecting only upon the extension and figure of matter, forms a set of notions more accurate and scientific than any which the senses exhibit, so the natural philosopher, reflecting upon other attributes of matter, forms another set, such as those of density, quantity of matter, velocity, momentum, fluidity, elasticity, centres of gravity, and of oscillation. These notions are accurate and scientific; but they cannot enter into a mind that has not some degree of judgment, nor can we make them intelligible to children, until they have some ripeness of understanding.

In navigation, the notions of latitude, longitude, course, leeway, cannot be made intelligible to children; and so it is with regard to the terms of every science, and of every art about which we can reason. They have had their five senses as perfect as men for years before they are capable of distinguishing, comparing, and perceiving the relations of things, so as to be able to form such notions. They acquire the intellectual powers by a slow progress, and by imperceptible degrees; and by means of them, learn to form distinct and accurate notions of things, which the senses could never have imparted.

Having said so much of the notions we get from the senses alone of the objects of sense, let us next consider what notions we can have from consciousness alone of the operations of our minds.

Mr Locke very properly calls consciousness an internal sense. It gives the like immediate knowledge of things in the mind—that is, of our own thoughts and feeling—as the senses give us of things external. There is this difference, however, that an external object may be at rest, and the sense may be employed about it for some time. But the objects of consciousness are never at rest: the stream of thought flows like a river, without stopping a moment; the whole train of thought passes in succession under the eye of consciousness, which is always employed about the present. But is it consciousness that analyses complex operations, distinguishes their different ingredients, and combines them in distinct parcels under general names? This surely is not the work of consciousness, nor can it be performed without reflection, recollecting and judging of what we were conscious of, and distinctly remember. This reflection does not appear in children. Of all the powers of the mind, it seems to be of the latest growth, whereas consciousness is coeval with the earliest.

Consciousness, being a kind of internal sense, can no more give us distinct and accurate notions of the operations of our minds, than the external senses can give of external objects. Reflection upon the operations of our minds is the same kind of operation with that by which we form distinct notions of external objects. They differ not in their nature, but in this only, that one is employed about external, and the other about internal objects; and both may, with equal propriety, be called reflection.

Mr Locke has restricted the word reflection to that which is employed about the operations of our minds, without any authority, as I think, from custom, the arbiter of language. For, surely, I may reflect upon what I have seen or heard, as well as upon what I have thought. The word, in its proper and common meaning, is equally applicable to objects of sense, and to objects of consciousness. He has likewise confounded reflection with consciousness, and seems not to have been aware that they are different powers, and appear at very different periods of life.

If that eminent philosopher had been aware of these mistakes about the meaning of the word reflection, he would, I think, have seen that, as it is by reflection upon the operations of our own minds that we can form any distinct and accurate notions of them, and not by consciousness without reflection, so it is by reflection upon the objects of sense, and not by the senses without reflection, that we can form distinct notions of them. Reflection upon anything, whether external or internal, makes it an object of our intellectual powers, by which we survey it on all sides, and form such judgments about it as appear to be just and true.

I proposed, in the *third* place, to consider our notions of the relations of things: and here I think, that, without judgment, we cannot have any notion of relations.

There are two ways in which we get the notion of relations. The first is, by comparing the related objects, when

we have before had the conception of both. By this comparison, we perceive the relation, either immediately, or by a
process of reasoning. That my foot is longer than my finger I
perceive immediately; and that three is the half of six. This
immediate perception is immediate and intuitive judgment.
That the angles at the base of an isosceles triangle are equal, I
perceive by a process of reasoning, in which it will be
acknowledged there is judgment.

Another way in which we get the notion of relations
(which seems not to have occurred to Mr Locke) is, when, by
attention to one of the related objects, we perceive or judge
that it must, from its nature, have a certain relation to something else, which before, perhaps, we never thought of; and
thus our attention to one of the related objects produces the
notion of a correlate, and of a certain relation between them.

Thus, when I attend to colour, figure, weight, I cannot
help judging these to be qualities which cannot exist without
a subject; that is, something which is coloured, figured,
heavy. If I had not perceived such things to be qualities, I
should never have had any notion of their subject, or of their
relation to it.

By attending to the operations of thinking, memory,
reasoning, we perceive or judge that there must be something which thinks, remembers, and reasons, which we call
the mind. When we attend to any change that happens in
Nature, judgment informs us that there must be a cause of
this change, which had power to produce it; and thus we get
the notions of cause and effect, and of the relation between
them. When we attend to body, we perceive that it cannot
exist without space; hence we get the notion of space, (which
is neither an object of sense nor of consciousness,) and of the
relation which bodies have to a certain portion of unlimited
space, as their place.

I apprehend, therefore, that all our notions of relations
may more properly be ascribed to judgment as their source
and origin, than to any other power of the mind. We must
first perceive relations by our judgment, before we can conceive them without judging of them; as we must first perceive colours by sight, before we can conceive them without
seeing them. I think Mr Locke, when he comes to speak of
the ideas of relations, does not say that they are ideas of sen-

sation or reflection, but only that they terminate in, and are concerned about, ideas of sensation or reflection.

The notions of unity and number are so abstract, that it is impossible they should enter into the mind until it has some degree of judgment. We see with what difficulty, and how slowly, children learn to use, with understanding, the names even of small numbers, and how they exult in this acquisition when they have attained it. Every number is conceived by the relation which it bears to unity, or to known combinations of units; and upon that account, as well as on account of its abstract nature, all distinct notions of it require some degree of judgment.

In its proper place, I shall have occasion to show that judgment is an ingredient in all determinations of taste, in all moral determinations, and in many of our passions and affections. So that this operation, after we come to have any exercise of judgment, mixes with most of the operations of our minds, and, in analysing them, cannot be overlooked without confusion and error.

Chapter IV

Of first principles in general.

One of the most important distinctions of our judgments is, that some of them are intuitive, others grounded on argument.

It is not in our power to judge as we will. The judgment is carried along necessarily by the evidence, real or seeming, which appears to us at the time. But, in propositions that are submitted to our judgment, there is this great difference — some are of such a nature that a man of ripe understanding may apprehend them distinctly, and perfectly understand their meaning, without finding himself under any necessity of believing them to be true or false, probable or improbable. The judgment remains in suspense, until it is inclined to one side or another by reasons or arguments.

But there are other propositions which are no sooner understood than they are believed. The judgment follows the apprehension of them necessarily, and both are equally the work of nature, and the result of our original powers. There is no searching for evidence, no weighing of arguments; the proposition is not deduced or inferred from another; it has the light of truth in itself, and has no occasion to borrow it from another.

Propositions of the last kind, when they are used in matters of science, have commonly been called *axioms*; and on whatever occasion they are used, are called *first principles, principles of common sense, common notions, self-evident truths*.[…]

What has been said, I think, is sufficient to distinguish first principles, or intuitive judgments, from those which may be ascribed to the power of reasoning; nor is it a just objection against this distinction, that there may be some judgments concerning which we may be dubious to which class they ought to be referred. There is a real distinction between persons within the house, and those that are without; yet it may be dubious to which the man belongs that stands upon the threshold.

The power of reasoning — that is, of drawing a conclusion from a chain of premises — may with some propriety be called an art. 'All reasoning,' says Mr Locke, 'is search and casting about, and requires pains and application.' It resembles the power of walking, which is acquired by use and exercise. Nature prompts to it, and has given the power of acquiring it; but must be aided by frequent exercise before we are able to walk. After repeated efforts, much stumbling, and many falls, we learn to walk; and it is in a similar manner that we learn to reason.

But the power of judging in self-evident propositions, which are clearly understood, may be compared to the power of swallowing our food. It is purely natural, and therefore common to the learned and the unlearned, to the trained and the untrained. It requires ripeness of understanding, and freedom from prejudice, but nothing else.

I take it for granted that there are self-evident principles. Nobody, I think, denies it. And if any man were so sceptical as to deny that there is any proposition that is self-evident, I see not how it would be possible to convince him by reasoning.[…]

[N]ature hath not left us destitute of means whereby the candid and honest part of mankind may be brought to unanimity when they happen to differ about first principles.

When men differ about things that are taken to be first principles or self-evident truths, reasoning seems to be at an end. Each party appeals to common sense. When one man's common sense gives one determination, another man's a contrary determination, there seems to be no remedy but to leave every man to enjoy his own opinion. This is a common observation, and, I believe, a just one, if it be rightly understood.

It is in vain to reason with a man who denies the first principles on which the reasoning is grounded. Thus, it would be in vain to attempt the proof of a proposition in Euclid to a man who denies the axioms. Indeed, we ought never to reason with men who deny first principles from obstinacy and unwillingness to yield to reason.

But is it not possible, that men who really love truth, and are open to conviction, may differ about first principles?

I think it is possible, and that it cannot, without great want of charity, be denied to be possible.

When this happens, every man who believes that there is a real distinction between truth and error, and that the faculties which God has given us are not in their nature fallacious, must be convinced that there is a defect or a perversion of judgment on the one side or the other

A man of candour and humility will, in such a case, very naturally suspect his own judgment, so far as to be desirous to enter into a serious examination, even of what he has long held as a first principle. He will think it not impossible, that, although his heart be upright, his judgment may have been perverted by education, by authority, by party zeal, or by some other of the common causes of error, from the influence of which neither parts nor integrity exempt the human understanding.[…]

It is true that, in other controversies, the process by which the truth of a proposition is discovered, or its falsehood detected, is by showing its necessary connection with first principles, or its repugnancy to them. It is true, likewise, that, when the controversy is whether a proposition be itself a first principle, this process cannot be applied. The truth, therefore, in controversies of this kind labours under a peculiar disadvantage. But it has advantages of another kind to compensate this.

1. For, in the *first* place, in such controversies, every man is a competent judge; and therefore it is difficult to impose upon mankind.

To judge of first principles, requires no more than a sound mind free from prejudice, and a distinct conception of the question.[…]

In matters beyond the reach of common understanding, the many are led by the few, and willingly yield to their authority. But, in matters of common sense, the few must yield to the many, when local and temporary prejudices are removed. No man is now moved by the subtle arguments of Zeno against motion, though, perhaps, he knows not how to answer them.

The ancient skeptical system furnishes a remarkable instance of this truth. That system, of which Pyrrho was reputed the father, was carried down, through a succession of ages, by very able and acute philosophers, who taught men to believe nothing at all, and esteemed it the highest pitch of human wisdom to withhold assent from every proposition whatsoever.[…]

Yet, as this system was an insult upon the common sense of mankind, it died away of itself; and it would be in vain to attempt to revive it. The modern skepticism is very different from the ancient, otherwise it would not have been allowed a hearing; and when it has lost the grace of novelty, it will die away also, though it should never be refuted.

The modern scepticism, I mean that of Mr Hume, is built upon principles which were very generally maintained by philosophers, though they did not see that they led to scepticism. Mr Hume, by tracing with great acuteness and ingenuity the consequences of principles commonly received, has shown that they overturn all knowledge, and at last overturn themselves, and leave the mind in perfect suspense.

2. *Secondly*, We may observe that opinions which contradict first principles, are distinguished, from other errors, by this:—That they are not only false but absurd; and, to discountenance absurdity, nature hath given us a particular emotion—to wit, that of ridicule—which seems intended for this very purpose of putting out of countenance what is absurd, either in opinion or practice.

This weapon, when properly applied, cuts with as keen an edge as argument. Nature hath furnished us with the first to expose absurdity; as with the last to refute error. Both are well fitted for their several offices, and are equally friendly to truth when properly used.

Both may be abused to serve the cause of error; but the same degree of judgment which serves to detect the abuse of argument in false reasoning, serves to detect the abuse of ridicule when it is wrong directed.[…]

But it must be acknowledged that the emotion of ridicule, even when most natural, may be stifled by an emotion of a contrary nature, and cannot operate till that is removed.

Thus, if the notion of sanctity is annexed to an object, it is no longer a laughable matter; and this visor must be pulled off before it appears ridiculous.[…]

But, if ever we are able to view it naked, and stripped of those adventitious circumstances from which it borrowed its importance and authority, the natural emotion of ridicule will exert its force. An absurdity can be entertained by men of sense no longer than it wears a mask. When any man is found who has the skill or the boldness to pull off the mask, it can no longer bear the light; it slinks into dark corners for a while, and then is no more heard of, but as an object of ridicule.[…]

3. *Thirdly*, It may be observed, that, although it is contrary to the nature of first principles to admit of direct or *apodictical* proof; yet there are certain ways of reasoning even about them, by which those that are just and solid may be confirmed, and those that are false may be detected. It may here be proper to mention some of the topics from which we may reason in matters of this kind.

First, It is a good argument *ad hominem,* if it can be shown that a first principle which a man rejects stands, upon the same footing with others which he admits; for, when this is the case, he must be guilty of an inconsistency who holds the one and rejects the other.[…]

Secondly, A first principle may admit of a proof *ad absurdum.*

In this kind of proof, which is very common in mathematics, we suppose the contradictory proposition to be true. We trace the consequences of that supposition in a train of reasoning; and, if we find any of its necessary consequences to be manifestly absurd, we conclude the supposition from which it followed to be false; and, therefore its contradictory to be true.[…]

Thirdly, I conceive that the consent of ages and nations, of the learned and unlearned, ought to have great authority with regard to first principles, where every man is a competent judge.

Our ordinary conduct in life is built upon first principles, as well as our speculations in philosophy; and every motive to action supposes some belief. When we find a general agreement among men, in principles that concern human life, this must have great authority with every sober mind that loves truth.

It is pleasant to observe the fruitless pains which Bishop Berkeley takes to show that his system of the non-existence of a material world did not contradict the sentiments of the vulgar, but those only of the philosophers.

With good reason he dreaded more to oppose the authority of vulgar opinion in a matter of this kind, than all the schools of philosophers.

Here, perhaps, it will be said, What has authority to do in matters of opinion? Is truth to be determined by most votes? Or is authority to be again raised out of its grave to tyrannise over mankind?

I am aware that, in this age, an advocate for authority has a very unfavourable plea; but I wish to give no more to authority than is its due.

Most justly do we honour the names of those benefactors to mankind who have contributed more or less to break the yoke of that authority which deprives men of the natural, the unalienable right of judging for themselves; but, while we indulge a just animosity against this authority, and against all who would subject us to its tyranny, let us remember how common the folly is, of going from one faulty extreme into the opposite.

Authority, though a very tyrannical mistress to private judgment, may yet, on some occasions, be a useful handmaid. This is all she is entitled to, and this is all I plead in her behalf.

The justice of this plea will appear by putting a case in a science, in which, of all sciences, authority is acknowledged to have least weight.

Suppose a mathematician has made a discovery in that science which he thinks important; that he has put his demonstration in just order; and, after examining it with an attentive eye, has found no flaw in it, I would ask, Will there not be still in his breast some diffidence, some jealousy, lest the ardour of invention may have made him overlook some false step? This must be granted.

He commits his demonstration to the examination of a mathematical friend, whom he esteems a competent judge, and waits with impatience the issue of his judgment. Here I would ask again, Whether the verdict of his friend, according as it is favourable or unfavourable, will not greatly increase or diminish his confidence in his own judgment? Most certainly it will, and it ought.

If the judgment of his friend agree with his own, especially if it be confirmed by two or three able judges, he rests secure of his discovery without further examination; but if it be unfavourable, he is brought back into a kind of suspense, until the part that is suspected undergoes a new and a more rigorous examination.[…]

In a matter of common sense, every man is no less a competent judge than a mathematician is in a mathematical demonstration; and there must be a great presumption that the judgment of mankind, in such a matter, is the natural issue of those faculties which God hath given them. Such a judgment can be erroneous only when there is some cause of the error, as general as the error is. When this can be shown to be the case, I acknowledge it ought to have its due weight. But, to suppose a general deviation from truth among mankind in things self-evident, of which no cause can be assigned, is highly unreasonable.[…]

There are other opinions that appear to be universal, from what is common in the structure of all languages.

Language is the express image and picture of human thoughts; and from the picture we may draw some certain conclusions concerning the original.

We find in all languages the same parts of speech; we find nouns, substantive and adjective; verbs, active and passive, in their various tenses, numbers, and moods. Some rules of syntax are the same in all languages.

Now, what is common in the structure of languages, indicates a uniformity of opinion in those things upon which that structure is grounded.

The distinction between substances and the qualities belonging to them; between thought and the being that thinks; between thought and the objects of thought; is to be found in the structure of all languages. And, therefore, systems of philosophy, which abolish those distinctions, wage war with the common sense of mankind.

We are apt to imagine that those who formed languages were no metaphysicians; but the first principles of all sciences are the dictates of common sense, and lie open to all men; and every man who has considered the structure of language in a philosophical light, will find infallible proofs that those who have framed it, and those who use it with understanding, have the power of making accurate distinctions, and of forming general conceptions, as well as philosophers. Nature has given those powers to all men, and they can use them when occasions require it, but they leave it to the philosophers to give names to them, and to descant upon their nature. In like manner, nature has given eyes to all men, and they can make good use of them; but the structure of the eye, and the theory of vision, is the business of philosophers.

Fourthly, Opinions that appear so early in the minds of men that they cannot be the effect of education or of false reasoning, have a good claim to be considered as first principles. Thus, the belief we have that the persons about us are living and intelligent beings, is a belief for which, perhaps, we can give some reason, when we are able to reason; but we had this belief before we could reason, and before we could learn it by instruction. It seems, therefore, to be an immediate effect of our constitution.

The *last topic* I shall mention is, when an opinion is so necessary in the conduct of life, that, without the belief of it, a man must be led into a thousand absurdities in practice, such an opinion, when we can give no other reason for it, may safely be taken for a first principle.

Thus I have endeavoured to show, that, although first principles are not capable of direct proof, yet differences, that may happen with regard to them among men of candour, are not without remedy; that Nature has not left us destitute of means by which we may discover errors of this kind; and that there are ways of reasoning, with regard to first principles, by which those that are truly such may be distinguished from vulgar errors or prejudices.

Chapter V

The first principles of contingent truths.

[I]t is necessary that the first principles of knowledge be distinguished from other truths, and presented to view, that they may be sifted and examined on all sides. In order to this end, I shall attempt a detail of those I take to be such, and of the reasons why I think them entitled to that character.[…]

The truths that fall within the compass of human knowledge, whether they be self-evident, or deduced from those that are self-evident, may be reduced to two classes. They are either necessary and immutable truths, whose contrary is impossible; or they are contingent and mutable, depending upon some effect of will and power which had a beginning, and may have an end.

That a cone is the third part of a cylinder of the same base and the same altitude, is a necessary truth. It depends not upon the will and power of any being. It is immutably true, and the contrary impossible. That the sun is the centre about which the earth, and the other planets of our system, perform their revolutions, is a truth; but it is not a necessary truth. It depends upon the power and will of that Being who made the sun and all the planets, and who gave them those motions that seemed best to him.[…]

As the minds of men are occupied much more about truths that are contingent than about those that are necessary, I shall first endeavour to point out the principles of the former kind.

1. *First*, then, I hold, as a first principle, the existence of everything of which I am conscious.

Consciousness is an operation of the understanding of its own kind, and cannot be logically defined. The objects of it are our present pains, our pleasures, our hopes, our fears, our desires, our doubts, our thoughts of every kind; in a word, all the passions and all the actions and operations of our own minds while they are present. We may remember them when they are past; but we are conscious of them only while they are present.

When a man is conscious of pain, he is certain of its existence; when he is conscious that he doubts or believes, he is certain of the existence of those operations.

But the irresistible conviction he has of the reality of those operations is not the effect of reasoning; it is immediate and intuitive. The existence therefore of those passions and operations of our minds, of which we are conscious, is a first principle which nature requires us to believe upon her authority.

If I am asked to prove that I cannot be deceived by consciousness—to prove that it is not a fallacious sense—I can find no proof. I cannot find any antecedent truth from which it is deduced, or upon which its evidence depends. It seems to disdain any such derived authority, and to claim my assent in its own right.

If any man could be found so frantic as to deny that he thinks, while he is conscious of it, I may wonder, I may laugh, or I may pity him, but I cannot reason the matter with him. We have no common principles from which we may reason, and therefore can never join issue in an argument.

This, I think, is the only principle of common sense that has never directly been called in question. It seems to be so firmly rooted in the minds of men, as to retain its authority with the greatest sceptics. Mr Hume, after annihilating body and mind, time and space, action and causation, and even his own mind, acknowledges the reality of the thoughts, sensations, and passions of which he is conscious.[…]

2. Another first principle, I think, is, *That the thoughts of which I am conscious are the thoughts of a being which I call myself, my mind, my person.*

The thoughts and feelings of which we are conscious are continually changing, and the thought of this moment is not the thought of the last; but something which I call myself, remains under this change of thought. This self has the same relation to all the successive thoughts I am conscious of— they are all my thoughts; and every thought which is not my thought, must be the thought of some other person.

If any man asks a proof of this, I confess I can give none; there is an evidence in the proposition itself which I am unable to resist. Shall I think that thought can stand by itself without a thinking being? or that ideas can feel pleasure or pain? My nature dictates to me that it is impossible.[…]

3. Another first principle I take to be — *That those things did really happen which I distinctly remember*.

This has one of the surest marks of a first principle; for no man ever pretended to prove it, and yet no man in his wits calls it in question: the testimony of memory, like that of consciousness, is immediate; it claims our assent upon its own authority.[…]

4. Another first principle is, *Our own personal identity and continued existence, as far back as we remember anything distinctly*.

This we know immediately, and not by reasoning. It seems, indeed, to be a part of the testimony of memory. Everything we remember has such a relation to ourselves as to imply necessarily our existence at the time remembered. And there cannot be a more palpable absurdity than that a man should remember what happened before he existed. He must therefore have existed as far back as he remembers anything distinctly, if his memory be not fallacious. This principle, therefore, is so connected with the last mentioned that it may be doubtful whether both ought not to be included in one. Let everyone judge of this as he sees reason.[…]

5. Another first principle is, *That those things do really exist which we distinctly perceive by our senses, and are what we perceive them to be*.

It is too evident to need proof, that all men are by nature led to give implicit faith to the distinct testimony of their senses, long before they are capable of any bias from prejudices of education or of philosophy.[…]

6. Another first principle, I think, is, *That we have some degree of power over our actions, and the determinations of our will*.

All power must be derived from the fountain of power, and of every good gift. Upon his good pleasure its continuance depends, and it is always subject to his control.

Beings to whom God has given any degree of power, and understanding to direct them to the proper use of it, must be accountable to their Maker. But those who are entrusted with no power can have no account to make; for all good conduct consists in the right use of power, all bad conduct in the abuse of it.[…]

It is not easy to say in what way we first get the notion or idea of *power*. It is neither an object of sense nor of consciousness. We see events, one succeeding another; but we see not the power by which they are produced. We are conscious of the operations of our minds; but power is not an operation of mind. If we had no notions but such as are furnished by the external senses, and by consciousness, it seems to be impossible that we should ever have any conception of power. Accordingly, Mr Hume, who has reasoned the most accurately upon this hypothesis, denies that we have any idea of power, and clearly refutes the account given by Mr Locke of the origin of this idea.

But it is in vain to reason from a hypothesis against a fact, the truth of which every man may see by attending to his own thoughts. It is evident that all men, very early in life, not only have an idea of power, but a conviction that they have some degree of it in themselves; for this conviction is necessarily implied in many operations of mind, which are familiar to every man, and without which no man can act the part of a reasonable being.

First, It is implied in every act of volition. 'Volition, it is plain,' says Mr Locke, 'is an act of the mind, knowingly exerting that dominion which it takes itself to have over any part of the man, by employing it in, or withholding it from, any particular action.' Every volition, therefore, implies a conviction of power to do the action willed. A man may desire to make a visit to the moon, or to the planet Jupiter; but nothing but insanity could make him will to do so. And, if even insanity produced this effect, it must be by making him think it to be in his power.

Secondly, This conviction is implied in all deliberation; for no man in his wits deliberates whether he shall do what he believes not to be in his power. *Thirdly*, The same conviction is implied in every resolution or purpose formed in consequence of deliberation. A man may as well form a resolution to pull the moon out of her sphere, as to do the most insignificant action which he believes not to be in his power. The same thing may be said of every promise or contract wherein a man plights his faith; for he is not an honest man who promises what he does not believe he has power to perform.

As these operations imply a belief of some degree of power in ourselves; so there are others equally common and familiar which imply a like belief with regard to others.

When we impute to a man any action or omission, as a ground of approbation or of blame, we must believe he had power to do otherwise. The same is implied in all advice, exhortation, command, and rebuke, and in every case in which we rely upon his fidelity in performing any engagement of executing any trust.[…]

7. Another first principle is — *That the natural faculties, by which we distinguish truth from error, are not fallacious.* If any man should demand a proof of this, it is impossible to satisfy him. For, suppose it should be mathematically demonstrated, this would signify nothing in this case; because, to judge of a demonstration, a man must trust his faculties, and take for granted the very thing in question.[…]

8. Another first principle relating to existence, is, *That there is life and intelligence in our fellow-men with whom we converse.*

As soon as children are capable of asking a question, or of answering a question, as soon as they show the signs of love, of resentment, or of any other affection, they must be convinced that those with whom they have this intercourse are intelligent beings.

It is evident they are capable of such intercourse long before they can reason. Every one knows that there is a social intercourse between the nurse and the child before it is a year old. It can, at that age, understand many things that are said to it.

It can by signs ask and refuse, threaten and supplicate. It clings to its nurse in danger, enters into her grief and joy, is happy in her soothing and caresses, and unhappy in her displeasure. That these things cannot be without a conviction in the child that the nurse is an intelligent being, I think must be granted.

Now, I would ask how a child of a year old comes by this conviction? Not by reasoning surely, for children do not reason at that age. Nor is it by external senses, for life and intelligence are not objects of the external senses.[…]

[…] This belief stands upon another foundation than that of reasoning; and therefore, whether a man can give good reasons for it or not, it is not in his power to shake it off.

Setting aside this natural conviction, I believe the best reason we can give, to prove that other men are living and intelligent, is, that their words and actions indicate like powers of understanding as we are conscious of in ourselves. The very same argument applied to the works of nature, leads us to conclude that there is an intelligent Author of nature, and appears equally strong and obvious in the last case as in the first; so that it may be doubted whether men, by the mere exercise of reasoning, might not as soon discover the existence of a Deity, as that other men have life and intelligence.[…]

9. Another first principle I take to be, *That certain features of the countenance, sounds of the voice, and gestures of the body, indicate certain thoughts and dispositions of mind*.[…]

10. Another first principle appears to me to be — *That there is a certain regard due to human testimony in matters of fact, and even to human authority in matters of opinion*.

11. *There are many events depending upon the will of man, in which there is a self-evident probability, greater or less, according to circumstances*.

There may be in some individuals such a degree of frenzy and madness, that no man can say what they may or may not do. Such persons we find it necessary to put under restraint, that as far as possible they may be kept from doing harm to themselves or to others. They are not considered as reasonable creatures, or members of society. But, as to men who have a sound mind, we depend upon a certain degree of regularity in their conduct; and could put a thousand different cases, wherein we could venture, ten to one, that they will act in such a way, and not in the contrary.

If we had no confidence in our fellow-men that they will act such a part in such circumstances, it would be impossible to live in society with them. For that which makes men capable of living in society, and uniting in a political body under government, is, that their actions will always be regulated, in a great measure, by the common principles of human nature.

It may always be expected that they will regard their own interest and reputation, and that of their families and friends; that they will repel injuries, and have some sense of good offices; and that they will have some regard to truth and justice, so far at least as not to swerve from them without temptation.

It is upon such principles as these, that all political reasoning is grounded. Such reasoning is never demonstrative; but it may have a very great degree of probability, especially when applied to great bodies of men.

12. The last principle of contingent truths I mention is, *That, in the phænomena of nature, what is to be will probably be like to what has been in similar circumstances.*

We must have this conviction as soon as we are capable of learning anything from experience; for all experience is grounded upon a belief that the future will be like the past. Take away this principle, and the experience of a hundred years makes us no wiser with regard to what is to come.

This is one of those principles which, when we grow up and observe the course of nature, we can confirm by reasoning. We perceive that Nature is governed by fixed laws, and that, if it were not so, there could be no such thing as prudence in human conduct; there would be no fitness in any means to promote an end, and what on one occasion promoted it might as probably, on another occasion, obstruct it.

But the principle is necessary for us before we are able to discover it by reasoning, and therefore is made a part of our constitution, and produces its effects before the use of reason.[…]

I do not at all affirm, that those I have mentioned are all the first principles from which we may reason concerning contingent truths. Such enumerations, even when made after much reflection, are seldom perfect.

Chapter VI

First principles of necessary truths.

About most of the first principles of necessary truths there has been no dispute, and therefore it is the less necessary to dwell upon them. It will be sufficient to divide them into different classes; to mention some, by way of specimen, in each class; and to make some remarks on those of which the truth has been called in question.

They may, I think, most properly be divided according to the sciences to which they belong.

1. There are some first principles that may be called *grammatical*: such as, *That every adjective in a sentence must belong to some substantive expressed or understood; That every complete sentence must have a verb.*[…]

2. There are *logical* axioms: such as, *That any contexture of words which does not make a proposition is neither true nor false; That every proposition is either true or false; That no proposition can be both true and false at the same time; That reasoning in a circle proves nothing; That whatever may be truly affirmed of a genus, may be truly affirmed of all the species, and all the individuals belonging to that genus.*

3. Everyone knows there are *mathematical* axioms. Mathematicians have, from the days of Euclid, very wisely laid down the axioms or first principles on which they reason. And the effect which this appears to have had upon the stability and happy progress of this science, gives no small encouragement to attempt to lay the foundation of other sciences in a similar manner, as far as we are able.[…]

4. I think there are axioms even in matters of *taste*. Notwithstanding the variety found among men in taste, there are, I apprehend, some common principles even in matters of this kind. I never heard of any man who thought it a beauty in a human face to want a nose, or an eye, or to have the mouth on one side.[…]

There is a taste that is acquired and a taste that is natural. This holds with respect both to the external sense of taste and the internal. Habit and fashion have a powerful influence upon both.

Of tastes that are natural, there are some that may be called rational, others that are merely animal.

Children are delighted with brilliant and gaudy colours, with romping and noisy mirth, with feats of agility, strength, or cunning; and savages have much the same taste as children.

But there are tastes that are more intellectual. It is the dictate of our rational nature that love and admiration are misplaced when there is no intrinsic worth in the object.

In those operations of taste which are rational, we judge of the real worth and excellence of the object, and our love or admiration is guided by that judgment. In such operations there is judgment as well as feeling, and the feeling depends upon the judgment we form of the object.

I do not maintain that taste, so far as it is acquired or so far as it is merely animal, can be reduced to principles. But, as far as it is founded on judgment, it certainly may.

The virtues, the graces, the muses, have a beauty that is intrinsic. It lies not in the feelings of the spectator, but in the real excellence of the object. If we do not perceive their beauty, it is owing to the defect or to the perversion of our faculties.[…]

[T]hat taste which we may call rational, is that part of our constitution by which we are made to receive pleasure from the contemplation of what we conceive to be excellent in its kind, the pleasure being annexed to this judgment, and regulated by it. This taste may be true or false, according as it is founded on a true or false judgment. And if it may be true or false, it must have first principles.

5. There are also first principles in *morals*.

That an unjust action has more demerit than an ungenerous one; That a generous action has more merit than a merely just one; That no man ought to be blamed for what it was not in his power to hinder; That we ought not to do to others what we would think unjust or unfair to be done to us in like circumstances. These are moral axioms, and many others might be named which appear to me to have no less evidence than those of mathematics.

Some perhaps may think that our determinations, either in matters of taste or in morals, ought not to be accounted necessary truths: That they are grounded upon the constitution of that faculty which we call taste, and of that which we call the moral sense or conscience; which faculties might have been so constituted as to have given determinations different, or even contrary to those they now give: That, as there is nothing sweet or bitter in itself, but according as it agrees or disagrees with the external sense called taste; so there is nothing beautiful or ugly in itself but according as it agrees or disagrees with the internal sense, which we also call taste; and nothing morally good or ill in itself, but according as it agrees or disagrees with our moral sense.

This indeed is a system, with regard to morals and taste, which hath been supported in modern times by great authorities. And if this system be true, the consequence must be, that there can be no principles, either of taste or of morals, that are necessary truths. For, according to this system, all our determinations, both with regard to matters of taste, and with regard to morals, are reduced to matters of fact — I mean to such as these, that by our constitution we have on such occasions certain agreeable feelings, and on other occasions certain disagreeable feelings.

But I cannot help being of a contrary opinion, being persuaded that a man who determined that polite behaviour has great deformity, and that there is great beauty in rudeness and ill-breeding, would judge wrong, whatever his feelings were.

In like manner, I cannot help thinking that a man who determined that there is more moral worth in cruelty, perfidy, and injustice, than in generosity, justice, prudence, and temperance would judge wrong, whatever his constitution was.

And, if it be true that there is judgment in our determinations of taste and of morals, it must be granted that what is true or false in morals, or in matters of taste, is necessarily so. For this reason, I have ranked the first principles of morals and of taste under the class of necessary truths.

6. The last class of first principles I shall mention we may call *metaphysical*.

I shall particularly consider three of these, because they have been called in question by Mr Hume.

The *first* is, *That the qualities which we perceive by our senses must have a subject, which we call body, and that the thoughts we are conscious of must have a subject, which we call mind.*

It is not more evident that two and two make four, than it is that figure cannot exist, unless there be something that is figured, nor motion without something that is moved. I not only perceive figure and motion, but I perceive them to be qualities. They have a necessary relation to something in which they exist as their subject. The difficulty which some philosophers have found in admitting this, is entirely owing to the theory of ideas. A subject of the sensible qualities which we perceive by our senses, is not an idea either of sensation or of consciousness; therefore say they, we have no such idea. Or, in the style of Mr Hume, from what impression is the idea of substance derived? It is not a copy of any impression; therefore there is no such idea.

The distinction between sensible qualities and the substance to which they belong, and between thought and the mind that thinks, is not the invention of philosophers; it is found in the structure of all languages, and therefore must be common to all men who speak with understanding. And I believe no man, however sceptical he may be in speculation, can talk on the common affairs of life for half an hour, without saying things that imply his belief of the reality of these distinctions.[…]

The *second* metaphysical principle I mention is — *That whatever begins to exist, must have a cause which produced it.*

Philosophy is indebted to Mr Hume in this respect among others, that, by calling in question many of the first principles of human knowledge, he hath put speculative men upon inquiring more carefully than was done before into the nature of the evidence upon which they rest. Truth can never suffer by a fair inquiry; it can bear to be seen naked and in the fullest light, and the strictest examination will always turn out in the issue to its advantage. I believe Mr Hume was the first who ever called in question whether things that begin to exist must have a cause.

With regard to this point, we must hold one of these three things, either that it is an opinion for which we have no evidence, and which men have foolishly taken up without ground; or, *secondly*, That it is capable of direct proof by argument; or, *thirdly*, That it is self-evident, and needs no proof, but ought to be received as an axiom, which cannot, by reasonable men, be called in question.

The first of these suppositions would put an end to all philosophy, to all religion, to all reasoning that would carry us beyond the objects of sense, and to all prudence in the conduct of life.

As to the second supposition, that this principle may be proved by direct reasoning, I am afraid we shall find the proof extremely difficult, if not altogether impossible.

I know only of three or four arguments that have been urged by philosophers, in the way of abstract reasoning, to prove that things which begin to exist must have a cause.

One is offered by Mr Hobbes, another by Dr Samuel Clarke, another by Mr Locke. Mr Hume in his *Treatise of Human Nature* has examined them all; and in my opinion has shown that they take for granted the thing to be proved; a kind of false reasoning, which men are very apt to fall into when they attempt to prove what is self-evident.

It has been thought, that, although this principle does not admit of proof from abstract reasoning, it may be proved from experience, and may be justly drawn by induction, from instances that fall within our observation.

I conceive this method of proof will leave us in great uncertainty, for these three reasons:

1st, Because the proposition to be proved is not a contingent but a *necessary* proposition. It is not that things which begin to exist commonly have a cause, or even that they always in fact have a cause; but that they must have a cause and cannot begin to exist without a cause.

Propositions of this kind, from their nature, are incapable of proof by induction. Experience informs us only of what *is* or *has been*, not of what *must be*; and the conclusion must be of the same nature with the premises.

For this reason, no mathematical proposition can be proved by induction. Though it should be found by experience in a thousand cases, that the area of a plane triangle is equal to the rectangle under the altitude and half the base, this would not prove that it must be so in all cases, and cannot be otherwise; which is what the mathematician affirms.

In like manner, though we had the most ample experimental proof that things which have begun to exist had a cause, this would not prove that they must have a cause. Experience may show us what is the established course of nature, but can never show what connections of things are in their nature necessary.

2ndly, General maxims, grounded on experience, have only a degree of probability proportioned to the extent of our experience, and ought always to be understood so as to leave room for exceptions, if future experience shall discover any such.

The law of gravitation has as full a proof from experience and induction as any principle can be supposed to have. Yet, if any philosopher should, by clear experiment, show that there is a kind of matter in some bodies which does not gravitate, the law of gravitation ought to be limited by that exception.

Now it is evident that men have never considered the principle of the necessity of cause, as a truth of this kind which may admit of limitation or exception; and therefore it has not been received upon this kind of evidence.

3rdly, I do not see that experience could satisfy us that every change in nature actually has a cause.

In the far greatest part of the changes in nature that fall within our observation, the causes are unknown; and, therefore, from experience, we cannot know whether they have causes or not.

Causation is not an object of sense. The only experience we can have of it, is in the consciousness we have of exerting some power in ordering our thoughts and actions. But this experience is surely too narrow a foundation for a general conclusion, that all things that have had or shall have a beginning, must have a cause.

For these reasons, this principle cannot be drawn from experience, any more than from abstract reasoning.

The *third* supposition is—That it is to be admitted as a first or self-evident principle. Two reasons may be urged for this.

1. The universal consent of mankind, not of philosophers only, but of the rude and unlearned vulgar.

Mr Hume, as far as I know, was the first that ever expressed any doubt of this principle. And when we consider that he has rejected every principle of human knowledge, excepting that of consciousness, and has not even spared the axioms of mathematics, his authority is of small weight.[...]

'It is', says he, 'a maxim in philosophy that whatever begins to exist must have a cause of existence. This is commonly taken for granted in all reasonings, without any proof given or demanded. It is supposed to be founded on intuition, and to be one of those maxims which, though they may be denied with the lips, it is impossible for men in their hearts really to doubt of. But, if we examine this maxim by the idea of knowledge above explained, we shall discover in it no mark of such intuitive certainty.' The meaning of this seems to be that it did not suit with his theory of intuitive certainty, and, therefore, he excludes it from that privilege.

The vulgar adhere to this maxim as firmly and universally as the philosophers. Their superstitions have the same origin as the systems of philosophers—to wit, a desire to know the causes of things. *Felix qui potuit rerum cognoscere causas*[5] is the universal sense of men; but to say that anything can happen without a cause, shocks the common sense of a savage.

This universal belief of mankind is easily accounted for, if we allow that the necessity of a cause of every event is obvious to the rational powers of a man. But it is impossible to account for it otherwise. It cannot be ascribed to education, to systems of philosophy, or to priestcraft. One would think that a philosopher who takes it to be a general delusion or prejudice, would endeavour to show from what causes in human nature such a general error may take its rise. But I forget that Mr Hume might answer upon his own principles, that since things may happen without a cause—this error and delusion of men may be universal without any cause.

2. A second reason why I conceive this to be a first principle, is, That mankind not only assent to it in speculation, but that the practice of life is grounded upon it in the most important matters, even in cases where experience leaves us doubtful; and it is impossible to act with common prudence if we set it aside.[…]

Suppose a man to be found dead on the highway, his skull fractured, his body pierced with deadly wounds, his watch and money carried off. The coroner's jury sits upon the body; and the question is put, What was the cause of this man's death?—was it accident, or *felo de se,*[6] or murder by persons unknown? Let us suppose an adept in Mr Hume's philosophy to make one of the jury, and that he insists upon the previous question, whether there was any cause of the event, and whether it happened without a cause.

Surely, upon Mr Hume's principles, a great deal might be said upon this point; and if the matter is to be determined by past experience, it is dubious on which side the weight of argument might stand. But we may venture to say, that, if

Mr Hume had been of such a jury, he would have laid aside his philosophical principles, and acted according to the dictates of common prudence.

Many passages might be produced, even in Mr Hume's philosophical writings, in which he, unawares, betrays the same inward conviction of the necessity of causes which is common to other men. I shall mention only one, in the *Treatise of Human Nature* and in that part of it where he combats this very principle: 'As to those impressions', says he, 'which arise from the senses, their ultimate cause is, in my opinion, perfectly inexplicable by human reason; and it will always be impossible to decide with certainty whether they arise immediately from the object, or are produced by the creative power of the mind, or are derived from the Author of our being.'

Among these alternatives he never thought of their not arising from any cause.[…]

The [*third* and] *last* metaphysical principle I mention, which is opposed by the same author, is, *That design and intelligence in the cause may be inferred, with certainty, from marks or signs of it in the effect.*

Intelligence, design, and skill, are not objects of the external senses, nor can we be conscious of them in any person but ourselves. Even in ourselves, we cannot, with propriety, be said to be conscious of the natural or acquired talents we possess. We are conscious only of the operations of mind in which they are exerted. Indeed, a man comes to know his own mental abilities, just as he knows another man's, by the effects they produce, when there is occasion to put them to exercise.

A man's wisdom is known to us only by the signs of it in his conduct; his eloquence by the signs of it in his speech. In the same manner, we judge of his virtue, of his fortitude, and of all his talents and virtues.

Yet it is to be observed that we judge of men's talents with as little doubt or hesitation as we judge of the immediate objects of sense.

One person, we are sure, is a perfect idiot; another, who feigns idiocy to screen himself from punishment, is found, upon trial, to have the understanding of a man and to be accountable for his conduct. We perceive one man to be open, another cunning; one to be ignorant, another very knowing; one to be slow of understanding, another quick. Every man forms such judgments of those he converses with; and the common affairs of life depend upon such judgments. We can as little avoid them as we can avoid seeing what is before our eyes.

From this it appears, that it is no less a part of the human constitution, to judge of men's characters, and of their intellectual powers, from the signs of them in their actions and discourse, than to judge of corporeal objects by our senses; that such judgments are common to the whole human race that are endowed with understanding; and that they are absolutely necessary in the conduct of life.

Now, every judgment of this kind we form is only a particular application of the general principle, that intelligence, wisdom, and other mental qualities in the cause, may be inferred from their marks or signs in the effect.

The actions and discourses of men are effects, of which the actors and speakers are the causes. The effects are perceived by our senses; but the causes are behind the scene. We only conclude their existence and their degrees from our observation of the effects.

From wise conduct, we infer wisdom in the cause; from brave actions, we infer courage; and so in other cases.

This inference is made with perfect security by all men. We cannot avoid it; it is necessary in the ordinary conduct of life; it has therefore the strongest marks of being a first principle.

Perhaps some may think that this principle may be learned either by reasoning or by experience, and therefore that there is no ground to think it a first principle.

If it can be shown to be got by reasoning, by all, or the greater part of those who are governed by it, I shall very readily acknowledge that it ought not to be esteemed a first principle. But I apprehend the contrary appears from very convincing arguments.

First, The principle is too universal to be the effect of reasoning. It is common to philosophers and to the vulgar; to the learned and to the most illiterate; to the civilised and to the savage. And of those who are governed by it, not one in ten thousand can give a reason for it.

Secondly, We find philosophers, ancient and modern, who can reason excellently in subjects that admit of reasoning, when they have occasion to defend this principle, not offering reasons for it, or any *medium* of proof, but appealing to the common sense of mankind; mentioning particular instances to make the absurdity of the contrary opinion more apparent, and sometimes using the weapons of wit and ridicule, which are very proper weapons for refuting absurdities, but altogether improper in points that are to be determined by reasoning.[…]

We are next to consider whether we may not learn this truth from experience, That effects which have all the marks and tokens of design, must proceed from a designing cause.

I apprehend that we cannot learn this truth from experience for two reasons.

First, Because it is a necessary truth, not a contingent one. It agrees with the experience of mankind since the beginning of the world, that the area of a triangle is equal to half the rectangle under its base and perpendicular. It agrees no less with experience, that the sun rises in the east and sets in the west. So far as experience goes, these truths are upon an equal footing. But every man perceives this distinction between them — that the first is a necessary truth, and that it is impossible it should not be true; but the last is not necessary, but contingent, depending upon the will of Him who made the world. As we cannot learn from experience that twice three must necessarily make six, so neither can we learn from experience that certain effects must proceed from a designing and intelligent cause. Experience informs us only of what has been, but never of what must be.

Secondly, It may be observed, that experience can show a connection between a sign and the thing signified by it, in those cases only where both the sign and thing signified are perceived and have always been perceived in conjunction. But, if there be any case where the sign only is perceived, experience can never show its connection with the thing signified. Thus, for example, thought is a sign of a thinking principle or mind. But how do we know that thought cannot be without a mind? If any man should say that he knows this by experience, he deceives himself. It is impossible he can have any experience of this; because, though we have an immediate knowledge of the existence of thought in ourselves by consciousness, yet we have no immediate knowledge of a mind. The mind is not an immediate object either of sense or of consciousness. We may, therefore, justly conclude that the necessary connection between thought and a mind, or thinking being, is not learned from experience.

The same reasoning may be applied to the connection between a work excellently fitted for some purpose, and design in the author or cause of that work. One of these—to wit, the work—may be an immediate object of perception. But the design and purpose of the author cannot be an immediate object of perception; and, therefore, experience can never inform us of any connection between the one and the other, far less of a necessary connection.

Thus, I think, it appears, that the principle we have been considering—to wit, that from certain signs or indications in the effect, we may infer that there must have been intelligence, wisdom, or other intellectual or moral qualities in the cause—is a principle which we get neither by reasoning nor by experience; and, therefore, if it be a true principle, it must be a first principle. There is in the human understanding a light, by which we see immediately the evidence of it, when there is occasion to apply it.

Of how great importance this principle is in common life we have already observed. And I need hardly mention its importance in natural theology.[…]

I know of no person who ever called in question the principle now under our consideration, when it is applied to the actions and discourses of men. For this would be to deny that we have any means of discerning a wise man from an idiot, or a man that is illiterate in the highest degree from a man of knowledge and learning, which no man has the effrontery to deny.

But, in all ages, those who have been unfriendly to the principles of religion, have made attempts to weaken the force of the argument for the existence and perfections of the Deity, which is founded on this principle.[…]

[T]he most direct attack has been made upon this principle by Mr Hume, who puts an argument in the mouth of an Epicurean on which he seems to lay great stress.

The argument is, That the universe is a singular effect, and, therefore, we can draw no conclusion from it, whether it may have been made by wisdom or not.

If I understand the force of this argument, it amounts to this, That, if we had been accustomed to see worlds produced, some by wisdom and others without it, and had observed that such a world as this which we inhabit was always the effect of wisdom, we might then, from past experience, conclude that this world was made by wisdom; but having no such experience, we have no means of forming any conclusion about it.

That this is the strength of the argument appears, because, if the marks of wisdom seen in one world be no evidence of wisdom, the like marks seen in ten thousand will give as little evidence, unless, in time past, we perceived wisdom itself conjoined with the tokens of it; and from their perceived conjunction in time past, conclude that, although in the present world we see only one of the two, the other must accompany it.

Whence it appears that this reasoning of Mr Hume is built on the supposition that our inferring design from the strongest marks of it, is entirely owing to our past experience of having always found these two things conjoined. But I hope I have made it evident that this is not the case. And, indeed, it is evident that, according to this reasoning, we can have no evidence of mind or design in any of our fellowmen.

How do I know that any man of my acquaintance has understanding. I never saw his understanding? I see only certain effects, which my judgment leads me to conclude to be marks and tokens of it.

But, says the sceptical philosopher, you can conclude nothing from these tokens, unless past experience has informed you that such tokens are always joined with understanding. Alas! sir, it is impossible I can ever have this experience. The understanding of another man is no immediate object of sight, or of any other faculty which God hath given me; and unless I can conclude its existence from tokens that are visible, I have no evidence that there is understanding in any man.

It seems, then, that the man who maintains that there is no force in the argument from final causes, must, if he will be consistent, see no evidence of the existence of any intelligent being but himself.

---

1   *An Enquiry concerning Human Understanding*, Section XII.
2   Virgil, *Æneid*, Book IV, line 159: '…wishes for a boar or a tawny lion to come down from the mountain'.
3   Christian Wolff, *Philosophia prima, sive Ontologia, methodo scientifica pertractata, qua omnis, cognitionis humanae principia continentur* (Francofurti et Lipsiae, 1731), Sects. 102, 103: 'That of which we cannot form any notion is impossible; that, on the contrary, is possible to which some notion corresponds.'
4   Ovid, *Metamorphoses*, trans. F.J. Miller (Cambridge, MA: Harvard University Press, 1994), I.7: 'a rough, unordered mass of things.'
5   Virgil, *The Georgics*, in *Eclogues, Georgics, Aeneid I–VI*, trans. H. Rushton Fairclough (Cambridge, MA: Harvard University Press, 1999), Book II: 'Blessed is he who has been able to win knowledge of the cause of things.' More simply: 'Happy is the one who can know the causes of things.'
6   Literally: felon on himself, i.e. suicide.

III

Essays on the Active Powers of Man

Essay I: Of Active Power in General

Chapter I

Of the notion of active power.

[…]

1. Power is not an object of any of our external senses, nor even an object of consciousness.

That it is not seen, nor heard, nor touched, nor tasted, nor smelt, needs no proof. That we are not conscious of it, in the proper sense of that word, will be no less evident, if we reflect, that consciousness is that power of the mind by which it has an immediate knowledge of its own operations. Power is not an operation of the mind, and therefore no object of consciousness. Indeed, every operation of the mind is the exertion of some power of the mind; but we are conscious of the operation only—the power lies behind the scene; and, though we may justly infer the power from the operation, it must be remembered, that inferring is not the province of consciousness, but of reason.

I acknowledge, therefore, that our having any conception or idea of power is repugnant to Mr Locke's theory, that all our simple ideas are got either by the external senses, or by consciousness. Both cannot be true. Mr Hume perceived this repugnancy, and consistently maintained, that we have no idea of power. Mr Locke did not perceive it. If he had, it might have led him to suspect his theory; for when theory is repugnant to fact, it is easy to see which ought to yield. I am conscious that I have a *conception* or *idea* of power; but, strictly speaking, I am not conscious that I have *power*.

I shall have occasion to show, that we have very early, from our constitution, a conviction or belief of some degree of active power in ourselves. This belief, however, is not consciousness—for we may be deceived in it; but the testimony of consciousness can never deceive. Thus, a man who is struck with a palsy in the night, commonly knows not that he has lost the power of speech till he attempts to speak: he knows not whether he can move his hands and arms till he makes the trial; and if, without making trial, he consults his consciousness ever so attentively, it will give him no information whether he has lost these powers, or still retains them.

From this we must conclude, that the powers we have are not an object of consciousness, though it would be foolish to censure this way of speaking in popular discourse, which requires not accurate attention to the different provinces of our various faculties. The testimony of consciousness is always unerring, nor was it ever called in question by the greatest sceptics, ancient or modern.

2. A *second* observation is—That, as there are some things of which we have a *direct*, and others of which we have only a *relative* conception; Power belongs to the latter class.

As this distinction is overlooked by most writers in logic, I shall beg leave to illustrate it a little, and then shall apply it to the present subject.

Of some things, we know what they are in themselves: our conception of such things I call *direct*. Of other things, we know not what they are in themselves, but only that they have certain properties or attributes, or certain relations to other things: of these our conception is only *relative*.

To illustrate this by some examples:—In the university library, I call for the book, press L, shelf 10, No. 10; the library-keeper must have such a conception of the book I want as to be able to distinguish it from ten thousand that are under his care. But what conception does he form of it from my words? They inform him neither of the author, nor the subject, nor the language, nor the size, nor the binding, but only of its mark and place. His conception of it is merely relative to these circumstances; yet this relative notion enables him to distinguish it from every other book in the library.

There are other relative notions that are not taken from accidental relations, as in the example just now mentioned, but from qualities or attributes essential to the thing.

Of this kind are our notions both of body and mind. What is body? It is, say philosophers, that which is extended, solid, and divisible. Says the querist, I do not ask what the properties of body are, but what is the thing itself; let me first know directly what body is, and then consider its properties? To this demand, I am afraid the querist will meet with no satisfactory answer; because our notion of body is not direct but relative to its qualities. We know that it is something extended, solid, and divisible, and we know no more.

Again, if it should be asked, What is mind? It is that which thinks. I ask not what it does, or what its operations are, but what it is. To this I can find no answer; our notion of mind being not direct, but relative to its operations, as our notion of body is relative to its qualities.

There are even many of the qualities of body, of which we have only a relative conception. What is heat in a body? It is a quality which affects the sense of touch in a certain way. If you want to know, not how it affects the sense of touch, but what it is in itself — this, I confess, I know not. My conception of it is not direct, but relative to the effect it has upon bodies. The notions we have of all those qualities which Mr Locke calls secondary, and of those he calls powers of bodies — such as the power of the magnet to attract iron, or of fire to burn wood — are relative.

Having given examples of things of which our conception is only relative, it may be proper to mention some of which it is direct. Of this kind, are all the primary qualities of body — figure, extension, solidity, hardness, fluidity, and the like. Of these we have a direct and immediate knowledge from our senses. To this class belong also all the operations of mind of which we are conscious. I know what thought is, what memory, what a purpose, what a promise.

There are some things of which we can have both a direct and a relative conception. I can directly conceive ten thousand men, or ten thousand pounds, because both are objects of sense, and may be seen. But, whether I see such an object, or directly conceive it, my notion of it is indistinct: it is only that of a great multitude of men, or of a great heap of money;

and a small addition or diminution makes no perceptible change in the notion I form in this way. But I can form a relative notion of the same number of men or of pounds, by attending to the relations which this number has to other numbers, greater or less. Then I perceive that the relative notion is distinct and scientific; for the addition of a single man, or a single pound, or even of a penny, is easily perceived.

In like manner, I can form a direct notion of a polygon of a thousand equal sides and equal angles. This direct notion cannot be more distinct, when conceived in the mind, than that which I get by sight, when the object is before me; and I find it so indistinct, that it has the same appearance to my eye, or to my direct conception, as a polygon of a thousand and one, or of nine hundred and ninety-nine sides. But, when I form a relative conception of it, by attending to the relation it bears to polygons of a greater or less number of sides, my notion of it becomes distinct and scientific, and I can demonstrate the properties by which it is distinguished from all other polygons. From these instances, it appears that our relative conceptions of things are not always less distinct, nor less fit materials for accurate reasoning than those that are direct; and that the contrary may happen in a remarkable degree.

Our conception of power is relative to its exertions or effects. Power is one thing; its exertion is another thing. It is true, there can be no exertion without power; but there may be power that is not exerted. Thus, a man may have power to speak when he is silent; he may have power to rise and walk when he sits still.

But, though it be one thing to speak, and another to have the power of speaking, I apprehend we conceive of the power as something which has a certain relation to the effect. And of every power we form our notion by the effect which it is able to produce.

3. It is evident that Power is a *quality*, and cannot exist without a subject to which it belongs.

That power may exist without any being or subject to which that power may be attributed, is an absurdity, shocking to every man of common understanding.

It is a quality which may be varied, not only in degree, but also in kind; and we distinguish both the kinds and degrees by the effects which they are able to produce.

Thus a power to fly, and a power to reason, are different kinds of power, their effects being different in kind. But a power to carry one hundred weight, and a power to carry two hundred, are different degrees of the same kind.

4. We cannot conclude the want of power from its not being exerted; nor from the exertion of a less degree of power, can we conclude that there is no greater degree in the subject. Thus, though a man on a particular occasion said nothing, we cannot conclude from that circumstance, that he had not the power of speech; nor from a man's carrying ten pound weight, can we conclude that he had not power to carry twenty.[…]

Chapter V

Whether beings that have no will nor understanding may have active power.

That active power is an attribute, which cannot exist but in some being possessed of that power, and the subject of that attribute, I take for granted as a self-evident truth. Whether there can be active power in a subject which has no thought, no understanding, no will, is not so evident.

The ambiguity of the words *power, cause, agent*, and of all the words related to these, tends to perplex this question. The weakness of human understanding, which gives us only an indirect and relative conception of power, contributes to darken our reasoning, and should make us cautious and modest in our determinations.

We can derive little light in this matter from the events which we observe in the course of nature. We perceive changes innumerable in things without us. We know that those changes must be produced by the active power of some agent; but we neither perceive the agent nor the power, but the change only. Whether the things be active, or merely passive, is not easily discovered. And though it may be an object of curiosity to the speculative few, it does not greatly concern the many.

To know the event and the circumstances that attended it, and to know in what circumstances like events may be expected, may be of consequence in the conduct of life; but to know the real efficient, whether it be matter or mind, whether of a superior or inferior order, concerns us little.

Thus it is with regard to all the effects we ascribe to nature.

Nature is the name we give to the efficient cause of innumerable effects which fall daily under our observation. But, if it be asked what nature is — whether the first universal cause or a subordinate one, whether one or many, whether intelligent or unintelligent — upon these points we find various conjectures and theories, but no solid ground upon which we can rest. And I apprehend the wisest men are they who are sensible that they know nothing of the matter.

From the course of events in the natural world, we have sufficient reason to conclude the existence of an eternal intelligent First Cause. But whether He acts immediately in the production of those events, or by subordinate intelligent agents, or by instruments that are unintelligent, and what the number, the nature, and the different offices, of those agents or instruments may be — these I apprehend to be mysteries placed beyond the limits of human knowledge. We see an established order in the succession of natural events, but we see not the bond that connects them together.

Since we derive so little light, with regard to efficient causes and their active power, from attention to the natural world, let us next attend to the moral, I mean to human actions and conduct.

Mr Locke observes very justly, 'That, from the observation of the operation of bodies by our senses, we have but a very imperfect obscure idea of active power, since they afford us not any idea in themselves of the power to begin any action, either of motion or thought.' He adds, 'That we find in ourselves a power to begin or forbear, continue or end, several actions of our minds and motions of our bodies, barely by a thought or preference of the mind, ordering, or, as it were, commanding the doing or not doing such a particular action. This power which the mind has thus to order the consideration of any idea, or the forbearing to consider it, or to prefer the motion of any part of the body to its rest, and *vice versa*, in any particular instance, is that which we call *the will*. The actual exercise of that power, by directing any particular action, or its forbearance, is that which we call *volition* or *willing*.'

According to Mr Locke, therefore, the only clear notion or idea we have of active power, is taken from the power which we find in ourselves to give certain motions to our bodies, or a certain direction to our thoughts; and this power in ourselves can be brought into action only by willing or volition.

From this, I think, it follows, that, if we had not will, and that degree of understanding which will necessarily implies, we could exert no active power, and, consequently, could have none; for power that cannot be exerted is no power. It follows, also, that the active power, of which only we can have any distinct conception, can be only in beings that have understanding and will.

Power to produce any effect, implies power not to produce it. We can conceive no way in which power may be determined to one of these rather than the other, in a being that has no will.

Whatever is the effect of active power, must be something that is contingent. Contingent existence is that which depended upon the power and will of its cause. Opposed to this, is necessary existence, which we ascribe to the Supreme Being, because his existence is not owing to the power of any being. The same distinction there is between contingent and necessary truth.

That the planets of our system go round the sun from west to east, is a contingent truth; because it depended upon the power and will of Him who made the planetary system, and gave motion to it. That a circle and a right line can cut one another only in two points, is a truth which depends upon no power nor will, and, therefore, is called necessary and immutable. Contingency, therefore, has a relation to active power, as all active power is exerted in contingent events, and as such events can have no existence but by the exertion of active power.

When I observe a plant growing from its seed to maturity, I know that there must be a cause that has power to produce this effect. But I see neither the cause nor the manner of its operation.

But, in certain motions of my body and directions of my thought, I know not only that there must be a cause that has power to produce these effects, but that I am that cause; and I am conscious of what I do in order to the production of them.

From the consciousness of our own activity, seems to be derived not only the clearest, but the only conception we can form of activity, or the exertion of active power.

As I am unable to form a notion of any intellectual power different in kind from those I possess, the same holds with respect to active power. If all men had been blind, we should have had no conception of the power of seeing, nor any name for it in language. If man had not the powers of abstraction and reasoning, we could not have had any conception of these operations. In like manner, if he had not some degree of active power, and if he were not conscious of the exertion of it in his voluntary actions, it is probable he could have no conception of activity, or of active power.

A train of events following one another ever so regularly, could never lead us to the notion of a cause, if we had not, from our constitution, a conviction of the necessity of a cause to every event.

And of the manner in which a cause may exert its active power, we can have no conception, but from consciousness of the manner in which our own active power is exerted.

With regard to the operations of nature, it is sufficient for us to know, that, whatever the agents may be, whatever the manner of their operation or the extent of their power, they depend upon the First Cause, and are under his control; and this indeed is all that we know; beyond this we are left in darkness. But, in what regards human actions, we have a more immediate concern.

It is of the highest importance to us, as moral and accountable creatures, to know what actions are in our own power, because it is for these only that we can be accountable to our Maker, or to our fellow-men in society; by these only we can merit praise or blame; in these only all our prudence, wisdom, and virtue must be employed; and, therefore, with regard to them, the wise Author of nature has not left us in the dark.

Every man is led by nature to attribute to himself the free determinations of his own will, and to believe those events to be in his power which depend upon his will. On the other hand, it is self-evident, that nothing is in our power that is not subject to our will.

We grow from childhood to manhood, we digest our food, our blood circulates, our heart and arteries beat, we are sometimes sick and sometimes in health; all these things must be done by the power of some agent; but they are not done by our power. How do we know this? Because they are not subject to our will. This is the infallible criterion by which we distinguish what is our doing from what is not; what is in our power from what is not.

Human power, therefore, can only be exerted by will, and we are unable to conceive any active power to be exerted without will. Every man knows infallibly that what is done by his conscious will and intention, is to be imputed to him, as the agent or cause; and that whatever is done without his will and intention, cannot be imputed to him with truth.

We judge of the actions and conduct of other men by the same rule as we judge of our own. In morals, it is self-evident that no man can be the object either of approbation or of blame for what he did not. But how shall we know whether it is his doing or not? If the action depended upon his will, and if he intended and willed it, it is his action in the judgment of all mankind. But if it was done without his knowledge, or without his will and intention, it is as certain that he did it not, and that it ought not to be imputed to him as the agent.

When there is any doubt to whom a particular action ought to be imputed, the doubt arises only from our ignorance of facts; when the facts relating to it are known, no man of understanding has any doubt to whom the action ought to be imputed.

The general rules of imputation are self-evident. They have been the same in all ages, and among all civilized nations. No man blames another for being black or fair, for having a fever or the falling sickness; because these things are believed not to be in his power; and they are believed not to be in his power, because they depend not upon his will. We can never conceive that a man's duty goes beyond his power, or that his power goes beyond what depends upon his will.

Reason leads us to ascribe unlimited power to the Supreme Being. But what do we mean by unlimited power? It is power to do whatsoever he wills. To suppose him to do what he does not will to do, is absurd.

The only distinct conception I can form of active power is, that it is an attribute in a being by which he can do certain things if he wills. This, after all, is only a relative conception. It is relative to the effect, and to the will of producing it. Take away these, and the conception vanishes. They are the handles by which the mind takes hold of it. When they are taken away, our hold is gone. The same is the case with regard to other relative conceptions. Thus velocity is a real state of a body, about which philosophers reason with the force of demonstration; but our conception of it is relative to space and time. What is velocity in a body? It is a state in which it passes through a certain space in a certain time. Space and time are very different from velocity; but we cannot conceive it but by its relation to them. The effect produced, and the will to produce it, are things different from active power, but we can have no conception of it, but by its relation to them.

Whether the conception of an efficient cause, and of real activity, could ever have entered into the mind of man, if we had not had the experience of activity in ourselves, I am not able to determine with certainty. The origin of many of our conceptions, and even of many of our judgments, is not so easily traced as philosophers have generally conceived. No man can recollect the time when he first got the conception of an efficient cause, or the time when he first got the belief that an efficient cause is necessary to every change in nature. The conception of an efficient cause may very probably be derived from the experience we have had in very early life of our own power to produce certain effects. But the belief, that no event can happen without an efficient cause, cannot be derived from experience. We may learn from experience what *is*, or what *was*, but no experience can teach us what *necessarily must be*.

In like manner, we probably derive the conception of pain from the experience we have had of it in ourselves; but our belief that pain can only exist in a being that hath life, cannot be got by experience, because it is a necessary truth; and no necessary truth can have its attestation from experience.

If it be so that the conception of an efficient cause enters into the mind, only from the early conviction we have that we are the efficients of our own voluntary actions, (which I think is most probable,) the notion of efficiency will be reduced to this, That it is a relation between the cause and the effect, similar to that which is between us and our voluntary actions. This is surely the most distinct notion, and, I think, the only notion we can form of real efficiency.

Now it is evident, that, to constitute the relation between me and my action, my conception of the action, and will to do it, are essential. For what I never conceived nor willed, I never did.

If any man, therefore, affirms, that a being maybe the efficient cause of an action, and have power to produce it, which that being can neither conceive nor will, he speaks a language which I do not understand. If he has a meaning, his notion of power and efficiency must be essentially different from mine; and, until he conveys his notion of efficiency to my understanding, I can no more assent to his opinion than if he should affirm that a being without life may feel pain.

It seems, therefore, to me most probable, that such beings only as have some degree of understanding and will, can possess active power; and that inanimate beings must be merely passive, and have no real activity. Nothing we perceive without us affords any good ground for ascribing active power to any inanimate being; and everything we can discover in our own constitution, leads us to think that active power cannot be exerted without will and intelligence.

Chapter VI

Of the efficient causes of the phænomena of nature.

If active power, in its proper meaning, requires a subject endowed with will and intelligence, what shall we say of those active powers which philosophers teach us to ascribe to matter—the powers of corpuscular attraction, magnetism, electricity, gravitation, and others? Is it not universally allowed, that heavy bodies descend to the earth by the power of gravity; that, by the same power, the moon, and all the planets and comets, are retained in their orbits? Have the most eminent natural philosophers been imposing upon us, and giving us words instead of real causes?

In answer to this, I apprehend, that the principles of natural philosophy have, in modern times, been built upon a foundation that cannot be shaken, and that they can be called in question only by those who do not understand the evidence on which they stand. But the ambiguity of the words *cause, agency, active power*, and the other words related to these, has led many to understand them, when used in natural philosophy, in a wrong sense, and in a sense which is neither necessary for establishing the true principles of natural philosophy, nor was ever meant by the most enlightened in that science.

To be convinced of this, we may observe that those very philosophers who attribute to matter the power of gravitation, and other active powers, teach us, at the same time, that matter is a substance altogether inert, and merely passive; that gravitation, and the other attractive or repulsive powers which they ascribe to it, are not inherent in its nature, but impressed upon it by some external cause, which they do not pretend to know or to explain. Now, when we find wise men ascribing action and active power to a substance which they expressly teach us to consider as merely passive and acted upon by some unknown cause, we must conclude that the action and active power ascribed to it are not to be understood strictly, but in some popular sense.

It ought likewise to be observed, that although philosophers, for the sake of being understood, must speak the language of the vulgar as when they say — the sun rises and sets, and goes through all the signs of the zodiac — yet they often think differently from the vulgar. Let us hear what the greatest of natural philosophers says, in the eighth definition prefixed to his *Principia*: — 'Voces autem attractionis, impulsus, vel propensionis cujuscunque in centrum, indifferenter et pro se mutuo promiscue usurpo; has voces non physice sed mathematice considerando. Unde caveat lector, ne per hujus modi voces cogitet me speciem vel modum actionis, causamve aut rationem physicam, alicubi definire; vel centris (quæ sunt puncta mathematica) vires vere et physice tribuere, si forte centra trahere, aut vires centrorum esse, dixero.'[1]

In all languages, action is attributed to many things which all men of common understanding believe to be merely passive. Thus, we say the wind blows, the rivers flow, the sea rages, the fire burns, bodies move, and impel other bodies.

Every object which undergoes any change must be either active or passive in that change. This is self-evident to all men from the first dawn of reason; and, therefore, the change is always expressed in language, either by an active or a passive verb. Nor do I know any verb, expressive of a change, which does not imply either action or passion. The thing either changes, or it is changed. But it is remarkable in language, that when an external cause of the change is not obvious, the change is always imputed to the thing changed, as if it were animated, and had active power to produce the change in itself. So we say, the moon changes, the sun rises and goes down.

Thus active verbs are very often applied, and active power imputed to things, which a little advance in knowledge and experience teaches us to be merely passive. This property, common to all languages, I endeavoured to account for in the second chapter of this Essay, to which the reader is referred.

A like irregularity may be observed in the use of the word signifying *cause*, in all languages, and of the words related to it.

Our knowledge of causes is very scanty in the most advanced state of society, much more is it so in that early period in which language is formed. A strong desire to know the causes of things, is common to all men in every state; but the experience of all ages shows, that this keen appetite, rather than go empty, will feed upon the husks of real knowledge where the fruit can not be found.

While we are very much in the dark with regard to the real agents or causes which produce the phænomena of nature, and have, at the same time, an avidity to know them, ingenious men frame conjectures, which those of weaker understanding take for truth. The fare is coarse, but appetite makes it go down.

Thus, in a very ancient system, love and strife were made the causes of things. Plato made the causes of things to be matter, ideas, and an efficient architect; Aristotle, matter, form, and privation; Des Cartes thought matter, and a certain quantity of motion given it by the Almighty at first, to be all that is necessary to make the material world; Leibnitz conceived the whole universe, even the material part of it, to be made up of *monades*, each of which is active and intelligent, and produces in itself, by its own active power, all the changes it undergoes from the beginning of its existence to eternity.

In common language, we give the name of a cause to a reason, a motive, an end, to any circumstance which is connected with the effect, and goes before it.

Aristotle, and the schoolmen after him, distinguished four kinds of causes — the Efficient, the Material, the Formal, and the Final. This, like many of Aristotle's distinctions, is only a distinction of the various meanings of an ambiguous word; for the Efficient, the Matter, the Form, and the End, have nothing common in their nature, by which they may be accounted species of the same *genus*; but the Greek word which we translate *cause*, had these four different meanings in Aristotle's days, and we have added other meanings. We do not indeed call the matter or the form of a thing its cause; but we have final causes, instrumental causes, occasional causes, and I know not how many others.

Thus the word *cause* has been so hackneyed, and made to have so many different meanings in the writings of philosophers, and in the discourse of the vulgar, that its original and proper meaning is lost in the crowd.

With regard to the phænomena of nature, the important end of knowing their causes, besides gratifying our curiosity, is, that we may know when to expect them, or how to bring them about. This is very often of real importance in life; and this purpose is served by knowing what, by the course of nature, goes before them and is connected with them; and this, therefore, we call the cause of such a phænomenon.

If a magnet be brought near to a mariner's compass, the needle, which was before at rest, immediately begins to move, and bends its course towards the magnet, or perhaps the contrary way. If an unlearned sailor is asked the cause of this motion of the needle, he is at no loss for an answer. He tells you it is the magnet; and the proof is clear; for, remove the magnet, and the effect ceases; bring it near, and the effect is again produced. It is, therefore, evident to sense, that the magnet is the cause of this effect.

A Cartesian philosopher enters deeper into the cause of this phænomenon. He observes, that the magnet does not touch the needle, and therefore can give it no impulse. He pities the ignorance of the sailor. The effect is produced, says he, by magnetic effluvia, or subtile matter, which passes from the magnet to the needle, and forces it from its place. He can even show you, in a figure, where these magnetic effluvia issue from the magnet, what round they take, and what way they return home again. And thus he thinks he comprehends perfectly how, and by what cause, the motion of the needle is produced.

A Newtonian philosopher inquires what proof can be offered for the existence of magnetic effluvia, and can find none. He therefore holds it as a fiction, a hypothesis; and he has learned that hypotheses ought to have no place in the philosophy of nature. He confesses his ignorance of the real cause of this motion, and thinks that his business, as a philosopher, is only to find from experiment the laws by which it is regulated in all cases.

These three persons differ much in their sentiments with regard to the real cause of this phænomenon; and the man who knows most is he who is sensible that he knows nothing of the matter. Yet all the three speak the same language, and acknowledge that the cause of this motion is the attractive or repulsive power of the magnet.

What has been said of this, may be applied to every phænomenon that falls within the compass of natural philosophy. We deceive ourselves if we conceive that we can point out the real efficient cause of any one of them.

The grandest discovery ever made in natural philosophy, was that of the law of gravitation, which opens such a view of our planetary system that it looks like something divine. But the author of this discovery was perfectly aware, that he discovered no real cause, but only the law or rule, according to which the unknown cause operates.

Natural philosophers, who think accurately, have a precise meaning to the terms they use in the science; and, when they pretend to show the cause of any phænomenon of nature, they mean by the cause, a law of nature of which that phænomenon is a necessary consequence.

The whole object of natural philosophy, as Newton expressly teaches, is reducible to these two heads: first, by just induction from experiment and observation, to discover the laws of nature; and then, to apply those laws to the solution of the phænomena of nature. This was all that this great philosopher attempted, and all that he thought attainable. And this indeed he attained in a great measure, with regard to the motions of our planetary system, and with regard to the rays of light.

But supposing that all the phænomena that fall within the reach of our senses, were accounted for from general laws of nature, justly deduced from experience — that is, supposing natural philosophy brought to its utmost perfection — it does not discover the efficient cause of any one phænomenon in nature.

The laws of nature are the rules according to which the effects are produced; but there must be a cause which operates according to these rules. The rules of navigation never navigated a ship; the rules of architecture never built a house.

Natural philosophers, by great attention to the course of nature, have discovered many of her laws, and have very happily applied them to account for many phænomena; but they have never discovered the efficient cause of any one phænomenon; nor do those who have distinct notions of the principles of the science make any such pretence.

Upon the theatre of nature we see innumerable effects, which require an agent endowed with active power; but the agent is behind the scene. Whether it be the Supreme Cause alone, or a subordinate cause or causes; and if subordinate causes be employed by the Almighty, what their nature, their number, and their different offices may be — are things hid, for wise reasons without doubt, from the human eye.

It is only in human actions, that may be imputed for praise or blame, that it is necessary for us to know who is the agent; and in this, nature has given us all the light that is necessary for our conduct.

Essay III. Part II: Of Animal Principles of Action

Chapter VIII

Of opinion.

When we come to explain the rational principles of action, it will appear that *Opinion* is an essential ingredient in them. Here we are only to consider its influence upon the animal principles. Some of those I have ranked in that class cannot, I think, exist in the human mind without it.

Gratitude supposes the opinion of a favour done or intended; resentment the opinion of an injury; esteem the opinion of merit; the passion of love supposes the opinion of uncommon merit and perfection in its object.

Although natural affection to parents, children, and near relations is not grounded on the opinion of their merit, it is much increased by that consideration. So is every benevolent affection. On the contrary, real malevolence can hardly exist without the opinion of demerit in the object.

There is no natural desire or aversion which may not be restrained by opinion. Thus, if a man were athirst, and had a strong desire to drink, the opinion that there was poison in the cup would make him forbear.

It is evident that hope and fear, which every natural desire or affection may create, depend upon the opinion of future good.

Thus it appears, that our passions, our dispositions, and our opinions, have great influence upon our animal principles, to strengthen or weaken, to excite or restrain them; and, by that means, have great influence upon human actions and characters.

That brute-animals have both passions and dispositions similar, in many respects, to those of men, cannot be doubted. Whether they have opinions is not so clear. I think they have not, in the proper sense of the word. But, waving all dispute upon this point, it will be granted that opinion in men has a much wider field than in brutes. No man will say that they have systems of theology, morals, jurisprudence, or politics; or that they can reason from the laws of nature, in mechanics, medicine, or agriculture.

They feel the evils or enjoyments that are present; probably they imagine those which experience has associated with what they feel. But they can take no large prospect either of the past or of the future, nor see through a train of consequences.

A dog may be deterred from eating what is before him by the fear of immediate punishment, which he has felt on like occasions; but he is never deterred by the consideration of health, or of any distant good.

I have been credibly informed, that a monkey, having once been intoxicated with strong drink, in consequence of which it burnt its foot in the fire, and had a severe fit of sickness, could never after be induced to drink anything but pure water. I believe this is the utmost pitch which the faculties of brutes can reach.

From the influence of opinion upon the conduct of mankind, we may learn that it is one of the chief instruments to be used in the discipline and government of men.

All men, in the early part of life, must be under the discipline and government of parents and tutors. Men who live in society must be under the government of laws and magistrates through life. The government of men is undoubtedly one of the noblest exertions of human power. And it is of great importance that those who have any share, either in domestic or civil government, should know the nature of man, and how he is to be trained and governed.

Of all instruments of government, opinion is the sweetest, and the most agreeable to the nature of man. Obedience that flows from opinion is real freedom, which every man desires. That which is extorted by fear of punishment is slavery, a yoke which is always galling, and which every man will shake off when it is in his power.

The opinions of the bulk of mankind have always been, and will always be, what they are taught by those whom they esteem to be wise and good; and, therefore, in a considerable degree, are in the power of those who govern them.

Man, uncorrupted by bad habits and bad opinions, is of all animals the most tractable; corrupted by these, he is of all animals the most untractable.

I apprehend, therefore, that, if ever civil government shall be brought to perfection, it must be the principal care of the state to make good citizens by proper education, and proper instruction and discipline.

The most useful part of medicine is that which strengthens the constitution, and prevents diseases by good regimen; the rest is somewhat like propping a ruinous fabric at great expense, and to little purpose. The art of government is the medicine of the mind, and the most useful part of it is that which prevents crimes and bad habits, and trains men to virtue and good habits by proper education and discipline.

The end of government is to make the society happy, which can only be done by making it good and virtuous.

That men in general will be good or bad members of society, according to the education and discipline by which they have been trained, experience may convince us.

The present age has made great advances in the art of training men to military duty. It will not be said that those who enter into that service are more tractable than their fellow-subjects of other professions. And I know not why it should be thought impossible to train men to equal perfection in the other duties of good citizens.

What an immense difference is there, for the purpose of war, between an army properly trained, and a militia hastily drawn out of the multitude? What should hinder us from thinking that, for every purpose of civil government, there may be a like difference between a civil society properly trained to virtue, good habits, and right sentiments, and those civil societies which we now behold? But I fear I shall be thought to digress from my subject into Utopian speculation.[…]

Essay III. Part III: Of the Rational Principles of Action

Chapter I

There are rational principles of action in man.

Mechanical principles of action produce their effect without any will or intention on our part. We may, by a voluntary effort, hinder the effect; but, if it be not hindered by will and effort, it is produced without them.

Animal principles of action require intention and will in their operation, but not judgment. They are, by ancient moralists, very properly called *cæcæ cupidines*, blind desires.

Having treated of these two classes, I proceed to the third —the *Rational* principles of action in man; which have that name, because they can have no existence in beings not endowed with reason, and, in all their exertions, require, not only intention and will, but judgment or reason.

That talent which we call *Reason*, by which men that are adult and of a sound mind are distinguished from brutes, idiots, and infants, has, in all ages, among the learned and unlearned, been conceived to have two offices — *to regulate our belief*, and *to regulate our actions and conduct*.

Whatever we believe, we think agreeable to reason, and, on that account, yield our assent to it. Whatever we disbelieve, we think contrary to reason, and, on that account, dissent from it. Reason, therefore, is allowed to be the principle by which our belief and opinions ought to be regulated.

But reason has been no less universally conceived to be a principle by which our actions ought to be regulated.

To act reasonably, is a phrase no less common in all languages, than to judge reasonably. We immediately approve of a man's conduct, when it appears that he had good reason for what he did. And every action we disapprove, we think unreasonable, or contrary to reason.

A way of speaking so universal among men, common to the learned and the unlearned in all nations and in all languages, must have a meaning. To suppose it to be words without meaning, is to treat, with undue contempt, the common sense of mankind.

Supposing this phrase to have a meaning, we may consider in what way reason may serve to regulate human conduct, so that some actions of men are to be denominated reasonable, and others unreasonable.

I take it for granted, that there can be no exercise of Reason without Judgment, nor, on the other hand, any judgment of things, abstract and general, without some degree of reason.

If, therefore, there be any principles of action in the human constitution, which, in their nature, necessarily imply such judgment, they are the principles which we may call rational, to distinguish them from animal principles, which imply desire and will, but not judgment.

Every deliberate human action must be done either as the means, or as an end; as the means to some end, to which it is subservient, or as an end, for its own sake, and without regard to anything beyond it.

That it is a part of the office of reason to determine what are the proper means to any end which we desire, no man ever denied. But some philosophers, particularly Mr Hume, think that it is no part of the office of reason to determine the ends we ought to pursue, or the preference due to one end above another. This, he thinks, is not the office of reason, but of taste or feeling.

If this be so, reason cannot, with any propriety, be called a principle of action. Its office can only be to minister to the principles of action, by discovering the means of their gratification. Accordingly, Mr Hume maintains, that reason is no principle of action; but that it is, and ought to be, the servant of the passions.

I shall endeavour to show that, among the various ends of human actions, there are some, of which, without reason, we could not even form a conception; and that, as soon as they are conceived, a regard to them is, by our constitution, not only a principle of action, but a leading and governing principle, to which all our animal principles are subordinate, and to which they ought to be subject.

These I shall call *rational* principles; because they can exist only in beings endowed with reason, and because, to act from these principles, is what has always been meant by acting according to reason.

The ends of human actions I have in view, are two — to wit, *What is good for us upon the whole*, and, *What appears to be our duty*. They are very strictly connected, lead to the same course of conduct, and cooperate with each other; and, on that account, have commonly been comprehended under one name — that of *reason*. But, as they may be disjoined, and are really distinct principles of action, I shall consider them separately.

Chapter III

The tendency of this principle.

[...] The sum of what has been said in these three chapters amounts to this: —

There is a principle of action in men that are adult and of a sound mind, which, in all ages, has been called *reason*, and set in opposition to the animal principles which we call the *passions*. The ultimate object of this principle is what we judge to be good upon the whole. This is not the object of any of our animal principles; they being all directed to particular objects, without any comparison with others, or any consideration of their being good or ill upon the whole.

What is good upon the whole cannot even be conceived without the exercise of reason, and therefore cannot be an object to beings that have not some degree of reason.

As soon as we have the conception of this object, we are led, by our constitution, to desire and pursue it. It justly claims a preference to all objects of pursuit that can come in competition with it. In preferring it to any gratification that opposes it, or in submitting to any pain or mortification which it requires, we act according to reason; and every such action is accompanied with self-approbation and the approbation of mankind. The contrary actions are accompanied with shame and self-condemnation in the agent, and with contempt in the spectator, as foolish and unreasonable.

The right application of this principle to our conduct requires an extensive prospect of human life, and a correct judgment and estimate of its goods and evils, with respect to their intrinsic worth and dignity, their constancy and duration, and their attainableness. He must be a wise man indeed, if any such man there be, who can perceive, in every instance, or even in every important instance, what is best for him upon the whole, if he have no other rule to direct his conduct.

However, according to the best judgment which wise men have been able to form, this principle leads to the practice of every virtue. It leads directly to the virtues of Prudence, Temperance, and Fortitude. And, when we consider ourselves as social creatures, whose happiness or misery is very much connected with that of our fellow-men; when we consider that there are many benevolent affections planted in our constitution, whose exertions make a capital part of our good and enjoyment: from these considerations, this principle leads us also, though more indirectly, to the practice of justice, humanity, and all the social virtues.

It is true, that a regard to our own good cannot, of itself, produce any benevolent affection. But, if such affections be a part of our constitution, and if the exercise of them make a capital part of our happiness, a regard to our own good ought to lead us to cultivate and exercise them, as every benevolent affection makes the good of others to be our own.

Chapter IV

Defects of this principle.

Having explained the nature of this principle of action, and shown in general the tenor of conduct to which it leads, I shall conclude what relates to it, by pointing out some of its defects, if it be supposed, as it has been by some philosophers, to be the only regulating principle of human conduct.

Upon that supposition, it would neither be a sufficiently plain rule of conduct, nor would it raise the human character to that degree of perfection of which it is capable, nor would it yield so much real happiness as when it is joined with another rational principle of action—to wit, a disinterested regard to duty.

First, I apprehend the greater part of mankind can never attain such extensive views of human life, and so correct a judgment of good and ill, as the right application of this principle requires.

[…] The ignorance of the bulk of mankind concurs with the strength of their passions to lead them into error in this most important point.

Every man, in his calm moments, wishes to know what is best for him on the whole, and to do it. But the difficulty of discovering it clearly, amidst such variety of opinions and the importunity of present desires, tempt men to give over the search, and to yield to the present inclination.

Though philosophers and moralists have taken much laudable pains to correct the errors of mankind in this great point, their instructions are known to few; they have little influence upon the greater part of those to whom they are known, and sometimes little even upon the philosopher himself.

Speculative discoveries gradually spread from the knowing to the ignorant, and diffuse themselves over all; so that, with regard to them, the world, it may be hoped, will still be growing wiser. But the errors of men, with regard to what is truly good or ill, after being discovered and refuted in every age, are still prevalent.

Men stand in need of a sharper monitor to their duty than a dubious view of distant good. There is reason to believe, that a present sense of duty has, in many cases, a stronger influence than the apprehension of distant good would have of itself. And it cannot be doubted, that a sense of guilt and demerit is a more pungent reprover than the bare apprehension of having mistaken our true interest.

The brave soldier, in exposing himself to danger and death, is animated, not by a cold computation of the good and the ill, but by a noble and elevated sense of military duty.

A philosopher shows, by a copious and just induction, what is our real good, and what our ill. But this kind of reasoning is not easily apprehended by the bulk of men. It has too little force upon their minds to resist the sophistry of the passions. They are apt to think that, if such rules be good in the general, they may admit of particular exceptions, and that what is good for the greater part, may, to some persons, on account of particular circumstances, be ill. Thus, I apprehend, that, if we had no plainer rule to direct our conduct in life than a regard to our greatest good, the greatest part of mankind would be fatally misled, even by ignorance of the road to it.

Secondly, Though a steady pursuit of our own real good may, in an enlightened mind, produce a kind of virtue which is entitled to some degree of approbation, yet it can never produce the noblest kind of virtue which claims our highest love and esteem.

We account him a wise man who is wise for himself; and, if he prosecutes this end through difficulties and temptations that lie in his way, his character is far superior to that of the man who, having the same end in view, is continually starting out of the road to it from an attachment to his appetites and passions, and doing every day what he knows he shall heartily repent.

Yet, after all, this wise man, whose thoughts and cares are all centred ultimately in himself, who indulges even his social affections only with a view to his own good, is not the man whom we cordially love and esteem.

Like a cunning merchant, he carries his goods to the best market, and watches every opportunity of putting them off to the best account. He does well and wisely. But it is for himself. We owe him nothing upon this account. Even when he does good to others, he means only to serve himself; and, therefore, has no just claim to their gratitude or affection.

This surely, if it be virtue, is not the noblest kind, but a low and mercenary species of it. It can neither give a noble elevation to the mind that possesses it, nor attract the esteem and love of others.

Our cordial love and esteem is due only to the man whose soul is not contracted within itself, but embraces a more extensive object: who loves virtue, not for her dowry only, but for her own sake: whose benevolence is not selfish, but generous and disinterested: who, forgetful of himself, has the common good at heart, not as the means only, but as the end: who abhors what is base, though he were to be a gainer by it; and loves that which is right, although he should suffer by it.

Such a man we esteem the perfect man, compared with whom he who has no other aim but good to himself is a mean and despicable character.

Disinterested goodness and rectitude is the glory of the Divine Nature, without which he might be an object of fear or hope, but not of true devotion. And it is the image of this divine attribute in the human character that is the glory of man.

To serve God and be useful to mankind, without any concern about our own good and happiness, is, I believe, beyond the pitch of human nature. But to serve God and be useful to men, merely to obtain good to ourselves, or to avoid ill, is servility, and not that liberal service which true devotion and real virtue require.

Thirdly, Though one might be apt to think that he has the best chance for happiness who has no other end of his deliberate actions but his own good, yet a little consideration may satisfy us of the contrary.

A concern for our own good is not a principle that, of itself, gives any enjoyment. On the contrary, it is apt to fill the mind with fear, and care, and anxiety. And these concomitants of this principle often give pain and uneasiness, that overbalance the good they have in view.

We may here compare, in point of present happiness, two imaginary characters: The first, of the man who has no other ultimate end of his deliberate actions but his own good; and who has no regard to virtue or duty, but as the means to that end. The second character is that of the man who is not indifferent with regard to his own good, but has another ultimate end perfectly consistent with it—to wit, a disinterested love of virtue, for its own sake, or a regard to duty as an end.

Comparing these two characters in point of happiness, that we may give all possible advantage to the selfish principle, we shall suppose the man who is actuated solely by it, to be so far enlightened as to see it his interest to live soberly, righteously, and godly in the world, and that he follows the same course of conduct from the motive of his own good only, which the other does, in a great measure, or in some measure, from a sense of duty and rectitude.

We put the case so as that the difference between these two persons may be, not in what they do, but in the motive from which they do it; and, I think, there can be no doubt that he who acts from the noblest and most generous motive, will have most happiness in his conduct.

The one labours only for hire, without any love to the work. The other loves the work, and thinks it the noblest and most honourable he can be employed in. To the first, the mortification and self-denial which the course of virtue requires, is a grievous task, which he submits to only through necessity. To the other it is victory and triumph, in the most honourable warfare.

It ought farther to be considered—That although wise men have concluded that virtue is the only road to happiness, this conclusion is founded chiefly upon the natural respect men have for virtue, and the good or happiness that is intrinsic to it and arises from the love of it. If we suppose a man, as we now do, altogether destitute of this principle, who considered virtue only as the means to another end, there is no reason to think that he would ever take it to be the road to happiness, but would wander for ever seeking this object, where it is not to be found.

The road of duty is so plain that the man who seeks it with an upright heart cannot greatly err from it. But the road to happiness, if that be supposed the only end our nature leads us to pursue, would be found dark and intricate, full of snares and dangers, and therefore not to be trodden without fear, and care, and perplexity.

The happy man, therefore, is not he whose happiness is his only care, but he who, with perfect resignation, leaves the care of his happiness to him who made him, while he pursues with ardour the road of his duty.

This gives an elevation to his mind, which is real happiness. Instead of care, and fear, and anxiety, and disappointment, it brings joy and triumph. It gives a relish to every good we enjoy, and brings good out of evil.

And as no man can be indifferent about his happiness, the good man has the consolation to know that he consults his happiness most effectually when, without any painful anxiety about future events, he does his duty.

Thus, I think, it appears—That, although a regard to our good upon the whole, be a rational principle in man, yet if it be supposed the only regulating principle of our conduct, it would be a more uncertain rule, it would give far less perfection to the human character, and far less happiness, than when joined with another rational principle—to wit, a regard to duty.

Chapter V

Of the notion of duty, rectitude, moral obligation.

A being endowed with the animal principles of action only, may be capable of being trained to certain purposes by discipline, as we see many brute-animals are, but would be altogether incapable of being governed by law.

The subject of law must have the conception of a general rule of conduct, which, without some degree of reason, he cannot have. He must likewise have a sufficient inducement to obey the law, even when his strongest animal desires draw him the contrary way.

This inducement may be a sense of *interest*, or a sense of *duty*, or both concurring.

These are the only principles I am able to conceive, which can reasonably induce a man to regulate all his actions according to a certain general rule or law. They may therefore be justly called the *rational* principles of action, since they can have no place but in a being endowed with reason, and since it is by them only that man is capable either of political or of moral government.

Without them human life would be like a ship at sea without hands, left to be carried by winds and tides as they happen. It belongs to the rational part of our nature to intend a certain port, as the end of the voyage of life; to take the advantage of winds and tides when they are favourable, and to bear up against them when they are unfavourable.

A sense of interest may induce us to do this, when a suitable reward is set before us. But there is a nobler principle in the constitution of man, which, in many cases, gives a clearer and more certain rule of conduct, than a regard merely to interest would give, and a principle, without which man would not be a moral agent.

A man is prudent when he consults his real interest; but he cannot be virtuous, if he has no regard to duty.

I proceed now to consider this *regard to Duty* as a rational principle of action in man, and as that principle alone by which he is capable either of virtue or vice.

I shall first offer some observations with regard to the *general notion of duty, and its contrary, or of right and wrong in human conduct*, and then consider, *how we come to judge and determine certain things in human conduct to be right, and others to be wrong.*

With regard to the notion or conception of Duty, I take it to be too simple to admit of a logical definition.

We can define it only by synonymous words or phrases, or by its properties and necessary concomitants, as when we say that it is *what we ought to do – what is fair and honest – what is approvable –* what *every man professes to be the rule of his conduct – what all men praise – and, what is in itself laudable, though no man should praise it.*

I observe, in the *next* place, That the notion of duty cannot be resolved into that of interest, or what is most for our happiness.

Every man may be satisfied of this who attends to his own conceptions, and the language of all mankind shows it. When I say, This is my interest, I mean one thing; when I say,

It is my duty, I mean another thing. And, though the same course of action, when rightly understood, may be both my duty and my interest, the conceptions are very different. Both are reasonable motives to action, but quite distinct in their nature.

I presume it will be granted, that, in every man of real worth, there is a principle of honour, a regard to what is honourable or dishonourable, very distinct from a regard to his interest. It is folly in a man to disregard his interest, but to do what is dishonourable, is baseness. The first may move our pity, or, in some cases, our contempt; but the last provokes our indignation.

As these two principles are different in their nature, and not resolvable into one, so the principle of honour is evidently superior in dignity to that of interest.

No man would allow him to be a man of honour who should plead his interest to justify what he acknowledged to be dishonourable; but to sacrifice interest to honour never costs a blush.

It likewise will be allowed by every man of honour, that this principle is not to be resolved into a regard to our reputation among men, otherwise the man of honour would not deserve to be trusted in the dark. He would have no aversion to lie, or cheat, or play the coward, when he had no dread of being discovered.

I take it for granted, therefore, that every man of real honour feels an abhorrence of certain actions, because they are in themselves base, and feels an obligation to certain other actions, because they are in themselves what honour requires, and this independently of any consideration of interest or reputation.

This is an immediate moral obligation. This principle of honour, which is acknowledged by all men who pretend to character, is only another name for what we call a regard to duty, to rectitude, to propriety of conduct. It is a moral obligation which obliges a man to do certain things because they are right, and not to do other things because they are wrong.

Ask the man of honour why he thinks himself obliged to pay a debt of honour? The very question shocks him. To suppose that he needs any other inducement to do it but the principle of honour, is to suppose that he has no honour, no worth, and deserves no esteem.

There is, therefore, a principle in man, which, when he acts according to it, gives him a consciousness of worth, and, when he acts contrary to it, a sense of demerit.

From the varieties of education, of fashion, of prejudices, and of habits, men may differ much in opinion with regard to the extent of this principle, and of what it commands and forbids; but the notion of it, as far as it is carried, is the same in all. It is that which gives a man real worth, and is the object of moral approbation.

Men of rank call it *honour*, and too often confine it to certain virtues that are thought most essential to their rank. The vulgar call it *honesty*, *probity*, *virtue*, *conscience*. Philosophers have given it the names of *the moral sense*, *the moral faculty*, *rectitude*.

The universality of this principle in men that are grown up to years of understanding and reflection, is evident. The words that express it, the names of the virtues which it commands, and of the vices which it forbids, the *ought* and *ought not* which express its dictates, make an essential part of every language. The natural affections of respect to worthy characters, of resentment of injuries, of gratitude for favours, of indignation against the worthless, are parts of the human constitution which suppose a right and a wrong in conduct. Many transactions that are found necessary in the rudest societies go upon the same supposition. In all testimony, in all promises, and in all contracts, there is necessarily implied a moral obligation on one party, and a trust in the other, grounded upon this obligation.

The variety of opinions among men in points of morality, is not greater, but, as I apprehend, much less than in speculative points; and this variety is as easily accounted for, from the common causes of error, in the one case as in the other; so that it is not more evident, that there is a real distinction between true and false, in matters of speculation, than that there is a real distinction between right and wrong in human conduct.

Mr Hume's authority, if there were any need of it, is of weight in this matter, because he was not wont to go rashly into vulgar opinions.

'Those,' says he, 'who have denied the reality of moral distinctions, may be ranked among the disingenuous disputants' (who really do not believe the opinions they defend, but engage in the controversy, from affectation, from a spirit of opposition, or from a desire of showing wit and ingenuity superior to the rest of mankind); 'nor is it conceivable, that any human creature could ever seriously believe that all characters and actions were alike entitled to the regard and affection of every one.

'Let a man's insensibility be ever so great, he must often be touched with the images of RIGHT and WRONG; and let his prejudices be ever so obstinate, he must observe that others are susceptible of like impressions. The only way, therefore, of convincing an antagonist of this kind, is to leave him to himself. For, finding that nobody keeps up the controversy with him, it is probable he will at last, of himself, from mere weariness, come over to the side of common sense and reason.' [*Principles of Morals*, § I.]

What we call *right* and *honourable* in human conduct, was, by the ancients, called *honestum* [...]; of which Tully says, 'Quod vere dicimus, etiamsi a nullo laudetur, natura esse laudabile.'[2] [*De Officiis*, L. I. c. iv.]

All the ancient sects, except the Epicureans, distinguished the *honestum* from the *utile*, as we distinguish what is a man's duty from what is his interest.

The word *officium* [...] extended both to the *honestum* and the *utile*: so that every reasonable action, proceeding either from a sense of duty or a sense of interest, was called *officium*. It is defined by Cicero to be—'Id quod cur factum sit ratio probabilis reddi potest.'[3] We commonly render it by the word *duty*, but it is more extensive; for the word *duty*, in the English language, I think, is commonly applied only to what the ancients called *honestum*. Cicero, and Panætius before him, treating of offices, first point out those that are grounded upon the *honestum*, and next those that are grounded upon the *utile*.

The most ancient philosophical system concerning the principles of action in the human mind, and, I think, the most agreeable to nature, is that which we find in some fragments of the ancient Pythagoreans, and which is adopted by Plato, and explained in some of his dialogues.

According to this system, there is a leading principle in the soul, which, like the supreme power in a commonwealth, has authority and right to govern. This leading principle they called *Reason*. It is that which distinguishes men that are adult from brutes, idiots, and infants. The inferior principles, which are under the authority of the leading principle, are our passions and appetites, which we have in common with the brutes.

Cicero adopts this system, and expresses it well in few words. 'Duplex enim est vis animorum atque naturæ. Una pars in appetitu posita est, quæ hominem huc et illuc rapit […]; altera in ratione, quæ docet, et explanat quid faciendum fugiendumve sit. Ita sit ut ratio præsit appetitus obtemperet.'⁴ [*De Officiis*, L. I. c. 28.]

This division of our active principles can hardly, indeed, be accounted a discovery of philosophy, because it has been common to the unlearned in all ages of the world, and seems to be dictated by the common sense of mankind.

What I would now observe concerning this common division of our active powers, is, that the leading principle, which is called *Reason*, comprehends both a regard to what is right and honourable, and a regard to our happiness upon the whole.

Although these be really two distinct principles of action, it is very natural to comprehend them under one name, because both are leading principles, both suppose the use of Reason, and, when rightly understood, both lead to the same course of life. They are like two fountains, whose streams unite and run in the same channel.

When a man, on one occasion, consults his real happiness in things not inconsistent with his duty, though in opposition to the solicitation of appetite or passion; and when, on another occasion, without any selfish consideration, he does what is right and honourable, because it is so — in both these cases, he acts reasonably; every man approves of his conduct, and calls it reasonable, or according to reason.

So that, when we speak of reason as a principle of action in man, it includes a regard both to the *honestum* and to the *utile*. Both are combined under one name; and, accordingly, the dictates of both, in the Latin tongue, were combined under the name *officium*.[…]

If we examine the abstract notion of Duty, or Moral Obligation, it appears to be neither any real quality of the action considered by itself, nor of the agent considered without respect to the action, but a certain relation between the one and the other.

When we say a man ought to do such a thing, the *ought*, which expresses the moral obligation, has a respect, on the one hand, to the person who ought; and, on the other, to the action which he ought to do. Those two correlates are essential to every moral obligation; take away either, and it has no existence. So that, if we seek the place of moral obligation among the categories, it belongs to the category of *relation*.

There are many relations of things, of which we have the most distinct conception, without being able to define them logically. Equality and proportion are relations between quantities, which every man understands, but no man can define.

Moral obligation is a relation of its own kind, which every man understands, but is, perhaps, too simple to admit of logical definition. Like all other relations, it may be changed or annihilated by a change in any of the two related things — I mean the agent or the action.

Perhaps it may not be improper to point out briefly the circumstances, both in the action and in the agent, which are necessary to constitute moral obligation. The universal agreement of men in these, shows that they have one and the same notion of it.

With regard to the action, it must be a voluntary action, or prestation of the person obliged, and not of another. There can be no moral obligation upon a man to be six feet high. Nor can I be under a moral obligation that another person should do such a thing. His actions must be imputed to himself, and mine only to me, either for praise or blame.

I need hardly mention, that a person can be under a moral obligation, only to things within the sphere of his natural power.

As to the party obliged, it is evident there can be no moral obligation upon an inanimate thing. To speak of moral obligation upon a stone or a tree is ridiculous, because it contradicts every man's notion of moral obligation.

The person obliged must have understanding and will, and some degree of active power. He must not only have the natural faculty of understanding, but the means of knowing his obligation. An invincible ignorance of this destroys all moral obligation.

The opinion of the agent in doing the action gives it its moral denomination. If he does a materially good action, without any belief of its being good, but from some other principle, it is no good action in him. And if he does it with the belief of its being ill, it is ill in him.

Thus, if a man should give to his neighbour a potion which he really believes will poison him, but which, in the event, proves salutary, and does much good; in moral estimation, he is a poisoner, and not a benefactor.

These qualifications of the action and of the agent, in moral obligation, are self-evident; and the agreement of all men in them shows that all men have the same notion, and a distinct notion of moral obligation.

Chapter VI

Of the sense of duty.

We are next to consider, how we learn to judge and determine, that this is right, and that is wrong.

The abstract notion of moral good and ill would be of no use to direct our life, if we had not the power of applying it to particular actions, and determining what is morally good, and what is morally ill.

Some philosophers, with whom I agree, ascribe this to an original power or faculty in man, which they call the *Moral Sense*, the *Moral Faculty*, *Conscience*. Others think that our moral sentiments may be accounted for without supposing any original sense or faculty appropriated to that purpose, and go into very different systems to account for them.

I am not, at present, to take any notice of those systems, because the opinion first mentioned seems to me to be the truth; to wit, That, by an original power of the mind, when we come to years of understanding and reflection, we not only have the notions of right and wrong in conduct, but perceive certain things to be right, and others to be wrong.

The name of the *Moral Sense*, though more frequently given to Conscience since Lord Shaftesbury and Dr

Hutcheson wrote, is not new. The *sensus recti et honesti*,[5] is a phrase not unfrequent among the ancients; neither is the *sense of duty*, among us.

It has got this name of *sense*, no doubt, from some analogy which it is conceived to bear to the external senses. And, if we have just notions of the office of the external senses, the analogy is very evident, and I see no reason to take offence, as some have done, at the name of the *moral sense*.

The offence taken at this name seems to be owing to this, That philosophers have degraded the senses too much, and deprived them of the most important part of their office.

We are taught, that, by the senses, we have only certain ideas which we could not have otherwise. They are represented as powers by which we have sensations and ideas, not as powers by which we judge.

This notion of the senses I take to be very lame, and to contradict what nature and accurate reflection teach concerning them.

A man who has totally lost the sense of seeing, may retain very distinct notions of the various colours; but he cannot judge of colours, because he has lost the sense by which alone he could judge. By my eyes I not only have the ideas of a square and a circle, but I perceive this surface to be a square, that to be a circle.

By my ear, I not only have the idea of sounds, loud and soft, acute and grave, but I immediately perceive and judge this sound to be loud, that to be soft, this to be acute, that to be grave. Two or more synchronous sounds I perceive to be concordant, others to be discordant.

These are judgments of the senses. They have always been called and accounted such, by those whose minds are not tinctured by philosophical theories. They are the immediate testimony of nature by our senses; and we are so constituted by nature, that we must receive their testimony, for no other reason but because it is given by our senses.

In vain do sceptics endeavour to overturn this evidence by metaphysical reasoning. Though we should not be able to answer their arguments, we believe our senses still, and rest our most important concerns upon their testimony.

If this be a just notion of our external senses, as I conceive it is, our moral faculty may, I think, without impropriety, be called the *Moral Sense*.

In its dignity it is, without doubt, far superior to every other power of the mind; but there is this analogy between it and the external senses, That, as by them we have not only the original conceptions of the various qualities of bodies, but the original judgment that this body has such a quality, that such another; so by our moral faculty, we have both the original conceptions of right and wrong in conduct, of merit and demerit, and the original judgments that this conduct is right, that is wrong; that this character has worth, that demerit.

The testimony of our moral faculty, like that of the external senses, is the testimony of nature, and we have the same reason to rely upon it.

The truths immediately testified by the external senses are the first principles from which we reason, with regard to the material world, and from which all our knowledge of it is deduced.

The truths immediately testified by our moral faculty, are the first principles of all moral reasoning, from which all our knowledge of our duty must be deduced.

By moral reasoning, I understand all reasoning that is brought to prove that such conduct is right, and deserving of moral approbation; or that it is wrong; or that it is indifferent, and, in itself, neither morally good nor ill.

I think, all we can properly call moral judgments, are reducible to one or other of these, as all human actions, considered in a moral view, are either good, or bad, or indifferent.

I know the term *moral reasoning* is often used by good writers in a more extensive sense; but, as the reasoning I now speak of is of a peculiar kind, distinct from all others, and, therefore, ought to have a distinct name, I take the liberty to limit the name of *moral reasoning* to this kind.

Let it be understood, therefore, that in the reasoning I call *moral*, the conclusion always is, That something in the conduct of moral agents is good or bad, in a greater or a less degree, or indifferent.

All reasoning must be grounded on first principles. This holds in moral reasoning, as in all other kinds. There must, therefore, be in morals, as in all other sciences, first or self-evident principles, on which all moral reasoning is grounded, and on which it ultimately rests. From such self-evident principles, conclusions may be drawn synthetically with regard to the moral conduct of life; and particular duties or virtues may be traced back to such principles, analytically. But, without such principles, we can no more establish any conclusion in morals, than we can build a castle in the air, without any foundation.

An example or two will serve to illustrate this.

It is a first principle in morals, That we ought not to do to another what we should think wrong to be done to us in like circumstances. If a man is not capable of perceiving this in his cool moments, when he reflects seriously, he is not a moral agent, nor is he capable of being convinced of it by reasoning.

From what topic can you reason with such a man? You may possibly convince him by reasoning, that it is his interest to observe this rule; but this is not to convince him that it is his duty. To reason about justice with a man who sees nothing to be just or unjust, or about benevolence with a man who sees nothing in benevolence preferable to malice, is like reasoning with a blind man about colour, or with a deaf man about sound.

It is a question in morals that admits of reasoning, Whether, by the law of nature, a man ought to have only one wife?

We reason upon this question, by balancing the advantages and disadvantages to the family, and to society in general, that are naturally consequent both upon monogamy and polygamy. And, if it can be shown that the advantages are greatly upon the side of monogamy, we think the point is determined.

But, if a man does not perceive that he ought to regard the good of society, and the good of his wife and children, the reasoning can have no effect upon him, because he denies the first principle upon which it is grounded.

Suppose, again, that we reason for monogamy from the intention of nature, discovered by the proportion of males and of females that are born—a proportion which corresponds perfectly with monogamy, but by no means with polygamy—this argument can have no weight with a man who does not perceive that he ought to have a regard to the intention of nature.

Thus we shall find that all moral reasonings rest upon one or more first principles of morals, whose truth is immediately perceived without reasoning, by all men come to years of understanding.

And this indeed is common to every branch of human knowledge that deserves the name of science. There must be first principles proper to that science, by which the whole superstructure is supported.

The first principles of all the sciences, must be the immediate dictates of our natural faculties; nor is it possible that we should have any other evidence of their truth. And in different sciences the faculties which dictate their first principles are very different.

Thus, in astronomy and in optics, in which such wonderful discoveries have been made, that the unlearned can hardly believe them to be within the reach of human capacity, the first principles are phænomena attested solely by that little organ, the human eye. If we disbelieve its report, the whole of those two noble fabrics of science, falls to pieces like the visions of the night.

The principles of music all depend upon the testimony of the ear. The principles of natural philosophy, upon the facts attested by the senses. The principles of mathematics, upon the necessary relations of quantities considered abstractly— such as, That equal quantities added to equal quantities make equal sums, and the like; which necessary relations are immediately perceived by the understanding.

The science of politics borrows its principles from what we know by experience of the character and conduct of man. We consider not what he ought to be, but what he is, and thence conclude what part he will act in different situations and circumstances. From such principles we reason concerning the causes and effects of different forms of government, laws, customs, and manners. If man were either a more perfect or a more imperfect, a better or a worse creature than he is, politics would be a different science from what it is.

The first principles of morals are the immediate dictates of the moral faculty. They show us, not what man is, but what he ought to be. Whatever is immediately perceived to be just, honest, and honourable, in human conduct, carries moral obligation along with it, and the contrary carries demerit and blame; and, from those moral obligations that are immediately perceived, all other moral obligations must be deduced by reasoning.

He that will judge of the colour of an object, must consult his eyes, in a good light, when there is no medium or contiguous objects that may give it a false tinge. But in vain will he consult every other faculty in this matter.

In like manner, he that will judge of the first principles of morals, must consult his conscience, or moral faculty, when he is calm and dispassionate, unbiassed by interest, affection, or fashion.

As we rely upon the clear and distinct testimony of our eyes, concerning the colours and figures of the bodies about us, we have the same reason to rely with security upon the clear and unbiassed testimony of our conscience, with regard to what we ought and ought not to do. In many cases, moral worth and demerit are discerned no less clearly by the last of those natural faculties, than figure and colour by the first.

The faculties which nature hath given us, are the only engines we can use to find out the truth. We cannot indeed prove that those faculties are not fallacious, unless God should give us new faculties to sit in judgment upon the old. But we are born under a necessity of trusting them.

Every man in his senses believes his eyes, his ears, and his other senses. He believes his consciousness with respect to his own thoughts and purposes; his memory, with regard to what is past; his understanding, with regard to abstract relations of things; and his taste, with regard to what is elegant and beautiful. And he has the same reason, and, indeed, is under the same necessity of believing the clear and unbiassed dictates of his conscience, with regard to what is honourable and what is base.

The sum of what has been said in this chapter is, That, by an original power of the mind, which we call *conscience*, or the *moral faculty*, we have the conceptions of right and wrong in human conduct, of merit and demerit, of duty and moral obligation, and our other moral conceptions; and that, by the same faculty, we perceive some things in human conduct to be right, and others to be wrong; that the first principles of morals are the dictates of this faculty; and that we have the same reason to rely upon those dictates, as upon the determinations of our senses, or of our other natural faculties.

Chapter VIII

Observations concerning conscience.

I shall now conclude this essay with some observations concerning this power of the mind which we call *Conscience*, by which its nature may be better understood.[…]

The *next* [*third*] observation is—That Conscience is evidently intended by nature to be the immediate guide and director of our conduct, after we arrive at the years of understanding.

There are many things which, from their nature and structure, show intuitively the end for which they were made.

A man who knows the structure of a watch or clock, can have no doubt in concluding that it was made to measure time. And he that knows the structure of the eye, and the properties of light, can have as little doubt whether it was made that we might see by it.

In the fabric of the body, the intention of the several parts is, in many instances, so evident as to leave no possibility of doubt. Who can doubt whether the muscles were intended to move the parts in which they are inserted? Whether the bones were intended to give strength and support to the body; and some of them to guard the parts which they enclose?

When we attend to the structure of the mind, the intention of its various original powers is no less evident. Is it not evident that the external senses are given, that we may discern those qualities of bodies which may be useful or hurtful to us?—Memory, that we may retain the knowledge we have acquired—judgment and understanding, that we may distinguish what is true from what is false?

The natural appetites of hunger and thirst; the natural affections of parents to their offspring, and of relations to each other; the natural docility and credulity of children; the affections of pity and sympathy with the distressed; the attachment we feel to neighbours, to acquaintance, and to the laws

and constitution of our country—these are parts of our constitution, which plainly point out their end, so that he must be
blind, or very inattentive, who does not perceive it. Even the
passions of anger and resentment appear very plainly to be a
kind of defensive armour, given by our Maker to guard us
against injuries, and to deter the injurious.

Thus it holds generally with regard both to the intellectual and active powers of man, that the intention for which
they are given is written in legible characters upon the face of
them.

Nor is this the case of any of them more evidently than of
conscience. Its intention is manifestly implied in its office;
which is, to show us what is good, what bad, and what
indifferent in human conduct.

It judges of every action before it is done. For we can
rarely act so precipitately but we have the consciousness that
what we are about to do is right, or wrong, or indifferent.
Like the bodily eye, it naturally looks forward, though its
attention may be turned back to the past.

To conceive, as some seem to have done, that its office is
only to reflect on past actions, and to approve or disapprove,
is, as if a man should conceive that the office of his eyes is
only to look back upon the road he has travelled, and to see
whether it be clean or dirty; a mistake which no man can
make who has made the proper use of his eyes.

Conscience prescribes measures to every appetite, affection, and passion, and says to every other principle of action—So far thou mayest go, but no farther.

We may indeed transgress its dictates, but we cannot
transgress them with innocence, nor even with impunity.

We condemn ourselves, or, in the language of scripture,
our heart condemns us, whenever we go beyond the rules of
right and wrong which conscience prescribes.

Other principles of action may have more strength, but
this only has authority. Its sentence makes us guilty to ourselves, and guilty in the eyes of our Maker, whatever other
principle may be set in opposition to it.

It is evident, therefore, that this principle has, from its
nature, an authority to direct and determine with regard to
our conduct; to judge, to acquit, or to condemn, and even to

punish; an authority which belongs to no other principle of the human mind.

It is the candle of the Lord set up within us, to guide our steps. Other principles may urge and impel, but this only authorizes. Other principles ought to be controlled by this; this may be, but never ought to be controlled by any other, and never can be with innocence.

The authority of conscience over the other active principles of the mind, I do not consider as a point that requires proof by argument, but as self-evident. For it implies no more than this — That in all cases a man ought to do his duty. He only who does in all cases what he ought to do, is the perfect man.

Of this perfection in the human nature, the Stoics formed the idea, and held it forth in their writings, as the goal to which the race of life ought to be directed. Their *wise man* was one in whom a regard to the *honestum* swallowed up every other principle of action.

The *wise man* of the Stoics, like the *perfect orator* of the rhetoricians, was an ideal character, and was, in some respects, carried beyond nature; yet it was perhaps the most perfect model of virtue that ever was exhibited to the heathen world; and some of those who copied after it, were ornaments to human nature.

The [*fourth* and] *last* observation is — That the Moral Faculty or Conscience is both an Active and an Intellectual power of the mind.

It is an *active* power, as every truly virtuous action must be more or less influenced by it. Other principles may concur with it, and lead the same way; but no action can be called morally good, in which a regard to what is right, has not some influence. Thus, a man who has no regard to justice, may pay his just debt, from no other motive but that he may not be thrown into prison. In this action there is no virtue at all.

The moral principle, in particular cases, may be opposed by any of our animal principles. Passion or appetite may urge to what we know to be wrong. In every instance of this kind, the moral principle ought to prevail, and the more difficult its conquest is, it is the more glorious.

In some cases, a regard to what is right may be the sole motive, without the concurrence or opposition of any other principle of action; as when a judge or an arbiter determines a plea between two different persons, solely from a regard to justice.

Thus we see that conscience, as an active principle, sometimes concurs with other active principles, sometimes opposes them, and sometimes is the sole principle of action.

I endeavoured before to show, that a regard to our own good upon the whole is not only a rational principle of action, but a leading principle, to which all our animal principles are subordinate. As these are, therefore, two regulating or leading principles in the constitution of man — a regard to what is best for us upon the whole, and a regard to duty — it may be asked, Which of these ought to yield if they happen to interfere?

Some well-meaning persons have maintained — That all regard to ourselves and to our own happiness ought to be extinguished; that we should love virtue for its own sake only, even though it were to be accompanied with eternal misery.

This seems to have been the extravagance of some Mystics, which perhaps they were led into in opposition to a contrary extreme of the schoolmen of the middle ages, who made the desire of good to ourselves to be the sole motive to action, and virtue to be approvable only on account of its present or future reward.

Juster views of human nature will teach us to avoid both these extremes.

On the on hand, the disinterested love of virtue is undoubtedly the noblest principle in human nature, and ought never to stoop to any other.

On the other hand, there is no active principle which God hath planted in our nature that is vicious in itself, or that ought to be eradicated, even if it were in our power.

They are all useful and necessary in our present state. The perfection of human nature consists, not in extinguishing, but in restraining them within their proper bounds, and keeping them in due subordination to the governing principles.

As to the supposition of an opposition between the two governing principles — that is, between a regard to our happiness upon the whole, and a regard to duty — this supposition is merely imaginary. There can be no such opposition.

While the world is under a wise and benevolent administration, it is impossible that any man should, in the issue, be a loser by doing his duty. Every man, therefore, who believes in God, while he is careful to do his duty, may safely leave the care of his happiness to Him who made him. He is conscious that he consults the last most effectually by attending to the first.

Indeed, if we suppose a man to be an atheist in his belief, and, at the same time, by wrong judgment, to believe that virtue is contrary to his happiness upon the whole, this case, as Lord Shaftesbury justly observes, is without remedy. It will be impossible for the man to act so as not to contradict a leading principle of his nature. He must either sacrifice his happiness to virtue, or virtue to happiness; and is reduced to this miserable dilemma, whether it be best to be a fool or a knave.

This shows the strong connection between morality and the principles of natural religion; as the last only can secure a man from the possibility of an apprehension, that he may play the fool by doing his duty.

Hence, even Lord Shaftesbury, in his gravest work, concludes, *That virtue without piety is incomplete*. Without piety, it loses its brightest example, its noblest object, and its firmest support.

I conclude with observing, That conscience, or the moral faculty, is likewise an *intellectual* power.

By it solely we have the original conceptions or ideas of right and wrong in human conduct. And of right and wrong there are not only many different degrees, but many different species. Justice and injustice, gratitude and ingratitude, benevolence and malice, prudence and folly, magnanimity and meanness, decency and indecency, are various moral forms, all comprehended under the general notion of right and wrong in conduct, all of them objects of moral approbation or disapprobation, in a greater or a less degree.

The conception of these, as moral qualities, we have by our moral faculty; and by the same faculty, when we compare them together, we perceive various moral relations among them. Thus, we perceive that justice is entitled to a small degree of praise, but injustice to a high degree of blame; and the same may be said of gratitude and its contrary. When justice and gratitude interfere, gratitude must give place to justice, and unmerited beneficence must give place to both.

Many such relations between the various moral qualities compared together, are immediately discerned by our moral faculty. A man needs only to consult his own heart to be convinced of them.

All our reasonings in morals, in natural jurisprudence, in the law of nations, as well as our reasonings about the duties of natural religion, and about the moral government of the Deity, must be grounded upon the dictates of our moral faculty, as first principles.

As this faculty, therefore, furnishes the human mind with many of its original conceptions or ideas, as well as with the first principles of many important branches of human knowledge, it may justly be accounted an intellectual as well as an active power of the mind.

Essay IV: Of the Liberty of Moral Agents

Chapter I

The notions of moral liberty and necessity stated.

By the *Liberty of a Moral Agent,* I understand, *a power over the determinations of his own Will.*

If, in any action, he had power to will what he did, or not to will it, in that action he is free. But if, in every voluntary action, the determination of his will be the necessary consequence of something involuntary in the state of his mind, or of something in his external circumstances, he is not free; he has not what I call the Liberty of a Moral Agent, but is subject to Necessity.

This Liberty supposes the agent to have Understanding and Will; for the determinations of the will are the sole object about which this power is employed; and there can be no will without such a degree of understanding, at least, as gives the conception of that which we will.

The liberty of a moral agent implies, not only a *conception* of what he wills, but some degree of practical *judgment* or *reason*.

For, if he has not the judgment to discern one determination to be preferable to another, either in itself or for some purpose which he intends, what can be the use of a power to determine? His determinations must be made perfectly in the dark, without reason, motive, or end. They can neither be right nor wrong, wise nor foolish. Whatever the consequences may be, they cannot be imputed to the agent, who had not the capacity of foreseeing them, or of perceiving any reason for acting otherwise than he did.

We may, perhaps, be able to conceive a being endowed with power over the determinations of his will, without any light in his mind to direct that power to some end. But such power would be given in vain. No exercise of it could be either blamed or approved. As nature gives no power in vain, I see no ground to ascribe a power over the determinations of the will to any being who has no judgment to apply it to the direction of his conduct, no discernment of what he ought or ought not to do.

For that reason, in this Essay, I speak only of the Liberty of Moral Agents, who are capable of acting well or ill, wisely or foolishly, and this, for distinction's sake, I shall call *Moral Liberty*.

What kind or what degree of liberty belongs to brute animals, or to our own species, before any use of reason, I do not know. We acknowledge that they have not the power of self-government. Such of their actions as may be called *voluntary* seem to be invariably determined by the passion, or appetite, or affection, or habit, which is strongest at the time.

This seems to be the law of their constitution, to which they yield, as the inanimate creation does, without any conception of the law, or any intention of obedience.

But of civil or moral government, which are addressed to the rational powers, and require a conception of the law and an intentional obedience, they are, in the judgment of all mankind, incapable. Nor do I see what end could be served by giving them a power over the determinations of their own will, unless to make them intractable by discipline, which we see they are not.

The effect of moral liberty is, *That it is in the power of the agent to do well or ill*. This power, like every other gift of God, may be abused. The right use of this gift of God is to do well and wisely, as far as his best judgment can direct him, and thereby merit esteem and approbation. The abuse of it is to act contrary to what he knows or suspects to be his duty and his wisdom, and thereby justly merit disapprobation and blame.

By *Necessity*, I understand the want of that moral liberty which I have above defined.

If there can be a better and a worse in actions on the system of Necessity, let us suppose a man necessarily determined in all cases to will and to do what is best to be done, he would surely be innocent and inculpable. But, as far as I am able to judge, he would not be entitled to the esteem and moral approbation of those who knew and believed this necessity. What was, by an ancient author, said of Cato, might, indeed, be said of him: *He was good because he could not be otherwise*. But this saying, if understood literally and strictly, is not the praise of Cato, but of his constitution, which was no more the work of Cato than his existence.

On the other hand, if a man be necessarily determined to do ill, this case seems to me to move pity, but not disapprobation. He was ill, because he could not be otherwise. Who can blame him? Necessity has no law.

If he knows that he acted under this necessity, has he not just ground to exculpate himself? The blame, if there be any, is not in him, but in his constitution. If he be charged by his Maker with doing wrong, may he not expostulate with him, and say — Why hast thou made me thus? I may be sacrificed at thy pleasure, for the common good, like a man that has the plague, but not for ill desert; for thou knowest that what I am charged with is thy work, and not mine.

Such are my notions of moral liberty and necessity, and of the consequences inseparably connected with both the one and the other.

This moral liberty a man may have, though it do not extend to all his actions, or even to all his voluntary actions. He does many things by instinct, many things by the force of habit, without any thought at all, and consequently without will. In the first part of life, he has not the power of self-government any more than the brutes. That power over the determinations of his own will, which belongs to him in ripe years, is limited, as all his powers are; and it is, perhaps, beyond the reach of his understanding to define its limits with precision. We can only say, in general, that it extends to every action for which he is accountable.

This power is given by his Maker, and at his pleasure whose gift it is it may be enlarged or diminished, continued or withdrawn. No power in the creature can be independent of the Creator. His hook is in its nose; he can give it line as far as he sees fit, and, when he pleases, can restrain it, or turn it whithersoever he will. Let this be always understood when we ascribe liberty to man, or to any created being.

Supposing it therefore to be true, *That man is a free agent*, it may be true, at the same time, that his liberty may be impaired or lost, by disorder of body or mind, as in melancholy, or in madness; it may be impaired or lost by vicious habits; it may, in particular cases, be restrained by divine interposition.

We call man a *free* agent in the same way as we call him a *reasonable* agent. In many things he is not guided by reason, but by principles similar to those of the brutes. His reason is weak at best. It is liable to be impaired or lost, by his own fault, or by other means. In like manner, he may be a free agent, though his freedom of action may have many similar limitations.

The liberty I have described has been represented by some philosophers as inconceivable, and as involving an absurdity.

'Liberty, they say, consists only in a power to act as we will; and it is impossible to conceive in any being a greater liberty than this. Hence it follows, that liberty does not extend to the determinations of the will, but only to the actions consequent to its determination, and depending upon the will. To say that we have power to will such an action, is to say, that we may will it, if we will. This supposes the will to be determined by a prior will; and, for the same reason, that will must be determined by a will prior to it, and so on in an infinite series of wills, which is absurd. To act freely, therefore, can mean nothing more than to act voluntarily; and this is all the liberty that can be conceived in man, or in any being.'

This reasoning — first, I think, advanced by Hobbes — has been very generally adopted by the defenders of necessity. It is grounded upon a definition of liberty totally different from that which I have given, and therefore does not apply to moral liberty, as above defined.

But it is said that this is the only liberty that is possible, that is conceivable, that does not involve an absurdity.

It is strange, indeed, if the word *Liberty* has no meaning but this one. I shall mention *three*, all very common. The objection applies to one of them, but to neither of the other two.

Liberty is sometimes opposed to external force or confinement of the body. Sometimes it is opposed to obligation by law, or by lawful authority. Sometimes it is opposed to necessity.

1. It is opposed to confinement of the body by superior force. So we say a prisoner is set at liberty when his fetters are knocked off, and he is discharged from confinement. This is the liberty defined in the objection; and I grant that this liberty extends not to the will, neither does the confinement, because the will cannot be confined by external force.

2. Liberty is opposed to obligation by law, or lawful authority. This liberty is a right to act one way or another, in things which the law has neither commanded nor forbidden; and this liberty is meant when we speak of a man's natural liberty, his civil liberty, his Christian liberty. It is evident that this liberty, as well as the obligation opposed to it, extends to the will: For it is the will to obey that makes obedience; the will to transgress that makes a transgression of the law. Without will there can be neither obedience nor transgression. Law supposes a power to obey or to transgress; it does not take away this power, but proposes the motives of duty and of interest, leaving the power to yield to them, or to take the consequence of transgression.

3. Liberty is opposed to Necessity, and in this sense it extends to the determinations of the will only, and not to what is consequent to the will.

In every voluntary action, the determination of the will is the first part of the action, upon which alone the moral estimation of it depends. It has been made a question among philosophers, *Whether, in every instance, this determination be the necessary consequence of the constitution of the person, and the circumstances in which he is placed; or whether he had not power, in many cases, to determine this way or that?*

This has, by some, been called the *philosophical* notion of liberty and necessity; but it is by no means peculiar to philosophers. The lowest of the vulgar have, in all ages, been prone to have recourse to this necessity, to exculpate themselves or their friends in what they do wrong, though, in the general tenor of their conduct, they act upon the contrary principle.

Whether this notion of moral liberty be *conceivable* or not, every man must judge for himself. To me there appears no difficulty in conceiving it. I consider the determination of the will as an effect. This effect must have a cause which had power to produce it; and the cause must be either the person himself, whose will it is, or some other being. The first is as easily conceived as the last. If the person was the cause of that determination of his own will, he was free in that action, and it is justly imputed to him, whether it be good or bad. But, if another being was the cause of this determination, either by producing it immediately, or by means and instruments under his direction, then the determination is the act and deed of that being, and is solely imputable to him.

But it is said—'That nothing is in our power but what depends upon the will, and therefore, the will itself cannot be in our power.'

I answer—That this is a fallacy arising from taking a common saying in a sense which it never was intended to convey, and in a sense contrary to what it necessarily implies.

In common life, when men speak of what is, or is not, in a man's power, they attend only to the external and visible effects, which only can be perceived, and which only can affect them. Of these, it is true that nothing is in a man's power but what depends upon his will, and this is all that is meant by this common saying.

But this is so far from excluding his will from being in his power, that it necessarily implies it. For to say that what depends upon the will is in a man's power, but the will is not in his power, is to say that the end is in his power, but the means necessary to that end are not in his power, which is a contradiction.

In many propositions which we express universally, there is an exception necessarily implied, and, therefore, always understood. Thus, when we say that all things depend upon God, God himself is necessarily excepted. In like manner, when we say, that all that is in our power depends upon the will, the will itself is necessarily excepted: for, if the will be not, nothing else can be in our power. Every effect must be in the power of its cause. The determination of the will is an effect, and, therefore, must be in the power of its cause, whether that cause be the agent himself, or some other being.

From what has been said in this chapter, I hope the notion of moral liberty will be distinctly understood, and that it appears that this notion is neither inconceivable, nor involves any absurdity or contradiction.

Chapter IV

Of the influence of motives.

The modern advocates for the doctrine of Necessity lay the stress of their cause upon the influence of *motives*.

'Every deliberate action, they say, must have a motive. When there is no motive on the other side, this motive must determine the agent: When there are contrary motives, the strongest must prevail. We reason from men's motives to their actions, as we do from other causes to their effects. If man be a free agent, and be not governed by motives, all his actions must be mere caprice, rewards and punishments can have no effect, and such a being must be absolutely ungovernable.'

In order, therefore, to understand distinctly, in what sense we ascribe moral liberty to man, it is necessary to understand what influence we allow to motives. To prevent misunderstanding, which has been very common upon this point, I offer the following observations:

1. I grant that all rational beings are influenced, and ought to be influenced, by motives. But the influence of motives is of a very different nature from that of efficient causes. They are neither causes nor agents. They suppose an efficient cause, and can do nothing without it. We cannot, without absurdity, suppose a motive either to act, or to be acted upon; it is equally incapable of action and of passion; because it is not a thing that exists, but a thing that is con-

ceived; it is what the schoolmen called an *ens rationis*. Motives, therefore, may *influence* to action, but they do not act. They may be compared to advice, or exhortation, which leaves a man still at liberty. For in vain is advice given when there is not a power either to do or to forbear what it recommends. In like manner, motives suppose liberty in the agent, otherwise they have no influence at all.

It is a law of nature with respect to matter, That every motion and change of motion, is proportional to the force impressed, and in the direction of that force. The scheme of necessity supposes a similar law to obtain in all the actions of intelligent beings; which, with little alteration, may be expressed thus:—Every action, or change of action, in an intelligent being, is proportional to the force of motives impressed, and in the direction of that force.

The law of nature respecting matter, is grounded upon this principle: That matter is an inert, inactive substance, which does not act, but is acted upon; and the law of necessity must be grounded upon the supposition, That an intelligent being is an inert, inactive substance, which does not act, but is acted upon.

2. Rational beings, in proportion as they are wise and good, will act according to the best motives; and every rational being who does otherwise, abuses his liberty. The most perfect being, in everything where there is a right and a wrong, a better and a worse, always infallibly acts according to the best motives. This, indeed, is little else than an identical proposition; for it is a contradiction to say, That a perfect being does what is wrong or unreasonable. But, to say that he does not act freely, because he always does what is best, is to say, That the proper use of liberty destroys liberty, and that liberty consists only in its abuse.

The moral perfection of the Deity consists, not in having no power to do ill, otherwise, as Dr Clarke justly observes, there would be no ground to thank him for his goodness to us, any more than for his eternity or immensity; but his moral perfection consists in this, that, when he has power to do everything, a power which cannot be resisted, he exerts that power only in doing what is wisest and best. To be subject to necessity, is to have no power at all; for power and necessity are opposites. We grant, therefore, that motives have influence, similar to that of advice or persuasion; but this influence is perfectly consistent with liberty, and, indeed, supposes liberty.

3. Whether every deliberate action must have a motive, depends on the meaning we put upon the word *deliberate*. If, by a deliberate action, we mean an action wherein motives are weighed, which seems to be the original meaning of the word, surely there must be motives, and contrary motives, otherwise they could not be weighed. But, if a deliberate action means only, as it commonly does, an action done by a cool and calm determination of the mind, with forethought and will, I believe there are innumerable such actions done without a motive.

This must be appealed to every man's consciousness. I do many trifling actions every day, in which, upon the most careful reflection, I am conscious of no motive; and to say that I may be influenced by a motive of which I am not conscious, is, in the first place, an arbitrary supposition without any evidence, and then, it is to say, that I may be convinced by an argument which never entered into my thought.

Cases frequently occur, in which an end that is of some importance, may be answered equally well by any one of several different means. In such cases, a man who intends the end finds not the least difficulty in taking one of these means, though he be firmly persuaded that it has no title to be preferred to any of the others.

To say that this is a case that cannot happen, is to contradict the experience of mankind; for surely a man who has occasion to lay out a shilling, or a guinea, may have two hundred that are of equal value, both to the giver and to the receiver, any one of which will answer his purpose equally well. To say, that, if such a case should happen, the man could not execute his purpose, is still more ridiculous, though it have the authority of some of the schoolmen, who determined that the ass, between two equal bundles of hay, would stand still till it died of hunger.

If a man could not act without a motive, he would have no power at all; for motives are not in our power; and he that has not power over a necessary mean, has not power over the end.

That an action, done without any motive, can neither have merit nor demerit, is much insisted on by the writers for necessity, and triumphantly, as if it were the very hinge of the controversy. I grant it to be a self-evident proposition, and I know no author that ever denied it.

How insignificant soever, in moral estimation, the actions may be which are done without any motive, they are of moment in the question concerning moral liberty. For, if there ever was any action of this kind, motives are not the sole causes of human actions. And, if we have the power of acting without a motive, that power, joined to a weaker motive, may counterbalance a stronger.

4. It can never be proved, That when there is a motive on one side only, that motive must determine the action.

According to the laws of reasoning, the proof is incumbent on those who hold the affirmative; and I have never seen a shadow of argument, which does not take for granted the thing in question — to wit, that motives are the sole causes of actions.

Is there no such thing as wilfulness, caprice, or obstinacy, among mankind? If there be not, it is wonderful that they should have names in all languages. If there be such things, a single motive, or even many motives, may be resisted.

5. When it is said, that of contrary motives the strongest always prevails, this can neither be affirmed nor denied with understanding, until we know distinctly what is meant by the strongest motive.

I do not find that those who have advanced this as a self-evident axiom, have ever attempted to explain what they mean by the strongest motive, or have given any rule by which we may judge which of two motives is the strongest.

How shall we know whether the strongest motive always prevails, if we know not which is strongest? There must be some test by which their strength is to be tried, some balance in which they may be weighed; otherwise, to say that the strongest motive always prevails, is to speak without any meaning. We must therefore search for this test or balance, since they who have laid so much stress upon this axiom, have left us wholly in the dark as to its meaning. I grant, that, when the contrary motives are of the same kind, and differ only in quantity, it may be easy to say which is the strongest.

Thus a bribe of a thousand pounds is a stronger motive than a bribe of a hundred pounds. But when the motives are of different kinds — as money and fame, duty and worldly interest, health and strength, riches and honour — by what rule shall we judge which is the strongest motive?

Either we measure the strength of motives merely by their prevalence, or by some other standard distinct from their prevalence.

If we measure their strength merely by their prevalence, and by the strongest motive mean only the motive that prevails, it will be true indeed that the strongest motive prevails; but the proposition will be identical, and mean no more than that the strongest motive is the strongest motive. From this surely no conclusion can be drawn.

If it should be said, That by the strength of a motive is not meant its prevalence, but the cause of its prevalence; that we measure the cause by the effect, and from the superiority of the effect conclude the superiority of the cause, as we conclude that to be the heaviest weight which bears down the scale: I answer, That, according to this explication of the axiom, it takes for granted that motives are the causes, and the sole causes, of actions. Nothing is left to the agent, but to be acted upon by the motives, as the balance is by the weights. The axiom supposes, that the agent does not act, but is acted upon; and, from this supposition, it is concluded that he does not act. This is to reason in a circle, or rather it is not reasoning but begging the question.

Contrary motives may very properly be compared to advocates pleading the opposite sides of a cause at the bar. It would be very weak reasoning to say, that such an advocate is the most powerful pleader, because sentence was given on his side. The sentence is in the power of the judge, not of the advocate. It is equally weak reasoning, in proof of necessity, to say, such a motive prevailed, therefore it is the strongest; since the defenders of liberty maintain that the determination was made by the man, and not by the motive.

We are therefore brought to this issue, that, unless some measure of the strength of motives can be found distinct from their prevalence, it cannot be determined whether the strongest motive always prevails or not. If such a measure can be found and applied, we may be able to judge of the truth of this maxim, but not otherwise.

Everything that can be called a motive, is addressed either to the animal or to the rational part of our nature. Motives of the former kind are common to us with the brutes; those of the latter are peculiar to rational beings. We shall beg leave, for distinction's sake, to call the former, *animal* motives, and the latter, *rational*.

Hunger is a motive in a dog to eat; so is it in a man. According to the strength of the appetite, it gives a stronger or a weaker impulse to eat. And the same thing may be said of every other appetite and passion. Such animal motives give an impulse to the agent, to which he yields with ease; and, if the impulse be strong, it cannot be resisted without an effort which requires a greater or a less degree of self-command. Such motives are not addressed to the rational powers. Their influence is immediately upon the will. We feel their influence, and judge of their strength, by the conscious effort which is necessary to resist them.

When a man is acted upon by contrary motives of this kind, he finds it easy to yield to the strongest. They are like two forces pushing him in contrary directions. To yield to the strongest, he needs only to be passive. By exerting his own force, he may resist; but this requires an effort of which he is conscious. The strength of motives of this kind is perceived, not by our judgment, but by our feeling; and that is the strongest of contrary motives, to which he can yield with ease, or which it requires an effort of self-command to resist; and this we may call the *animal test* of the strength of motives.

If it be asked, whether, in motives of this kind, the strongest always prevails, I would answer, that in brute-animals I believe it does. They do not appear to have any self-command; an appetite or passion in them is overcome only by a stronger contrary one. On this account, they are not accountable for their actions, nor can they be the subjects of law.

But in men who are able to exercise their rational powers, and have any degree of self-command, the strongest animal motive does not always prevail. The flesh does not always prevail against the spirit, though too often it does. And if men were necessarily determined by the strongest animal motive, they could no more be accountable, or capable of being governed by law, than brutes are.

Let us next consider rational motives, to which the name of *motive* is more commonly and more properly given. Their influence is upon the judgment, by convincing us that such an action ought to be done; that it is our duty, or conducive to our real good, or to some end which we have determined to pursue.

They do not give a blind impulse to the will, as animal motives do. They convince, but they do not impel, unless, as may often happen, they excite some passion of hope, or fear, or desire. Such passions may be excited by conviction, and may operate in its aid as other animal motives do. But there may be conviction without passion; and the conviction of what we ought to do, in order to some end which we have judged fit to be pursued, is what I call a *rational motive*.

Brutes, I think, cannot be influenced by such motives. They have not the conception of *ought* and *ought not*. Children acquire these conceptions as their rational powers advance; and they are found in all of ripe age, who have the human faculties.

If there be any competition between rational motives, it is evident that the strongest, in the eye of reason, is that which it is most our duty and our real happiness to follow. Our duty and our real happiness are ends which are inseparable; and they are the ends which every man, endowed with reason, is conscious he ought to pursue in preference to all others. This we may call the *rational test* of the strength of motives. A motive which is the strongest, according to the animal test, may be, and very often is, the weakest according to the rational.

The grand and the important competition of contrary motives is between the animal, on the one hand, and the rational on the other. This is the conflict between the flesh and the spirit, upon the event of which the character of men depends.

If it be asked, Which of these is the strongest motive? The answer is, That the first is commonly strongest, when they are tried by the animal test. If it were not so, human life would be no state of trial. It would not be a warfare, nor would virtue require any effort or self-command. No man would have any temptation to do wrong. But, when we try the contrary motives by the rational test, it is evident that the rational motive is always the strongest.

And now, I think, it appears, that the strongest motive, according to either of the tests I have mentioned, does not always prevail.

In every wise and virtuous action, the motive that prevails is the strongest according to the rational test, but commonly the weakest according to the animal. In every foolish and in every vicious action, the motive that prevails is commonly the strongest according to the animal test, but always the weakest according to the rational.

6. It is true that we reason from men's motives to their actions, and, in many cases, with great probability, but never with absolute certainty. And to infer from this, that men are necessarily determined by motives, is very weak reasoning.

For let us suppose, for a moment, that men have moral liberty, I would ask, what use may they be expected to make of this liberty? It may surely be expected, that, of the various actions within the sphere of their power, they will choose what pleases them most for the present, or what appears to be most for their real, though distant good. When there is a competition between these motives, the foolish will prefer present gratification; the wise the greater and more distant good.

Now, is not this the very way in which we see men act? Is it not from the presumption that they act in this way, that we reason from their motives to their actions? Surely it is. Is it not weak reasoning, therefore, to argue, that men have not liberty, because they act in that very way in which they would act if they had liberty? It would surely be more like reasoning to draw the contrary conclusion from the same premises.

7. Nor is it better reasoning to conclude that, if men are not necessarily determined by motives, all their actions must be capricious.

To resist the strongest animal motives when duty requires, is so far from being capricious that it is, in the highest degree, wise and virtuous. And we hope this is often done by good men.

To act against rational motives, must always be foolish, vicious, or capricious. And, it cannot be denied, that there are too many such actions done. But is it reasonable to conclude, that, because liberty may be abused by the foolish and the vicious, therefore it can never be put to its proper use, which is to act wisely and virtuously?

8. It is equally unreasonable to conclude—That, if men are not necessarily determined by motives, rewards and punishments would have no effect. With wise men they will have their due effect; but not always with the foolish and the vicious.

Let us consider what effect rewards and punishments do really, and in fact, produce, and what may be inferred from that effect upon each of the opposite systems of liberty and of necessity.

I take it for granted that, in fact, the best and wisest laws, both human and divine, are often transgressed, notwithstanding the rewards and punishments that are annexed to them. If any man should deny this fact, I know not how to reason with him.

From this fact, it may be inferred with certainty, upon the supposition of necessity, That, in every instance of transgression, the motive of reward or punishment was not of sufficient strength to produce obedience to the law. This implies a fault in the lawgiver; but there can be no fault in the transgressor, who acts mechanically by the force of motives. We might as well impute a fault to the balance when it does not raise a weight of two pounds by the force of one pound.

Upon the supposition of necessity, there can be neither reward nor punishment, in the proper sense, as those words imply good and ill desert. Reward and punishment are only tools employed to produce a mechanical effect. When the effect is not produced, the tool must be unfit or wrong applied.

Upon the supposition of liberty, rewards and punishments will have a proper effect upon the wise and the good; but not so upon the foolish and the vicious, when opposed by their animal passions or bad habits; and this is just what we see to be the fact. Upon this supposition, the transgression of the law implies no defect in the law, no fault in the lawgiver; the fault is solely in the transgressor. And it is upon this supposition only, that there can be either reward or punishment, in the proper sense of the words, because it is only on this supposition that there can be good or ill desert.

Chapter VI

First argument [for moral liberty].

We have, by our constitution, a natural conviction or belief that we act freely—a conviction so early, so universal, and so necessary in most of our rational operations, that it must be the result of our constitution, and the work of Him that made us.

Some of the most strenuous advocates for the doctrine of necessity acknowledge that it is impossible to act upon it. They say that we have a natural sense or conviction that we act freely, but that this is a fallacious sense.

This doctrine is dishonourable to our Maker, and lays a foundation for universal scepticism. It supposes the Author of our being to have given us one faculty on purpose to deceive us, and another by which we may detect the fallacy, and find that he imposed upon us.

If any one of our natural faculties be fallacious, there can be no reason to trust to any of them; for He that made one made all.

The genuine dictate of our natural faculties is the voice of God, no less than what he reveals from heaven; and to say that it is fallacious, is to impute a lie to the God of truth.

If candour and veracity be not an essential part of moral excellence, there is no such thing as moral excellence, nor any reason to rely on the declarations and promises of the Almighty. A man may be tempted to lie, but not without being conscious of guilt and of meanness. Shall we impute to the Almighty what we cannot impute to a man without a heinous affront?

Passing this opinion, therefore, as shocking to an ingenuous mind, and, in its consequences, subversive of all religion, all morals, and all knowledge, let us proceed to consider the evidence of our having a natural conviction that we have some degree of active power.

The very conception or idea of active power must be derived from something in our own constitution. It is impossible to account for it otherwise. We see events, but we see not the power that produces them. We perceive one event to follow another, but we perceive not the chain that binds them together. The notion of power and causation, therefore, cannot be got from external objects.

Yet the notion of causes, and the belief that every event must have a cause which had power to produce it, is found in every human mind so firmly established, that it cannot be rooted out.

This notion and this belief must have its origin from something in our constitution; and that it is natural to man, appears from the following observations.

1. We are conscious of many voluntary exertions, some easy, others more difficult, some requiring a great effort. These are exertions of power. And, though a man may be unconscious of his power when he does not exert it, he must have both the conception and the belief of it, when he knowingly and willingly exerts it, with intention to produce some effect.

2. Deliberation about an action of moment, whether we shall do it or not, implies a conviction that it is in our power. To deliberate about an end, we must be convinced that the means are in our power; and to deliberate about the means, we must be convinced that we have power to choose the most proper.

3. Suppose our deliberation brought to an issue, and that we resolve to do what appeared proper, can we form such a resolution or purpose, without any conviction of power to execute it? No; it is impossible. A man cannot resolve to lay out a sum of money which he neither has nor hopes ever to have.

4. Again, when I plight my faith in any promise or contract, I must believe that I shall have power to perform what I promise. Without this persuasion, a promise would be downright fraud.

There is a condition implied in every promise, *if we live* and *if God continue with us the power which he hath given us.* Our conviction, therefore, of this power derogates not in the least from our dependence upon God. The rudest savage is taught by nature to admit this condition in all promises, whether it be expressed or not. For it is a dictate of common sense, that we can be under no obligation to do what it is impossible for us to do.

If we act upon the system of necessity, there must be another condition implied in all deliberation, in every resolution, and in every promise; and that is, *if we shall be willing.* But the will not being in our power, we cannot engage for it.

If this condition be understood, as it must be understood if we act upon the system of necessity, there can be no deliberation, or resolution, nor any obligation in a promise. A man might as well deliberate, resolve, and promise, upon the actions of other men as upon his own.

It is no less evident that we have a conviction of power in other men, when we advise, or persuade, or command, or conceive them to be under obligation by their promises.

5. Is it possible for any man to blame himself for yielding to necessity? Then he may blame himself for dying, or for being a man. Blame supposes a wrong use of power; and, when a man does as well as it was possible for him to do, wherein is he to be blamed? Therefore, all conviction of wrong conduct, all remorse and self-condemnation, imply a conviction of our power to have done better. Take away this conviction, and there may be a sense of misery, or a dread of evil to come; but there can be no sense of guilt or resolution to do better.

Many who hold the doctrine of necessity, disown these consequences of it, and think to evade them. To such, they ought not to be imputed; but their inseparable connection with that doctrine appears self-evident; and, therefore, some late patrons of it have had the boldness to avow them. 'They cannot accuse themselves of having done anything wrong, in the ultimate sense of the words. In a strict sense, they have nothing to do with repentance, confession, and pardon — these being adapted to a fallacious view of things.'

Those who can adopt these sentiments, may, indeed, celebrate, with high encomiums, '*the great and glorious doctrine of necessity.*' It restores them, in their own conceit, to the state of innocence. It delivers them from all the pangs of guilt and remorse, and from all fear about their future conduct, though not about their fate. They may be as secure that they shall do nothing wrong as those who have finished their course. A doctrine so flattering to the mind of a sinner, is very apt to give strength to weak arguments.

After all, it is acknowledged, by those who boast of this glorious doctrine, 'That every man, let him use what efforts he can, will necessarily feel the sentiments of shame, remorse, and repentance, and, oppressed with a sense of guilt, will have recourse to that mercy of which he stands in need.'

The meaning of this seems to me to be, That, although the doctrine of necessity be supported by invincible arguments, and though it be the most consolatory doctrine in the world; yet no man, in his most serious moments, when he sits himself before the throne of his Maker, can possibly believe it, but must then necessarily lay aside this glorious doctrine, and all its flattering consequences, and return to the humiliating conviction of his having made a bad use of the power which God had given him.

If the belief of our having active power be necessarily implied in those rational operations we have mentioned, it must be coeval with our reason; it must be as universal among men, and as necessary in the conduct of life, as those operations are.

We cannot recollect by memory when it began. It cannot be a prejudice of education, or of false philosophy. It must be a part of our constitution, or the necessary result of our constitution and therefore the work of God.

It resembles, in this respect, our belief of the existence of a material world; our belief that those we converse with are living and intelligent beings; our belief that those things did really happen, which we distinctly remember; and our belief that we continue the same identical persons.

We find difficulty in accounting for our belief of these things; and some philosophers think that they have discovered good reasons for throwing it off. But it sticks fast, and the greatest sceptic finds that he must yield to it in his practice, while he wages war with it in speculation.

If it be objected to this argument, That the belief of our acting freely cannot be implied in the operations we have mentioned, because those operations are performed by them who believe that we are, in all our actions, governed by necessity—the answer to this objection is, That men in their practice may be governed by a belief which in speculation they reject.

However strange and unaccountable this may appear, there are many well-known instances of it.

I knew a man who was as much convinced as any man of the folly of the popular belief of apparitions in the dark; yet he could not sleep in a room alone, nor go alone into a room in the dark. Can it be said, that his fear did not imply a belief of danger? This is impossible. Yet his philosophy convinced him that he was in no more danger in the dark when alone, than with company.

Here an unreasonable belief, which was merely a prejudice of the nursery, stuck so fast as to govern his conduct, in opposition to his speculative belief as a philosopher and a man of sense.

There are few persons who can look down from the battlement of a very high tower without fear, while their reason convinces them that they are in no more danger than when standing upon the ground.

There have been persons who professed to believe that there is no distinction between virtue and vice, yet in their practice they resented injuries, and esteemed noble and virtuous actions.

There have been sceptics who professed to disbelieve their senses and every human faculty; but no sceptic was ever known, who did not, in practice, pay a regard to his senses and to his other faculties.

There are some points of belief so necessary, that, without them, a man would not be the being which God made him. These may be opposed in speculation, but it is impossible to root them out. In a speculative hour they seem to vanish, but in practice they resume their authority. This seems to be the case of those who hold the doctrine of necessity, and yet act as if they were free.

This natural conviction of some degree of power in ourselves and in other men, respects voluntary actions only. For, as all our power is directed by our will, we can form no conception of power, properly so called, that is not under the direction of will. And therefore our exertions, our deliberations, our purposes, our promises, are only in things that depend upon our will. Our advices, exhortations, and commands, are only in things that depend upon the will of those to whom they are addressed. We impute no guilt to ourselves, nor to others, in things where the will is not concerned.

But it deserves our notice, that we do not conceive everything, without exception, to be in a man's power which depends upon his will. There are many exceptions to this general rule. The most obvious of these I shall mention, because they both serve to illustrate the rule, and are of importance in the question concerning the liberty of man.

In the rage of madness, men are absolutely deprived of the power of self-government. They act voluntarily, but their will is driven as by a tempest, which, in lucid intervals, they resolve to oppose with all their might, but are overcome when the fit of madness returns.

Idiots are like men walking in the dark, who cannot be said to have the power of choosing their way, because they cannot distinguish the good road from the bad. Having no light in their understanding, they must either sit still, or be carried on by some blind impulse.

Between the darkness of infancy, which is equal to that of idiots, and the maturity of reason, there is a long twilight, which, by insensible degrees, advances to the perfect day.

In this period of life, man has but little of the power of self-government. His actions, by nature, as well as by the laws of society, are in the power of others more than in his own. His folly and indiscretion, his levity and inconstancy, are considered as the fault of youth, rather than of the man. We consider him as half a man and half a child, and expect that each by turns should play its part. He would be thought a severe and unequitable censor of manners, who required the same cool deliberation, the same steady conduct, and the same mastery over himself, in a boy of thirteen, as in a man of thirty.

It is an old adage, That violent anger is a short fit of madness. If this be literally true in any case, a man, in such a fit of passion, cannot be said to have the command of himself. If real madness could be proved, it must have the effect of madness while it lasts, whether it be for an hour or for life. But the madness of a short fit of passion, if it be really madness, is incapable of proof; and therefore is not admitted in human tribunals as an exculpation. And, I believe, there is no case where a man can satisfy his own mind that his passion, both in its beginning and in its progress, was irresistible. The Searcher of hearts alone knows infallibly what allowance is due in cases of this kind.

But a violent passion, though it may not be irresistible, is difficult to be resisted: And a man, surely, has not the same power over himself in passion, as when he is cool. On this account it is allowed by all men to alleviate, when it cannot exculpate; and has its weight in criminal courts, as well as in private judgment.

It ought likewise to be observed, That he who has accustomed himself to restrain his passions, enlarges by habit his power over them, and consequently over himself. When we consider that a Canadian savage can acquire the power of defying death in its most dreadful forms, and of braving the most exquisite torment for many long hours, without losing the command of himself; we may learn from this, that, in the constitution of human nature, there is ample scope for the enlargement of that power of self-command without which there can be no virtue nor magnanimity.

There are cases, however, in which a man's voluntary actions are thought to be very little, if at all, in his power, on account of the violence of the motive that impels him. The magnanimity of a hero, or of a martyr, is not expected in every man, and on all occasions.

If a man trusted by the government with a secret which it is high treason to disclose, be prevailed upon by a bribe, we have no mercy for him, and hardly allow the greatest bribe to be any alleviation of his crime.

But, on the other hand, if the secret be extorted by the rack, or by the dread of present death, we pity him more than we blame him, and would think it severe and unequitable to condemn him as a traitor.

What is the reason that all men agree in condemning this man as a traitor in the first place, and, in the last, either exculpate him, or think his fault greatly alleviated? If he acted necessarily in both cases, compelled by an irresistible motive, I can see no reason why we should not pass the same judgment on both.

But the reason of these different judgments is evidently this — That the love of money, and of what is called a man's interest, is a cool motive, which leaves to a man the entire power over himself; but the torment of the rack, or the dread of present death, are so violent motives that men who have not uncommon strength of mind, are not masters of themselves in such a situation, and, therefore, what they do is not imputed, or is thought less criminal.

If a man resist such motives, we admire his fortitude, and think his conduct heroical rather than human. If he yields, we impute it to human frailty, and think him rather to be pitied than severely censured.

Inveterate habits are acknowledged to diminish very considerably the power a man has over himself. Although we may think him highly blameable in acquiring them, yet, when they are confirmed to a certain degree, we consider him as no longer master of himself, and hardly reclaimable without a miracle.

Thus we see that the power which we are led, by common sense, to ascribe to man respects his voluntary actions only, and that it has various limitations even with regard to them. Some actions that depend upon our will are easy, others very difficult, and some, perhaps, beyond our power. In different men, the power of self-government is different, and in the same man at different times. It may be diminished, or perhaps lost, by bad habits; it may be greatly increased by good habits.

These are facts attested by experience, and supported by the common judgment of mankind. Upon the system of Liberty they are perfectly intelligible; but, I think, irreconcileable to that of Necessity; for, How can there be an easy and a difficult in actions equally subject to necessity? — or, How can power be greater or less, increased or diminished, in those who have no power?

This natural conviction of our acting freely, which is acknowledged by many who hold the doctrine of necessity, ought to throw the whole burden of proof upon that side; for, by this, the side of liberty has what lawyers call a *jus quæsitum*, or a right of ancient possession, which ought to stand good till it be overturned. If it cannot be proved that we always act from necessity, there is no need of arguments on the other side to convince us that we are free agents.

To illustrate this by a similar case: — If a philosopher would persuade me that my fellow-men with whom I converse are not thinking, intelligent beings, but mere machines, though I might be at a loss to find arguments against this strange opinion, I should think it reasonable to hold the belief which nature gave me before I was capable of weighing evidence, until convincing proof is brought against it.

Chapter VII

Second argument [for moral liberty].

That there is a real and essential distinction between right and wrong conduct, between just and unjust—That the most perfect moral rectitude is to be ascribed to the Deity—That man is a moral and accountable being, capable of acting right and wrong and answerable for his conduct to Him who made him, and assigned him a part to act upon the stage of life; are principles proclaimed by every man's conscience— principles upon which the systems of morality and natural religion, as well as the system of revelation, are grounded, and which have been generally acknowledged by those who hold contrary opinions on the subject of human liberty. I shall therefore here take them for granted.

These principles afford an obvious, and, I think, an invincible argument, that man is endowed with Moral Liberty.

Two things are implied in the notion of a moral and accountable being—*Understanding* and *Active Power*.

First, He must *understand the law to which he is bound, and his obligation to obey it*. Moral obedience must be voluntary, and must regard the authority of the law. I may command my horse to eat when he hungers, and drink when he thirsts. He does so; but his doing it is no moral obedience. He does not understand my command, and therefore can have no will to obey it. He has not the conception of moral obligation, and therefore cannot act from the conviction of it. In eating and drinking, he is moved by his own appetite only, and not by my authority.

Brute-animals are incapable of moral obligation, because they have not that degree of understanding which it implies. They have not the conception of a rule of conduct, and of obligation to obey it, and therefore, though they may be noxious, they cannot be criminal.

Man, by his rational nature, is capable both of understanding the law that is prescribed to him, and of perceiving its obligation. He knows what it is to be just and honest, to injure no man, and to obey his Maker. From his constitution, he has an immediate conviction of his obligation to these things. He has the approbation of his conscience when he acts by these rules; and he is conscious of guilt and demerit when he transgresses them. And, without this knowledge of his duty and his obligation, he would not be a moral and accountable being.

Secondly, Another thing implied in the notion of a moral and accountable being, *is power to do what he is accountable for*.

That no man can be under a moral obligation to do what it is impossible for him to do, or to forbear what it is impossible for him to forbear, is an axiom as self-evident as any in mathematics. It cannot be contradicted, without overturning all notion of moral obligation; nor can there be any exception to it, when it is rightly understood.

Some moralists have mentioned what they conceived to be an exception to this maxim. The exception is this. When a man, by his own fault, has disabled himself from doing his duty, his obligation, they say, remains, though he is now unable to discharge it. Thus, if a man by sumptuous living has become bankrupt, his inability to pay his debt does not take away his obligation.

To judge whether, in this and similar cases, there be any exception to the axiom above mentioned, they must be stated accurately.

No doubt a man is highly criminal in living above his fortune, and his crime is greatly aggravated by the circumstance of his being thereby unable to pay his just debt. Let us suppose, therefore, that he is punished for this crime as much as it deserves; that his goods are fairly distributed among his creditors, and that one half remains unpaid. Let us suppose also, that he adds no new crime to what is past, that he becomes a new man, and not only supports himself by honest industry, but does all in his power to pay what he still owes.

I would now ask, Is he further punishable, and really guilty for not paying more than he is able? Let every man consult his conscience, and say whether he can blame this man for not doing more than he is able to do. His guilt before his bankruptcy is out of the question, as he has received the punishment due for it. But that his subsequent conduct is unblameable, every man must allow; and that, in his present state, he is accountable for no more than he is able to do. His obligation is not cancelled, it returns with his ability, and can go no farther.

Suppose a sailor, employed in the navy of his country, and longing for the ease of a public hospital as an invalid, to cut off his fingers, so as to disable him from doing the duty of a sailor; he is guilty of a great crime; but, after he has been punished according to the demerit of his crime, will his captain insist that he shall still do the duty of a sailor? Will he command him to go aloft when it is impossible for him to do it, and punish him as guilty of disobedience? Surely, if there be any such thing as justice and injustice, this would be unjust and wanton cruelty.

Suppose a servant, through negligence and inattention, mistakes the orders given him by his master, and, from this mistake, does what he was ordered not to do. It is commonly said that culpable ignorance does not excuse a fault. This decision is inaccurate, because it does not show where the fault lies. The fault was solely in that inattention, or negligence, which was the occasion of his mistake. There was no subsequent fault.

This becomes evident, when we vary the case so far as to suppose that he was unavoidably led into the mistake without any fault on his part. His mistake is now invincible, and, in the opinion of all moralists, takes away all blame; yet this new case supposes no change, but in the cause of his mistake. His subsequent conduct was the same in both cases. The fault therefore lay solely in the negligence and inattention which was the cause of his mistake.

The axiom, *That invincible ignorance takes away all blame*, is only a particular case of the general axiom, That there can be no moral obligation to what is impossible; the former is grounded upon the latter, and can have no other foundation.

I shall put only one case more. Suppose that a man, by excess and intemperance, has entirely destroyed his rational faculties, so as to have become perfectly mad or idiotical; suppose him forewarned of his danger, and that, though he foresaw that this must be the consequence, he went on still in his criminal indulgence. A greater crime can hardly be supposed, or more deserving of severe punishment. Suppose him punished as he deserves; will it be said, that the duty of a man is incumbent upon him now, when he has not the faculties of a man, or that he incurs new guilt when he is not a moral agent? Surely we may as well suppose a plant, or a clod of earth, to be a subject of moral duty.

The decisions I have given of these cases, are grounded upon the fundamental principles of morals, the most immediate dictates of conscience. If these principles are given up, all moral reasoning is at an end, and no distinction is left between what is just and what is unjust. And it is evident that none of these cases furnishes any exception to the axiom above mentioned. No moral obligation can be consistent with impossibility in the performance.

Active power, therefore, is necessarily implied in the very notion of a moral accountable being. And if man be such a being, he must have a degree of active power proportioned to the account he is to make. He may have a model of perfection set before him which he is unable to reach; but, if he does to the utmost of his power, this is all he can be answerable for. To incur guilt, by not going beyond his power, is impossible.

What was said, in the first argument, of the limitation of our power, adds much strength to the present argument. A man's power, it was observed, extends only to his voluntary actions, and has many limitations, even with respect to them.

His *accountableness* has the same extent and the same limitations.

In the rage of madness he has no power over himself, neither is he accountable, or capable of moral obligation. In ripe age, man is accountable in a greater degree than in nonage, because his power over himself is greater. Violent passions and violent motives alleviate what is done through their influence, in the same proportion as they diminish the power of resistance.

There is, therefore, a perfect correspondence between *power*, on the one hand, and *moral obligation* and *accountableness*, on the other. They not only correspond in general, as they respect voluntary actions only, but every limitation of the first produces a corresponding limitation of the two last. This, indeed, amounts to nothing more than that maxim of common sense, confirmed by Divine authority, 'That to whom much is given, of him much will be required.'

The sum of this argument is — that a certain degree of active power is the talent which God hath given to every rational accountable creature, and of which he will require an account. If man had no power, he would have nothing to account for. All wise and all foolish conduct, all virtue and vice, consist in the right use or in the abuse of that power which God hath given us. If man had no power, he could neither be wise nor foolish, virtuous nor vicious.

If we adopt the system of necessity, the terms *moral obligation* and *accountableness*, *praise* and *blame*, *merit* and *demerit*, *justice* and *injustice*, *reward* and *punishment*, *wisdom* and *folly*, *virtue* and *vice*, ought to be disused, or to have new meanings given to them when they are used in religion, in morals, or in civil government; for, upon that system, there can be no such things as they have beer always used to signify.

Chapter VIII

Third argument [for moral liberty].

That man has power over his own actions and volitions appears, because he is capable of carrying on, wisely and prudently, a system of conduct, which he has before conceived in his mind, and resolved to prosecute.

I take it for granted, that, among the various characters of men, there have been some who, after they came to years of understanding, deliberately laid down a plan of conduct, which they resolve to pursue through life; and that of these, some have steadily pursued the end they had in view, by the proper means.

It is of no consequence in this argument, whether one has made the best choice of his main end or not; whether his end be riches, or power, or fame, or the approbation of his Maker. I suppose only, that he has prudently and steadily pursued it; that, in a long course of deliberate actions, he has taken the means that appeared most conducive to his end, and avoided whatever might cross it.

That such conduct in a man demonstrates a certain degree of wisdom and understanding, no man ever doubted; and I say it demonstrates, with equal force, a certain degree of power over his voluntary determinations.

This will appear evident, if we consider, that understanding without power may project, but can execute nothing. A regular plan of conduct, as it cannot be contrived without understanding, so it cannot be carried into execution without power; and, therefore, the execution, as an effect, demonstrates, with equal force, both power and understanding in the cause. Every indication of wisdom, taken from the effect, is equally an indication of power to execute what wisdom planned. And, if we have any evidence that the wisdom which formed the plan is in the man, we have the very same evidence that the power which executed it is in him also.

In this argument, we reason from the same principles as in demonstrating the being and perfections of the First Cause of all things.

The effects we observe in the course of nature require a cause. Effects wisely adapted to an end, require a wise cause. Every indication of the wisdom of the Creator is equally an indication of His power. His wisdom appears only in the works done by his power; for wisdom without power may speculate, but it cannot act; it may plan, but it cannot execute its plans.

The same reasoning we apply to the works of men. In a stately palace we see the wisdom of the architect. His wisdom contrived it, and wisdom could do no more. The execution required both a distinct conception of the plan, and power to operate according to that plan.

Let us apply these principles to the supposition we have made—That a man, in a long course of conduct, has determined and acted prudently in the prosecution of a certain end. If the man had both the wisdom to plan this course of conduct, and that power over his own actions that was necessary to carry it into execution, he is a free agent, and used his liberty, in this instance, with understanding.

But, if all his particular determinations, which concurred in the execution of this plan, were produced, not by himself, but by some cause acting necessarily upon him, then there is no evidence left that he contrived this plan, or that he ever spent a thought about it.

The cause that directed all these determinations so wisely, whatever it was, must be a wise and intelligent cause;

it must have understood the plan, and have intended the execution of it.

If it be said that all this course of determination was produced by Motives, motives, surely, have not understanding to conceive a plan, and intend its execution. We must, therefore, go back beyond motives to some intelligent being who had the power of arranging those motives, and applying them in their proper order and season, so as to bring about the end.

This intelligent being must have understood the plan, and intended to execute it. If this be so, as the man had no hand in the execution, we have not any evidence left that he had any hand in the contrivance, or even that he is a thinking being.

If we can believe that an extensive series of means may conspire to promote an end without a cause that intended the end, and had power to choose and apply those means for the purpose, we may as well believe that this world was made by a fortuitous concourse of atoms, without an intelligent and powerful cause.

If a lucky concourse of motives could produce the conduct of an Alexander or a Julius Caesar, no reason can be given why a lucky concourse of atoms might not produce the planetary system.

If, therefore, wise conduct in a man demonstrates that he has some degree of wisdom, it demonstrates, with equal force and evidence, that he has some degree of power over his own determinations.

All the reason we can assign for believing that our fellow-man think and reason, is grounded upon their actions and speeches. If they are not the cause of these, there is no reason left to conclude that they think and reason.

Des Cartes thought that the human body is merely a mechanical engine, and that all its motions and actions are produced by mechanism. If such a machine could be made to speak and to act rationally, we might, indeed, conclude with certainty, that the maker of it had both reason and active power; but, if we once knew that all the motions of the machine were purely mechanical, we should have no reason to conclude that the man had reason or thought.

The conclusion of this argument is—That, if the actions and speeches of other men give us sufficient evidence that they are reasonable beings, they give us the same evidence, and the same degree of evidence, that they are free agents.

There is another conclusion that may be drawn from this reasoning, which it is proper to mention.

Suppose a Fatalist, rather than give up the scheme of necessity, should acknowledge that he has no evidence that there is thought and reason in any of his fellow-men, and that they may be mechanical engines for all that he knows, he will be forced to acknowledge that there must be active power, as well as understanding, in the maker of those engines, and that the first cause is a free agent. We have the same reason to believe this as to believe his existence and his wisdom. And, if the Deity acts freely, every argument brought to prove that freedom of action is impossible, must fall to the ground.

The First Cause gives us evidence of his power by every effect that gives us evidence of his wisdom. And, if he is pleased to communicate to the work of his hands some degree of his wisdom, no reason can be assigned why he may not communicate some degree of his power, as the talent which wisdom is to employ.

That the first motion, or the first effect, whatever it be, cannot be produced necessarily, and, consequently, that the First Cause must be a free agent, has been demonstrated so clearly and unanswerably by Dr Clarke, both in his *Demonstration of the Being and Attributes of God*, and in the end of his *Remarks on Collins's Philosophical Enquiry concerning Human Liberty*, that I can add nothing to what he has said; nor have I found any objection made to his reasoning, by any of the defenders of necessity.

Essay V: Of Morals

Chapter V

Whether justice be a natural or an artificial virtue.

[…] I shall now make some observations upon the reasoning of this author [David Hume], in proof of his favourite principle, That justice is not a natural but an artificial virtue; or, as it is expressed in the *Enquiry*, That public utility is the sole origin of justice, and that reflections on the beneficial consequences of this virtue, are the sole foundation of its merit.[6]

1. It must be acknowledged that this principle has a necessary connection with his system concerning the foundation of all virtue; and, therefore, it is no wonder that he hath taken so much pains to support it; for the whole system must stand or fall with it.

If the *dulce* and the *utile* — that is, pleasure, and what is useful to procure pleasure — be the whole merit of virtue, justice can have no merit beyond its utility to procure pleasure. If, on the other hand, an intrinsic worth in justice, and demerit in injustice, be discerned by every man that hath a conscience; if there be a natural principle in the constitution of man by which justice is approved, and injustice disapproved and condemned — then the whole of this laboured system must fall to the ground.

2. We may observe, That, as justice is directly opposed to injury, and as there are various ways in which a man may be injured, so there must be various branches of justice opposed to the different kinds of injury.

A man may be injured, *first*, in his person, by wounding, maiming, or killing him; *secondly*, in his family, by robbing him of his children, or any way injuring those he is bound to protect; *thirdly*, in his liberty, by confinement; *fourthly*, in his reputation; *fifthly*, in his goods, or property; and, *lastly*, in the violation of contracts or engagements made with him. This enumeration, whether complete or not, is sufficient for the present purpose.

The different branches of justice, opposed to these different kinds of injury, are commonly expressed by saying, that an innocent man has a right to the safety of his person and family, a right to his liberty and reputation, a right to his goods, and to fidelity to engagements made with him. To say that he has a right to these things, has precisely the same meaning as to say that justice requires that he should be permitted to enjoy them, or that it is unjust to violate them; for injustice is the violation of right, and justice is to yield to every man what is his right.

These things being understood as the simplest and most common ways of expressing the various branches of justice, we are to consider how far Mr Hume's reasoning proves any or all of them to be artificial, or grounded solely upon public utility. The last of them, fidelity to engagements, is to be the subject of the next chapter, and, therefore, I shall say nothing of it in this.

The four first named—to wit, the right of an innocent man to the safety of his person and family, to his liberty and reputation, are, by the writers on jurisprudence, called *natural* rights of man, because they are grounded in the nature of man as a rational and moral agent, and are by his Creator committed to his care and keeping. By being called *natural* or *innate*, they are distinguished from acquired rights, which suppose some previous act or deed of man by which they are acquired; whereas natural rights suppose nothing of this kind.

When a man's natural rights are violated, he perceives intuitively, and he feels that he is injured. The feeling of his heart arises from the judgment of his understanding; for, if he did not believe that the hurt was intended, and unjustly intended, he would not have that feeling. He perceives that injury is done to himself, and that he has a right to redress. The natural principle of resentment is roused by the view of its proper object, and excites him to defend his right. Even the injurious person is conscious of his doing injury; he dreads a just retaliation; and, if it be in the power of the injured person, he expects it as due and deserved.

That these sentiments spring up in the mind of man as naturally as his body grows to its proper stature; that they are not the birth of instruction, either of parents, priests, philosophers, or politicians, but the pure growth of nature—cannot, I think, without effrontery, be denied. We find them equally strong in the most savage and in the most civilized tribes of mankind; and nothing can weaken them but an inveterate habit of rapine and bloodshed, which benumbs the conscience, and turns men into wild beasts.

The public good is very properly considered by the judge who punishes a private injury, but seldom enters into the thought of the injured person. In all criminal law, the redress due to the private sufferer is distinguished from that which is due to the public; a distinction which could have no foundation, if the demerit of injustice arose solely from its hurting the public. And every man is conscious of a specific difference between the resentment he feels for an injury done to himself, and his indignation against a wrong done to the public.

I think, therefore, it is evident that, of the six branches of justice we mentioned, four are natural, in the strictest sense, being founded upon the constitution of man, and antecedent to all deeds and conventions of society; so that, if there were but two men upon the earth, one might be unjust and injurious, and the other injured.

But does Mr Hume maintain the contrary?

To this question I answer, That his doctrine seems to imply it; but I hope he meant it not.

He affirms, in general, that justice is not a natural virtue; that it derives its origin solely from public utility; and that reflections on the beneficial consequences of this virtue, are the sole foundation of its merit. He mentions no particular branch of justice as an exception to this general rule; yet justice, in common language, and in all the writers on jurisprudence I am acquainted with, comprehends the four branches above mentioned. His doctrine, therefore, according to the common construction of words, extends to these four, as well as to the two other branches of justice.

On the other hand, if we attend to his long and laboured proof of this doctrine, it appears evident that he had in his eye only two particular branches of justice. No part of his reasoning applies to the other four. He seems, I know not why, to have taken up a confined notion of justice, and to have restricted it to a regard to property and fidelity in contracts. As to other branches he is silent. He nowhere says, that it is not naturally criminal to rob an innocent man of his life, of his children, of his liberty, or of his reputation; and I am apt to think he never meant it.

The only philosopher I know who has had the assurance to maintain this, is Mr Hobbes, who makes the state of nature to be a state of war, of every man against every man; and of such a war in which every man has a right to do and to acquire whatever his power can, by any means, accomplish — that is, a state wherein neither right nor injury, justice nor injustice, can possibly exist.

Mr Hume mentions this system of Hobbes, but without adopting it […].

3. As Mr Hume, therefore, has said nothing to prove the four branches of justice which relate to the innate rights of men, to be artificial, or to derive their origin solely from public utility, I proceed to the fifth branch, which requires us not to invade another man's property.

The right of property is not innate, but acquired. It is not grounded upon the constitution of man; but upon his actions. Writers on jurisprudence have explained its origin in a manner that may satisfy every man of common understanding.

The earth is given to men in common for the purposes of life, by the bounty of Heaven. But, to divide it, and appropriate one part of its produce to one, another part to another, must be the work of men who have power and understanding given them, by which every man may accommodate himself without hurt to any other.

This common right of every man to what the earth produces, before it be occupied and appropriated by others, was, by ancient moralists, very properly compared to the right which every citizen had to the public theatre, where every man that came might occupy an empty seat, and thereby acquire a right to it while the entertainment lasted, but no man had a right to dispossess an other.

The earth is a great theatre, furnished by the Almighty, with perfect wisdom and goodness, for the entertainment and employment of all mankind. Here every man has a right to accommodate himself as a spectator, and to perform his part as an actor, but without hurt to others.

He who does so is a just man, and thereby entitled to some degree of moral approbation; and he who not only does no hurt, but employs his power to do good, is a good man, and is thereby entitled to a higher degree of moral approbation. But he who jostles and molests his neighbour, who deprives him of any accommodation which his industry has provided without hurt to others, is unjust, and a proper object of resentment.

It is true, therefore, that property has a beginning from the actions of men, occupying, and, perhaps, improving by their industry, what was common by nature. It is true, also, that, before property exists, that branch of justice and injustice which regards property cannot exist. But it is also true, that, where there are men, there will very soon be property of one kind or another, and, consequently, there will be that branch of justice which attends property as its guardian.

There are *two kinds of property* which we may distinguish.

The *first* is *what must presently be consumed to sustain life*; the *second*, which is more permanent, is, *what may be laid up and stored for the supply of future wants*.

Some of the gifts of nature must be used and consumed by individuals for the daily support of life; but they cannot be used till they be occupied and appropriated. If another person may, without injustice, rob me of what I have innocently occupied for present subsistence, the necessary consequence must be, that he may, without injustice, take away my life.

A right to life implies a right to the necessary means of life. And that justice which forbids the taking away the life of an innocent man, forbids no less the taking from him the necessary means of life. He has the same right to defend the one as the other; and nature inspires him with the same just resentment of the one injury as of the other.

The natural right of liberty implies a right to such innocent labour as a man chooses, and to the fruit of that labour. To hinder another man's innocent labour, or to deprive him of the fruit of it, is an injustice of the same kind, and has the same effect as to put him in fetters or in prison, and is equally a just object of resentment.

Thus it appears, that some kind, or some degree, of property must exist wherever men exist, and that the right to such property is the necessary consequence of the natural right of men to life and liberty.

It has been further observed, that God has made man a sagacious and provident animal, led by his constitution not only to occupy and use what nature has provided for the supply of his present wants and necessities, but to foresee future wants, and to provide for them; and that not only for himself, but for his family, his friends, and connections.

He therefore acts in perfect conformity to his nature, when he stores, of the fruit of his labour, what may afterwards be useful to himself or to others; when he invents and fabricates utensils or machines by which his labour may be facilitated, and its produce increased; and when, by exch-

anging with his fellow-men commodities or labour, he acc-
ommodates both himself and them. These are the natural
and innocent exertions of that understanding wherewith his
Maker has endowed him. He has therefore a right to exercise
them, and to enjoy the fruit of them. Every man who imp-
edes him in making such exertions, or deprives him of the
fruit of them, is injurious and unjust, and an object of just
resentment.

Many brute-animals are led by instinct to provide for fut-
urity, and to defend their store, and their store-house, against
all invaders. There seems to be in man, before the use of
reason, an instinct of the same kind. When reason and conscience grow up, they approve and justify this provident
care, and condemn, as unjust, every invasion of others, that
may frustrate it.

Two instances of this provident sagacity seem to be peculiar to man: I mean the invention of utensils and machines
for facilitating labour, and the making exchanges with his
fellow-men for mutual benefit. No tribe of men has been
found so rude as not to practise these things in some degree.
And I know no tribe of brutes that was ever observed to
practise them. They neither invent nor use utensils or machines, nor do they traffic by exchanges.

From these observations, I think it evident that man, even
in the state of nature, by his powers of body and mind, may
acquire permanent property, or what we call *riches*, by which
his own and his family's wants are more liberally supplied,
and his power enlarged to requite his benefactors, to relieve
objects of compassion, to make friends, and to defend his
property against unjust invaders. And we know from history, that men, who had no superior on earth, no connection
with any public beyond their own family, have acquired
property, and had distinct notions of that justice and injustice
of which it is the object.

Every man, as a reasonable creature, has a right to gratify
his natural and innocent desires, without hurt to others. No
desire is more natural, or more reasonable, than that of
supplying his wants. When this is done without hurt to any
man, to hinder or frustrate his innocent labour, is an unjust
violation of his natural liberty. Private utility leads a man to

desire property, and to labour for it; and his right to it is only a right to labour for his own benefit.

That public utility is the sole origin, even of that branch of justice which regards property, is so far from being true, that, when men confederate and constitute a public, under laws and government, the right of each individual to his property is, by that confederation, abridged and limited. In the state of nature every man's property was solely at his own disposal, because he had no superior. In civil society it must be subject to the laws of the society. He gives up to the public part of that right which he had in the state of nature, as the price of that protection and security which he receives from civil society. In the state of nature, he was sole judge in his own cause, and had right to defend his property, his liberty, and life, as far as his power reached. In the state of civil society, he must submit to the judgment of the society, and acquiesce in its sentence, though he should conceive it to be unjust.

What was said above, of the natural right every man has to acquire permanent property, and to dispose of it, must be understood with this condition, That no other man be thereby deprived of the necessary means of life. The right of an innocent man to the necessaries of life, is, in its nature, superior to that which the rich man has to his riches, even though they be honestly acquired. The use of riches, or permanent property, is to supply future and casual wants, which ought to yield to present and certain necessity.

As, in a family, justice requires that the children who are unable to labour, and those who, by sickness, are disabled, should have their necessities supplied out of the common stock, so, in the great family of God, of which all mankind are the children, justice, I think, as well as charity, requires, that the necessities of those who, by the providence of God, are disabled from supplying themselves, should be supplied from what might otherwise be stored for future wants.

From this it appears, That the right of acquiring and that of disposing of property, may be subject to limitations and restrictions, even in the state of nature, and much more in the state of civil society, in which the public has what writers in jurisprudence call an *eminent dominion* over the property, as well as over the lives of the subjects, as far as the public good requires.

If these principles be well founded, Mr Hume's arguments to prove that justice is an artificial virtue, or that its public utility is the sole foundation of its merit, may be easily answered.

He supposes, *first*, a state in which nature has bestowed on the human race, such abundance of external goods, that every man, without care or industry, finds himself provided of whatever he can wish or desire. It is evident, says he, that, in such a state, the cautious, jealous virtue of justice would never once have been dreamed of.

It may be observed, *first*, That this argument applies only to one of the six branches of justice before mentioned. The other five are not in the least affected by it; and the reader will easily perceive that this observation applies to almost all his arguments, so that it needs not be repeated.

Secondly, All that this argument proves is, That a state of the human race may be conceived wherein no property exists, and where, of consequence, there can be no exercise of that branch of justice which respects property. But does it follow from this, that where property exists, and must exist, that no regard ought to be had to it?

He next supposes that the necessities of the human race continuing the same as at present, the mind is so enlarged with friendship and generosity, that every man feels as much tenderness and concern for the interest of every man, as for his own. It seems evident, he says, that the use of justice would be suspended by such an extensive benevolence, nor would the divisions and barriers of property and obligation have ever been thought of.

I answer, The conduct which this extensive benevolence leads to, is either perfectly consistent with justice, or it is not. *First*, If there be any case where this benevolence would lead us to do injustice, the use of justice is not suspended. Its obligation is superior to that of benevolence; and, to show benevolence to one, at the expense of injustice to another, is immoral. *Secondly*, Supposing no such case could happen, the use of justice would not be suspended, because by it we must distinguish good offices to which we had a right, from those to which we had no right, and which therefore require a return of gratitude. *Thirdly*, Supposing the use of justice to be suspended, as it must be in every case where it cannot be exercised, Will it follow, that its obligation is suspended, where there is access to exercise it?

A *third* supposition is, the reverse of the first, That a society falls into extreme want of the necessaries of life: The question is put, Whether, in such a case, an equal partition of bread, without regard to private property, though effected by power, and even by violence, would be regarded as criminal and injurious? And the author conceives that this would be a suspension of the strict laws of justice.

I answer, That such an equal partition as Mr Hume mentions, is so far from being criminal or injurious, that justice requires it; and surely that cannot be a suspension of the laws of justice which is an act of justice. All that the strictest justice requires in such a case, is, That the man whose life is preserved at the expense of another, and without his consent, should indemnify him when he is able. His case is similar to that of a debtor who is insolvent, without any fault on his part. Justice requires that he should be forborne till he is able to pay. It is strange that Mr Hume should think that an action, neither criminal nor injurious, should be a suspension of the laws of justice. This seems to me a contradiction; for *justice* and *injury* are contradictory terms.

The next argument is thus expressed: — 'When any man, even in political society, renders himself, by crimes, obnoxious to the public, he is punished in his goods and person — that is, the ordinary rules of justice are, with regard to him, suspended for a moment, and it becomes equitable to inflict on him what otherwise he could not suffer without wrong or injury.'

This argument, like the former, refutes itself. For that an action should be a suspension of the rules of justice, and at the same time equitable, seems to me a contradiction. It is possible that equity may interfere with the letter of human laws, because all the cases that may fall under them, cannot be foreseen; but that equity should interfere with justice is impossible. It is strange that Mr Hume should think that justice requires that a criminal should be treated in the same way as an innocent man.

Another argument is taken from public war. What is it, says he, but a suspension of justice among the warring parties? The laws of war, which then succeed to those of equity and justice, are rules calculated for the advantage and utility of that particular state in which men are now placed.

I answer, when war is undertaken for self-defence, or for reparation of intolerable injuries, justice authorizes it. The laws of war, which have been described by many judicious moralists, are all drawn from the fountain of justice and equity; and every thing contrary to justice, is contrary to the laws of war. That justice which prescribes one rule of conduct to a master, another to a servant; one to a parent, another to a child — prescribes also one rule of conduct towards a friend, another towards an enemy. I do not understand what Mr Hume means by the *advantage* and *utility* of a state of war, for which he says the laws of war are calculated, and succeed to those of justice and equity. I know no laws of war that are not calculated for justice and equity.

The next argument is this — Were there a species of creatures intermingled with men, which, though rational, were possessed of such inferior strength, both of body and mind, that they were incapable of all resistance, and could never, upon the highest provocation, make us feel the effects of their resentment; the necessary consequence, I think, is, that we should be bound, by the laws of humanity, to give gentle usage to these creatures, but should not, properly speaking, lie under any restraint of justice with regard to them, nor could they possess any right or property, exclusive of such arbitrary lords.

If Mr Hume had not owned this sentiment as a consequence of his Theory of Morals, I should have thought it very uncharitable to impute it to him. However, we may judge of the Theory by its avowed consequence. For there cannot be better evidence that a theory of morals, or of any particular virtue, is false, than when it subverts the practical rules of morals. This defenceless species of rational creatures, is doomed by Mr Hume to have no rights. Why? Because they have no power to defend themselves. Is not this to say — That right has its origin from power; which, indeed, was the doctrine of Mr Hobbes. And to illustrate this doctrine, Mr Hume adds — That, as no inconvenience ever results from the exercise of a power so firmly established in nature, the restraints of justice and property being totally useless, could never have place in so unequal a confederacy; and, to the same purpose, he says, that the female part of our own species owe the share they have in the rights of society, to the power which their address and their charms give them. If this be sound morals, Mr Hume's Theory of Justice may be true.

We may here observe, that, though, in other places, Mr Hume founds the obligation of justice upon its utility to *ourselves* or to *others*, it is here founded solely upon utility to *ourselves*. For surely to be treated with justice would be highly useful to the defenceless species he here supposes to exist. But, as no inconvenience to ourselves can ever result from our treatment of them, he concludes, that justice would be useless, and therefore can have no place. Mr Hobbes could have said no more.

He supposes, in the *last* place, a state of human nature wherein all society and intercourse is cut off between man and man. It is evident, he says, that so solitary a being would be as much incapable of justice as of social discourse and conversation.

And would not so solitary a being be as incapable of friendship, generosity, and compassion, as of justice? If this argument prove justice to be an artificial virtue, it will, with equal force, prove every social virtue to be artificial.

These are the arguments which Mr Hume has advanced in his *Enquiry*, in the first part of a long section upon justice.

In the *second* part, the arguments are not so clearly distinguished, nor can they be easily collected. I shall offer some remarks upon what seems most specious in this second part.

He begins with observing – 'That, if we examine the particular laws by which justice is directed and property determined, they present us with the same conclusion. The good of mankind is the only object of all those laws and regulations.'

It is not easy to perceive where the stress of this argument lies. *The good of mankind is the object of all the laws and regulations by which justice is directed and property determined; therefore, justice is not a natural virtue, but has its origin solely from public utility, and its beneficial consequences are the sole foundation of its merit.*

Some step seems to be wanting to connect the antecedent proposition with the conclusion, which, I think, must be one or other of these two propositions – first, *All the rules of justice tend to public utility;* or, secondly, *Public utility is the only standard of justice, from which alone all its rules must be deduced.*

If the argument be, That justice must have its origin solely from public utility, because all its rules tend to public utility, I cannot admit the consequence; nor can Mr Hume admit it without overturning his own system; for the rules of benevolence and humanity do all tend to the public utility; and yet, in his system, they have another foundation in human nature; so likewise may the rules of justice.

I am apt to think, therefore, that the argument is to be taken in the last sense, That public utility is the only standard of justice, from which all its rules must be deduced; and therefore justice has its origin solely from public utility.

This seems to be Mr Hume's meaning, because, in what follows, he observes, That, in order to establish laws for the regulation of property, we must be acquainted with the nature and situation of man; must reject appearances which may be false though specious; and must search for those rules which are, on the whole, most useful and beneficial; and endeavours to show, that the established rules which regard property are more for the public good than the system, either of those religious fanatics of the last age who held that saints only should inherit the earth, or of those political fanatics who claimed an equal division of property.

We see here, as before, that, though Mr Hume's conclusion respects justice in general, his argument is confined to one branch of justice—to wit, the right of property; and it is well known that to conclude from a part to the whole is not good reasoning.

Besides, the proposition from which his conclusion is drawn cannot be granted, either with regard to property, or with regard to the other branches of justice.

We endeavoured before to show that property, though not an innate but an acquired right, may be acquired in the state of nature, and agreeably to the laws of nature; and that this right has not its origin from human laws, made for the public good, though, when men enter into political society, it may and ought to be regulated by those laws.

If there were but two men upon the face of the earth, of ripe faculties, each might have his own property, and might know his right to defend it, and his obligation not to invade the property of the other. He would have no need to have recourse to reasoning from public good, in order to know when he was injured, either in his property or in any of his natural rights, or to know what rules of justice he ought to observe towards his neighbour.

The simple rule, of not doing to his neighbour what he would think wrong to be done to himself, would lead him to the knowledge of every branch of justice, without the consideration of public good, or of laws and statutes made to promote it.

It is not true, therefore, that public utility is the only standard of justice, and that the rules of justice can be deduced only from their public utility.

Aristides, and the people of Athens, had surely another notion of justice, when he pronounced the counsel of Themistocles, which was communicated to him only, to be highly useful, but unjust; and the assembly, upon this authority, rejected the proposal unheard. These honest citizens, though subject to no laws but of their own making, far from making utility the standard of justice, made justice to be the standard of utility.

'*What is a man's property?* Anything which it is lawful for him, and for him alone, to use. *But what rule have we by which we can distinguish these objects?* Here we must have recourse to statutes, customs, precedents, analogies, &c.'

Does not this imply that, in the state of nature, there can be no distinction of property? If so, Mr Hume's state of nature is the same with that of Mr Hobbes.

It is true that, when men become members of a political society, they subject their property, as well as themselves, to the laws, and must either acquiesce in what the laws determine, or leave the society. But justice, and even that particular branch of it which our author always supposes to be the whole, is antecedent to political societies and to their laws; and the intention of these laws is, to be the guardians of justice, and to redress injuries.

As all the works of men are imperfect, human laws may be unjust; which could never be, if justice had its origin from law, as the author seems here to insinuate.

Justice requires that a member of a state should submit to the laws of the state, when they require nothing unjust or impious. There may, therefore, be statutory rights and statutory crimes. A statute may create a right which did not before exist, or make that to be criminal which was not so before. But this could never be, if there were not an antecedent obligation upon the subjects to obey the statutes. In like manner, the command of a master may make that to be the servant's duty which, before, was not his duty, and the servant may be chargeable with injustice if he disobeys, because he was under an antecedent obligation to obey his master in lawful things.

We grant, therefore, that particular laws may direct justice and determine property, and sometimes even upon very slight reasons and analogies, or even for no other reason but that it is better that such a point should be determined by law than that it should be left a dubious subject of contention. But this, far from presenting us with the conclusion which the author would establish, presents us with a contrary conclusion. For all these particular laws and statutes derive their whole obligation and force from a general rule of justice antecedent to them — to wit, That subjects ought to obey the laws of their country.

The author compares the rules of justice with the most frivolous superstitions, and can find no foundation for moral sentiment in the one more than in the other, excepting that justice is requisite to the well-being and existence of society.

It is very true that, if we examine *mine* and *thine* by the senses of *sight, smell,* or *touch,* or scrutinize them by the sciences of *medicine, chemistry* or *physics,* we perceive no difference. But the reason is, that none of these senses or sciences are the judges of right or wrong, or can give any conception of them any more than the ear of colour, or the eye of sound. Every man of common understanding, and every savage, when he applies his moral faculty to those objects, perceives a difference as clearly as he perceives day-light. When that sense or faculty is not consulted, in vain do we consult every other, in a question of right and wrong.

To perceive that justice tends to the good of mankind, would lay no moral obligation upon us to be just, unless we be conscious of a moral obligation to do what tends to the good of mankind. If such a moral obligation be admitted, why may we not admit a stronger obligation to do injury to no man? The last obligation is as easily conceived as the first, and there is as clear evidence of its existence in human nature.

The last argument is a dilemma, and is thus expressed: — 'The dilemma seems obvious. As justice evidently tends to promote public utility, and to support civil society, the sentiment of justice is either derived from our reflecting on that tendency, or, like hunger, thirst, and other appetites, resentment, love of life, attachment to offspring, and other passions, arises from a simple original instinct in the human breast, which nature has implanted for like salutary purposes. If the latter be the case, it follows, That property, which is the object of justice, is also distinguished by a simple original instinct, and is not ascertained by any argument or reflection. But who is there that ever heard of such an instinct,' &c.

I doubt not but Mr Hume has heard of a principle called *conscience*, which nature has implanted in the human breast. Whether he will call it a simple original instinct I know not, as he gives that name to all our appetites, and to all our passions. From this principle, I think, we derive the sentiment of justice.

As the eye not only gives us the conception of colours, but makes us perceive one body to have one colour, and another body another; and as our reason not only gives us the conception of true and false, but makes us perceive one proposition to be true and another to be false; so our conscience, or moral faculty, not only gives us the conception of honest and dishonest, but makes us perceive one kind of conduct to be honest, another to he dishonest. By this faculty we perceive a merit in honest conduct, and a demerit in dishonest, without regard to public utility.

That these sentiments are not the effect of education or of acquired habits, we have the same reason to conclude as that our perception of what is true and what false, is not the effect of education or of acquired habits. There have been men who professed to believe that there is no ground to assent to any one proposition rather than its contrary; but I never yet heard of a man who had the effrontery to profess himself to be under no obligation of honour or honesty, of truth or justice, in his dealings with men.

Nor does this faculty of conscience require *innate ideas of property, and of the various ways of acquiring and transferring it, or innate ideas of kings and senators, of prætors, and chancellors, and juries,* any more than the faculty of seeing requires innate ideas of colours, or than the faculty of reasoning requires innate ideas of cones, cylinders, and spheres.

---

1   Isaac Newton, *Mathematical Principles of Natural Philosophy,* trans. I. B. Cohen and A. Whitman (Berkeley and Los Angeles, CA: 1999), p. 408: 'Further, it is in this sense that I call attractions and impulses accelerative and motive. Moreover, I use interchangeably and indiscriminately words signifying attraction, impulse, or any sort of propensity toward a centre, considering these forces not from a physical but only from a mathematical point of view. Therefore, let the reader beware of thinking that by words of this kind I am anywhere defining a species or mode of action or a physical cause or reason, or that I am attributing forces in a true and physical sense to centres (which are mathematical points) if I happen to say that centres attract or that centres have forces.' In the critical edition of the *Essays on the Active Powers of Man*, Haakonssen and Harris note that Reid made a mistake in the transcription of the first sentence: the second 'voces' (words) should be 'vires' (forces).

2   Cicero, *De Officiis*, trans. W. Miller (Cambridge, MA: Harvard University Press, 1975) I.iv (14), p. 17: 'what we correctly maintain merits praise, even though it be praised by no one.'

3   Cicero, *De Officiis*, I.iii (8), p. 11: 'That for the performance of which an adequate reason may be rendered.'

4   Cicero, *De Officiis* I.xxviii (101), p. 103: 'Now we find that the essential activity of the spirit is twofold: one force is appetite[…], which impels a man this way and that; the other is reason, which teaches and explains what should be done and what should be left undone. The result is that reason commands, appetite obeys.'

5   'The sense of right and duty'.

6   See David Hume, *Enquiry concerning the Principles of Morals*, Section 3, Part 1.

Bibliography

Reid's Works

The Edinburgh Edition of Thomas Reid (General Editor: Knud Haakonssen) is the definitive critical edition of Reid's works. Volumes in this edition are published by the Edinburgh University Press in the United Kingdom, and by the Pennsylvania State University Press in the United States.

Reid, Thomas, *The Works of Thomas Reid, D.D., with Notes and Supplementary Dissertations*, 2 vols., ed. William Hamilton, 8th edition, Edinburgh: MacLachlan and Stewart, 1880 [the 1st edition by Hamilton appeared in 1846].

---, *Philosophical Orations of Thomas Reid*, [in Latin], ed. W.R. Humphries, Aberdeen: Aberdeen University Press, 1937.

---, *Essays on the Intellectual Powers of Man*, abridged, ed. A.D. Woozley, London: MacMillan, 1941.

---, *Essays on the Intellectual Powers of Man*, ed. Baruch A. Brody, Cambridge, MA: MIT Press, 1969.

---*, *Lectures on the Fine Arts*, ed. Peter Kivy, The Hague: Martinus Nijhoff, 1973.

---*, *Lectures on Natural Theology*, ed. Elmer H. Duncan, Washington, DC: University Press of America, 1981.

---, *Inquiry and Essays*, abridged, eds. Ronald E. Beanblossom and Keith Lehrer, Indianapolis, IN: Hackett, 1983.

---, *Philosophical Orations of Thomas Reid, delivered at Graduation Ceremonies in King's College, Aberdeen, 1753, 1756, 1759, 1762*, ed. D.D. Todd, trans. S. Duncan, Carbondale, IL: Southern Illinois University Press, 1989.

---, *Practical Ethics, Being Lectures and Papers on Natural Religion, Self-Government, Natural Jurisprudence, and the Law of Nations*, ed. Knud Haakonssen, Princeton, NJ: Princeton University Press, 1990.

---, *Thomas Reid on the Animate Creation: Papers Relating to the Life Sciences*, ed. Paul Wood, Edinburgh: Edinburgh University Press, 1996.

---, *An Inquiry into the Human Mind on the Principles of Common Sense*, ed. Derek R. Brookes, Edinburgh: Edinburgh University Press, 1997.

---, 'Of Power', ed. John Haldane, *The Philosophical Quarterly*, **51** (2001): 3–12.

---, *Essays on the Intellectual Powers of Man*, ed. Derek R. Brookes, Edinburgh: Edinburgh University Press, 2002.

---, *The Correspondence of Thomas Reid*, ed. Paul Wood, Edinburgh: Edinburgh University Press, 2002.

---, *Thomas Reid on Logic, Rhetoric and the Fine Arts*, ed. Alexander Broadie, Edinburgh: Edinburgh University Press, 2004.

---, *Thomas Reid on Practical Ethics: Lectures and Papers on Natural Religion, Self-Government, Natural Jurisprudence, and the Law of Nations*, ed. Knud Haakonssen, Edinburgh: Edinburgh University Press, 2007.

---, 'Some Thoughts on the Utopian System (1794)', in *Politics and Society in Scottish Society*, ed. Shinichi Nagao, Exeter: Imprint Academic, 2007.

---, *Essays on the Active Powers of Man*, eds. Knud Haakonssen and James A. Harris, Edinburgh: Edinburgh University Press, 2010.

* N.B. These collections are composed of manuscript writings that are not in Thomas Reid's handwriting; they represent student transcriptions of his lectures at University of Glasgow.

Bibliographies

Squillante, Martino, 'Thomas Reid: An Updated Bibliography. Part I: Reid's Works', *Reid Studies,* **1** (1998): 71–81.

---, 'Thomas Reid: An Updated Bibliography. Part II: Critical Studies', *Reid Studies,* **2** (1998): 57–78.

Books, Dissertations, and Collections of Articles

Barker, Stephen and Thomas Beauchamp, eds., *Thomas Reid: Critical Interpretations*, Philadelphia, PA: Philosophical Monographs, 1976.

Berkeley, George, *The Works of George Berkeley, Bishop of Cloyne*, eds. A.A. Luce and T.E. Jessop, London: Thomas Nelson and Sons, 9 vols., 1948–1957.

Broadie, Alexander, *A History of Scottish Philosophy*, Edinburgh: Edinburgh University Press, 2009 (esp. pp. 235–272).

Callergård, Robert, 'An Essay on Thomas Reid's Philosophy of Science', Doctoral Thesis, Stockholm University, 2006.

Cuneo, Terence and René Van Woudenberg, eds., *The Cambridge Companion to Thomas Reid*, Cambridge: Cambridge University Press, 2004.

Dalgarno, Melvin and Eric Matthews, eds., *The Philosophy of Thomas Reid*, Dordrecht: Kluwer, 1989.

Daniels, Norman, *Thomas Reid's Inquiry: The Geometry of Visibles and the Case for Realism*, New York, NY: Burt Franklin, 1974.

Davis, William C., *Thomas Reid's Ethics: Moral Epistemology on Legal Foundations*, London: Continuum International, 2006.

De Bary, Philip, *Thomas Reid and Scepticism: His Reliabilist Response*, London: Routledge, 2002.

Diamond, Peter J., *Common Sense and Improvement: Thomas Reid as Social Theorist*, Bern: Peter Lang, 1998.

Fraser, A. Campbell, *Thomas Reid*, Edinburgh and London: Oliphant, Anderson and Ferrier, 1898.

Gallie, Roger, *Thomas Reid and 'The Way of Ideas'*, Dordrecht: Kluwer, 1989.

---, *Thomas Reid: Ethics, Aesthetics and the Anatomy of the Self*, Dordrecht: Kluwer, 1998.

Grave, S.A., *The Scottish Philosophy of Common Sense*, Oxford: Oxford University Press, 1960.

Haldane, John and Stephen Read, eds., *The Philosophy of Thomas Reid*, Oxford: Blackwell, 2003.

Harris, James, *Of Liberty and Necessity: the Free Will Debate in Eighteenth-Century British Philosophy*, Oxford: Oxford University Press, 2008 (esp. pp. 179–202).

Houston, Joseph, ed., *Thomas Reid: Context, Influence, Significance*. Edinburgh: Dunedin Academic, 2004.

Hume, David, *An Enquiry concerning the Principles of Morals*, ed. T. Beauchamp, Oxford: Oxford University Press, 1998.

---, *An Enquiry concerning Human Understanding*, ed. T. Beauchamp, Oxford: Oxford University Press, 2000.

---, *A Treatise of Human Nature*, eds. D.F. Norton and M. Norton, Oxford: Oxford University Press, 2000.

Kant, Immanuel, *Prolegomena to any Future Metaphysics*, trans. Lewis White Beck, Indianapolis, IN: Bobbs-Merrill, 1955.

Kuehn, Manfred, *Scottish Common Sense in Germany: A Contribution to the History of Critical Philosophy*, Montreal and Kingston: McGill-Queen's University Press, 1987.

Lehrer, Keith, *Thomas Reid*, London: Routledge, 1989.

Ledwig, Marion, *Reid's Philosophy of Psychology*, Lanham, MD: University Press of America, 2005.

Locke, John, *An Essay Concerning Human Understanding*, ed. P. Nidditch, Oxford: Oxford University Press, 1975.

Manns, James W., *Reid and his French Disciples: Aesthetics and Metaphysics*, Leiden: E.J. Brill, 1994.

Marcil-Lacoste, Louise, *Claude Buffier and Thomas Reid: Two Common-Sense Philosophers*, Montreal and Kingston: McGill-Queen's University Press, 1982.

McCosh, James, *The Scottish Philosophy: Biographical, Expository, Critical from Hutcheson to Hamilton*, London: MacMillan, 1875.

Newton, Isaac, *The* Principia*: Mathematical Principles of Natural Philosophy*, trans. I. Bernard Cohen and Anne Whitman, Berkeley, CA: University of California Press, 1999.

Ni, Peimin, *On Reid*, Belmont, CA: Wadsworth, 2002.

Nichols, Ryan, *Thomas Reid's Theory of Perception*, Oxford: Oxford University Press, 2007.

Roeser, Sabine, ed., *Reid on Ethics*, Basingstoke: Palgrave Macmillan, 2010.

Rowe, William, *Thomas Reid on Freedom and Morality*, Ithaca, NY: Cornell University Press, 1991.

Schneewind, J.B., *The Invention of Autonomy: A History of Modern Moral Philosophy*, Cambridge: Cambridge University Press, 1998 (esp. pp. 395–403).

Schultess, Daniel, *Philosophie et sens commun chez Thomas Reid (1710–1796)* Berne: Peter Lang, 1983.

Smith, John C., *Companion to the Works of Philosopher Thomas Reid, 1710–1796*, Lewiston, NY: E. Mellen Press, 2000.

Wolterstorff, Nicholas, *Thomas Reid and the Story of Epistemology*, Cambridge: Cambridge University Press, 2001.

Wood, Paul B., 'Thomas Reid Natural Philosopher: A Study of Science and Philosophy in the Scottish Enlightenment', PhD Dissertation, University of Leeds, 1984.

Yaffe, Gideon, *Manifest Activity: Thomas Reid's Theory of Action*, Oxford: Oxford University Press, 2004.

Yolton, John W., *Perceptual Acquaintance from Descartes to Reid*, Minneapolis, MN: University of Minnesota Press, 1984.

Special Issues of Journals on Reid

American Catholic Philosophical Quarterly, **74** (3), 2000.

Journal of Scottish Philosophy, **6** (1), 2008.

The Monist, **70** (4), 1987.

The Monist, **61** (2), 1978.

Philosophical Quarterly, **52** (209), 2002.

Selected Articles Not Appearing in the Collections Listed Above

Alston, William P., 'Thomas Reid On Epistemic Principles', *History of Philosophy Quarterly*, **2** (1985): 435–452.

Anstey, Peter, 'Thomas Reid and the Justification of Induction', *History of Philosophy Quarterly*, **12** (1995): 77–93.

Benbaji, Hagit, 'Reid's View of Aesthetic and Secondary Qualities', *Reid Studies*, **2** (1999): 31–46.

---, 'Reid on Causation and Action', *Journal of Scottish Philosophy*, **1** (2003): 1–19.

---, 'Is Thomas Reid a Direct Realist about Perception?', *European Journal of Philosophy*, **17** (2009): 1–29.

Bourdillon, Philip, 'Thomas Reid's Account of Sensation as a Natural Principle of Belief', *Philosophical Studies*, **27** (1975): 19–36.

Buras, Todd, 'The Nature of Sensations in Reid', *History of Philosophy Quarterly*, **22** (2005): 221–238.

---, 'Three Grades of Immediate Perception: Thomas Reid's Distinctions', *Philosophy and Phenomenological Research*, **76** (2008): 603–632.

---, 'The Function of Sensations in Reid', *Journal of the History of Philosophy*, **47** (2009): 329–353.

Callergård, Robert, 'Thomas Reid's Newtonian Theism: His Differences with the Classical Arguments of Richard Bentley and William Whiston', *Studies in History and Philosophy of Science*, **41** (2010): 109–119.

Castagnetto, Susan, 'Reid's Answer to Abstract Ideas', *Journal of Philosophical Research*, **17** (1992): 39–60.

Chisholm, Roderick M., 'Keith Lehrer and Thomas Reid', *Philosophical Studies*, **60** (1990): 33–38.

Copenhaver, Rebecca, 'A Realism for Reid: Mediated but Direct', *British Journal for the History of Philosophy*, **12** (2004): 61–74.

---, 'Thomas Reid's Theory of Memory', *History of Philosophy Quarterly*, **23** (2006): 171–189.

---, 'Is Thomas Reid a Mysterian?', *Journal of the History of Philosophy*, **44** (2006): 449–466.

---, 'Thomas Reid's Philosophy of Mind: Consciousness and Intentionality', *Philosophy Compass*, **1** (2006): 279–289.

---, 'Reid on Consciousness, Hop, Hot or For', *Philosophical Quarterly*, **57** (2007): 613–634.

---, 'Thomas Reid on Acquired Perception', *Pacific Philosophical Quarterly*, **91** (2010): 285–312

Cummins, Phillip D., 'Reid's Realism', *Journal of the History of Philosophy*, **12** (1974): 317–340.

Cuneo, Terence, 'Reidian Moral Perception', *Canadian Journal of Philosophy*, **33** (2003): 229–258.

---, 'Signs of Value: Reid on the Evidential Role of Feelings in Moral Judgement', *British Journal for the History of Philosophy*, **14** (2006): 69–91.

Daniels, Norman, 'Thomas Reid's Discovery of a Non-Euclidean Geometry', *Philosophy of Science*, **3** (1972): 219–234.

David, Marian, 'Nonexistence and Reid's Conception of Conceiving', *Grazer Philosophische Studien*, **25–6** (1985–6): 585–599.

De Rose, Keith, 'Reid's Anti-Sensationalism and His Realism', *Philosophical Review*, **98** (1989): 313–348.

Duggan, Timothy J., 'Thomas Reid's Theory of Sensation', *Philosophical Review*, **69** (1960): 90–100.

Falkenstein, Lorne, 'Hume and Reid on the Simplicity of the Soul', *Hume Studies*, **21** (1995): 24–45.

---, 'Reid's Account of Localization', *Philosophy and Phenomenological Research*, **61** (2000): 305–328.

---, 'Reid's Critique of Berkeley's Position on the Inverted Image', *Reid Studies*, **4** (2000): 35–51.

---, 'Hume and Reid on the Perception of Hardness', *Hume Studies*, **28** (2002): 27–48.

---, 'Reid and Smith on Vision', *Journal of Scottish Philosophy*, **2** (2004): 103–118.

---, 'Condillac's Paradox', *Journal of the History of Philosophy*, **43** (2005): 403–435.

Falkenstein, Lorne and Giovanni Grandi, 'The Role of Material Impressions in Reid's Theory of Vision', *Journal of Scottish Philosophy*, **1** (2001): 117–133.

Gallie, Roger, 'Reid: Conception, Representation and Innate Ideas', *Hume Studies*, **23** (1997): 315–335.

Grandi, Giovanni, 'Reid's Geometry of Visibles and the Parallel Postulate', *Studies in History and Philosophy of Science*, **36** (2005): 79–103.

---, 'Reid's Direct Realism about Vision', *History of Philosophy Quarterly*, **23** (2006): 225–238.

---, 'Reid and Condillac on Sensation and Perception: A Thought Experiment on Sensory Deprivation', *Southwest Philosophy Review,* **24** (2008): 191–200.

Haakonssen, Knud, 'Introduction to Reid's Practical Ethics', in *Reid's Practical Ethics,* Princeton, NJ: Princeton University Press, 1990, pp. 1–99.

Haldane, John, 'Whose Theory? Which Representations?', *Pacific Philosophical Quarterly*, **74** (1993): 247–257.

Hamilton, Andy, '"Scottish Commonsense" about Memory: A Defence of Thomas Reid's Direct Knowledge Account', *Australasian Journal of Philosophy*, **81** (2003): 229–245.

Harris, James A., 'Reid and Religion', *Eighteenth-Century Thought*, **3** (2007): 415–426.

Hoffman, Paul, 'Thomas Reid's Notion of Exertion', *Journal of the History of Philosophy*, **44** (2006): 431–447.

Kivy, Peter, 'Lectures on the Fine Arts: an Unpublished Manuscript of Thomas Reid's', *Journal of the History of Ideas*, **31** (1970): 17–32.

Lopston, Peter, 'Locke, Reid and Personal Identity', *The Philosophical Forum*, **35** (2004): 51-63.

Lehrer, Keith, 'Conception Without Representation, Justification Without Inference: Reid's Theory', *Nous*, **23** (1989): 145-154.

McDermid, Douglas, 'Thomas Reid on Moral Liberty and Common Sense', *British Journal for the History of Philosophy*, **7** (1999): 275-303.

Madden, Edward H., 'Commonsense and Agency Theory', *Review of Metaphysics*, **36** (1982): 319-342.

---, 'Was Reid a Natural Realist?', *Philosophy and Phenomenological Research*, **47** (1986): 255-276.

Manns, James, 'Beauty and Objectivity in Thomas Reid', *British Journal of Aesthetics*, **28** (1988): 119-131.

Nadler, Steven M., 'Reid, Arnauld, and the Objects of Perception', *History of Philosophy Quarterly*, **3** (1986): 165-174.

Nagao, Shinichi, 'The Political Economy of Thomas Reid', *Journal of Scottish Philosophy*, **1** (2003): 21-33.

Nauckhoff, Josefine C., 'Objectivity and Expression in Thomas Reid's Aesthetics', *Journal of Aesthetics and Art Criticism*, **52** (1994): 183-191.

Nichols, Ryan, 'Visible Figure and Reid's Theory of Visual Perception', *Hume Studies*, **28** (2002): 49-82.

---, 'Learning and Conceptual Content in Reid's Theory of Perception', *British Journal for the History of Philosophy*, **10** (2002): 561-590.

---, 'Reid's Inheritance from Locke, and How He Overcomes It', *Journal of the History of Philosophy*, **41** (2003): 471-491.

O'Connor, Timothy, 'Thomas Reid on Free Agency', *Journal of the History of Philosophy*, **32** (1994): 605-622.

Pappas, George S., 'Sensation and Perception in Reid', *Nous*, **23** (1989): 155-167.

---, 'Causation and Perception in Reid', *Philosophy*, **50** (1990): 763-766.

Rysiew, Patrick, 'Reidian Evidence', *Journal of Scottish Philosophy*, **3** (2005): 107-121.

Robbins, David O., 'The Aesthetics of Thomas Reid', *Journal of Aesthetics and Art Criticism*, **2** (1942): 30-41.

Roeser, Sabine, 'Reid and Moral Emotions', *Journal of Scottish Philosophy*, **7** (2009): 177-192

Schumann, Karl, 'Elements of Speech Act Theory in the Work of Thomas Reid', *History of Philosophy Quarterly*, **7** (2009): 47-66.

Van Cleve, James, 'Reid on the First Principles of Contingent Truths', *Reid Studies*, **3** (1999): 3-30.

---, 'Thomas Reid's Geometry of Visibles', *Philosophical Review*, **111** (2002): 373-416.

---, 'Reid versus Berkeley on the Inverted Retinal Image', *Philosophical Topics*, **31** (2005): 425–455.

---, 'Reid on the Credit of Human Testimony', in *The Epistemology of Testimony*, ed. Jennifer Lackey, Oxford: Clarendon Press, 2006, pp. 50–74.

---, 'Touch, Sound, and Things without the Mind', *Metaphilosophy*, **37** (2006): 162–182.

---, 'Reid's Answer to Molyneux's Question', *Monist*, **90** (2007): 251–270.

Van Woudenberg, René, 'Thomas Reid on Memory', *Journal of the History of Philosophy*, **37** (1999): 117–133.

Weldon, Susan, 'Direct Realism and Visual Distortion: A Development of Arguments from Thomas Reid', *Journal of the History of Philosophy*, **20** (1982): 355–368.

Wood, Paul, 'Thomas Reid's Critique of Joseph Priestley: Context and Chronology', *Man and Nature/L'homme et la nature: Yearbook of the Canadian Society for Eighteenth-Century Studies*, **4** (1985): 29–45.

---, 'Introduction to Thomas Reid', *An Inquiry into the Human Mind on the Principles of Common Sense*, facsimile reprint of the 1785 edition, Bristol: Thoemmes, 1990.

---, 'Hume, Reid and the Science of the Mind', in *Hume and Hume's Connexions*, ed. M.A. Stewart, University Park, PA: Pennsylvania State University Press, 1995, pp. 119–139.

---, 'The Fittest Man in the Kingdom and the Glasgow Chair of Moral Philosophy', *Hume Studies*, **23** (1997): 277–313.

---, 'Thomas Reid and the Tree of the Sciences', *Journal of Scottish Philosophy*, **2** (2004): 119–136.

Wright, John P., 'Hume versus Reid on Ideas: the New Hume Letter', *Mind*, **96** (1987): 392–398.

Yaffe, Gideon, 'Reid on the Perception of Visible Figure', *Journal of Scottish Philosophy*, **1** (2) (2003): 103–115.

---, 'The Office of an Introspectible Sensation: A Reply to Falkenstein and Grandi', *Journal of Scottish Philosophy*, **1** (2003): 135–140.

---, 'Promises, Social Acts, and Reid's First Argument for Moral Liberty', *Journal of the History of Philosophy*, **45** (2007): 267–289.

---, 'Thomas Reid on Consciousness and Attention', *Canadian Journal of Philosophy*, **39** (2009): 165–194.

Index

Paracelsus, 28
Peripatetics, 54, 66, 93, 95–96, 98–99, 147–48
Plato, 45, 197, 199, 261, 279
Porterfield, William, 14, 163–64
prejudice, 2, 31, 75–76, 160, 165, 173, 180, 194–96, 198–99, 224, 229, 231, 242, 278–79, 311
Priestley, Joseph, 1, 3, 16
Pyrrho, 224
Pythagoreans, 197, 279

qualities
primary 6–7, 9–10, 12–13, 65–67, 71, 78–80, 97, 148, 251
secondary 7, 9–10, 12–13, 43, 59, 66, 78, 90, 92–93, 97–98, 147–48, 251

Raeburn, Henry, 24
reason
analogical, 2, 82, 139, 141, 143–50, 154–55, 164–66, 188–91, 194–96, 201, 336–37
deductive, 42, 61, 63, 71, 77, 98–99, 111, 146–48, 221, 229–30, 264, 287, 335–36
inductive, 28, 51, 116, 139–41, 144, 240–41, 264, 272, 343
liberty, sign of, 296
mathematical, 11, 33, 77, 98–100, 106–09, 124, 149, 162, 168–69, 206–07, 217, 225, 227, 233, 236–37, 240–41, 260, 286, 317, 339
moral, 16, 56, 136, 238, 265, 275–77, 279, 283–87, 293–94, 299, 319
Reid, Elizabeth, 23
Reid, Lewes, 22

Saturn, 120
Saunderson, Nicholas, 23, 69, 82, 99, 157n2
scepticism, 2, 4–5, 11, 25–26, 28, 32–34, 37, 75–76, 96, 99, 115, 120–22, 146, 150–51, 153, 161, 222, 224, 239, 247, 308, 311–12
Scholastics (schoolmen), 167, 189, 262, 291, 300–01
self-evidence, 2, 61, 80–81, 113, 138, 164, 186, 209, 222–23, 227, 229, 234, 239–41, 253, 257, 261, 282, 285, 290, 302, 317
Shaftesbury, Anthony Ashley Cooper, Lord, 282, 292
Shakespeare, William, 157n1
Smith, Adam, 15
Smith, Richard, 13–14
Stewart, John, 22–23
Stoics, 290
Swift, Jonathan, 189

Themistocles, 336
Titian, 133
Turnbull, George, 3, 22

utility, 279, 280, 323–24, 326–27, 329–31, 333–36, 338

Venus, 23, 175
Virgil, 248n2, 248n5
visible figure, 6–7, 14, 20n35, 23, 82, 84, 87, 99–102, 104–07, 109–10, 123, 129

Wolfius, Christian, 204

Zeno, 224